MW00862173

comp it up:
a studio skills foundation

comp it up:
a studio skills foundation

rose gonnella

christopher j. navetta

 DELMAR
CENGAGE Learning

Australia • Brazil • Japan • Korea • Mexico • Singapore • Spain • United Kingdom • United States

Comp It Up: A Studio Skills Foundation
Rose Gonnella and Christopher J. Navetta

Vice President, Career and Professional
Editorial: Dave Garza

Director of Learning Solutions: Sandy Clark

Senior Acquisitions Editor: Jim Gish

Managing Editor: Larry Main

Associate Product Manager:
Meaghan O'Brien

Editorial Assistant: Sarah Timm

Vice President, Career and Professional
Marketing: Jennifer Baker

Marketing Director: Deborah Yarnell

Marketing Manager: Erin Brennan

Production Director: Wendy Troeger

Senior Content Project Manager:
Kathryn B. Kucharek

Senior Art Director: Joy Kocsis

For product information and technology assistance, contact us at
Cengage Learning Customer & Sales Support, 1-800-354-9706

For permission to use material from this text or product,
submit all requests online at **www.cengage.com/permissions**.
Further permissions questions can be e-mailed to
permissionrequest@cengage.com.

Adobe® Photoshop®, Adobe® InDesign®, Adobe® Illustrator®, Adobe® Flash®, Adobe® Dreamweaver® Adobe® Creative Suite®, Adobe® Acrobat®, and Adobe® InCopy® are trademarks or registered trademarks of Adobe Systems, Inc. in the United States and/or other countries. Third party products, services, company names, logos, design, titles, words, or phrases within these materials may be trademarks of their respective owners.

FrogTape® is a registered trademark of FrogTape & Shurtape Technologies, LLC Company in the United States and/or other countries and its use herein shall not be deemed to imply endorsement or sponsorship of this publicity product.

Crop-A-Dile® is a registered trademark of We R Memory Keepers in the United States and/or other countries and its use herein shall not be deemed to imply endorsement or sponsorship of this publicity product.

Fastenator® is a registered trademark of EK Success LTD in the United States and/or other countries and its use herein shall not be deemed to imply endorsement or sponsorship of this publicity product.

Galaxy Gauge™ is a registered trademark of Scientific Illustration Services Corp., in the United States and/or other countries and its use herein shall not be deemed toimply endorsement or sponsorship of this publicity product.

Schaedler Precision Rule © Schaedler Quinzel Inc., in the United States and/or other countries and its use herein shall not be deemed toimply endorsement or sponsorship of this publicity product.

All images owned by Delmar, Cengage Learning unless otherwise noted.

Library of Congress Control Number: 2010921312
ISBN-13: 978-1-4283-2235-6
ISBN-10: 1-4283-2235-3

Delmar
5 Maxwell Drive, Clifton Park, NY 12065-2919, USA

Cengage Learning is a leading provider of customized learning solutions with office locations around the globe, including Singapore, the United Kingdom, Australia, Mexico, Brazil, and Japan. Locate your local office at: **international.cengage.com/region**

Cengage Learning products are represented in Canada by Nelson Education, Ltd.

To learn more about Delmar, visit **www.cengage.com/delmar**

Purchase any of our products at your local college store or at our preferred online store **www.ichapters.com**

NOTICE TO THE READER

Publisher and authors do not warrant or guarantee any of the products described herein or perform any independent analysis in connection with any of the product information contained herein. Publisher and authors do not assume, and expressly disclaims, any obligation to obtain and include information other than that provided to it by the manufacturer. The reader is expressly warned to consider and adopt all safety precautions that might be indicated by the activities described herein and to avoid all potential hazards. By following the instructions contained herein, the reader willingly assumes all risks in connection with such instructions. The publisher and authors make no representations or warranties of any kind, including but not limited to, the warranties of fitness for particular purpose or merchantability, nor are any such representations implied with respect to the material set forth herein, and the publisher and authors take no responsibility with respect to such material. The publisher and authors shall not be liable for any special, consequential, or exemplary damages resulting, in whole or part, from the readers' use of, or reliance upon, this material.

Printed in the United States of America
1 2 3 4 5 6 7 14 13 12 11 10

To my father Joseph, an old world tradesman/printer/dad, and to my mother Josie, an extraordinary mom, seamstress, cook, gardener, and craftsman, who taught me to "do it myself" and all else I needed to know to pursue a creatively fulfilling life. And, to Frank, who helps me to live a creative life, I extend my sincere, three-dimensional thanks.

—*Rose Mary Gonnella*

To my parents, Mario and Judi, who never stifled my creativity and let me build a Batcave in the basement when I was young. To my sister, Jean-Marie, who always serves as a sounding board for everything I do in design. To Michael Evans and Gregg Iveson—a pair of friends who unfortunately are no longer with us—for always being two of my biggest fans and never doubting my Photoshop skills. And to *Star Trek*. Everything else I need to know about life I learned from *Star Trek*.

—*Christopher J. Navetta*

preface

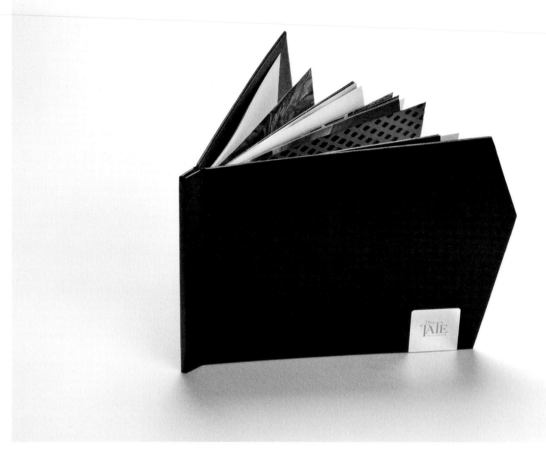

Figure P-1
Promotional Book: The Tate Residences
Studio: Kinetic, Singapore
Creative Director: Roy Poh
Client: Hong Leong Holdings, LTD

The book pictured is an exquisitely designed book promoting an urban, residential luxury condominium complex. The book includes a variety of carefully selected papers and substrates and both traditional printing and specialty printing effects. These special elements reflect the luxury of the subject matter. Note the staggered and diagonally cut pages that conceptually echo the sleek and contemporary architectural style of the buildings.

Comp It Up: A Studio Skills Foundation was written for graphic design students and curious professionals as a how-to textbook and resource that explains and explores the use of tools, materials, techniques, and processes relative to studio craftsmanship and desktop production for the comprehensive mock-up of graphic design solutions.

Our focus is on glorious paper and ink that when combined lead to the tangible ("holdable") printed matter of design. Yet, nonprint, action-packed, screen-based processes are also discussed when relevant.

Developing excellence in craftsmanship is paramount whether using screen-based or traditional hand tools and techniques because it speaks of the thoughtfulness, care, and integrity of the designer and consequently of the concept presented to the instructor, creative director, potential employer, or client.

As an adjunct to developing skill in craftsmanship, creativity can expand as the processes covered in the text reveal lush information that leads to pointedly interesting format options for both traditional and nonconventional design solutions.

Although this book does not specifically address the step-by-step development of ideas and concepts regarding design solutions (we leave that to Professor Robin Landa and her many excellent books) the text does remind its readers to always relate to the client, the problem to be solved, the message to and communication with the audience, and the context and culture in which the solution will be seen. It also reminds readers that personal expression can always be folded in.

intended audience

Comp It Up is a textbook and long-lasting resource that reaches out to an audience of design students (and curious professionals) with a relaxed tone. The informal and personal instruction in this book developed because we (the authors) know from our experience that so many students find the tone of most textbooks dry and unappealing. We intend to talk *with* the audience and nurture and guide through the techniques required for craftsmanship of the myriad three-dimensional objects of graphic design—whether for a class presentation, for a final portfolio presentation, or simply for the self-interest of making things.

If, while studying design, there is an interest in also gaining in-depth awareness of paper and becoming knowledgeable of a great variety of materials, construction and production techniques, and processes needed to make a design solution tangible, then potentially, *Comp It Up* can lead the way and provide both a creative and "crafty" competitive edge.

where and when

This book could be used in conjunction with either foundation or advanced design concept and application courses such as a creative and visual thinking course, promotional design, editorial and publication design, packaging design, or environmental design. It also stands alone as a course in itself. *Comp It Up* fits with the DIY movement—that is, "design it yourself": books, booklets, wearables, hand and tote bags, invitations, announcements, cards, stationery, stickers, magnets, buttons, posters, storage boxes, photo albums, kids' stuff, games, zines, newsletters, CD and DVD packaging, functional domestic stuff, and nonfunctional-oriented art gifts.

We hope the overarching objective of this book—learning the mechanics of construction and their application to a great variety of design formats and techniques—leads to a lifelong pursuit of the creative pleasure found through the exploration of handcraftsmanship . . . or simply having fun making things for others and yourself.

new media and emerging trends

Creativity and design are fluid and dynamic. There are frequent new technologies (and ways to use them). New conceptual and visual trends pop up and evolve. Even new media with which to bring ideas to the public emerge with surprising frequency.

Therefore, every designer has quite the enormous task to stay informed and be adept at all the tools that are available—both the traditional and the new. Despite the constant *mantra* of design students and professional designers—"there is not enough time" (for everything we are assigned to do)—great craftsmanship develops only with painstaking practice. A significant commitment of time is necessary with a payoff that is priceless. The reward: a timeless skill.

textbook organization

The pedagogy in *Comp It Up* is a bit eclectic: traditionally focused and guided discussion, conversational explanations and references, exploratory and playful directives, demonstrative illustrations, and intuition-nurturing exercises.

Comp It Up relies on the best practices of the industry and business of design, its artistry, and craftsmanship to engage readers with creative and practical information. It offers professional insights, illustrative models, step-by-step diagrams, convenient resource lists, and professional examples.

We can all learn through observation and analysis of graphic design solutions. Classroom critiques on the work of peers, field discovery on the web, and the professional examples in this book can inspire you. The professional exemplars and excellent student work are notably and purely *role models*. There are nearly infinite solutions to any design assignment.

Some professional design and art works are contemporary whereas others have been created in the recent past. We think that the examples presented are, in essence, classic or iconic; their solutions and approach will remain creatively relevant for many years to come. We also mix in references to mathematicians, engineers, and fine artists (painters, book artists, printmakers, etc.) as well, believing that innovation and inspiration rises from a crucible of diverse minds.

an orderly study

The three parts of the book—Part 1: Foundation in Craftsmanship (Digital and Traditional); Part 2: Application of Basic Skills; and Part 3: Presentation—should be read overall to get a clear idea of the purpose and interconnectivity of each. Once the whole is generally understood, the three parts should be considered and studied in order. It is best to thoroughly understand each part and chapter before proceeding to the next but to also refer back to each section, if necessary, to review and subsequently move forward.

Each topic is the subject of an isolated study as well as considered a potential element of the whole. For example, in Chapter 7 on bookbinding, the materials and techniques of crafting bound, multipage design solutions are explored, explained, demonstrated (when necessary and possible), and followed with practice exercises. Basic practical considerations are covered such as standards in the industry and relative cost. The investigation of binding techniques creates interest and excitement in itself while providing a catalyst for the use of binding in various design solutions and in conjunction with other materials and techniques.

In addition, information is cross-referenced, with other sections and chapters where appropriate, reinforcing the thinking that the materials and techniques of design are not used in isolation.

specific order

We had a specific order in mind when compiling the chapters, outlined as follows:

Part 1: Foundation in Craftsmanship (Digital and Traditional)

- **Chapter 1**: Essential and Helpful Tools; **Chapter 2**: Paper and Alternative Substrates; **Chapter 3**: Basic Techniques; and **Chapter 4**: Software Basics are the core of the textbook. The foundation of great craftsmanship begins with a thorough understanding of the materials, tools, and corresponding basic techniques for their use.

- Discussion includes selection of hand tools and digital tools as well as a guide to understanding paper—the basic material for printed design solutions. Basic techniques for handling the tools and materials are also included here. These techniques must be well understood, practiced, and retained before moving forward into applications.

Part 2: Application of Basic Skills

- **Chapter 5**: A Folded Finish; **Chapter 6**: Within: Envelopes and Folders; **Chapter 7:** Binding Together; **Chapter 8:** Packaging All Around; and **Chapter 9:** Specialty Printing and Postpress Special Effects present and guide the construction of application formats (folded objects, folders, and envelopes for brochures, posters, direct mail promotions, etc.), booklet and bookbinding methods, packaging formats, and specialty printing methods. There are literally thousands of options for these objects and surely not enough space in this textbook to cover them all. We believe we have included a well-researched selection of standard and traditional industry formats and methods as well as examples of the unconventional and experimental—this leads to invention and paths for a student or professional's ever-expanding visual vocabulary.

- All design elements should certainly contribute to and perhaps enhance or enrich the design concept. Hence, reference is made to remember the connection between the materials and techniques and design concept development.

- Throughout Parts 1 and 2, instruction includes explanation, illustration, example, and/or step-by-step demonstration. We talk you through a variety of options and techniques presented; then you must practice to evolve and become a great craftsman and creative designer. You learn by doing. So, please *do*.

Part 3: Portfolio Presentation

- In **Chapter 10**: Present Well, we conclude with guidance and options for presentation of an overall body of student design solutions—a career-launching portfolio. The focus is on presentation, and not concept development of individual applications. But at the end of most chapters, and in the exercise and practice sections of Chapters 5 through 9, we do include suggested assignments that could be developed into finished design solutions.

- We recommend that Chapters 1 through 4 are considered in order and as a group. Chapters 5 through 9 could be studied in a different order than what is presented, yet these chapters were written to build from the simple to the complex. We suggest that you at least start with Chapter 5 and then reorder to include those topics of most interest, if time is indeed restricted. Do finish with Chapter 10; portfolio presentation is our summarizing application.

features

Comp It Up: A Studio Skills Foundation contains these features:

- A step-by-step image guide of procedures for each technique

- Helpful notations on industry standards regarding materials and formats

- Practice exercises titled "Exercise Knowledge Gained" to help readers put to use the techniques they have learned within each chapter

- Hundreds of examples of related design solutions

- A relaxed tone and easy-to-follow explanations

- Helpful resource lists in each chapter

- A combination of traditional techniques with new technologies: handcrafted design solutions accompanied by contemporary techniques, such as digital imagery and printing

- Information on portfolio presentation

- Special feature articles throughout the book to focus readers' attention on important related topics

- Small boxed features in each chapter (Professional Notes, Green Thoughts, Tech Tips, etc.) to provide additional information about relevant issues

about the authors

rose gonnella

An educator, artist, designer, and writer, Rose Gonnella is a professor in the Robert Busch School of Design at Kean University (NJ). She teaches courses in design theory (identity design, editorial design, and senior design portfolio), studio skills, and computer technology courses, inclusive of developing the school's web design curriculum. Professor Gonnella's interests also extend to traditional media, such as hand-papermaking, drawing, painting, and book arts. She promotes student design work in handcraftsmanship and personal expression in her studio skills course and other areas of the design curriculum.

Professor Gonnella has been awarded membership to two scholarly academic organizations—Phi Beta Kappa National Honor Society (1980) and Phi Kappa Phi National Honor Society (2001). She has received grants from the Mid-America Arts Alliance International Residency Project, the Mid-Atlantic Residency Grant Project, and the New Jersey State Council on the Arts Fellowship. In addition, she has received several awards from Kean University, including the Presidential Award for Distinguished Research/Creative Work, the Computers in Curriculum Released Time Award, the Alumni Association Grant, the Faculty-Student Research Award, and the Alumni Association Teacher of the Year.

She is currently on the executive board of the Art Directors Club of New Jersey (ADCNJ) and serves as the coordinator and chairperson of the Kean University/ADCNJ "Thinking Creatively" design conference (www.thinkingcreatively.org).

A practicing artist and designer, Rose has exhibited her drawings both nationally and internationally for over 20 years. Her drawings are included in the permanent collections of the Smithsonian National Museum of American Art (Washington, DC), the Museum of Art and Archaeology (Columbia, MO), and other public and private collections.

Rose also serves as the creative editor of the university's intellectual journal: *The Kean Review*.

Rose's published writing includes the co-authored *2D: Visual Basics for Designers* (Delmar Cengage Learning) with Professor Robin Landa and Steven Brower, the co-authored set with Robin Landa—*Creative Jolt* and its companion, *Creative Jolt Inspirations* (North Light Publications)—and *Visual Workout Creativity Workbook* (Thomson Delmar Learning). Other books include *Sea Captains' Houses and Rose-Covered Cottages: The Architectural Heritage of Nantucket Island* (Rizzoli, co-authored with Margaret Booker and Patricia Butler), *summer nantucket drawings* (Waterborn), and several artists book collaborations (privately published and held).

Rose has also written numerous magazine articles on creativity, art, and architecture for the regional publications *Nantucket Magazine* and *Cape Cod Life*, and several articles for national publications, including *Hand Papermaking* and *Raw Vision*. She was a part-time arts journalist for the *Nantucket Beacon* and the *Nantucket Independent* newspapers for nine years and has written over 250 articles on art, design, and architecture.

Aspiration: Shieldmaiden of Rohan. Given the unlikely goal of the aforementioned, she'll take twice removed, fourth assistant to Julie Taymor.

christopher j. navetta

Christopher J. Navetta has been a professional freelance graphic designer for over 15 years. His diverse career boasts an eclectic group of clients and employers—from large corporations to small businesses and individual customers—which have given him a unique sampling of the multifarious facets of design.

Christopher's earliest experience in the world of graphic design came years before any formal scholastic training in the field. Starting in the early 1990s, he was a regular participant in computer-generated graphic competitions on Quantum Computer Services' Q-Link, an early online service for the Commodore computer platform (a service that eventually became known as America Online). He later became a judge for some of those competitions, and through his exposure there, got his first taste of the professional graphic design world when he started freelancing for companies such as Wendy's and Long John Silver's.

Throughout the next several years, Christopher continued to freelance, particularly for national retail franchises such as Kay-Bee Toys, Natural Wonders, and New York/New Jersey comic book/collectible chain Comic Attitudes. It was then that he assumed the position of digital colorist for the New Jersey–based comic and magazine publisher Southpaw Publishing (later Axess Comics). His duties there quickly expanded to complete book layout, advertising, packaging, public relations, web design, and story/script editing.

After his stint in the comic book world, Christopher returned to school and spent the next years at Kean University, where he earned a BFA in Visual Communications/Graphic Design. During that time, he was awarded two Art Directors Club of New Jersey (ADCNJ) scholarships for design and a Phi Kappa Phi Honor Society writing scholarship. All the while at Kean, he continued his freelancing, gaining clients of all sizes such as Jersey City Public Schools, Thomson Delmar Learning, music promoter TigerClaw Enterprises, PFLAG, Prentice Hall, and the ADCNJ. In 2004, he became an executive board member of the ADCNJ (and is currently serving as vice president), and a designer for the 2005 Awards Show and Exhibition, as well as being involved with the Kean University/ADCNJ "Thinking Creatively" annual design conference. He has been a member of the American Institute of Graphic Arts (AIGA) and the Graphic Artists Guild (GAG). He has continued working for many of the aforementioned clients, adding new ones such as Six Flags, the Mall of America, and Nickelodeon.

In September of 2007, Christopher became a professor of design at Kean University, and has instructed courses including digital prepress, promotional design, and—of course—studio skills.

On the personal side, Christopher is a lifelong student of history, fine art, literature, and film. Bastien-Lepage, Dürer, van Gogh, Munch, Boccioni, Lichtenstein, and Warhol rank among his influencing artists. Also included are eclectic interests such as Gothic and Baroque architecture, and medieval European and Japanese armor/swordcraft. His studies in history have included heavy focus on the Roman Empire, the Hundred Years War, and the history of New Jersey. Most recently, modern film costume/set/prop design has come to the forefront of his artistic endeavors, with particular focus on the design and fabrication of science fiction and fantasy-based film props. This appreciation and unyielding love of history and popular culture has guided his design style throughout the years, and serves as an ever-changing source of artistic inspiration.

Most importantly, both Christopher and Rose are DIY geeks—and proud of it.

acknowledgments

The authors gratefully acknowledge and sincerely thank all the creative directors, art directors, designers, illustrators, photographers, artists, mathematicians, engineers, computer science pros, web developers, printers, design managers, business owners, writers, interns, student research assistants, DIY geeks, and our esteemed colleagues for their generous assistance and goodwill in contributing to this book.

Great thanks to the team at Cengage whose dedicated work, intelligence, patience, and faith in us made this book (finally) happen. Thank you so much: Jim Gish, Senior Acquisitions Editor, and Meaghan O'Brien, Associate Product Manager, at the lead of the project; Larry Main, Managing Editor; Joy Kocsis, Senior Art Director; Sarah Timm, Editorial Assistant; Kathy Kucharek, Senior Content Project Manager; and Margaret Moore Booker, Permissions Editor.

We respectfully acknowledge (in alphabetical order) these talented, kind, and generous people who have helped us in many ways and without whose help this book would not be possible: Neil Adelantar, Steven Brower, Martin Holloway, Michele Kathoff, Robin Landa, Dawnmarie McDermid, Captain Redskirt (Jean-Marie Navetta), Debra Rizzi, Alan Robbins, Erin Smith, James Smith, Michele Santo, Janine Toro, and Jody Williams.

And finally but not least, we thank our crafty DIY team of students (now pro designers): Rich Arnold ("Yes, I know how to read"), Michael Boos ("I have not a life, therefore I craft"), Allison Grow ("Chicadachicada"), Danny Virasawmi ("Yes boss!"), Iee Ling Yee ("Yeah, I do too know how to think"), Neil Adelantar ("Huh? How would I know?"), and Jason Alejandro ("Let me ponder that . . .").

Delmar Cengage Learning and the authors would also like to thank the reviewers for their valuable suggestions and expertise:

Daniel Bouweraerts
Professor
Truckee Meadows Community College
Reno, New York

Scott Carnz
Associate Dean of Academic Affairs
The Art Institute of Seattle
Seattle, Washington

William Lancaster
Faculty
Santa Monica College
Santa Monica, California

Myung Hae Park
Associate Professor
California State University, Sacramento
Sacramento, California

Thomas Sakoulas
Associate Professor
State University of New York at Oneonta
Oneonta, New York

questions and feedback

Cengage and the authors welcome your questions and feedback. If you have suggestions that you think others would benefit from, please let us know and we will try to include them in the next edition.

To send us your questions and/or feedback, you can contact the publisher at:

Delmar Cengage Learning
Executive Woods
5 Maxwell Drive
Clifton Park, NY 12065
Attn: Media Arts and Design Team
800-998-7498

Or the authors at:
rgonnell@kean.edu
navettac@kean.edu

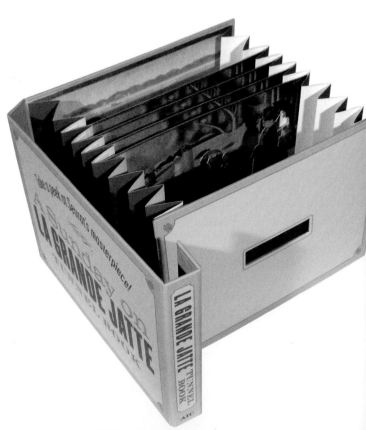

"I am rarely happier than when spending an entire day
programming my computer to perform automatically a task that
it would otherwise take me a good ten seconds to do by hand."
—*Douglas Adams, author*

comp it up:
an introduction

what are studio skills?

Hello, why are we asking *you* a question?

We ask because right from the start we want you to think. Start your brain engine.

You need to be curious to be a good learner:

- Ask a question. Get an answer.

- Put it in your head (knowledge bank deposit).

- Crank it up with all the other information in your head.

- Pull knowledge out when you need it.

- You are so smart to ask a question.

- Okay, you are still trying to confirm your answer to the initial question. Did you ponder and answer for yourself?

Good, but let us also tell you what we are thinking.

Studio skills is a traditional and fairly broad term that in the field of design could refer to everything from the fluent use of computer graphics software and drawing ability, to research savvy, and the ideation process, writing skill, hand craftsmanship, and digital production skills needed for both print and web. In other words, studio skills could include every piece of knowledge that may be employed in a large or small professional design studio.

However, relative to our direction for this textbook (and our sanity), our focused definition of **studio skills** refers to the ability to successfully choose and use, both creatively and practically,

the tools, materials, and techniques needed to physically create the elements of a design solution and construct a professional-level, comprehensive mock-up of that solution.

Although we have included pertinent information on digital elements and processes, the emphasis of our direction is on hand-craftsmanship rather than software instruction.

not a dummy

Printed on the desktop or digitally at a service bureau or built solely for use on a computer, a **comprehensive mock-up** is a visual, tangible (two- or three-dimensional) **simulation** of the proposed outcome of a professionally printed or digitally created design solution. See Figure I-2 for a professional comprehensive mock-up.

Stop. In this text, the term *comprehensive mock-up* is shortened to **comp** for ease of reading and because the majority of professional designers surveyed use the short version.

The full phrase "comprehensive mock-up" could also be shortened to "mock-up." "Dummy" is another word in use by professional designers to describe the objective result of the simulation of a design solution. In our opinion, neither of these two short terms (mock-up or dummy) defines the full scope and importance (or seriousness) of the object in discussion.

We will occasionally remind you of the shortened label of *comprehensive mock-up*—because we are teachers (and really nice ones too) and know that a bit of repetition and an occasional reminder can be helpful.

Go. Since we are humbly certain that we are both creative and sensible, the text also includes practical information on industry standards regarding paper, application formats, printing, postpress applications, and their resources.

creativity is precious

Ugh! You might say, "Practical information and standardization on formats, shapes, sizes, and techniques? Rigid charts, tables, and lists!" We venture to say that we can hear your possible thoughts: "What is the purpose of knowing so much practical information? Limitations are stifling."

We can also hear some of you say, "I'm creative; standardization and practicalities is the antithesis of creativity. Don't stifle me with rules, guidelines, and textbooks full of grey words and more blah, blah, blah. I'm an artist, a designer!"

Wait. We think that you might be somewhat mistaken. You are perhaps an artist. But you have also chosen to study design with the goal of practicing in this vast creative field. And if you want to practice this profession with personal integrity and earned respect,

Figure I-1
Kelly (Mangels) Koching, former design student (cranking it up), and currently art director, Oxford Communications.

Photography by Kelly Koching.

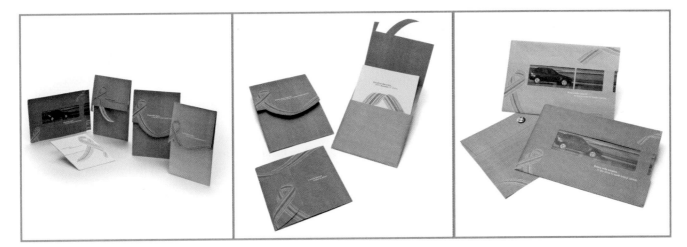

Figure I-2

Direct mail: Every Mile Counts in the Drive to Cure Breast Cancer

Art Direction and Design: Cesar Rubin

Studio: Ritta & Associates

Client: BMW

Comprehensive mock-ups help to determine both the success of the design aesthetic and the functionality of a design solution. Pictured are three design concepts, one variation of a single concept, and the final printed direct mail piece (a fund-raising call).

Left to right:

Variations within one concept. In the design format showing an open flap (right), it was discovered that the ribbon element was too fragile (likely to tear quickly upon opening the envelope). A second design was conceived to enhance the flowing of the illustrated ribbon but with greater physical strength. The third format was also rejected given that envelope flaps weren't contributing well enough to the form of the ribbon element.

Variations within one concept using black and white as well as color desktop printing. This design was rejected in favor of one placing emphasis on the form of the illustrated ribbon—a symbol and focal point of the fund-raising purpose of the application.

put it in your head that design is a business. You will be working under tight deadlines, within limited budgets, and for clients who are not always sympathetic to your expansive (but justifiable) use of negative space—that precious so connected to your basic artistic knowledge.

We are sympathetic. We love unbounded creativity. We love play and fun. We thrive on the experimental pursuit of a design solution and revel in the art and artistry of design. We live for it!

And yet we are successful (and sane and happy) because we can accept the balance of creating within the limits (when necessary), playing with the boundaries (nearly always), and pushing beyond the boundaries (when the door opens).

Business is not the enemy of creativity. Focus on the positive. Breakout creativity happens.

How? Use analytical thinking skills and your nonconformist nature in combination to help convince clients to follow offbeat routes. Read the biography of the late Tibor Kalman, a master of compelling clients to accept smart, imaginatively experimental design concepts. Keep in mind that there are thoughtful and learned clients who do connect with creative thinking—find them and stick with them.

Practice and hone the art of ingenuous persuasion during classroom critique. When fledged into the professional field, seek to work in agencies and studios where the policy is to gently and convincingly challenge clients to understand on-target creativity and value it. Listen not to the naysayers—designers who believe that clients will never understand a creative approach. Look around. Fresh, experimental, offbeat, nonconformist, gloriously imaginative design exists! Behind every smart, original, creative design there is a designer (and client) who aspired to creativity and didn't allow the naysayers to dampen their spirit.

with intent and purpose

Developing into a great craftsman takes time. If you are to make a sincere commitment to the significant amount of time it takes to develop skill in crafting a comprehensive mock-up, then you need to know why one is needed in the first place.

The purpose and importance of creating a comprehensive mock-up are threefold:

1. *Testing.* For the designer, this is a critical test stage needed to determine the success of the visual and physical functioning of the design solution.

2. *Presentation.* For the instructor or client who commissioned the design solution, the simulated version provides a tangible object to experience, comment upon, and eventually approve. Often, the comp is used as a contract between client and designer—at times with the client's signature written directly onto the comprehensive mock-up itself.

As a student, the comp is visible and tangible proof of your knowledge and skill. You will need to build a comp in order to photograph it for your printed portfolio and website, for presentation to potential employers. After that, you *may* not need to make another comp (depending on what the practice is within the studio or agency).

3. *Guidance.* The comp is given to the professional printer for use as a guide to ensure the finished work is exactly as the designer created.

The comp also may become part of a legally binding contract, this time between the designer and the printer (or with the web and computer science professionals, if a website is developed).

test, present, and guide: portable document format (PDF)

Not all comps need to be printed or tangibly constructed. The comprehensive mock-up can also be a screen representation of a design solution and is usually presented as a PDF or printed to remain as single, flat sheets but not constructed in three dimension or printed.

A PDF or flat, single sheets of paper printed using desktop technology are often adequate to present many design solutions, especially those that are essentially two dimensional such as posters, book covers, magazine spreads, and print ads. See Figure I-3 for both single flat sheets and fully constructed flats.

a case for comps: direct mail

You create a spectacular direct mail piece for the client, obtain final approvals, get it printed, and proudly send it to the mail house for final distribution only to find that the post office is rejecting it or needs to apply a postage upcharge. We all have been there at one point or another.

The solution? Always consult your mail house or post office representative throughout the creative process to avoid errors and save valuable time and money. Don't be fooled—a small change in size, weight, or dimensions could negatively impact the mailing—especially with postage that typically is a substantial portion of the entire budget.

Use the provided tips to manage direct mail campaigns successfully.

1. Measure Twice, Cut Once
It might sound like an old adage, but Dad was right on this one! Review your piece with your mail house representative or the post office before going to press. Correct sizing decreases your chances of your mailing deadline being compromised at the post office.

2. Verify Your Weights
Keep in mind that ink on paper, mailing labels, and postage all contribute to the final weight of a direct mail piece. The maximum weight for a standard #10 envelope is 1.0 ounce = $0.47 rate. A preprinted mock-up is a good preliminary troubleshooting measure, but weighing the final end product will ensure that you don't have any surprises at the mailbox.

3. Trim the Fat
Ensure that you confirm your scores/perforations/folds carefully. If you design a piece to meet postal regulations, ensure that your bindery is dead on. The slightest change, even 1/16 of an inch, can open the door for the post office to impose the higher applicable rate. Double-check your trim size!

4. Unique Sizes = More Money
Square envelopes gain a great amount of attention through the mail, but surcharges usually apply. Be prepared to pay more postage if you decide to go that route.

5. Differentiate Your Design
While getting direct mail opened is a high priority, still use your judgment and don't ignore your instincts. When designing your mailing labels, make sure that your mailing and return addresses are distinct and can be differentiated. Avoid frantic calls from the client about receiving numerous returns, to find out that the post office read your return address as the delivery address!

—Debra Rizzi
Rizco Design
www.rizcodesign.com

Invitation with envelope for ADCNJ Awards Dinner.

Art Director and Designer: Keith Rizzi
Studio: Rizco Design
Client: Art Directors Club of New Jersey. As noted by Debra Rizzi: [Y]our key responsibilities are to create compelling end products that convey a key message and positively impact the bottom line. The client is also relying that the end product will deliver! Please rely on your mailing team to assist you during every step of the design process.

Figure I-3
Journal: *The Kean Review*
Creative Editor: Rose Gonnella
Art Direction and Design: Erin Smith
Client: Kean University
Left to right:
Single-page proofs printed on the desktop (scattered).

Finished and professionally printed journal.
Cover comp.
A blank paper and binding dummy provided by the printer.
When a large multiple-page document is in the proofing stage,
a fully bound and realized comprehensive mock-up may not be
necessary. Unbound single-page spreads printed on the desktop
will suffice. However, a blank paper comp was also made to test the
binding and paper quality. A simple cover comp was made to test
the type spacing on the binding.

Of course, anything that isn't meant to be seen anywhere else but on screen (such as websites and video games) is simulated digitally and usually remains on screen for testing and presentation.

digital pdf or physical comps?

Why produce a physical comp when a PDF steps up to simulate a design solution? Why aren't *all* design solutions presented in a PDF?

A significant number of presentations shown to the client are in digital form only. Sent via e-mail or uploaded to a web server via FTP (file transfer protocol), PDFs are delivered fast.

Using PDFs also contributes to the "greening" of design—an environmental consciousness and a desire to be less wasteful of paper and consume fewer products that won't biodegrade or that harm the earth. We encourage environmentally responsible practices as much as possible.

Yet, there are situations when a comp is necessary and could also help in controlling overuse of paper, perhaps stopping waste. A well-crafted, tangible simulation of a great design solution can help win the client. Trust and confidence are gained because a comp shows the client *exactly* how the end product will appear—there is no guessing the final solution. The comp not only helps the client see the design solution but also feel it, use it, and understand it. Approval or disapproval happens at this test stage rather than at the printer or on delivery of the final professionally printed product.

In the long run, a comp may contribute to controlling waste by helping ensure that costly errors are caught before going to print.

When would a designer need a three-dimensional comp rather than a PDF? We recommend a three-dimensional comp when the design solution uses more than one paper type or is folded or contains multiple pages that are bound, or if the design solution employs single sheets contained in a folder or an envelope, or if the design involves special effects such as a cutout of some sort.

To summarize and reconfirm, a physical, three-dimensional comp is an essential test, presentation model, and guide for all involved in its production and outcome.

a professional point of view

When you engage in conversation with full-time professional designers, studio and agency managers, printers, and paper company representatives, you will quickly realize the value of excellent craftsmanship and the use of comps.

In small studios, often the person who originated the design solution would prepare and construct the comp. Having good craftsmanship adds to your repertoire of skills and contributions to the studio. On the other hand, large graphic design studios and advertising agencies often hire freelance comp technicians on site or hire out to companies that specialize in constructing comps—the latter especially applies to packaging design. For more information, research companies such as Comp24 or Creative Comps Inc. Both specialize in comps of packaging and printing effects.

get to it

The following guide will familiarize you with the process of executing the application exercises found at the end of each chapter in this book. The exercises apply the knowledge gained in the chapters.

step 1: read the directions carefully

When necessary, ask questions. A full understanding of the directions and assignment leads to successful execution without frustration and redoing. In addition, following directions is good practice for the professional level. Imagine if you did not follow the client's wishes or directives. If you fail to do so, you're fired. You are not entitled to keep your job if you can't follow directions because you didn't care to listen and take the time to understand.

step 2: think with a pencil (or a computer, or a marker)

For many designers, solutions happen when they are sketching (on paper, on screen, or on a napkin). Small, quick, unrefined drawings or sketches (a.k.a. thumbnails) allow time for creative experimentation, happy accidents (that can differentiate a design from the masses), and a visibly logical evolution leading to a smart solution. Sketch. Draw. You will learn how to recognize a good solution when you see it.

And when moving that solution to execution, take the time to also use thumbnails to "storyboard" or lay out a sequence of any multiple-part or paginated composition. Sketching the sequence of a multiple-part composition is a preliminary to the "first final stage" of executing a design solution.

step 3: know the three stages for success

As our friend Professor Alice Drueding of Tyler University states to her students, there are three levels of execution in regard to solving the design problem: the first final stage, the second final stage, and the third final stage.

We heartily agree. Create the solution to the problem, critique and refine it, and build the design solution to a tight finish. There is no great design; there is only great redesign.

critique and assessment

A **critique** (a.k.a. crit) is a written or verbal assessment of the design solution. Assessing your solution forces you to learn how well you followed directives, solved the objectives, and executed or crafted the solution.

Once you have finished the first final stage of the execution of the assignment, you can use the following brief critique guidelines to self-evaluate your process:

- ▢ Did you follow the directions carefully and meet the objectives and parameters of the assignment? No? Reread and try again.

- ▢ Is your approach to the solution creative? Did you take time to experiment? One way to test whether your solution is fresh, original, or creative is to observe how many of your peers created similar solutions. A creative idea is outstanding.

- ▢ Is the execution well crafted? There is nothing sloppy about a well-presented design solution. It should be accurate in its measurements, precise and neat in construction, and clean—free of smudges, glue blobs, and fingerprints.

This critique guide is placed in the introduction so you can use it for all the exercises in this book. It will make a great deal more sense once you actually apply it.

beyond business

Having developed excellent craftsmanship, you can also apply the skills to both personal projects and your own creative ventures. Be seriously entrepreneurial or just have fun and make things.

Finally, the desire to learn and develop excellence in craftsmanship contributes to a professional attitude—an eager and unstinting willingness to reach for greatness, to reach beyond your grasp rather than settling for what is satisfactory, or worse, settling for mediocrity.

Take your craftsmanship skill, combine it with creative thinking, and enjoy a life of constructive fun; see Figure I-4 for an example.

Read on to develop your skills as a designer craftsman.

Figure I-4
Handmade book: *A Scandal in Bohemia*
Creative Director: Rose Gonnella
Art Director and Designer: Erin Smith
Client: Self
This one-of-a-kind book was created for the simple joy of making a designed object by hand (and for eventual gift giving). The bulk paper for the interior of the book was cut smoothly with a small guillotine cutter (found in hand bookbinding studios or at printers). Binding was accomplished with glue and archival linen tape. The spine is covered with store-bought, handmade paper. The cover is bookboard covered with a flocked, milled specialty paper, and the title plate was printed on a desktop inkjet printer on archival paper using archival ink and then glued onto the surface of the cover using archival glue.
Cost? Priceless.

part one:
foundation in craftsmanship
(digital and traditional)

"There is no creative aspect of graphic design more enjoyable or rewarding than the indulgence of play."
—*Bradbury Thompson*

First row, left to right:
Detail of bone folder and ballpoint embossing tool.

Packaging: Bo Lings Chinese Restaurant
Studio: Design Ranch
Creative Directors: Michelle Sonderegger, Ingred Sidie
Client: Bo Lings Chinese Restaurant

Detail of metal ruler.

Second row, left to right:
Brochure: Delta Asset Management
Studio: And Partners, NY
Creative Director: David Schimmel
Designer: Aimee Sealfon Eng
Photographer: Vincent Ricardel (Executive Photography)
Illustrator: Photonica (stock)
Paper Selection: Mohawk Superfine; Canson Satin
Printer: Dickson's Inc.
Client: Delta Asset Management

Brand Collateral: Forecast retail clothing (business card, label, and table tent)
Creative Director: Jim Rivett
Art Director: Jim Rivett
Designers: Laura Treichel, Luis Avalos, and DeGaull Vang
Photographer: 44 inc.
Printer: Gift Box Corporation of America
Studio: Archetype
Client: Forecast

Business cards: Presidio Social Club
Studio: Mucca Design
Creative Director: Matteo Bologna
Designer: Christine Celic Strohl
Photographer: Christina Ottolini
Illustrator: Christine Celic Strohl

Third row, left to right:
Detail of a metal set square.

Book: MAP Financial Strategies
Studio: Voice
Creative Director: Scott Carslake
Art Directors: Scott Carslake, Stuart Gluth
Designer: Scott Carslake
Copywriter: Jemma Guthrie
Paper Artist: Stuart Gluth
Illustrator: Stuart Gluth
Lettering: Don Hatcher
Paper selection: Uncoated board
Printer: Regal Printing, Hong Kong
Bindery: Regal Printing, Hong Kong
Client: MAP Financial Strategies

Craft knife.

one
essential and helpful tools

chapter one: essential and helpful tools

learning objectives

- Create a "toolbox" with the traditional tools needed for constructing comps.
- Become aware of helpful tools that reach beyond basic needs.
- Learn the safety issues involved with the tools.

into the box: traditional tools of hand craftsmanship

Excellence in craftsmanship begins with traditional tools that should, at a minimum, include handheld tools for measuring, cutting, scoring, folding, and burnishing, along with traditional imaging tools and materials (pencils, pens, markers, etc.). Adhesives are also necessary construction materials.

In addition, the toolbox can be augmented with materials and tools that go beyond the basics to assist with constructing comps and any other project that inspires you to craft it up. Tools such as a saddle stapler, a bookbinder sewing awl, handheld punches, and perhaps a grommet tool are among many specialty tools that are handy and helpful; these extra tools will be noted after the essentials.

N.B. The *use* of the tools will be discussed in Chapter 3.

quality time

Buy the best quality tools possible that your budget allows. If stored, maintained, and treated with respect, most tools will be with you throughout your career. If you skimp on quality or leave out the essential basics, your results will likely also be at a loss in quality.

Employ the right tool. Of course you can use a shoe heel to knock a nail into the wall, but isn't a hammer the better tool for the purpose? Isn't the hammer made specifically for banging away at a nail even if the shoe heel can, in a way (or not really), accomplish the job?

Have the best tool for the job (as much as possible, but adapt when necessary). Once the toolbox is complete, you can be ready to comp any format and be most efficient with your work time.

You can purchase your tools (and additional supplies) from more than one source or any trusted source already in use. We do have favorites and offer some suggestions (alphabetically) for tools and additional materials:

- A.C. Moore Arts & Crafts
- BindingStuff
- Blick Art Materials
- The Container Store
- Harbor Freight Tools
- Hollander's Decorative Papers and Bookbinding Supplies
- The Home Depot
- Jo-Ann Fabric and Craft Stores
- Lowe's
- Michael's Arts and Crafts
- New York Central Art Supply
- The Paper Studio
- Pearl Fine Art Supplies
- Talas Bookbinding Supplies
- Utrecht Art Supplies
- Wet Paint Artists' Materials and Framing

We suggest that you consider purchasing the tools that will last a lifetime such as those made from stainless steel.

Also consider storing your tools in a box made of metal, untreated wood, or organic fabric. Hard plastic is the standard these days, but why not start a backward and thoughtfully earth-sustainable trend?

If you use plastic tools, take care and also keep them for a lifetime.

Since so many tools are made of plastic (as are food containers, boxes, ad infinitum) at least try to recycle them. We like the philosophy of Recycline, a company founded in 1996, which transforms recycled plastic into personal care and household items that can be sent back to the company and recycled again. Recycline's products, sold under the Preserve brand, make new products from items that would otherwise end up in the landfill. Recycline does not yet make scissors, triangles, or toolboxes, but perhaps some time in the near future, there will be tools made of recycled plastic—if we urgently request them.

For more thoughts on going green, see the feature article by Debra Rizzi, the founder of *Beleaf*.

store and organize tools

You will need a storage box to organize and contain your tools. Select one with handles that is easy to transport and perhaps another to store larger tools that are not frequently employed (see Figure 1-1). The following are suggestions:

- Metal box
- Sturdy canvas bag
- Zipper case or fabric tool roll

Lightweight metal boxes for storing tools can be found at a hardware store, a container store, or a department/variety store. Get one that has at least two tiers. The top tier is good for small items; the bottom for bulky tools. If you want to personalize the box, apply stickers or use paint (enamel) to make it the color of your choice. We also use the services of auto body repair shops to paint metal objects. Buy used, recycle, and refresh!

Want to avoid heavy metal? An alternative or adjunct to the toolbox, sturdy canvas bags (with shoulder strap) can be found in an outdoor or sports equipment store, container store, or variety store.

To further divide and organize small and frequently used tools, fabric tool rolls or zipper cases (the latter shown in Figure 1-1) can be handmade if you have sewing machine skills. Or, you can purchase a tool roll from a hardware store, stationery store, or bookbinding supplier.

be precise: measuring tools and cutting guides

You will need tools for measuring and for use as a straightedge while cutting. We suggest several essential tools and helpful additions to your toolbox when funds allow:

- Steel rulers
- Straightedge
- Galaxy Gauge or Schaedler Rule
- Triangle

A sturdy steel ruler with *incised* numbers and measurement lines is the optimum and essential measuring tool. Rulers with a cork backing are not recommended because they do not allow for direct contact with the surface that is being measured and therefore may cause the measurement mark to be less than perfectly accurate. However, you can remove the cork and save it for use when it seems necessary. Figure 1-2 has a selection of rulers pictured. If possible within your budget, include 12-, 24-, and 36-inch rulers in your collection for ease of measuring at a variety of lengths.

Figure 1-1
Left to right:
Metal box.
Sturdy canvas bag.
Zipper case.

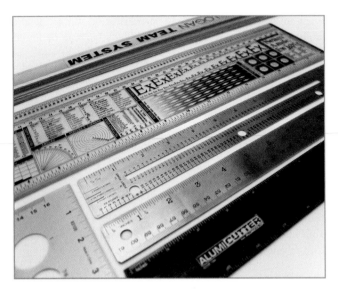

Figure 1-2
Straightedge, Galaxy Gauge, steel rulers, raised-edge ruler, triangle.

We urge you to purchase a steel ruler. An aluminum ruler is not satisfactory because the lines marking the increments of measurement are printed on the surface and can be more easily worn away or chipped off. In addition, the lines are usually thicker than the steel ruler's incised line and therefore slightly less precise—the line itself might be 1/64 inch and skew measurements (more on the use of rulers in Chapter 3).

A ruler can also double as a **straightedge** for use as a cutting guide; see also Figure 1-2.

Strongly suggested, however, is a *raised-edge* cutting guide or a ruler with a raised edge along the top. Most important, the raised-edge top can help to protect fingers and thumbs from being nicked or sliced by a cutting blade.

We use aluminum raised-edge cutters for thick board (this tool is also known as a mat cutter) and an aluminum raised-edge cutter with a ruler and steel insert for cutting thin paper (see the black ruler in Figure 1-2).

Precision rulers such as a **Galaxy Gauge** (Figure 1-2; note translucent ruler) and a **Schaedler Rule** are thin, plastic, highly precise measurement tools. There are inch, printer point/pica, metric, decimal-inch, agate line, and DTP point/pica calibrations on these rulers. In addition, several models include an angle-measuring guide (protractor) along with various other helpful measurements. If you want grand master accuracy, you might consider either a Galaxy Gauge or a Schaedler Rule.

triangles

A rigid metal drafting **triangle** (Figure 1-3) can assist as a guide to ensure that your measurements are square (corner edges meet at a perfect 90-degree angle). The triangle also assists with measuring, drawing, and cutting angles in a variety of degrees: 90 with 45 and 60.

If you like the possibility of using a triangle for extensive measuring of angles, we suggest a designer's triangle providing for the selection of angles from 15 to 90 degrees in a single implement (in increments of 15 degrees or less, and further including provisions for taper angles to vary the aforesaid angles).

helpful extra tools

The following group of measuring tools is handy but not essential:

¤ Set dividers

¤ Caliper

¤ T-square

Our recommendation is to purchase within your budget. Consider forgoing a few extraneous luxuries in favor of a good tool that will last a lifetime.

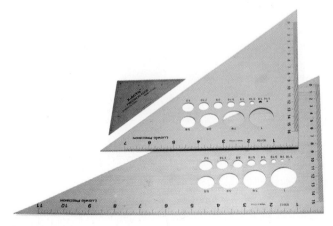

Figure 1-3
Triangles.

Set dividers (also known as spring dividers) are two-prong, sharply pointed tools that can be set and locked in place at a given width (usually less than 3 inches); see Figure 1-4. Once the measurement is set, the tool is used with a ruler or straightedge to mark or check multiple units of the set measurement. The sharp point of the tool slightly punctures the substrate to record the point of measurement. We like to use it to speed the process of measuring a line of set increments and to double-check measurements for pinpoint accuracy.

Calipers are particularly useful for measuring round and unusual-shaped objects and the thickness of paperboard. They're good for packaging measurements or measuring the lightsaber hilt tubes (the latter illustrated in Chapter 3).

Although the highly respected and personable master designer Michael Bierut, Principal at Pentagram, New York, humorously stated that his once important T-square is now handy only for back scratching ("Drawing Board to the Desktop: A Designer's Path," *New York Times*, February 7, 2009), we have nonetheless counted on our T-square for construction purposes on many occasions.

Disclaimer noted, a steel **T-square** (for technical drafting rather than a carpenter's version, see Figure 1-4) can also be included in your toolbox but is not absolutely critical. Rather, it is helpful for working with a triangle to draw straight and 90-degree (square) lines.

N.B. Paper is manufactured with precise 90-degree corner angles. However, once cut by hand, the sheet of paper may have lost its manufactured precision. Employing a triangle and a T-square allows you to check that all angles of the substrate have 90-degree corners.

Figure 1-4
T-square, set dividers, protractor, caliper.

score and fold

You will need tools with which to score, fold, and flatten a crease. We suggest you consider the following types of tools:

- ¤   Scoring tool

- ¤   Folding tool

- ¤   Burnishing tools

A **scoring tool** is used to incise a line that is to be folded. If scoring is not implemented, it is nearly impossible to have a clean, precise, and neat fold. The point of the tool should not be as sharp as a blade but should be thin and sturdy enough to incise the fold line without actually cutting through it.

We also use a craft knife (discussed further along in this chapter) for scoring, but we use the blunt side of the blade. If you choose this method, be sure to handle the razor edge carefully to avoid cutting yourself in the process.

We are guessing that you think folding tools look like tongue depressors. There is a similarity in shape, but these tools are heavier and should never be stuck in your classmate's throat!

A **folding tool** (also known as a **bone folder**) is used to rub over the edge of a fold to make it crisp and permanent. The tool can be employed to flatten the crease, tighten the fold, and smooth slight wrinkles. It is indispensable.

The folding tool can also be used to **burnish**—that is, to rub across a surface to make it smooth. A folding tool assists in pressing two glued surfaces together for evenly distributed adhesion.

You can buy hard plastic folding tools or choose to purchase one made of animal bone. If you are a political vegetarian, select the former. If you are concerned about the environment and biodegradable products, select the latter. If you are both, use a large spoon (it will sort of work, but it is not the best tool for the purpose). But do use a folder. Your fingers are not acceptable substitutes! See Figure 1-5 for scoring, folding, and burnishing tools.

handy burnishing tools

Tools such as those listed in the following group are helpful and handy for constructing comps and simulating specialty printing techniques. We list them to make you aware in the event you have the funds to add them to your toolbox:

- ¤   Embossing tools

- ¤   Rubber and wooden brayers (a.k.a. rollers)

- ¤   Spatula

beleaf: preserving the environment one design at a time

Debra Rizzi

Have you ever considered what role paper plays in shaping environmental change?

Similar to the creative process, the impact starts from the ground up. Forests store 50% of the world's terrestrial carbon. (In other words, they are awfully important "carbon sinks" that hold onto pollution that would otherwise lead to global warming.)[1]

The paper industry is the fourth largest contributor to greenhouse gas emissions among manufacturing industries in the United States, and contributes 9% of the manufacturing sector's carbon emissions.[2] Therefore, design and printing decisions that are made during the creative process directly impact the environment. There's a positive message in this. The paper and printing industries alike have made proactive efforts to reduce overall emissions through many combined efforts, one of which is being certified by the Forest Stewardship Council (FSC). This international organization supports responsible forestry practices through a heavily regulated chain of custody in which resources are monitored from the forest, to the pulp, to the mill that converts pulp into paper, to the merchant that sells the paper, and finally to the printer that prints on that paper.

The designer and client hold the key to the door that opens this positive chain reaction. All they need to do is specify certified products. But while this is one small component, what can designers do to inspire further change? The answer is different for each company, but in May of 2007, Rizco Design took action and launched a measurable plan of action, Beleaf, which has been utilized to transform the way they do business and educate other designers, clients, and end users along the way.

The design challenge includes the following points:

• Influence potential and existing clients to understand their impactand create a cycle of change thatencourages environmentally responsible graphic design, paper, and printing decisions.

• Help clients understand that "going green" does not impact the quality of their end product and can be accomplished with a limited (if not any) increase in cost to their bottom line.

• Avoid statements; instead, provide a measurable tool that showcases Rizco's commitment to producing a sustainable end product.

[1] Did you know? Approximately 16 million tons of high-grade fiber from offices and printers go into landfills annually that could be recovered.

[2] Environmental Paper Network (American Forest & Paper Association, 2006)

Various printed materials: Beleaf
Studio: Rizco Design
Creative Director: Keith Rizzi
Client: Beleaf (Rizco Design)

solution: beleaf and the beleaf report card

Rizco Design's Beleaf program is a three-tiered program that measures environmental decision making throughout the creative process in the firm—starting with how the office operates, to how the design is established, and finally, to how projects are printed. After a project is completed, Rizco Design grades the end product through a web-based tool. An electronic report card is distributed to the client to showcase the decisions that went into the project and measure the sustainability of the job, enabling the client to witness the impact firsthand.

how it works

The Beleaf report card is structured into three tiers based upon Green Office (20%), Green Design (30%), and Green Printing (50%).

To make *Tier One: Green Office* come to life, necessary changes were made to the internal day-to-day policies and procedures, such as implementing paperless paychecks, analyzing shipping and supply vendors, switching to eco-friendly cleaning products, and purchasing 100% green power (50/50 split between wind and hydro). Each of these has become "a way of doing business" and contributes to 20% of each job. The grading system gets tougher as the process progresses since each designer is responsible for making decisions and guiding the client to make sustainable choices.

Tier Two: Green Design accounts for 30% of the total score. Out of the seven criteria, the categories of "end product being recyclable" and "resources needed to produce the end product" have the highest percentages attached to them because they directly impact the sustainability of a job.

Lastly, *Tier Three: Green Printing* accounts for 50% of the total score since it relies heavily on natural resources. Seven key areas of print production are examined, including how files are released, colorization, paper stock, printing process, certified printers, coatings, and bindery. These main categories are broken down into subcategories that are individually analyzed and ranked with point values by how eco-friendly they are. In areas where nonrecyclable printing processes are selected, such as lamination, no points are awarded.

Additionally, major emphasis is placed on sustainable paper decision making such as specifying stocks that are FSC-certified and/or recycled. Purchasing paper through certified channels or with high recycled content helps to reduce unnecessary tree consumption, which in turn, lowers CO_2 levels and helps to reverse the negative effects of deforestation. Overall, the bottom-line total for any print project will reflect some negative impact on the environment and thus will never reach a score of 100% sustainability on the Beleaf report card.

results

The online report card has become a favorite among clients, with many of them taking their grades seriously. Between May and December of 2007, 74 print projects were recorded under the Beleaf program, with 47% meeting a score of 70–96. The average overall score for 2007 was 73.7.

Rizco Design continues to research and identify new eco-friendly products, like biodegradable lamination and foamboard, which lower the overall impact that their end products place on the environment. Additionally, education has become a key focus of the Beleaf program. Other initiatives include pro bono presentations on green design initiatives, the rollout of Beleaf Kids eco-educational T-shirts, and Project Give Back, a pro bono effort for eco-conscious nonprofit firms.

For more information, visit www.rizcodesign.com and www.beleaf.com.

eco-tips for designers

in the office

1. When commuting, try to be carbon neutral. Carpool or ride a bike. Offset your CO_2 if possible. (For more information, visit www.carbonfund.org.)

2. Go digital. Reduce printouts and share files electronically. Produce paperless paychecks and pay bills online. If you have to print, make it double-sided with smaller margins.

3. Choose green suppliers. Purchase "green" office supplies and work with eco-conscious vendors. Visit www.climate counts. org and download the pocket guide.

4. Use green power. Purchase renewable energy such as wind, biogas, biomass, solar, and hydro for your office and home. (For more information, visit www.epa.gov.)

   —Search online for "Green Power Locator" for information on how to convert.

5. Recycle, recycle, recycle.

design

1. Consider whether the product is truly necessary.

2. Design a recyclable end product.

3. Make longevity a priority. Design a piece that can be updated or used again.

4. Streamline printing processes. Less is more if it aligns with the overall strategy of the project.

5. Minimize colors and limit metallic/fluorescent inks.

6. Utilize PDFs versus printed proofs.

7. Remember that size matters. Smaller can be better.

8. When selecting paper, remember that lighter weights use less wood fiber.

9. Print several components at the same time (gang run) to lower costs and eliminate waste.

10. Advise clients on recycling steps for items that contain metal, plastic, or glue.

about rizco design

Rizco Design is an eco-conscious branding and design firm located in Manasquan, New Jersey. Featured in the 2007 "People to Watch Edition" of GDUSA, the team is known for the launch of Beleaf, a measurable sustainability program that ensures that a percentage of each client's job is environmentally friendly. Since its inception, the program has obtained over 24 million media impressions, including features in GDUSA, Print Professional, Renourish.com, GreenBiz Radio, and HOW Magazine's blog.

In August 2008, Rizco Design became the first design firm to be admitted into the EPA's Climate Leaders program where the company's environmental footprint is measured and a five-year plan of action is generated to reduce emissions. Rizco Design also participates in other eco-organizations, including the Designers Accord, EPA Green Power Partnership, Design Can Change, and One Percent for the Planet.

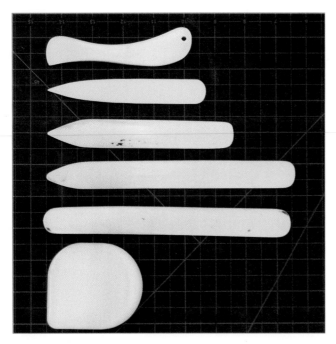

Figure 1-5
Top to bottom:
Scoring tools (2).
Folding and burnishing tools (bone) (3).
Folding and burnishing tool (plastic).

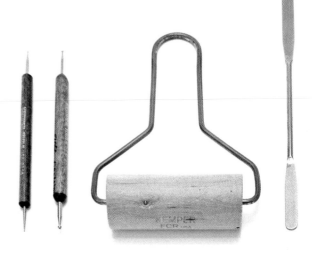

Figure 1-6
Left to right:
Ballpoint embossing stylus.
Brayer (roller).
Spatula.

An **embossing tool** is a ballpoint stylus that is primarily used to push paper into a stencil to create an embossed surface. The tool can also burnish into tight corners. We use them for "pushing" into tight corners. Because of the smooth ballpoint, there is less risk of tearing paper.

Brayers are excellent for burnishing and adhering two flat substrates together. The tool is especially good for rolling over large areas and for use with thick materials.

A **spatula** is a bookbinder's tool and can be used for lifting a glued paper up off the table without getting fingers sticky. It is also used for some types of burnishing. We use it for working with glue. See Figure 1-6 for burnishing tools.

finding the tools

Many tools are specialty items and, therefore, may not be found in just fine art supply stores. You may need multiple sources for purchasing tools. For instance, look for scoring, folding, burnishing, and embossing tools in the bookbinding section of your local or online craft supply store rather than with basic fine art supplies. Look for T-squares, triangles, and rulers with drafting supplies.

cutting tools

There is a great variety of cutting tools available for a wide assortment of purposes. We have grouped these tools by use and listed the options for each category:

- Single-blade knives (utility and craft)
- Scissors
- Circle and oval cutters
- Hole punchers

single-blade knives

A handheld tool for cutting paper is essential. The blade of the tool should be very sharp and remain sharp throughout the cutting process. Very sharp blades cut smoothly, neatly, and precisely and, therefore, are critically necessary. However, a very sharp blade is also the cause of many sliced fingertips. For safety purposes, we recommend using a large-handle **utility knife** for the vast majority of cutting; see Figure 1-7 for this category of cutting tool. There are many types of utility knives. If you can afford one with an ergonomic handle, we urge you to buy it for comfort and ease of use. Also purchase a bulk supply of blades because it is less expensive to buy them in quantity.

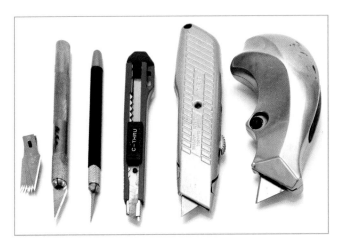

Figure 1-7
Left to right:
Craft knife blades.
Craft knives: heavy-duty and lightweight.
Utility knives: breakaway blade, standard utility,
and ergonomic handle.

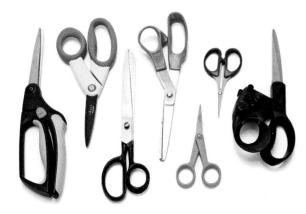

Figure 1-8
Left to right:
Spring-hinged scissors.
Serrated scissors for heavy cutting.
Two kinds of standard scissors.
Two kinds of precision scissors.
Laser guide scissors.

Craft knives are lightweight, slim-handle cutting tools. These tools allow for cutting small curves and small or complex shapes on lightweight material. However, they should not be used with heavyweight boards, foamboards, bulky stacks of paper, or large paper because the delicate handle and ultrasharp blade offer less control and strength than a utility knife. Less control may lead to a cutting accident—nicking or slicing into your fingers or hand.

Get a plastic sleeve to keep the slim cylinder from rolling off the drafting table and into your foot. As an alternative, select one with a retractable blade or a cap for storage. Or, put tape around the cylinder so that it doesn't roll. Purchase blades in bulk for a steady supply. A blade dispenser will keep the blades out of harm's way, before and after use.

scissors

A sturdy pair of standard **scissors** or larger shears is helpful for quickly cutting into large areas that do not require a precise measurement. When some precision is necessary, there is a scissor that uses a beam of light to assist in cutting along a straight line; we are craft enthusiasts so tools such as this one simply intrigue at the start but do eventually prove to be helpful.

> ### safety note
>
> The cutting tool is not ultimately responsible for a skin wound. You should be wide awake and aware at all times and use precaution when working with cutting tools of any sort. Safety issues in the use of cutting tools will be further discussed in Chapter 3.

Spring-hinged scissors and **serrated scissors** are good for heavy work and thick paper. **Precision scissors** are perfect for snipping away in tiny areas. All three types of scissors are shown in Figure 1-8.

circle and oval cutters

Cutting accurate and perfect circles and ovals is nearly impossible without a specialized knife and cutting guides. You can use hand-held knives as shown previously (Figure 1-7) or select from the many handheld circle and oval cutting tools available; see Figure 1-9. You do not need elaborate equipment, but do buy a tool that is adjustable in order to cut a variety of sizes.

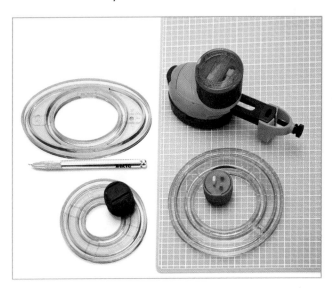

Figure 1-9
Shown are three circle and oval cutting tools with templates (translucent plastic), and a swivel craft knife (cuts curves). A small cutting mat can be seen underneath the tools.

Keep safety in mind when selecting a circle cutter. Look for a tool that has a retractable blade or protective storage covering. The blades on these tools are crazy sharp.

hole punching

We are constantly punching holes in all sorts of things (mostly paper) for a variety of construction techniques. You can't craft bookbindings without a hole puncher. Therefore, use single-hole, handheld punching tools to cut holes in paper, heavy board, fabric, and leather; see Figure 1-10. The essentials include:

◻ Leather punch (with craft hammer and anvil)

◻ Awl

◻ Single-hole punches (slot, circle, square, adjustable size circles)

Select a variety of diameters for circular holes. You should have at least one 1/16-inch punch. Shaped hole punches are not essential, but we find the simple square hole punch and slot punch a valuable alternative to a circular hole.

Alternately, an **awl** is a tool that can be used to poke tiny holes to assist in sewing or as a marking tool in measuring or both. Although not essential, a two- and three-hole punch can make multiple hole punching easier.

specialty cutters

Although not essential for a basic toolbox, the following specialized cutting tools can be helpful for specific jobs:

◻ Decorative edger

◻ Rotary cutter

◻ Bevel or mat cutter

◻ Foamboard cutter

◻ Razor saw and miter box

◻ Perforator

◻ Rounded corner cutter

There are a great variety of scissors that have blades molded into shapes to cut a decorative edge; see Figure 1-11. This type of specialty scissors is called a **decorative edger**. We recommend using *only* simple forms such as scallop, pinking (zigzag), and "mountain and valley." Elaborate decorative edges are difficult to reproduce in a commercial cost-effective way. In addition, there is a danger of the design looking amateurish and inappropriately silly if the decorative edge is overused. Use wisely. Design smartly.

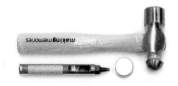
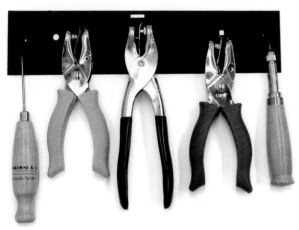

Figure 1-10
Top row:
Leather punch with hammer and anvil.
Bottom row, left to right:
Awl.
Single-hole punches: circle, slot, square.
Japanese single-action, adjustable, circle punch.

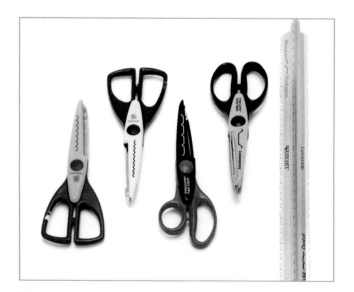

Figure 1-11
Decorative edgers.
Left to right:
Scallop.
Pinking.
"Mountain and valley."
"Mountain and valley" variation.
Deckle-edge ripper.

A **deckle-edge ripper** is a nonessential tool but can be useful for simulating the edge found on actual handmade paper. A straightedge can also rip paper for a handmade look, but it is smooth and less random in appearance; see Figure 1-11. The soft and uneven edge of handmade paper (**deckle**) is further noted in Chapter 2 on paper.

Specialty cutters and knives make construction easier and faster. They perform operations that can perhaps be accomplished with a craft knife or a utility knife, but the latter is a lot more work.

The primary purpose of a **rotary cutter** is to cut fabric. And we do use it for this purpose. We also use a rotary cutter for paper because it is fast. When we have multiple sheets of paper to cut and time is of the essence, a rotary cutter is a handy tool; see Figure 1-12.

A **bevel or mat cutter** will cut board at a 45-degree angle. The primary purpose is for cutting an angled edge for the inside of a picture mat, but we use it for other projects as well. The angle that can be obtained with this tool is more satisfactory than a bevel angle cut with a handheld utility knife.

Cutting foamboard is a tricky task. The foam and paper coating often tear in the process of cutting. The **foamboard cutter** makes for quick and clean-cut lines on this spongy substrate.

A **razor saw** cuts metal, wood, and plastic. The miter box keeps the substrate steady. Beyond paper, if you need to cut thick and rigid materials, a razor saw is the best tool. Be aware, however, that it does not cut glass.

The **perforator** is a little single-blade tool that cuts a perforated line. Try cutting a "perf" without one—tedious indeed.

We love our **rounded-corner cutter**. This little contraption cuts rounded corners with ease. If you are designing and crafting your own business card (or invitations, etc.) and have conceived a format with rounded corners, this tool becomes a must (unless you want to spend five weeks measuring the arc for 100 business cards and cutting a quarter-inch rounded corner with a craft knife).

working surfaces

You will need a sturdy worktable and clean, appropriate working surfaces to build and otherwise execute your comps. We recommend a dedicated work area for well-organized and safe construction. The following tools are essential for the work area:

- Drafting table

- Cutting mat

- Paperboard or heavyweight cardboard

We shouldn't assume you have a flat, adjustable **drafting table** as a surface for all your sketching, drawing, and production work. But if you are in design, it is likely that you have a table with an adjustable top that allows you to tilt the work surface toward you or make

Figure 1-12
Left to right:
Foamboard cutter.
Bevel or mat cutter.
Razor saw and miter box.
Rounded-corner cutter.
Perforator.
Rotary cutter.

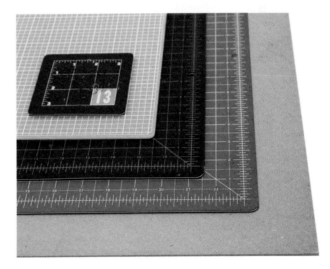

Figure 1-13
Self-healing cutting mats and cardboard
(also known as paperboard).

it flat for cutting and construction projects. If you do not have this type of table, we strongly suggest that you get one. A surface that tilts (for sketching and drawing) and lays flat (for cutting and construction) is essential.

To protect the top of your worktable when cutting or otherwise constructing your comps, it is necessary to have a smooth, movable surface.

Alas, the PVC that gives **cutting mats** maximum self-healing capability and a smooth cutting surface is the same substance that will not biodegrade; see Figure 1-13. However, cutting mats are nearly indispensable. They can be used forever if stored in a cool, dry place. Don't leave a cutting mat in a car that is baking in the hot sun. Once the mat warps, it is not easy (or not possible) to return to perfect flatness.

Since it is good idea to protect your cutting table and keep a clean and smooth cutting surface, an alternative to the PVC mat is recycled paperboard or cardboard. Paperboard is multiple-ply paper that makes a good clean and smooth surface. Unfortunately, using paperboard or cardboard as a cutting surface quickly dulls the cutting blade, whereas the PVC mats do not. PVC mats are also known as "self-healing." That is, when a blade slices the mat, the "wound" closes or self-heals. Paperboard and cardboard do not self-heal.

first aid

Because you will be working with cutting tools, you need to keep a standard first aid kit readily available in your studio; see the accompanying image. The kit should contain hydrogen peroxide and sterile gauze to clean a superficial wound caused by a cutting tool accident. There should also be antibacterial ointment and adhesive bandages to treat and cover the affected area.

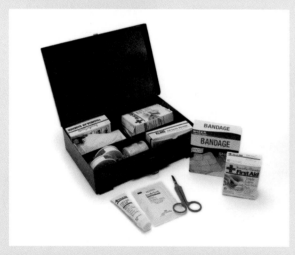

First aid kits are available at most office supply stores and pharmacies. Don't cut anything without one.

We can't tell you exactly at what point you should visit a hospital emergency room or doctor because we are not with you. If a wound is deep enough to require stitches or seems to become infected (red, swollen, sore to the touch), please use safe judgment and visit a doctor or nurse to determine what treatment you should receive for the wound.

Use stiff cardboard as a gluing surface. And save any scrap copier paper or other clear newsprint for a protective barrier while working with adhesives.

imaging tools

Standard or traditional dry and wet media are of course essential for imaging (drawing) and for practical use in sketching, measuring, and rendering textures for comps. Examples include:

- Pencils
- Erasers
- Pens and markers
- Crayons
- Acrylic paint
- Specialty texture paints
- Ink and stamp pads

Pencils are good tools for sketching, of course, but they are also necessary for marking a line of measurement. The graphite contained in your pencils should have a range of hardness. Include those that are hard (H) to soft (B): 5H, HB, 2B, 6B.

Erasers clean away graphite and can be used to assist with image making as well. Have several types of erasers in your toolbox. The different types of erasers will be used for a variety of purposes and in conjunction with a variety of papers. Select at least a kneaded eraser, a white eraser, and a gum eraser.

Also include with your tools a piece of paper of medium grit and very light jeweler's **sandpaper** to use as a cleaning surface to remove (by rubbing) graphite or other substances from the eraser. Light grit sandpaper is also helpful to smooth rough edges of paper and other materials.

Pens and **markers** are tools for sketching and visualizing. Select both fine points and thick points. Permanent markers are used for labeling tools with your name.

We like to use pens and markers for a continuous line sketch and for pressing and indenting into paper for an embossed technique (see later chapters on simulating embossing).

Crayons are those waxy playful visualizing tools used to produce a particular type of line that we find interesting for image creation and rendering textures. For imaging tools and erasers, see Figures 1-14 and 1-15.

Figure 1-14
Left to right:
Crayons (2).
Metal nib "quill" pens (2).
Ballpoint pens (2).
Rollerball pen.
Markers (chisel point, extra fine point, fine point, silver ink fine point).
White pencil.
Graphite pencils (5).
Mechanical pencil.
Drafting pencil with graphite refills (for the latter).

wet media

Paints can expand the visual range of images and are also useful for simulating textures. We suggest the following types:

- Acrylic paint
- Enamel paint
- Texture or puff paint
- Spray paint (enamels and specialty finishes)

Synthetic **acrylic paint** is a water-soluble imaging medium that can be used in a wide range of techniques that yield a variety of interesting results. We use it for simulating textured surfaces, for image making, and for mixed media projects (such as painting on photos). For a good range of color mixing, at a minimum select acrylic paint in basic red, red-orange, crimson, cobalt blue, ultramarine blue, yellow, yellow ochre, burnt ochre, white, and black.

Specialty paints such as oil-based **enamels** or **texture** (or puff) **paint** are useful for painting on metal, glass, or plastic. Use oil-based paints and their solvents only with great care in a well-ventilated area. See Figure 1-16 for some examples of these types of paints.

Figure 1-15
Top, left to right:
White plastic eraser.
Kneaded eraser.
Gum eraser.
Bottom:
Eraser pencil.

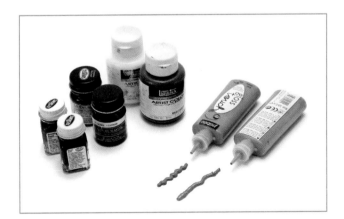

Figure 1-16
Left to right:
Enamel paint.
Acrylic paints.
Puff (or texture) paint.

Specialty spray paints can be found in various colors and finishes (gloss, satin, matte) and can simulate finishes such as metal/metallic/hammered metal, sandstone, granite, marble, frosted glass, translucent, terra cotta, chalkboard, suede, magnetized, phosphorescent, fluorescent, reflective, spray-on rubber . . . and we reluctantly end there. See Figure 1-17 for samples.

The caveat here is that brush-on enamel paints or spray paints often require a toxic solvent for cleaning off brushes and hands. We repeat for emphasis: Use spray and enamel paints with great care and clean up with as little solvent as possible.

Include a variety of sizes of acrylic and bristle brushes for applying paint and glue (paperboard chips are also good for the latter); see Figure 1-18. When simply thinking creatively, we recommend going beyond standard (and at times very expensive) artists' paintbrushes. Have fun with inexpensive sponge brushes, foam brushes, forks, twigs, and so on; see Figure 1-19.

Found in the supermarket with kitchen supplies, **parchment** (waxy) **paper** can be used as a surface on which to mix paints. A small glass pane (taped along the edges for safety) can work as a mixing surface as well. Recycle large yogurt containers to hold water for cleaning brushes and have plenty of soft cotton rags for cleanup.

stamping and thermography

To simulate specialty printing processes, we suggest the following supplies and tools:

- ¤ Foam stamp pads with pigmented ink

- ¤ Craft foam

- ¤ Adhesive ink pens

- ¤ Rosin powder (a.k.a. thermography or embossing powder)

- ¤ Heat gun

Foam stamp pads (with pigmented ink), craft foam or carveable rubber, powdered rosin, and a heat gun are necessary for simple desktop **stamping** (printing) techniques and for simulating **thermography**—a specialty printing technique discussed further in Chapter 10.

Select **stamp pads** (in a plastic case) that have a *foam* base for holding *pigmented* ink. These pads can get expensive, so plan ahead and select those colors that you are sure to use; see Figure 1-20. Ink can be purchased separately from the pad and used with **craft foam** (thin, compressed sponge) or carveable rubber. The ink gets a bit messy without a case, however. We recommend soap and lots of time in order to clean stamping ink off your fingers—avoid the use of toxic solvents whenever possible. Craft foam and carveable rubber are used to make your own stamps. This material can be cut with a sharp scissors or craft knife into shapes and letters. Or, you can carve your own from a linoleum block or have a rubber stamp made through an office supply store or a small printer.

Figure 1-17
Specialty paints.
Left to right:
Metallic gold.
Blue satin.
Hammered silver (for plastic surfaces).
Stone.
Clear matte.

Figure 1-18
Left to right:
Paperboard chips for spreading glue (or paint).
Brushes for various purposes: natural bristle, soft acrylic bristle, sable, flat bristle (wide), cylinder handle bristle (with attached stand and burnisher at the tip of the handle for gluing).

Figure 1-19
Collection of inexpensive brushes and various image making tools.

Figure 1-20
Left to right:
Craft foam sheets (2).
Pigmented foam stamp pad.
Craft knife.
Handmade stamp (crafted from gum eraser and craft foam).
Commercially made stamp mounted on wood block (the letter O).
Sample stamping.

term). Rather, the rosin is called thermography powder because of its relationship to the specialty printing process of the same name. The specialty printing (or imprinting) processes of thermography and embossing are discussed in Chapter 10. Even though the rosin is sold as embossing powder, we will use the term *thermography powder* as it is used in the industry, when discussed further in this book.

You will also need a **heat gun** for melting the thermography powder. A heat gun is a handheld tool that generates a low level of heat but does not blow air. You might think a hair dryer is a good substitute—it is not. The high velocity of the dryer fan will blow away the thermography powder before it melts.

stick to it

The vast majority of three-dimensional comps need some kind of adhesive to hold the parts (usually paper) together. You should consider including the following types of adhesives for your toolbox:

- ▢ Adhesive-backed transfer sheets/dry mount
- ▢ Adhesive applicator tool or glue spreader
- ▢ Glue dots
- ▢ Glue stick
- ▢ Liquid glue and applicators
- ▢ Paste glue
- ▢ Tapes

Figure 1-21
Thermography powders.

Figure 1-22
Left to right:
Heat gun.
Adhesive ink pens.
Thermography powder (and sample image).

Adhesive ink pens are good for drawing lines of clear ink to which the rosin or thermography powder will stick; see Figures 1-21 and 1-22.

Desktop embossing or **thermography powder** is a hobby-grade rosin (Figure 1-21) that will melt when light heat is applied over it. The term **embossing** refers to the raised surface it creates, but the term is confusing relative to commercial printing that defines and creates embossing (a raised surface) *without* the use of melted rosin. The term *embossing* is not used to describe the use of rosin relative to commercial use (it is an art supply store and hobbyist's

safety note

With glue there are safety issues. Many types of glue are toxic. For instance, we say absolutely no rubber cement. Spray adhesives are also usually avoidable. The fumes, spray, and chemicals of rubber cement and spray adhesives are airborne and stick to human lungs, well, like glue. Even with proper ventilation that is needed when gluing, the chemicals found in rubber cement and its cleaner are not good for a healthy body.

Although chemically based, stick and liquid glues are much less toxic than rubber cement and spray adhesives. Read the label on the container of the adhesive to learn about its ingredients and toxicity level. Especially note any warning label information on the adhesive container. If you have allergies and are not sure if you will have an adverse reaction, contact the manufacturer of the adhesive for information in this regard. Use adhesives in a well-ventilated area. Wear a face mask for protection when gluing extensively.

Adhesive sheets (a.k.a. dry-mount adhesives) usually come in packages of 20 and in various sizes. Peeling off the overlay sheet exposes the non-repro white adhesive below.

The sheets come in light and heavy (permanent bond) adhesive layers. The latter is good for gluing heavyweight papers and for some other heavyweight materials. You can also find acid-free, archival adhesive sheets.

Since the adhesive sheets are simple (and not as messy as sprays or liquids) and comps are not generally meant to be archival, they are useful for a great majority of projects. Be sure to read all information provided by the distributor and manufacturer to understand the ingredients and possible hazards of the products.

An **adhesive applicator tool** (a.k.a. glue spreader) lays down a dot pattern (2- and 4-inch versions) of glue that remains repositionable for approximately 12 hours and then forms a permanent bond. The tool is usually preloaded with 20 to 50 feet of acid-free adhesive. Refill cartridges are sold separately. We recommend it for its fast action and for use with large projects.

Glue sticks are simple, relatively mess-free, almost all-purpose adhesive. We like 3M wrinkle-free glue sticks. This clear formula glue stick is acid-free and goes on smoothly and cleanly. It is initially repositionable and has a high potential for a wrinkle-free surface. When dry, it creates a strong bond to most papers and photos and it is nontoxic. Get a bunch for your toolbox.

There are additional tape-like and adhesive "sticky" substances that are useful. We use double-sided glue "dots" and peel-and-stick dot tabs for various jobs that need only a small dab in a discreet area. Some glue dots are repositionable.

You may also like the purple color glue sticks. The color guides the application, helping to see those areas covered sufficiently and those areas that are not. Purple color glue sticks are helpful but not critical. See Figure 1-23 for adhesive sheets, glue spreader, and glue dots.

The only general-purpose white glue that we suggest using is **PVA (polyvinyl acetate)**. PVA glue is fast drying and creates a strong permanent bond; see Figure 1-24. PVA or PVAc is a rubbery synthetic polymer. Sold as an adhesive, PVA is a liquid white glue used for paper and more importantly for porous materials, particularly wood and fabric. PVA is widely used in bookbinding and book arts due to its flexibility and because it is nonacidic and archival unlike many other polymers. In addition, PVA creates a strong, permanent bond. But don't expect to add water because diluting negates the strength of the bond.

Given that PVA glue is less expensive when purchased in a large quantity, we suggest that you pour the glue into a small container so that you are not working from the cumbersome large jar. Glues should be kept in a cool and dry location.

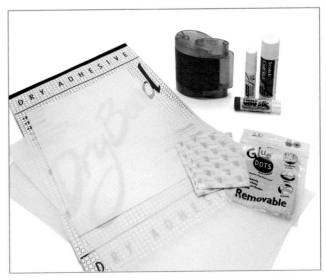

Figure 1-23
Left to right:
Adhesive sheets (dry mount).
Glue spreader.
Glue dots.
Glue sticks.

Figure 1-24
Left to right:
Glass plate for holding glue.
Gluing brushes (on top of plate).
Paperboard spreaders.
PVA liquid white glue.
Gel super glue (for instant bonds).

Glue brushes are needed to spread the substance. We recommend stiff, round and/or flat bristle brushes. Wash brushes between use and you will have them for a long time. You can buy brushes specifically made for liquid white (PVA) glue.

Paste glue is an all-purpose clear paste that is thick and sticky. We like YES brand. Paste glue can be substituted for liquid white glue but it is not archival. It is a bit easier to control because of the thick consistency rather than a flowing liquid.

Also suggested for spreading paste and liquid glue are 3" × 4" (or thereabout) scraps of small leftover pieces (a.k.a. chips) of stiff cardboard or illustration board. The scraps can be cut back after use in order to reuse. Or, simply recycle after using all sides of the scrap board.

Hot glue (and the applicator known as a glue gun) is not essential but is included here because it is handy for adhering small, three-dimensional objects such as buttons, beads, trinkets, and other "doodads" to a sturdy surface. It bonds instantly and dries in seconds; see Figure 1-25.

tapes

For temporary and permanent purposes, tape is an essential construction supply. When funds allow, specialty tapes for specific purposes can also be very helpful. Some suggestions include those in the following group:

- Drafting tape
- Double-stick tape
- Linen tape
- Specialty tapes: paint-resistant masking tape, masking, frosted, heavy-duty clear or duct, metal tape, pigmented

Drafting tape assists with *temporarily* securing a substrate to a surface or for testing the construction before applying glue. **Double-stick tape** is useful when you need to adhere only one edge of a paper (it has a stronger adhesive than drafting tape). Additional uses for these tapes may arise as you work. Double-stick tape is also a relatively mess-free, quick, and handy adhesive for small areas. **Linen tape** is an adhesive-backed strip of fabric that is good for bookbinding.

Specialty tapes such as masking, frosted, heavy-duty clear or duct, metallic coated, and pigmented (color) have sticky or superadhesive qualities that are meant to be strong or nearly permanent and/or meant for decorative purposes. However, don't expect any tape to completely take the place of glue. Tapes leave visible seams; when used properly, glue binds seamlessly. See Figure 1-26 for examples of tape products.

staplers and fasteners

Staplers are essential tools for binding multiple pages of paper and assisting with or simulating several types of bookbinding. There are several types:

- Cinch stapler
- Saddle stapler
- Long-handle stapler
- Staple-free "stapler"

Figure 1-26
Specialty tapes.
Left to right:
FrogTape (paint-resistant masking tape).
Black masking.
Frosted cellophane (in dispenser).
Double-sided.
Heavy-duty clear.
White cloth.
White drafting.
Metal tape (like having adhesive aluminum foil).

Figure 1-25
Battery-operated and electric glue guns.

A **long-handle stapler** is excellent for securing a small stack of text weight papers and reaching beyond what the usual 5-inch standard stapler can accomplish. It is best to have a long-handle stapler—it is more versatile than the standard size.

Heavy-duty **cinch staplers** are handy and helpful; they perform special tasks such as stapling through thick material.

A **saddle stapler** is not essential but is handy for stapling along a fold of several sheets of paper; see Figure 1-27 for examples of staplers.

Beyond the essential, and for creative fun (and small jobs of three or less pieces of lightweight paper), try color staples such as used with a hobbyist stapler (brand name: Fastenator) or color staples with a ministapler, the latter being small and convenient enough to fit in a portable toolbox; see Figure 1-28.

In addition, a **staple-free "stapler"** is a tool that creates a flap-joint to hold several sheets of paper together; see Figure 1-29.

miscellaneous tools for binding

Not essential for all construction projects, yet helpful for simulating particular binding styles, the following tools and materials can expand your creative potential:

- ☐ Grommets and grommet punch
- ☐ Tweezers
- ☐ Needle, thread, thimble, beeswax
- ☐ Sewing machine
- ☐ Spiral, Wire-O, and hot glue binding machines
- ☐ Electric drill and clamps

Grommets are circular metal loops that are primarily used for strengthening a hole cut in paper or fabric (sneakers with laces often have grommet holes). For desktop implementation of grommets, special tools (punches) for the purpose can be purchased in craft stores, art supply stores, or outlets selling bookbinding supplies; see Figure 1-30.

We recommend having small tweezers in your toolbox. Tweezers are not essential but very helpful for a variety of tasks—especially removing lint from sticky surfaces.

Sewing tools such as needles and thread are helpful for hand bookbinding. **Beeswax** is a substance applied to thread as a coating to help it pass through a stack of paper easily and smoothly. Use a **thimble** as protection while sewing so you don't poke your skin.

A sewing machine fitted with a leather foot is helpful too. If there is a theater program and costume shop in your college or university, there may be a sewing machine available for students.

Figure 1-27
Left to right:
Saddle stapler.
Long-handle stapler.
Heavy-duty cinch stapler.

Figure 1-28
The Fastenator and mini-stapler with decorative color staples.

Figure 1-29
Staple-free stapler and results.

Figure 1-30

Left to right:

Spring-hinged needle-nose pliers.

Standard needle-nose pliers.

Grommets of several colors; Crop-A-Dile grommet tool.

Screw and posts (a.k.a. Chicago screws).

Sewing tools (left to right): beeswax, darning needles, linen bookbinding thread, embroidery thread with large-eye needles, and thimble.

Figure 1-31

Left to right:

Double-loop Wire-O binding machine.

Spiral binding machine pictured with binding elements.

Spiral binding, double-loop **"Wire-O" binding**, and hot glue binding machines are not the usual tools found on a desktop and are certainly beyond what is critically essential. However, these specialty machines can produce commercial-level, mechanical bookbinding results; see Figure 1-31 for examples of the spiral and double-loop Wire-O binding machines. When your budget allows, a basic toolbox can be augmented to cover a variety of specialized tasks or make the working process easier.

Finally, it takes some heavy-duty drilling to make the holes for binding big, thick books, so an electric drill can be helpful. You will need clamps to hold the pages steady while drilling (and for general construction purposes). Use two small pieces of a hardwood (like poplar) at the top and bottom of book pages to distribute the pressure while clamping; see Figure 1-32. Reminder: These techniques are discussed in Chapter 3.

summary: set, ready, go

Traditional craft tools for measuring, cutting, scoring, and folding are the essential basics of a designer's desktop toolbox. Heavy-duty staplers and desktop cutting and binding machines facilitate large jobs and make bookbinding easier. Tools abound for various specific specialized tasks that can be added to the basics as needed and desired.

Having the best tools and the right ones to do the jobs efficiently, safely, and correctly are key to developing into a skilled designer-craftsman.

Excellent craftsmanship skills contribute to building your worth as a practical and functioning designer. As an added value, the pride that comes with completing a well-crafted comprehensive mock-up deservedly feeds your self-worth.

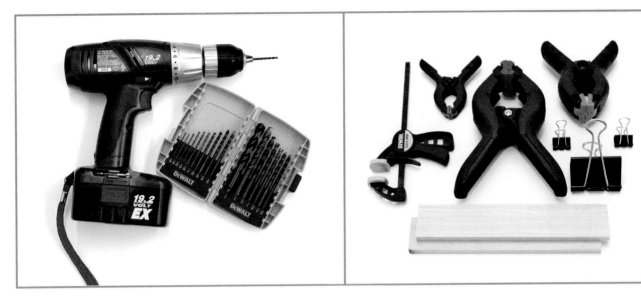

Figure 1-32
Left to right:
Electric drill and bits.
Clamps: ratcheting squeeze clamp, spring clamps (three sizes), binder clips (two small, one large).
Small pieces of poplar wood.

Figure 1-33
Crafty college students.

And, yes, it is simply fun to design and craft it yourself.

Set up the work area, ready the tools, and go for it!

exercise knowledge gained

Once your tools are purchased, you will learn basic techniques for their use in Chapter 3. However, at this point, we have some suggestions before you buy the tools and for simple practice.

1. observe

Observe professors and advanced students using the tools. If appropriate, ask questions on the ease and comfort of using the particular tool.

2. borrow

Perhaps you are not certain as to what style tool to purchase. If possible, borrow the tool to check out how it works and feels in your hand. Determine what style tool works best for you. Perhaps an ergonomic handle on a utility knife is the best fit. Maybe not. Rulers vary in style as well. Make sure that you can clearly read the instrument.

3. shop around

Not every art supply store carries the same products. Find stores that are close to you and see what they stock. Compare that to the inventories of online retailers. In both cases, keep an eye on price. And don't limit your search to art supply stores. As we've mentioned, you'll find some of these tools and supplies at hardware stores, home centers, and other locations.

"Rags are as beauties which concealed lie,
But when in paper, how it charms the eye!
Pray save your rags, new beauties to discover,
For of paper, truly every one's a lover.
By the pen and press such knowledge is displayed
As wouldn't exist if paper were not made.
Wisdom of things, mysterious, divine
Illustriously doth on paper shine."
—*Author Unknown, Advertisement in* The Boston News-Letter, *1769*

First row, left to right:
Photograph: *Old Colored Comics*
© Mietitore | Dreamstime.com
Great fun on paper.

Specialty milled paper.
Impressed textures can be wonderful to see and touch.

Book: Istvan Orosz
Studio: Design Ranch
Creative Directors: Ingred Sidie, Michelle Sonderegger
Illustrator: Istvan Orosz
Printer: Hammerpress (all hand letterpress)
Paper: Various French and vellum
Client: Istvan Orosz
Compelling the viewer to touch, the designers used a contrast of
textures: translucent vellum and paperboard.

Second row, left to right:
Photograph: *Newspaper*
© Milosluz | Dreamstime.com
Pictured is newsprint paper without the news.

Photograph: *Background of Handmade Paper*
© Linnea | Dreamstime.com
Beautiful to see and touch.

Crumpled milled paper ball. Paper can be a printed design substrate,
instant toy, sculpture, or tension release instrument.

Third row, left to right:
Identity system: Broadfoam
Studio: And Partners
Creative Director: David Schimmel
Designer: David Schimmel
Printer: Dickson's Inc.
Paper: Fibermark, and Neenah Paper Classic Cotton
Client: Broadform
A color and texture combine to enhance and make memorable this
identity system.

Book with deckle edges; this is a book all about its paper.
Student designer: lee Ling Yee

Invitation: Su-zen
Studio: Mucca Design
Creative Director: Matteo Bologna
Art Director and Designer: Matteo Bologna
Photograper: Steven Gross
Client: Su-zen
Brilliant ideas are obvious. For a new store opening, the designers
created a tailor's label to the size of a postcard, to serve as the
invitation. A note from the designers: Su-zen is a fashion brand . . .
the company specializes in tailored fashions using the finest fabrics,
handmade tailored knits, and elegantly detailed designs.

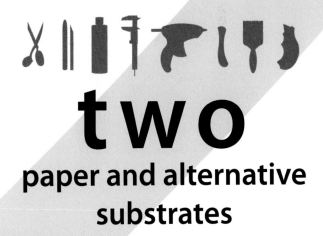

two
paper and alternative
substrates

learning objectives

- Learn basic industry information regarding paper features, properties, and attributes.
- Explore paper and alternative substrates and their use and limitations in regard to both desktop comps and professional printing.
- Acquire basic skills needed for simulating specialty features and properties of paper.
- Start a library of paper and substrate samples.

paper inside and out

Acquiring an understanding of technical, functional, and practical aspects of paper is basic to operating successfully as a professional print designer.

With this broad knowledge of paper, you will also be able to grasp its creative, visual, and tactile potential. Paper affects how the audience responds to a design concept as much as the typography or images. You see paper and touch it. Paper is an integral element in a printed design solution such as the stationery seen in Figure 2-1.

So go ahead and use Neenah Classic Columns, Pistachio (color), Recycled, 80# cover paper for a design. (Note: Weight in pounds is denoted with a # sign after the number.)

Figure 2-1

Stationery and brochure: Matta
Studio: Mucca Design
Creative Director: Matteo Bologna
Designers: Christine Celic Strohl and Christina Gitti
Photographer: Luca Pioltelli
Illustrator: Christine Celic Strohl
Paper: Various handmade papers
Printer: Inhouse and Almar Graphics
Client: Matta
Noted by the designers: "All of Matta's clothing is hand made using bright colors and patterns. It was important to communicate that aesthetic with all of the design and photography. Although the client does not have a large budget for printed promotional materials, she is able to add finishing touches to all of the pieces, making each one unique.
The business cards were printed in house on various colored handmade papers. Another piece of paper was hand stamped, and then the two colored pieces were sewn together.
The brochure was printed offset 4c [four color] process by Almar graphics, they were then hand stamped and bound using pieces of *sarong* from Matta's design collection."

Figure 2-2
Japanese *Chiyogami* paper (always printed on one side) and yellow *daiishu chiri* (kozo fibers) Japanese handmade paper.

Or incorporate and accent element using Japanese *Chiyogami* paper or other handmade paper into a design—rather than miss an opportunity simply because you were not aware that these papers exist; see Figure 2-2 for an example of both.

Whether tediously technical or gloriously inspirational, the more knowledge gained concerning paper, the greater the opportunity of expanding success with a design solution both functionally and creatively.

Since a smart thinking designer is also an aware and curious one, begin the study of paper with an overview of its history. Although we can't possibly cover the vast history and the world-changing impact of paper, we do offer a guide to its study.

In the study of the history and evolution of paper, you would gain an appreciation of the impact of paper on civilization, its importance to human communication, and its fascinating aesthetic complexity.

See the sidebar information for a *brief* history of paper as gleaned from the Forest Stewardship Council website. Use the information to guide further study. See Figure 2-3 for a photo of an old-fashioned papermaking mill.

Figure 2-3
Old Fashioned Paper Mill
© Elsen029 | Dreamstime.com
Papermaking has a 2000 year history.

a brief history of paper

"Paper has been around for nearly 2000 years! Try to imagine life without it."
The Forest Stewardship Council

A Chinese court official, Ts'ai Lun, has been credited with the invention of the papermaking process circa A.D. 105. Ts'ai most likely used a mixture of pulverized mulberry bark, hemp, and rags with water. The fibers were suspended in the water, drained, and pressed, and the resulting thin mat was hung in the sun to dry. So perhaps began a giant step in the evolution of human communication.

Fast forward to 1690. William Rittenhouse and William Bradford established the first North American paper mill, Wissachikon Creek, near Philadelphia. Through the recycling (gathered, categorized, cleaned) of cloth rags, the men successfully manufactured America's first writing papers.

By the early 1800s in France, Nicholas-Louis Robert engineered the Fourdrinier papermaking machine, which produces paper with the use of a continuous wire screen. By the mid-1800s, paper was being fabricated using wood pulp. This technique spread to the United States by the early 1900s. With the inclusion of wood pulp, paper became less expensive to produce and thus more widely available.

Continuous developments in the manufacture of paper improved speed of production and quality, as well as expanded variety. Yet, the basic ingredient (cellulose fiber) and the basic process involving a screen-based (for draining water) mechanism are still in use, albeit in a highly advanced state.

get physical with paper

Although considerably updated since its invention in the nineteenth century, the Fourdrinier paper machine is still in use at commercial paper manufacturers. The companies that make paper are known as **paper mills**. The paper produced by machine is called **milled paper**. Naturally, with the study of paper, you will want some understanding of how paper is currently manufactured—a complicated undertaking with impressively large machines. See Figure 2-4 for an example of contemporary papermaking machinery.

resources: making paper

Since paper is a critical aspect of both desktop comps and professional printed matter, we encourage further study of the commercial papermaking process. The extent of the information to be learned is vast and impossible to cover in the scope of this textbook, so we urge further independent study with some suggestions for sources. For research into *commercial* papermaking, the Sappi paper company offers a very good diagrammatic explanation of the paper manufacturing process. Go to the Sappi North America website and click on "Paper Insight" and then click on "Life Cycle" and look for the .pdf download titled "The Papermaking Process." In addition, Mohawk Paper has a rich library of information on paper including papermaking. On the main menu of the Mohawk website, click on "Ask Mohawk" and then click on "Paper Basics." Read on.

Since we know that seeing is an alternative road to understanding, there are also several YouTube video explanations of commercial papermaking that could be viewed. Search on YouTube for "commercial papermaking" with the following words as a guide: "Neenah paper mill visit."

Figure 2-4
Paper [making] *machine*
© Deg | Dreamstime.com

basic ingredients

There are aspects to the physical fabrication of paper that you need to understand for optimum use and results in building studio desktop comps. This information is also helpful when ordering paper for the final professional-level job. The most basic ingredients in papermaking include the following substances:

¤   Cellulose fiber

¤   Fillers

¤   Dyes and pigments

Although there are instances of the use of synthetics, the basic ingredient of paper is natural (virgin, or recycled/postconsumer waste) cellulose **fiber**. The fibers are either hardwood, softwood, cotton, hemp, bamboo, sugar cane, or another cellulose product. Tear a small piece of paper and note the tiny fibers slightly protruding from the torn edge. The fibers are about the length of a grain of rice, finer than human hair, and hollow. Before it is made into the finished product, fiber mass is referred to as **pulp;** see Figure 2-5. Paper mills do not necessarily manufacture the pulp (although some do).

Raw cellulose fiber or recycled fiber is not the only ingredient in the recipe that makes paper. As noted on the Mohawk Paper website, ". . . each paper requires its own special mix of fibers and fillers to achieve its unique characteristics. The **furnish**, [or recipe] which consists of the finest available wood *pulps, fillers,* and internal sizing, is mixed with *water* [as much as 99.5%] in large beaters until the mixture (a slurry called stock or stuff) resembles oatmeal." You could think of the papermaker as a chef—combining fibers, fillers, and water, and then cooking it (literally) to make the paper.

Fillers are minerals, other organic substances such as starch and clay, and chemical agents added to pulp to improve the opacity, smoothness, brightness, printing capabilities, and archival value of paper. For instance, **calcium carbonate**, an alkaline filler, buffers the acidic nature of cellulose and makes the paper relatively archival. The mineral also increases the brightness of paper. **Clay** (kaolin) may be added for smoothness and helps ink to adhere. The clay also adds density and bulk, making the paper more opaque.

Additional **optical brightening agents** work by absorbing invisible ultraviolet light and converting the energy to a visible bluish white light. The process results in a paper that appears brighter.

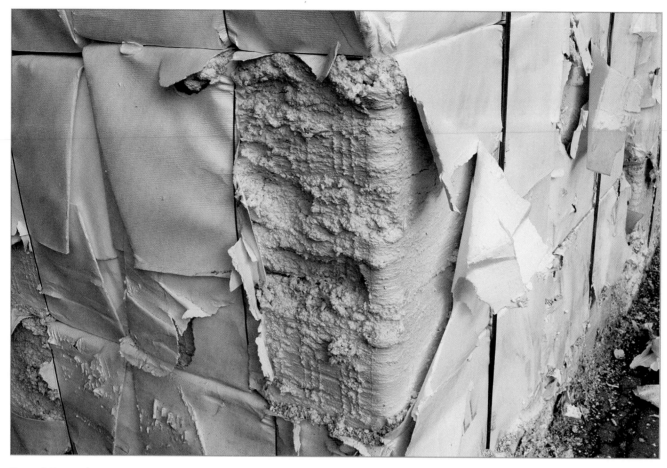

Figure 2-5
Paper and Pulp Mill [detail of cellulose]
© Morenosoppelsa | Dreamstime.com
Paper pulp massed and ready to be mixed with water and processed.

Finally but not least, **dyes and pigments** (natural or synthetic coloring agents; see Figure 2-6) are added to the fibers and fillers to create color. And we all love color, don't we?

In order to elicit public trust, paper companies often get national certification in regard to the use of ingredients in their products. The American National Standards Institute (www.ansi.org) is one such governing board.

relevant features, properties, and attributes

A significant group of physical *features*, *properties*, and *attributes* of paper is relevant to both constructing desktop comps and professionally designed work.

We use this set of terms commonly found in the paper industry in order to organize the information into related groups. The category names may not be the words used by local paper representatives.

Even if you were to look in a dictionary, the definitions of the words overlap in meaning and can get confusing in comparison. In addition, all the terms defined could be grouped into one category labeled *properties*. However, we have created three groups to help a beginner to put in order the information for ease of understanding.

Therefore we offer an explanation of our labeling system. The term *features* refers to the physicality of paper, *properties* refers to variable aspects and qualities of paper, and *attributes* refers to paper industry categories of the various additional characteristics of paper beyond features and properties.

No single feature, property, or attribute is independent of the rest. Nor can one be changed without affecting another. And, there are more not included. We note those that have the most impact on printing and design applications.

physical features

Being aware of the physicality (or physical character and response) of paper expands critical practical knowledge and assists in enhancing creative options.

Figure 2-6
Red Ochre Pigment Pile
© Erichn | Dreamstime.com

Features and properties generally include the following:

- Deckle edge

- Grain

- Formation

- Side-to-side consistency

- Watermark

- Brightness and whiteness

- Opacity

- Base size

- Basis weight and grammage

- Thickness

Physical features occur during the laying down of fibers in the papermaking process.

A deckle edge is the rough or feathered edge on paper created where the fibers meet the **deckle** (papermaking equipment). The deckle is a feature of handmade paper but is simulated on machine-made paper; see Figure 2-7. Paper companies produce simulated deckle edges for aesthetic purposes; a deckle edge is found especially on formal stationery and announcements.

The **grain** is the direction in which the majority of fibers lie, corresponding with the direction the paper is made on a paper machine; see Figure 2-8. The term **grain long** is used when the grain of the

paper runs parallel to the longest measurement of a sheet of paper (the fibers align parallel to the length of the sheet). The term **grain short** is used when the grain of the paper runs at a right angle to the longest dimension of the sheet. The fibers parallel the sheet's shortest dimension.

Formation is the uniformity or lack of it in the distribution of fibers during the manufacturing or handmade process. The feature can be observed by holding a sheet up to a light; a good formation is uniform or "close," whereas a poor formation has clumpy or mottled fibers (that look like swirling clouds). Most important, sheets with good formation hold ink uniformly. There is no official rating for formation—you just have to look for yourself.

Side-to-side consistency refers to the uniformity of quality on the top and bottom of the sheet of paper. The **felt side** or "top" of the paper sheet comes in contact with the felt rollers during manufacture. The top can be somewhat stronger and is generally a slightly textured (felt) surface *relative* to the bottom of the paper. The **wire side** or "bottom" of the paper sheet is created against the wire (screen) during manufacture. The wire side may be slightly weaker and more vulnerable than the felt side. However, papers with good side-to-side consistency should print evenly on both sides.

A **watermark** is created in the fabrication process. It is a recognizable image or pattern in the paper that is created by varying the thickness of fibers in a given area. Watermarks are used to identify the maker or owner of the paper (private watermark) and are most visible when a light shines through the paper.

Writing paper often has a watermark—a historic distinction and symbol of quality and beauty. Desktop printing papers (quality is not so important) do not usually have a watermark. Some specialty

Figure 2-7
Handmade paper and milled paper showing actual deckle and
simulated deckle edges.

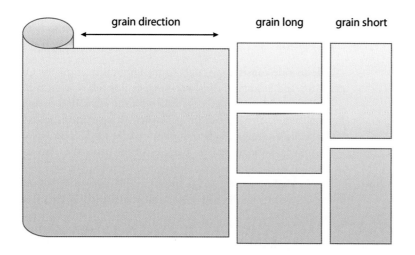

grain direction

grain long   grain short

milled paper

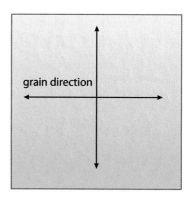

grain direction

handmade paper

Figure 2-8
Paper grain noted for milled papers and handmade papers.
Handmade papers do *not* have a one-directional grain; instead
they have an allover grain direction.

Figure 2-9
Paper company watermark on stationery for Kean University.
Proprietary watermark: Kean University Foundation stationery

milled papers and handmade papers may have watermarks to denote the maker (the former imitating the latter). See Figure 2-9 for examples of watermarks.

N.B. Understanding grain direction is absolutely critical for scoring and folding paper comps. More on paper grain will be discussed in Chapter 3 on techniques.

properties

Variable physical properties (or qualities or characteristics) occur during the papermaking process.

Brightness and whiteness are two paper properties that can be confusing. Two papers can have the same brightness but look different because of their whiteness. **Brightness** is the measure of the paper's reflectance (light reflected from the surface) or luminosity. Papers are rated in brightness in a range from 1 to 100. A paper near 100 will have almost all light reflected back to the viewer, making color images seem to "pop" off the page. Bright white papers also seem to enhance the luminosity of transparent printing inks. For design solutions with many pages of text, a paper with less brightness is best because the softer luminosity helps to minimize the eyestrain on the reader. **Whiteness** refers to the color of the sheet of paper. The three predominant colors are neutral white, warm white, and blue white. See Figure 2-10 for paper samples to compare brightness and whiteness (and limited color).

Opacity refers to the amount of light that passes through a sheet of paper and determines whether the image printed on one side of the page will show through on the reverse side or the sheet below. Opacity is rated from 1%, which is the most transparent, to 100%, which is the most opaque. Paper with a high percentage of opacity will have little show through, meaning colors printing on either side won't be seen through the sheet of paper. Adding fillers, dyes, and pigments to the paper mix can increase opacity as can the paper thickness and any coating on the paper. Selecting a paper with good opacity is essential for projects that have fine images and deep colors so the images won't interfere with text or images on the following pages.

neenah paper on watermarks

"Watermark is a term referring to the impression of a design, pattern or symbol in a sheet while it is being formed on the paper machine wire. It appears in the finished sheet as either a lighter or darker area than the rest of the paper. Two types of watermarks are available. A shaded watermark is produced by a dandy roll located at or near the suction box on the Fourdrinier. The desired design is pressed into the wire covering the surface of the dandy roll similar to an intaglio engraving. As the wet pulp moves along the web the dandy roll presses down and creates an accumulation of fibers, thus the watermark is seen as being darker than the rest of the sheet. The second type of watermark, called a wire mark, is accomplished by impressing a dandy roll with a raised surface pattern into the moving paper web in a similar manner to the shaded mark. This creates an area with less fiber making it lighter and more translucent."
From the Neenah Paper website

Figure 2-10
Paper samples showing a range of tones.

base size and basis weight

Base size is the industry-established (and regulated) standard size of a sheet of paper relative to either the United States or internationally (designated by the International Standards Organization/ISO).

According to the experts at Neenah Paper, paper types (in the United States) are categorized by base size. For example, the base size of cover weight paper (heavier than the type used for magazines)

is 20" × 26". Bond paper (a standard type used for copy machines) has a base size of 17" × 22". Text (paper for use in books) has a base size of 25" × 38".

Standardization of base sizes is necessary to determine how many pieces can be had from a single sheet of a particular type of paper. Standardization allows for the predetermination of the cost of a quantity of paper and related printing cost; see Figure 2-11 for a diagram of North American standard sheet sizes.

A designer needs to know the cost of a printed matter before proceeding with an application in order to remain within the client's budget. The designer works with both the paper company representative and the printing company representative to determine the most efficient use of the single sheet of paper. See Figure 2-12 for a diagram of how a base size of a single sheet of paper can be divided efficiently. The diagrams are meant to raise your awareness of the process but not for a definitive use in the field.

Figure 2-12 (right)
Four-page 9" x 12" finished (folded) application based on a 28"x 40" sheet.
Twelve-page 7" x 7" finished (booklet) application based on a 23" x 35" sheet.
Six-page 8.5" x 11" finished (folded) application based on a 23" x 35" sheet.
Sixteen-page 6" x 9" finished (booklet) application based on a 28" x 40" size sheet.
Noted in the diagrams are several ways to lay out pages for a design application (booklet, folded brochure, etc.) on a single sheet of paper of a particular base size. Calculating the placement of pages to fit on the single sheet of printing paper going to press (a press form) is called *imposition*. It will take study and practice before you can "wrap your head around" press form imposition. Gain awareness, but work must be accomplished by the professionals at the printing company.

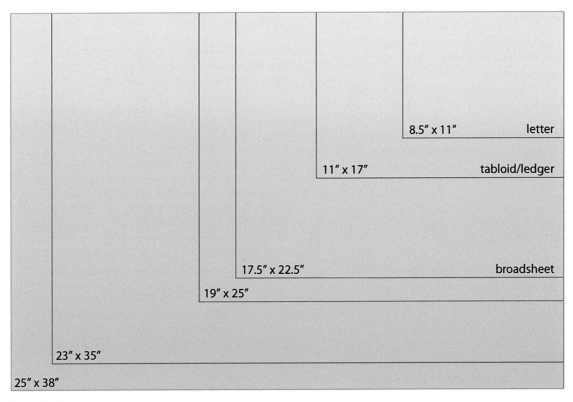

Figure 2-11
North American sheet sizes.

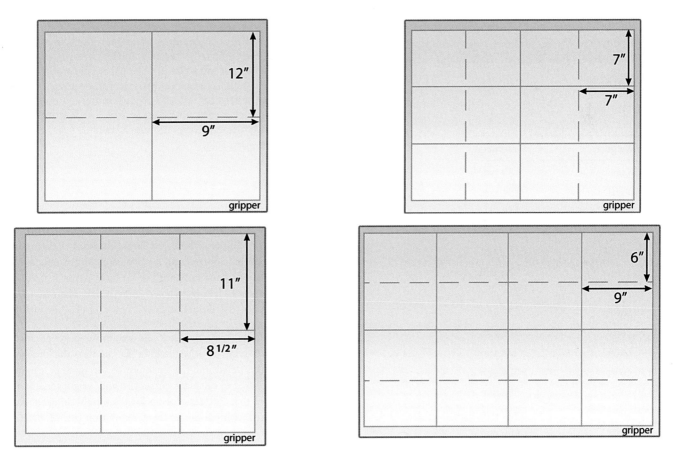

Figure 2-12

reams and basis weight

The base sizes are also used to calculate a paper's basis weight. The **basis weight** equals the **ream** (500 sheet) weight of the base size. Because the starting base size is not the same between paper types, the basis weights do not correspond directly (80# text is much lighter than 80# cover).

You must also understand, however, that weight is always determined using the paper's *original* base size and not the final cut size. A ream of 20#, 8½" × 11" paper actually weighs 5 pounds—it has been cut from larger sheets (17" × 22") into four equal pieces.

Note: As mentioned earlier, weight in pounds is sometimes denoted with a # sign after the number, for example 24#.

Paper's weight is related to its use (heavier paper for book covers, for instance). The weight is also a factor related to shipping costs. Design is a business, after all, and money is an important factor.

international grammage

You may notice the abbreviation **GSM** when researching paper types. This is the abbreviation for grams per square meter, or grammage. **Grammage** is the metric equivalent of basis weight, and it is the system used outside of North America (in other words, most of the world). The alternative abbreviation used is g/m². See the following chart for a sample of basis weight to grammage comparison. (Note: More on weight and paper types such as text and cover will be discussed further along in the section on paper attributes.)

Basis Weights	Grammage
60 text	89 gsm
70 text	104 gsm
80 text	118 gsm
100 text	148 gsm
60 cover	162 gsm
65 cover	176 gsm
80 cover	216 gsm
88 cover	238 gsm
90 cover	243 gsm
100 cover	270 gsm
120 cover	324 gsm
130 cover	352 gsm
160 cover	432 gsm
180 cover	486 gsm

why 8½" × 11"?

Does 8½" × 11" seem like an arbitrary size for paper? Why are those particular proportions so common in US paper usage? Why not some other size?

As it turns out, the size was not arbitrary. There is a very logical reason. We turn to the American Forest & Paper Association for the answer:

"Back in the late 1600s, the Dutch invented the two-sheet mold. The average maximum stretch of an experienced vat man's arms was 44". Many molds at that time were around 17" front to back because the laid lines and watermarks had to run from left to right. Sounds big? Well, to maximize the efficiency of papermaking, a sheet this big was made, and then quartered, forming four 8½" × 11" pieces.

This was well before paper machines dominated hand-made paper labor. A couple centuries later when machines dominated the trade (although many hand made paper makers still existed), and the United States decided on a standard paper size, they stuck with the same size so as to keep the hand made paper makers in business."
From the American Forest & Paper Association website

Noted without comment, a related observation from design great, Massimo Vignelli:

"The international standard paper sizes, called the A series, is based on a golden rectangle, the divine proportion. It is extremely handsome and practical as well. It is adopted by many countries around the world and is based on the German DIN metric standards. The United States uses a basic letter size (8½" × 11") of ugly proportions, and results in complete chaos with an endless amount of paper sizes. It is a by-product of the culture of free enterprise, competition and waste. Just another example of the misinterpretations of freedom."
From The Vignelli Canon

paper thickness

Closely related to basis weight is the **thickness** of paper. The thickness refers to the **caliper** or bulk of a sheet. Thickness is measured using a caliper or micrometer and is noted in points or mils. One point or mil equals one-thousandth of an inch (1 pt. = 0.001). Some thick papers such as paperboard and cards are manufactured by caliper and not basis weight, such as a 7 pt. card or 10 pt. board.

N.B. In book publishing, the thickness determines pages per inch (**PPI**) or the number of pages making up one inch thickness of pages. PPI helps determine the thickness of the spine of a book that is in turn used to calculate carton size and weight for shipping costs. Note that PPI designation for book publishing should not be confused with ppi digital image resolution (mentioned in Chapter 4).

attributes

In addition to features and properties, designers are most concerned with paper attributes. Milled paper has attributes characterized and categorized by the following criteria:

▢   Content

▢   Grade

▢   Basis weight

▢   Finish

▢   Shade or color

▢   Size (in sheets and rolls)

▢   Paper company proprietary name (e.g., Neenah Classic Crest)

See Figure 2-13 for a professional design solution and accompanying caption that lists the paper used and its attributes.

content and grade (distinguished type and rank)

Content is usually noted relative to the percentage of cotton versus other fibers such as wood, hemp, bamboo, and postconsumer pulp.

The American Forest & Paper Association describes a **grade** as follows:

"[A] class or level of quality of a paper or pulp is ranked, or distinguished from other papers or pulps, on the basis of its use, appearance, quality, manufacturing history, raw materials, or a combination of these factors. Some grades have been officially identified and described; others are commonly recognized but lack official definition."

Figure 2-13
Exhibition catalog: Punc't
Studio: And Partners
Creative Director: David Schimmel
Art Director and Designer: David Schimmel
Poster designs (visible): David Schimmel, Micheal Beirut

The catalog pictured uses the following Neenah Paper: Dust jacket: Environment Text, Cosmos Black 80#; Cover: Environment Cover, Irish Crème, 100#; Black text pages: Environment Text, Cosmos Black 80#; White text pages: Environment Text, Irish Crème, 80#; Overleaves: UV Ultra II, white 17#.

grades

Commonly recognized milled (printing) grades and their basic use are listed as follows:

Bond/writing	Copier paper, forms, newsletters
Text	Books, direct mail, posters, brochures, reports
Book	Books, reports, magazines, catalogs, brochures
Cover	Business cards, postcards, greeting cards, folders, covers of printed matter
Index/Bristol	Postcards, folders, cards, boxes, tags, tickets (index has a smooth finish; Bristol is less so)
Newsprint	Newspapers, drawing paper
Kraft	Bags, envelopes
Translucent vellum	Overlay sheets, envelopes, and other specialty purposes needing translucency (see Figure 2-14 for vellum in application)
Cardboard/paperboard	Boxes, packaging, shipping
Digital	Guaranteed to perform in digital printing
Offset	Guaranteed to perform in offset lithographic printing
Duplex	Two sheets of paper laminated together
Synthetic	A substrate that behaves like paper but is made from noncellulose material and made to be extra durable and waterproof (Think Tyvek.)

Paper is also manufactured in two broad categories of grade that affect the finished product. Those categories and resulting use include:

Coated paper	Ink sits on the surface and tends to look brighter. Coated papers can range from matte to high-gloss.
Uncoated paper	Ink tends to penetrate the surface of the paper and therefore tends to look deeper. Uncoated papers can have textures lightly embossed or impressed into them as they dry.

corresponding grades, weights, and sizes

As noted previously and expanded here in regard to application, the grade of the paper and its corresponding weight was developed and established for specific purposes—writing paper, paper for book covers, paper for interior of books (text), paper for index cards, and so on. Grading helps to quickly understand both the use and the general weight of a given paper for specific applications. A given paper grade also has corresponding base sizes.

Figure 2-14
Brochure: NHK Laboratories
Studio: IE Designs + Communications
Creative Director: Marci Carson
Art Director: Jane Lee
Designers: Jane Lee and Nicole Bednarz
Paper: Outer wrap: CT Soft Clear Reich Translucent; cover/text: Topkote Dull
Noted by designers: "Designing the capabilities brochure of NHK labs was a very collaborative process. We wanted to capture the company's unique turn-key manufacturing capabilities—taking ideas from concept to store shelf. Their process of bringing ideas to life posed the question, What's your big idea? This question was used as the concept for the piece and resulted in an oversized-format brochure with a gatefold center spread. The gatefold spread was used as an opportunity to showcase their process. The finished size was designed for visual impact as well as maximized the press sheet. A provocative vellum outer wrap envelops the cover with ethereal imagery overlaying the logo and type. Printed entirely in metallic inks, the design is smart, cutting-edge and innovative as the NHK Labs brand."

See Figure 2-15 for examples of a label on a ream of paper. Note that not all of the paper features and properties are listed on the package label. The buyer of the paper can get all the specifications on a specific paper from the paper mill website or through the company's representative.

Find an example of a paper specification sheet on a paper mill website. Visit the Domtar paper company website and search for the "spec sheet" on a particular type of paper to further your understanding of paper specifications.

finish

The **finish** refers to the surface qualities or attributes of the paper. Paper finishes range from matte to glossy, highly textured to completely smooth, and much in between. Each paper company may have its own proprietary process and name for a particular finish with the names usually defining the attribute. Don't be daunted—knowing the variations expands your creative potential.

 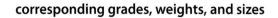

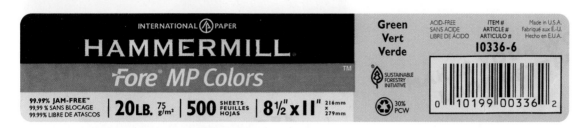

Figure 2-15

Examples of labels found on individual reams of paper. Note that not all of the paper features and properties are listed. Before purchasing, the buyer of paper can get all the specifications on a specific paper from the mill.

Common finishes include:

Felt	Slight texture (handmade look and feel)
Laid	Vertical line pattern (simulates a historic, handmade look)
Linen	Has the look of the fabric
Smooth	As stated
Supercalendered	Ultrasmooth
Vellum	Toothy texture
Wove	Smoothly toothy

Additional miscellaneous finishes (names vary with manufacturer) include:

Antique	Slight texture
Eggshell	As stated (texture)
Cockle	Pebbly
Linen on one side	As stated by name
Lines	Vertical line pattern
Pinstripe	Tight vertical pattern
Silk	Simulates the texture of the fabric
Squares	Impressed grid pattern of small squares

color

The color of paper ranges from bright white to black and most hues, but paper is primarily an obvious white or some variation of it or another lighter-value pigment such as pale blue or pale yellow. See Figure 2-16 for colorful paper samples.

Because of the very few individual names of colors in the English language and because of the vast number of labels in use, there appears to be a scramble from the paper companies to find the most charming and evocative names to describe variations of white, yellow, red, blue, and so on, such as ivory, pearl, cloud, cream, sea mist, and periwinkle. Realize that each paper company will have its own set of color names.

the greening of paper

For any contemporary designer or aspiring designer, the paper-buying decision includes thoughts of going "green"—that is, working with paper that was manufactured with the least amount of adverse impact to our natural environment.

Concerning protection of the natural environment, individuals must make their own choices based on conscience and budget. We try to make as many environmentally sound choices as we can. Following is a list of several important environmental designations that any smart designer (student or professional) should be aware of.

Figure 2-16

Paper can be found in a variety of grades, weights, finishes, and colors.

First row:

Sweet pastels and earth tones.

Second row:

Subtly pale hues and screaming brights.

The explanations were summarized or quoted from information on the Mohawk Paper Company website:

¤ *PCW (Post Consumer Waste/Recycled)*

¤ *Carbon Neutral* "Carbon Neutral describes products, operations, and activities that have had their carbon dioxide and greenhouse emissions (1) calculated, (2) reduced, and (3) where possible "offset" through credits that fund renewable, emission-free energy products."

¤ *FSC Certified (Forest Stewardship Council)* "The Forest Stewardship Council certifies wood and wood products that are responsibly harvested and processed. Their goal is to shift the market to eliminate habitat destruction, water pollution, and displacement of indigenous peoples. Use of the FSC label must be arranged with an FSC-certified printer when using FSC-certified paper purchased through an FSC-certified merchant."

¤ *ECF (Elemental Chlorine Free)* "This paper is made from virgin fiber and bleached using compounds that are alternative chlorine compounds rather than elemental chlorine. The former helps to reduce harmful by-products."

¤ *PCF (Processed Chlorine Free)* "These papers contain postconsumer recycled fiber that was processed without the use of any additional chlorine or chlorine compounds. If these papers also contain virgin fiber, the virgin fiber must have been processed without the use of any chlorine or chlorine compounds."

Green-e Certified Renewable Energy Green-e is the nation's leading independent certification and verification program for renewable energy products. Green-e verifies purchases of renewable energy certificates (RECs) and certifies the RECs to be sure they meet strict environmental and consumer protection standards. See www.green-e.org.

We the authors know that all our practices are not yet 100% "green." Yet, we try to be as green as possible in our own studios. Our hope is that all manufacturers and designers push toward the goal until paper, glues, and printing are all 100% green.

For instance, almost all paper companies manufacture papers that are recycled. Some companies are more advanced in their offerings than other companies. Use recycled paper whenever possible. Carefully reuse and recycle your own desktop paper waste.

Some printing and binding processes are more green than others—manufacturers of ink and adhesives are working on developing environmentally friendly products. You can encourage them through your requests.

Also, use PDF comps and websites when appropriate. But don't hesitate to make your own books, booklets, packages, collages, drawings, paintings, and so forth. A green world does not necessarily mean that we can't have printed matter, design, and art. Instead, be concerned about efficiency and decreasing waste while we wait for all manufacturers to go green. For more information on what designers are advocating relative to environmental issues and the profession, see the following websites: Designers Accord and Design Can Change.

In addition, please see Debra Rizzi's feature article in Chapter 1 about Beleaf, an advocacy group that is educating designers on "going green."

milling about to expand knowledge

To make sense of the vast array of information available for the professional and aspiring designer, further research into paper mills is essential for gaining an understanding of what is current, what is available, and what is possible.

The representatives and salespeople of paper mills and paper **distributors** (who buy from the mills and distribute to printers, designers, etc.) can provide a huge amount of practical and easy-to-understand technical information for understanding, using, and buying paper. These companies usually provide the information freely.

As mentioned previously in this chapter, the Sappi paper company has a superb website filled with informational PDF documents that can be downloaded from their website, saved on your computer notebook, and/or printed. The Sappi Knowledge Bank is worth a visit right now!

But don't stop at one paper mill. It is important to cross-reference information to gain the greatest breadth of knowledge and to make critical comparisons. Much that is technical is standard in the paper industry. However, terms, titles, and naming conventions can vary. Also mentioned previously, Mohawk Paper offers a website deep in content for both professional and aspiring designers. Visit www.mohawkpaper.com and click on "Ask Mohawk."

Many of the paper mills also have a glossary of paper terms. Neenah Paper has an excellent glossary. Rather than using printing paper, keep the glossary on your computer desktop in a virtual folder for quick reference. There is much to learn and not all need be committed to memory. Just be aware.

The following is an alphabetical (very short) list of paper mills:

- Curious Collection, Arjo Wiggins Fine Papers Ltd, Manchester, England

- Crane & Co. Inc., Dalton, MA, USA

- Domtar Inc., Montreal, Canada

- Fiber Mark Inc., Brattleboro, VT, USA

- Fraser Papers Inc., Toronto, ON, Canada

- French Paper Co., MI, USA (Don't miss their Sample Room.)

- Gmund, Germany

- Mohawk Paper Mills Inc., Cohoes, NY, USA

- Monadnock Paper Mills Inc., Bennington, NH, USA

- Neenah Paper Inc., Alpharetta, GA, USA

- New Leaf Paper, NY, USA

- NewPage Corp., Dayton, OH, USA

- Sappi North America

For additional paper-related information also visit these web resources:

- Paper Online (Confederation of European Paper Industries)

- PaperSpecs

- PaperOnWeb

a paper toolbox

Beyond the traditional toolbox of measuring, cutting, and folding tools, most professional designers keep a "library" or "toolbox" of paper samples. To call upon as reference and resource, the toolbox would consist of paper sample booklets (a.k.a. swatchbooks; see Figure 2-17), samples of blank and preprinted paper, and additional samples of construction materials and other alternative

Figure 2-17
Neenah swatchbooks.

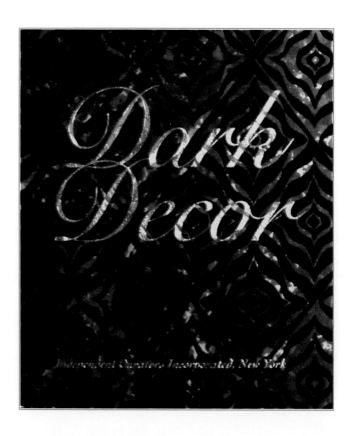

Figure 2-18
Exhibition catalog: Dark Decor
Studio: Russell Hassell
Creative Director: Russell Hassell
Designer: Russell Hassell
Client: Independent Curators Incorporated (ICI)
Cover paper: Flocked wallpaper
Noted by the designer: "Dark Décor was a traveling exhibition of works
by artists who use pattern and decorative elements as devices to
camouflage the more sinister aspects of their work. The concept was
reinforced by the catalog's dust jacket, actual wallpaper in a lurid bronze
and black metallic pre-pasted paper with black flocking. Since the taste
police had been through Manhattan, I had to go out to Brooklyn to find
something this wonderfully awful. The paper had been discontinued but
there was enough left in the supplier's warehouse to fill my needs—an
overage from the redecorating efforts of a local cocktail lounge."

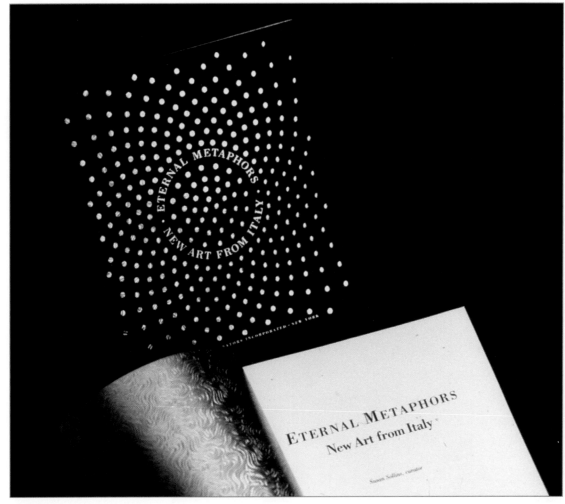

Figure 2-19

Exhibition catalog: Eternal Metaphors
Studio: Russell Hassell
Creative Director: Russell Hassell
Designer: Russell Hassell
Client: Independent Curators Incorporated (ICI)
Cover paper: Strathmore navy cover stock
Inside first sheet: Candy wrapper foil
Noted by the designer: "Eternal Metaphors was an exhibition of works by contemporary Italian artists. The concept was to try to visually convey the metaphysical, mythological, religious and contemporary concerns of the participating artists. To echo these themes in the catalog, the inspiration came from the star-mosaic of the cupola in the *Mausoleum of Galla Placidia in Ravenna*, Italy. It was also subliminally reminiscent of my grandmother's spaghetti colanders.

In keeping with the Byzantine spirit, comps for this job were rather laser intensive—I sat on my kitchen floor and stamped those holes one by one with a leather punch. The points were hand plotted and spaced. The accomplishment means little when you consider that 1000 years earlier, the same pattern had been plotted on the inside of a dome."

substrates such as bookcloth (for an example of the latter, see also Figures 2-30 and 2-31).

Since we use the word **substrate** often throughout the textbook, in context it can be defined as the material on which the design solution is created (paper or otherwise).

Whether you are a professional designer or a student of design, a sample library of paper **stock** (paper of a given grade and variation, available at any given time from a manufacturer) and resource links will provide you access to much practical information about the grade, weight, color, finish, and use of printing paper and alternative substrates.

Samples also provide a ready supply for printing and constructing comprehensive mock-ups and beyond.

There may be instances where a design solution is inspired by the paper itself, or the paper may be the driving force behind a concept. See Figures 2-18 through 2-20 for professional examples from a true paper aficionado. And do read what the designer, Russell Hassell, has to say about the comps and the process of design—he lives a "greener" life these days.

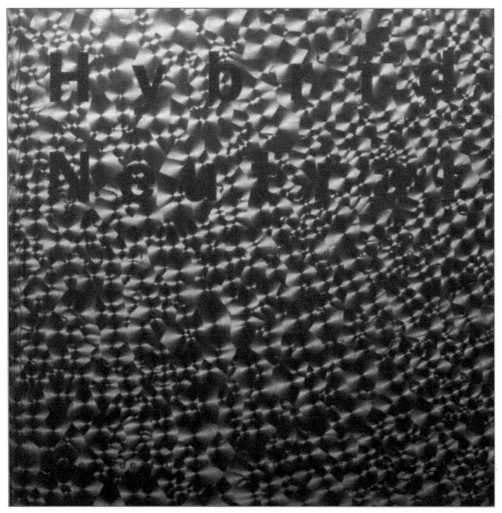

Figure 2-20
Exhibition catalog: Hybrid Neutral
Studio: Russell Hassell
Creative Director: Russell Hassell
Designer: Russell Hassell
Client: Independent Curators Incorporated (ICI)
Cover paper: Crystallized paper
Noted by the designer: "*Hybrid Neutral* was my baptism by fire. As my first big job for Independent Curators Incorporated (ICI), it was axiomatically cursed. The crystallized paper just seemed right for an exhibition full of artists who use wood-grained plastic laminate and lava lamps as their medium. Four-inch endflaps with bright yellow endpages were planned to help give the book a bit more structure. The paper manufacturer sent along the ink specifications for offset lithographic printing on this unusual crystallized paper to Studley Press [Dalton, MA]. Studley followed the directions exactly and—you guessed it—the ink never dried. It was decided to try silkscreening. The dense color of the silkscreened type looked even better than the offset litho version and had the added bonus of actually drying."

the paper's the thing

For the purposes of constructing comps of design solutions in which the printing is primarily accomplished on desktop inkjet printers and laser printers or at a small printing service provider, the printing paper or substrates employed may be somewhat limited. Although there is a vast amount of papers manufactured for commercial printing, much of the paper or other substrates (cloth or heavy acetate for instance) that might be employed for a comp needs to be compatible with the desktop printer hardware. If not compatible, then alternative printing options need to be explored. Some of these options are noted further along in this chapter and in Chapter 10 on specialty printing. Additionally, be aware that paperboard or bookboard can be employed for covers, boxes, and so on. However, you cannot print directly on these types of board using a desktop printer. Their thickness and rigidity make it impossible for the printer to accept the substrates.

As with so many of the tools noted in the previous chapter, it is most important to get paper that is compatible with your personal printer.

Figure 2-21

You will need high-quality inkjet or laser paper for desktop printing. The image color and quality will vary relative to the paper type.

Left to right:

Luster photo paper: 260 gsm, 97 ISO brightness, luster finish.

Premium glossy photo paper: 68#, 92 ISO brightness, high-gloss finish.

Photo paper: 60#, 89 ISO brightness, gloss finish.

Photo-quality (or presentation) paper: 27#, 90 ISO brightness, matte finish.

Heavyweight matte paper: 45#, 97 ISO brightness, matte finish.

Plain paper (bright white): 22#, 98 ISO brightness, matte finish (uncoated).

Every manufacturer of desktop printers has its corresponding and proprietary brand of paper, and those manufacturers usually state that their printers work best with their own paper. For example, Epson will probably tell you that Epson printers yield the best results with Epson paper. That is often true. However, desktop printers do of course work with paper beyond the proprietary brand. But there is testing needed to see what kind of paper or substrate may or may not work and what the results yield.

Also note that there is the possibility of error (even to the point of damaging the printer) if you misuse hardware. To avoid damage, read the instructions for the printer carefully and proceed with caution when using alternatives to the proprietary paper.

As for the printers, inkjet printers prove to be much cheaper in initial cost than their laser counterparts, particularly if opting for a color laser. For that reason, the focus in this section is on the inkjet varieties of paper, which in the end seem to give more versatility for the buck. Furthermore, there is significantly more variety in the inkjet selections as opposed to laser-compatible paper.

Since paper is by far the substrate most employed for desktop printing, understanding the limitations and learning about the choices are paramount to creative and functional design solutions and the subsequent comps needed to make them physical.

Some of the most common types of desktop printing paper include the following:

¤   Standard (plain, bright white) inkjet or laser paper

¤   Coated inkjet or laser paper

¤   Inkjet photo paper (glossy, semigloss, matte)

¤   Card stock (glossy, matte)

¤   Specialty media

See also Figure 2-21 for printed examples of desktop inkjet papers.

plain paper

The most basic type of desktop printing paper is the standard (or "plain" or "bright white") inkjet or laser paper. Plain inkjet paper is usually slightly heavier than standard copy paper (20#) and has a slightly brighter surface. Although bright white inkjet paper is lightweight and cheap, it is also the worst in terms of image quality. Inks tend to bleed (spread out diffusely from the edge of a shape), and double-sided printing is almost impossible. Okay, don't use cheap inkjet paper for final comps. However, plain paper is okay for preliminary work, especially if the first round of the comp is blank or black and white.

Coated inkjet or laser papers are a definite step up in quality from standard or plain, bright white paper. The light coatings add a bit of surface strength to a sheet. Coated paper usually provides a finer printing surface too—that is, colors are richer and bleed less. Depending on the weight, thickness, and opacity, double-sided printing may be possible.

photo families

One of the largest categories of inkjet papers is the photo family of coated papers. There are numerous varieties from equally as numerous manufacturers. Photo papers can boast the best image reproduction quality of all the inkjet media because the smooth coatings of photo-grade inkjet paper hold ink exceptionally well. In addition, sheets have more weight and are thicker than plain paper and thus more substantial for construction of comps.

The finishes in the photo family range from matte to satin, semigloss to gloss, as well as some super-glossy varieties. The variety of finishes within the photo group allows for the potential of expanded creative choices. Mix and match finishes within one design solution to achieve a variety of effects for visual communication purposes.

heavyweights

Inkjet card stock is also available, likewise in a number of finishes and weights. In general, card stock tends to be thicker and heavier than most desktop printing papers (even some photo papers) but often sacrifices image quality for weight. That is, many (but not all) varieties of card stock don't have coatings. Without a coating, an image could be dull because the ink bleeds into the paper and becomes diffused in hue saturation. Naturally, we recommend testing! Does the heavyweight paper produce an image of acceptable quality? If the answer is no, but a heavyweight paper is still desired, print on a lighter weight and then glue to another sheet of paper to strengthen.

specialty and alternative substrates

One of the best features of the newest desktop inkjet printers is their ability to print on a number of specialty substrates. This opens up creative output possibilities in so many ways; see Figure 2-22 for samples. From the more common types of vellum and transparency media (acetate), desktop printers can often work with many of the following:

- Foils and metallics
- Magnetic surfaces
- Printable fabrics
- Translucent vellum
- Backlight films
- Plastics/acetate
- Iron-on
- Adhesive-backed
- Printable CD/DVD media (print directly on disc)

Although many paper manufacturers offer a selection of specialty substrates, and even more third-party companies offer a wide range of these unusual media, not every desktop (or commercial) printer can handle every kind of these specialty substrates. Always use them with caution. Understand the capabilities and limitations of the desktop printer. When working with a desktop printer, realize that no type of paper reacts exactly the same way to any two printer brands or models. Testing and experimentation is key to successful use.

thinking about the design solution

There are numerous factors to consider when selecting a desktop printing paper or substrate, starting with what is needed for the design concept through production at the commercial printer. But on a simple, practical level, consider the following factors and use them as a checklist when testing paper on a desktop printer:

- What paper does the printer manufacturer recommend?
- Is an alternative available that is less expensive?
- How will the ink hold to the substrate selected? Does the ink stay on? Or does it smear, rub off, or "run" or "bleed"?
- How quickly does the ink dry? Will it dry at all?
- How does the paper/substrate fold? Does it crack?
- How does this small-scale paper/substrate compare if the design is to go to commercial-scale printing? Are the differences too great to simulate the final product? Or does paper simulate the final product well?

All of these questions must be addressed with every project. Without proper planning and forethought, a wonderfully designed piece housed in the computer can be damagingly stalled in the output printing process. See Figure 2-23 for an example of variable printing results—an image printed on the same paper, but from two different printers.

We also recommend comparative shopping for your inkjet papers. We often use Inkpress papers because of their relatively competitive pricing, but do shop around. The following sources have proved reliable for desktop printing paper:

Proprietary Brands

- Cannon
- Epson
- Hewlett-Packard

Figure 2-22
Alternative or specialty substrates for inkjet printers.
Left to right:
Foil.
Metallic (silver, gold).
Holographic foil.
Magnetic sheet.
Translucent vellum.
Backlight film.
Printable canvas.
Transparency.
Clear static-cling decal (acetate).
Iron-on (heat transfer) paper.
Glossy white label.
Printable DVD.

Figure 2-23
In this photograph, we can see an image printed on the same "Photo Quality Inkjet Paper," but from two different printers (of the same manufacturer). Despite using the printer manufacturer's proprietary paper, the two models yield different results.

specialty milled and handmade papers

Standard milled grades such as writing, text, and cover are not the only papers employed by professional designers. For use in both finished design solutions and comps, there are many occasions when a designer thoughtfully and successfully integrates a specialty milled substrate such as metallic foil or canvas, a dark color paper, a specialty texture, or a fancy finish such as flocking (raised velveteen).

Albeit (and unfortunately) rare, there may be occasions for the use of a *handmade* paper in professional design—as an accent page or book cover slip jacket, or for small quantities of applications such as an invitation to a special event or a tipped-on texture.

Handmade paper can fulfill on a personally expressive level. Not all the objects and printed matter that you make need be for a commercial purpose or for a client. Explore your creative impulses through making "self-commissioned" design objects with handmade paper or specialty milled papers.

See Figures 2-24 and 2-25 for samples of specialty milled and handmade papers. But realize that you cannot fully appreciate the subtle tactile qualities of these substrates through photographs.

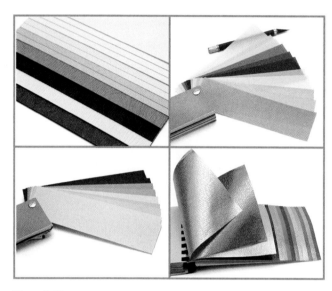

Figure 2-24
A select few specialty milled papers.
First row, left to right:
Impressed textures.
Translucents.
Second row, left to right:
Particles.
Candy wrapper foils.

touching is believing

You really need to hold (and hug) handmade paper to appreciate its lovable textural qualities and compelling tactile sensation. If you do not have a handmade or specialty milled paper source locally, shop online and get samples before investing in large sheets for your comps. Handmade paper is not inexpensive.

Figure 2-25
Handmade papers made from a variety of plant sources.

In alphabetical order, a few of our favorite retail sources for hand-made papers and specialty milled papers include:

- Creative Papers Online
- Green Field Paper Company
- Hollander's Decorative Paper and Bookbinding Supplies
- HQ PaperMaker
- New York Central Art Supply
- Paper Arts
- The Paper Mill Store
- The Paper Studio
- Talas Bookbinding Supplies
- Wet Paint Artists' Materials & Framing

simulated specials

Handmade papers, highly textured milled papers, and dark color papers are usually not compatible with desktop printing for a variety of reasons. The textured paper jams the printer, the handmade papers do not have fillers and rip during printing, formation may be mottled, and light color inks can't be effectively printed on dark color paper. The limitations and problems vary and may go beyond what was named. Yet, there are a few fairly satisfactory ways to simulate the color, texture, or other surface quality by working around the limitations.

Simulating specialty papers, textures, and other substrates is one such purpose; see Figure 2-26 for a professional design application.

scan for texture

A scanner is a tool in the comping process that a designer can use for multiple purposes. On the desktop, for instance, find the paper that is appropriate for the design solution. Scan the specialty substrate. Print the scanned image on desktop printing paper and proceed with the composition of the design solution.

To work around the inability to print light ink on dark color textured paper, compromise. Select a light color or white, textured paper that is compatible with your desktop printer. Second, scan your concept-appropriate dark paper (handmade or specialty milled), next design with the scanned color image, and finally print the resulting image on the actual, compatible textured paper.

digital use

Once a texture, paper, or other substrate is scanned, it is a digital file that can stay on the computer for use in nonprint design applications. Simulated tactile qualities are not as powerful as the actual sense of touching. But with scanned imagery, there can be some texture on the web! See Figure 2-27 for an example of scanned paper and a cork substrate used on the web.

Figure 2-26
Hang tags: Meangirl
Studio: Design Ranch
Creative Directors: Michelle Sonderegger, Ingred Sidie
Copywriter: Kerri Conan
Illustrator: Michelle Sonderegger
Printer: M-Press
Client: Design Ranchables
To simulate the woodgrain texture, real wood was imaged and then printed on the paperboard tags.

Figure 2-27
Website: Thinking Creatively Design Conference
Creative Director: Neil Adelantar
Designer and Developer: Neil Adelantar
Client: Kean University, Department of Design
Cork and paper scanned and incorporated into this website design for depth and illusionary texture.

parchment and aging effects: techniques and pitfalls

To simulate an "aged" look on a piece of paper, to make convincing parchments, vellums, antique writing surfaces of all kinds—how is it done? The film industry standard method—to this day—is to stain a piece of paper with tea and/or coffee! Well, being a watercolor artist, I thought I might try to push the envelope a bit. . . .

Before we begin, I should point out that tea-staining actually gives a pretty good result. The color produced is lovely—just a little one-dimensional.

[Instead], I use watercolor paint, usually (but not always) on watercolor paper. Although the overall color of the finished piece is dominated by earth colors—yellows, browns, siennas, sepia tones—I find that other colors are needed to provide richness and depth. And because the "earth" pigments tend to be nonstaining (they lift, move, and wash out upon subsequent wettings), I apply transparent, staining varieties of red, green, and blue first, to give the piece a background that will stay where I put it!

Let's take a moment to examine pigments, papers, and brushes.

For my underlying base, I use Alizarin Crimson, Phthalo blue, and Viridian green. As well as permanently staining the paper, these pigments have very good transparency; and for both of these reasons, these colors will make a better base than, say, Cadmium red, Cerulean blue, and Emerald green.

My mainstay earth color is Raw Sienna—I probably use twice as much of this as anything else. Burnt Sienna, Raw Umber, and Burnt Umber are used in varying proportions, depending on the required look. The two Burnt earths are often reserved for darkening the paper edges and creating "foxing" stains.

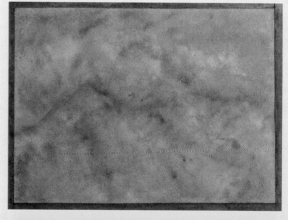

Recently, I've also been adding hints of Indigo and Payne's Grey, which, being compound colors themselves, create very rich blends with other pigments.

Repeated and prolonged wettings mean that it's almost always best to stretch the paper before you start—soak the paper in cold water, then tape it to a board using gummed paper tape. This prevents the paper from cockling (which then causes all the colors to run into the "valleys"). Mostly I'm using a soft-pressed or cold-pressed watercolor paper, 300 gsm, but all of these techniques work with any kind of paper.

I always use a hake (pronounced ha-kay) brush for creating soft washes. This oriental styled goat-hair brush holds a huge amount of water and easily avoids hard edges.

Top to bottom:
White start, Stage two, Stage three, Stage four.

Left:
Map of Cape Cod (USA) using watercolor texture to simulate the quality of aged paper. Artist and Designer: Daniel Reeve

Above:
Daniel Reeve and a tool of his craft.

So, back to work. My first layer is an uneven mottling of red, blue, and green, applied separately (but all in one session) onto prewetted paper. I allow the colors to mix together in some areas, in other places keep them separate, and I also ensure that I leave some paper white. Once dry, I follow this with a fairly even wash of an earth color or two, then two or three more layers of other earth colors, always allowing each layer to dry first. Now, even though some color will be washed out each time, some will also stay put, and each layer will soften any hard edges of the layers underneath, so that eventually, layer by layer, the parchment "look" will start to appear.

The fact that earth colors lift can be used to advantage during this process. I flick clear water onto the still-damp paint: the droplets force the pigment out where they land, creating lighter patches surrounded by darker tide marks. Timing is important: if this is attempted while the paint is too wet, it'll continue to run freely in the extra water and the effect will be lost, whereas if the paint is too dry it may not move at all.

Now all this sounds like a lot of work, and it certainly needs much trial and error to get it right, and it is easy to get carried away, ending up with so much color on the paper that it is all a bit muddy—it's important to retain some "lightness" to allow the white of the paper to shine through. It's also difficult to get matching effects if the piece needs to be double-sided. But the most specific pitfall is that too many wettings wash the sizing agents out of the paper, rendering it useless for subsequent linework! There are several solutions to this problem. . . .

1. Spraying the painted paper with fixative—this restores (to a large extent) the ability of the paper to take ink without it bleeding into the surrounding area.

2. Doing all the linework and calligraphy first, then "aging" it. This is what I usually do, although of course it carries the greatest risk, in that all the hours and hours of beautiful calligraphy and linework can be ruined in seconds by bad watercolor technique! Also, not all inks are waterproof. It is vital to test them first if you intend to use this method (although you can also get some very convincing aging effects by having the ink run and bleed).

3. If the final piece is to be digital or printed, the various layers—parchment, linework, calligraphy, borders, etc.—can all be prepared separately and combined on a computer.

There is also the option of using paper that already has the required look. Sometimes these papers are unsuitable for penwork because the ink bleeds into their "open" surfaces, but again, this can be mitigated by first spraying it with fixative (or applying some kind of sizing agent).

After all of this comes the decision about whether to further distress the piece or not. This can involve folds, creases, dog-eared corners, tears, burns, "real" stains, abrasions, crumplings, etc. Many of these effects, being so overt themselves, render the previous, subtle "aging" almost invisible. This is also true of the effect of calligraphy and linework on aged paper—what had seemed like extreme yellowing and mottling virtually disappears to the eye once the inkwork goes on.

All in all, the choices are almost limitless—there is a huge variety of paper to work on, different color palettes to try, and many of these techniques can be used with acrylic paint also. Painting techniques and effects make an inexhaustible subject—but if all else fails, you can always get a load of teabags and put that kettle on to boil. . . .

Daniel Reeve

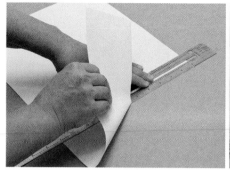 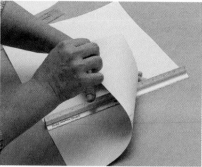 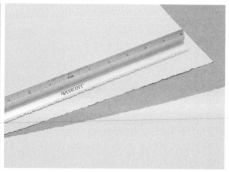

Figure 2-28
Simulating a deckle edge.
Left to right:
Tearing with a ruler.
Tearing with a deckle edger.
Final result.

rip the deckle

One technique from us just for fun: The "deckle-edge" paper is rather simple to simulate and worth a try. The simulated deckle provides a tactile and personal handmade feel not possible by scanning and printing. The deckle is simulated but the texture is real; see Figure 2-28 for a simple procedure for simulating a deckle edge.

Any paper can be torn to create a ragged edge that simulates a deckle edge. However, we recommend using 100% cotton paper because it rips smoothly and reveals its long soft fibers that most resemble the deckle edge of handmade papers. You will also need a steel ruler or a deckle-edge ripper (note in Chapter 1 on tools).

Follow these steps:

- On the bottom of the paper (the wire side), measure and mark the edge line. It is along this line that the paper will be torn.

- Place a ruler along the edge line on the back of the paper. Put the ruler on the long side of the edge line so that the greatest quantity of paper is below the ruler.

- Hold the ruler firmly in one hand and the top right corner of the paper in the other hand.

- Pull the paper toward you and into the ruler using a continuous motion.

- Remove the ruler and note that it leaves a tiny lip at the line of tearing. However, the reverse side (the top side) is perfectly smooth.

paint the texture

If the paper desired for a design concept is not available for scanning (too expensive?), simulate the decorative or textural quality on printer-compatible paper using drawing or painting techniques (don't forget to test for printer compatibility or scan the image if necessary and proceed).

Even if you lack skill and training in painting, have fun figuring out a method for your desired texture, as did famed prop designer, Daniel Reeve. Take a look at the finishes accomplished by Reeve for the maps he created for the film version of *The Lord of the Rings,* the 2005 version of *King Kong,* and *The Chronicles of Narnia* film series, among others. A bit of Reeve's magic is revealed in the special feature article and the step-by-step guide provided by the artist/designer.

paper tricks

We can't possibly give you all our tricks at this point (we need an additional book for that!) but we do include a few and leave you with this advice: Use everything in your brain's imagination skill box to pull off the texture, color, and finish needed to implement the concept. If the knowledge is not in your brain already, experiment and research! Use sponges, twigs, inked fabric, sandpaper, dirt, and glitter (just kidding, don't use glitter). Want to know how to marbleize paper? Want to know what we mean by marbleize? Go to the Blick Art Materials website and search for lesson plans on marbleizing paper. Want to create "flocking"? Try using sheets of adhesive-backed flocked paper and make your own patterns with it. Explore. Create. Have fun.

actual texture—gotta have it!

There are situations where the actual texture or color or substrate cannot be printed on the desktop or satisfactorily simulated—yet a tactile quality, rich color, or other quality is a must-have to serve the design solution. What to do about the comp? At times, you simply may not be able to comp it. (Although we are loath to say "never.") However, necessity is the mother of invention. Yes, we have some thoughts on the matter that may lead to experimentation on your part.

go naked

Consider using exotic handmade paper or other substrate such as bookcloth *without* printing on it. Leave the **bookcloth** (fabric adhered to paper for use specifically in bookbinding), paper, or other alternative substrate *blank* and let the texture and colors speak for themselves. See Figure 2-29 for a professional example.

nearly naked

Several specialty printing techniques can be applied either on the desktop or through a commercial printer. Specialty printing techniques are discussed in Chapter 10. See Figure 2-30 for a professional example and Figure 2-31 for a swatchbook of bookcloth—the textural substrate used in the professional design solution.

glue it on

When the milled paper or handmade paper can't be printed by hand, on a desktop printer, or at a commercial printer, but both a full-color image and a textured paper are desired and integral to the design solution, the image can be printed separately, cut to the size needed, and glued to the textured surface. See Figure 2-32 for a professional example of printed imagery glued to a textured surface.

a few final questions

Both students of design and pros must be aware of the power of paper and its functional variables. With only a few differences between student and pro, the following are some of the questions you should ask (of yourself and of the paper mill representatives) when selecting paper:

Student—Which paper is conceptually appropriate for my design solution?

Pro—Which paper is conceptually appropriate for my design solution?

Student—How well does it print on my desktop laser or inkjet?

Pro—How well does it print using offset printing? Digital printing? Specialty printing?

Student—How does it function after printing: cut, perforate, score, fold?

Pro—How does it function after printing: cut, perforate, score, fold?

Student—What is the life span of the printed piece? Is it a draft comp or a final comp?

Pro—What is the life span of the final printed piece? Is it archival or ephemeral?

Student—How environmentally sustainable is the paper?

Figure 2-29
Annual Report: Amara *Ascend*
Studio: Kinetic, Singapore
Creative Director: Roy Poh
Client: Amara
Cover substrate: *Faux* grass
Noted by the designer: "The theme of ascendance was the central thought behind this work. And because the impulse to reach upwards is common to all plants, the design brings the concept to life with expressive use of plant images and associated colours."

Pro—How environmentally sustainable is the paper?

Student—How fast can I purchase the paper? Is it readily available?

Pro—How fast can I purchase the paper? Is it readily available?

Student—Can I afford it?

Pro—Can the client afford it?

Figure 2-30

Catalog: The Mall at Short Hills
Studio: Brogan Tennyson Group Inc.
Creative Director: Jen Battle
Designer/Production Artist: Laura Menza
Client: The Mall at Short Hills

The professionally designed catalog for an upscale shopping mall. The cover was made with bookcloth over paperboard. Debossing was used for the type—a specialty printing technique discussed in Chapter 9.

Figure 2-31
Bookcloth sample swatches, showing the range of colors available.

Figure 2-32

Packaging: Fervere
Studio: Design Ranch
Creative Directors: Michelle Sonderegger, Ingred Sidie
Illustrator: Michelle Sonderegger
Copywriter: Kerri Conan
Printer: Hammerpress
Paper: French Paper
Client: Fervere

The decorative wrap, the identifying label (featuring the company's name and logo), and the label used to seal the box were all printed separately and adhered to the textured box.

summary: paper set; go

Paper is the primary foundation for printing a design solution. Additional substrates expand creative potential. The paper sample "toolbox" or library kept can be an inspiration to the design concepts you develop.

Awareness of industry standards and printing conventions in regard to paper and alternative substrates along with learning the basic technical aspects of working with paper on desktop printers for comps helps to build your worth as a practical and functioning designer.

Becoming aware of the art of paper use will help build your mind as a creative designer.

exercise knowledge gained

The very first step in your knowledge of paper and its many uses is a bit of research, immediately followed by some hands-on experience. The following exercises are simple projects that do not need to be brought to fruition as finished design solutions—but rather are designed to start you on the path of greater understanding of paper, alternative substrates, and their uses. Gain some knowledge and then get tactile!

1. resources at the ready

Research the paper supply stores in your immediate environment. Visit the stores and learn as much as you can about their inventory. Having a good supplier at hand is essential in meeting deadlines for practice design projects. Do not depend on mail order through the web for all your supplies. Shipping takes time and mail order fees can add up.

2. "bookmark" paper company websites; gather a paper library

Using the professional paper companies, hand-bookbinding and paper supply stores, and art supply stores listed in this chapter as your source, or through research on your own, gather and establish a library of paper samples for inspiration in concept development and for awareness of practical use. See Figure 2-33 for some paper samples. Nourish curiosity.

3. do the deckle

If you haven't tried the deckle-edge simulation (Figure 2-28) or textural painting (by Daniel Reeve) mentioned in this chapter, try them now. You will learn by doing. See also Figure 2-34 for a student example involving a simulated deckle edge and printed color over textured paper.

Figure 2-33
Paper samples: milled, specialty milled, and handmade.

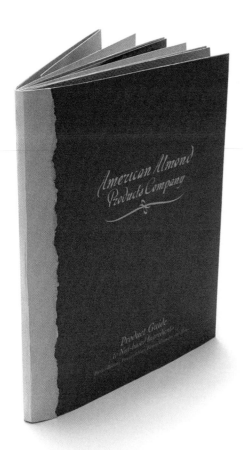

4. if you can't beat 'em, scan 'em!

So, you can't print on the texture or finish of your heart's desire, and it will kill your concept if you don't, right? Scan textures and keep them in a digital library for future use. See Figure 2-35 for samples of scanned textures.

5. visit a papermaking studio

Visit a fine arts center where books and paper are created. See a sheet of paper made. You may be allowed to observe or, better, enroll in a workshop and make your own paper—just for the fun of it. Don't think about application. The joy is in the process.

Figure 2-34
Simulating light ink on dark paper.
Student project: Promotional booklet.
Student designer: Jennifer Sencion
In this student design of a promotional catalog for almond paste
(a specialty bakery item), a cream color Canson paper was selected
as the textured substrate (compatible with the desktop printer
in use). Orange color Canson paper was scanned and used as a
background color.
The deckle is a physical (rather than scanned) simulation. The resulting
design solution and comp have both real and simulated textures. The
earthy orange color with its lightly speckled surface and the actual
pebbly texture of the paper express a warm (baked) feeling that echoes
the subject matter and helps to enhance the message (almond paste
adds depth of texture and taste to bakery products). The script typeface
is a counterbalance to the earthy color and texture, suggesting the
elegance of the bakery products created with almond paste.

Figure 2-35
Student project: Scanned textures and various other surfaces and things.
Student designer: Allison Grow

"There's nothing you can make that can't be made . . . It's easy."
—*John Lennon/Paul McCartney*

three
basic techniques

chapter three: plan, measure, think, measure again, score, cut, fold, and glue

learning objectives

- Learn relevant use of tools.
- Develop skill in using tools and materials.
- Explore the safe and effective use of materials and techniques.

foundation skills

Once the toolbox is complete and a library of paper is collected (or its sources known), proper and safe skill in using the basic tools and materials should be developed. Possibly, you think it easy to use craft tools and other crafting materials with no guidance or practice. Surely you know how to use a ruler (but maybe not with speed). We have tips that will help. To best understand this chapter, review Chapters 1 and 2 and refer back to those chapters for additional information on tools and materials.

N.B. The authors are right-handed. A reminder (and apology) to our left-handed readers—all instructions in this text are based on right-handed use.

get organized

It is likely that you can pick up basic craft tools and materials and use them, but probably not efficiently and expertly. Even if you have been using the tools for some time, maybe there are some new tricks or tips to learn.

Throughout this chapter, each relevant use of the basic tools is explained and most are visually demonstrated in photographs. Read each explanation carefully and study the photographic guides.

After you have some understanding of what we are demonstrating, reread and then practice the process on scrap paper, paperboard, and other substrates.

practice paper

We recommend using practice paper in standard 11" × 17" sheet sizes. Specifically, we suggest the following:

- ▢ 70#–80# text weight, smooth white paper, and various colors
- ▢ 70#–80# cover weight, smooth white paper, and various colors

---

green thought

Please do not waste fresh paper for practice purposes. And do not practice on finished printed design solutions. Use scrap or recycled paper. Trust that you need to learn the basics first and apply the knowledge once you have practiced. Rather than make mistakes and waste time, paper, and ink—practice on scrap. Be sure to recycle in any case.

Use an inexpensive neutral white paper that folds easily and cleanly. For color variety, Strathmore and Canson papers are easily accessible and come in a variety of interesting hues.

clear the area!

Save time and frustration by efficiently preparing and organizing the work area. Arrange a place for at least two flat-top tables (at home) and keep all tools and materials in organized containers. In the studio classroom setting, organization is also important.

The following checklist notes what is generally recommended to have at the ready in the working environment for constructing desktop comprehensive mock-ups:

- ▢ A well-lighted work area. Place lights to the right and left of the work surfaces to reduce cast shadows that could interfere with measurements and assembly.

- ▢ Three clean, flat, smooth work surfaces, either on one table using separate boards or at separate stations:

  A clean construction area and surface

  A smooth cutting surface (a self-healing mat is best)

  A gluing surface

- A small table (or box) exclusively to keep basic tools and materials at the ready:

  ➤ Practice paper and other substrates

  ➤ Drawing, erasing, cutting, scoring, folding, and measuring tools

  ➤ A raised straightedge cutting guide

  ➤ Adhesives and tapes

  ➤ A small, flat glass, ceramic, or paper plate for liquid glue (for separating glue into small batches)

  ➤ 3" × 2" pieces of stiff paperboard and/or brushes for spreading glue

  ➤ Dry and damp rags and/or paper towels (Keep rags ready on a plate so they do not dampen work surfaces.)

  ➤ Newsprint scrap and tracing paper ready to use for gluing and folding

- Keep a first aid kit ready or know where to find one. Before you begin, remember to use your tools and materials with caution.

- Finally, we recommend peace, quiet, privacy, and no cell phones. We know you can't bear to live without your text messages and cell phones for anything less than ²⁴⁄₇, but try! In solitude there is focused vision and far less margin for error.

mark it up and then erase it

We know you can use a pencil and an eraser for drawing. However, we have a few points to make in regard to their relevance in crafting a comp.

When marking an area for cutting or scoring a fold line, use a sharp, hard pencil such as a 5H. The 5H pencil leaves a very light mark that is obvious if left on the page. But do not add pressure to make the line darker as this will make an indentation in the paper. If you can't see the mark well enough, use a sharp 2H pencil instead. Do not use markers or pens. Pencils are employed for the obvious reason—the mark can be erased if necessary and for removal at finish.

A soft pencil (6B, 5B, HB) will yield a highly visible line, but it may smudge and cannot be erased totally. In addition, the thicker line made with soft pencil may also cause inaccuracy in measurements since it has a width that may exponentially, through the process, add up and skew the distance from one given point to the next. Use a soft pencil for marking textured or dark surfaces (so the mark is visible). Use a 5H for most other measurement marks where less visibility is needed.

To mark the desired measurement, place the ruler along the edge and make a dot with the pencil tip. Do not draw a line because it may skew the point of measurement. A dot is pointedly precise; see Figure 3-1 for a visual guide to placing measurement marks.

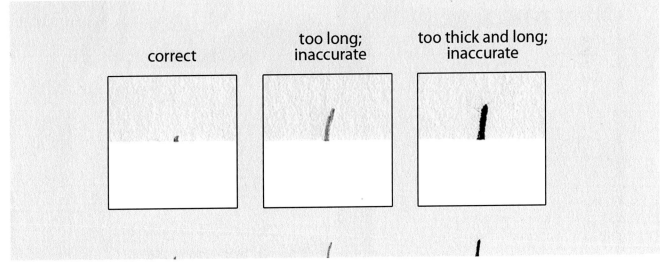

Figure 3-1
To place the measurement mark, use a sharp 5H (hard) graphite pencil or a mechanical pencil to make a dot. A dot is most accurate. Thick or curvy lines are unacceptable marks that will skew measurement. Excessively heavy or dark marks may also be difficult to erase cleanly.

now erase it

An **eraser** removes pencil from the surface of paper and other substrates. Erasers are not all the same. Note the type of erasers we recommended for the toolbox and their response to graphite (pencil). Always apply a test using an inconsequential substrate before applying an eraser (or any other tool for that matter) to finished, printed work.

With patience, a kneaded eraser (the type that stretches) will remove graphite and it can remove some pen ink. This eraser also gently pulls off stray bits of lint, dust, or other unwanted particles because it is slightly sticky.

A kneaded eraser is best used by pressing into the graphite and pulling up to remove. Additionally, this eraser can remove bits of printing ink. Push lightly into the surface and pull up and away rather than rub or grind. With a push-pulling action, there is less chance of grinding the graphite into the surface or smudging the graphite or ink during the erasing action.

However, a kneaded eraser can also pull paper fibers and powdered laser ink and inkjet ink off the surface and will cause surface changes if not used carefully. Or perhaps the damage is acceptable with the trade being that removing some fibers of the paper surface will clean unwanted marker or pen ink marks. Be aware. The kneaded eraser is also conveniently self-cleaning—stretch and knead.

A white eraser is the best thorough cleaner for most graphite on paper. Rub to erase. White erasers can cause some surface damage and will only smudge the graphite if they are not kept clean while in use. Clean a used eraser on a rough surface (paper or light grit sandpaper) before reusing.

Use a gum eraser for a gentle touch on soft substrates. It is non-greasy and will erase graphite from paper. A gum eraser cleans fairly easily by rubbing with paper towel or rubbing along clear scrap paper; it crumbles as it is cleaned and used.

when to rule

Fortunately, the measurements needed for your graphic design solutions and subsequent comps can be calculated in the inch or metric system and indicated from within graphic design software programs while working on your computer; see Figure 3-2.

Within the software program command dialogue boxes, measurements can be set using the base 10 decimal system, corresponding with the fractions of an inch on an English/Imperial ruler.

Rulers also appear visually on the computer screen running along both the top horizontal and the left vertical edge of the program window. For the highest accuracy, use the digital screen rulers along with the software to measure and mark cut and fold lines.

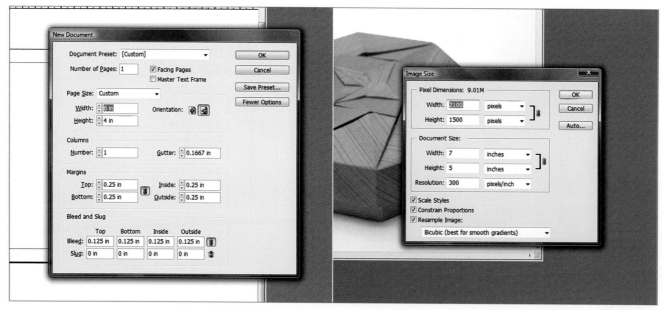

Figure 3-2
Pictured here are screenshots of the software command/entry boxes for various measurements. On the left is a Document Size dialogue box from Adobe InDesign; on the right is an Image Size dialogue from Adobe Photoshop.

desktop rulers

You may be wondering why you need a ruler when your graphics software can so accurately set measurements. First of all, understanding a measurement system is necessary in order to use it correctly, whether the system appears on the screen or on a ruler.

There will be occasions when you need to use a ruler to measure paper for a blank comp or check measurements after printing pages or to mark up pages that will be processed into a comp. You cannot be a great technician of comprehensive mock-ups if you do not understand inch (and decimal) measurements or how to read a ruler.

english or imperial rules

The following discussion on learning to read a ruler pertains to the United States system of measurements, that being called the English, US, or Imperial system of inches and feet.

Standard steel rulers will have the smallest unit of measurement as ¹⁄₁₆ inch. The first inch should also indicate the smaller unit of ¹⁄₃₂ inch.

For use of an Imperial ruler, you need to know that inches are divided into fractions: one-half (½), one-quarter (¼), one-eighth (⅛), and one-sixteenth (¹⁄₁₆).

The lowest fraction of an inch in use for this text is ¹⁄₃₂. Anything smaller than ¹⁄₃₂ is barely visible to the human eye or not absolutely critical for handcraftsmanship of comps.

Refer to Figure 3-3; the measurements are noted on a ruler as follows:

¤ One-half inch (½") divides the inch into two equal units.

¤ One-quarter inch (¼") divides the half inch into two equal units, which would be four equal units to the inch.

¤ One-eighth inch (⅛") divides the quarters into half again, which would be eight equal units to the inch.

¤ One-sixteenth inch (¹⁄₁₆") divides the eighths into half, which would be 16 equal units to the inch.

¤ One thirty-second inch (¹⁄₃₂") divides the sixteenths into half, which would be 32 equal units to the inch.

The precision ruler in Figure 3-3 displays both ¹⁄₃₂" indicator lines and ¹⁄₆₄" indicator lines. As noted from the Galaxy Gauge website: "[The Ruling] Tool includes: points, picas, centimeters, inches (with built-in conversion tool), bullets, rule weights, fraction to decimal conversions, leading, angles, circles, FTP clock, scan sizes, serif & sans serif type sizes, screen densities, screen frequencies, line work resolutions, enlargement/reductions and precision decimal inch & millimeters"—all the measurements a graphic designer may desire.

Your eye and hand are not machines, thankfully. But do strive for the greatest precision and accuracy in crafting the comps for your graphic design solutions because you are trying to *simulate* what a machine will accomplish. Precision will impress clients and potential employers. Sloppy craftsmanship never will.

reading a ruler

"Excuse me," you may say when looking at the awkward system of inches and feet on your new steel ruler. "Where are the numbers written for one-eighth inch? Where is one-quarter inch noted? What is one foot? The words and numbers for these measurements are not indicated."

Usually, only the numbers for inches are indicated on a standard ruler. A standard ruler of 1 foot (12 inches), 2 feet (24 inches), or 3 feet (36 inches) indicates the breakdown of inches using Arabic numbers. The fractions of inches are indicated using a hierarchical system of straight, vertical lines of differing lengths (not numbers).

When writing measurements, the word *inches* is indicated with the inch mark (") and the word *feet* is indicated with the foot mark ('). For instance, 2 feet and 3 inches is indicated as 2' 3". Because comps are relatively small, the measurements discussed in this textbook will be inches.

With ruler in hand, count all the small vertical lines between the 2" and 3" lines and you will note that there are 16. This is because an inch has 16 units measuring ¹⁄₁₆" each. Sixteen units of 1 inch can be written: ¹⁶⁄₁₆". Because fractional numbers are expressed in the largest unit possible, ¹⁶⁄₁₆" is simplified and written as 1 inch or 1".

Next, count 8 vertical lines (⁸⁄₁₆") between the 2" and 3" lines. Eight vertical lines equal one-half inch or ½" (expressed in the largest unit possible). Stay within 2" and 3" and count four of the shortest lines: ⁴⁄₁₆" equals a quarter of an inch or ¼".

We hope you know how to add fractions of an inch such as ½" plus ¼". If not, get tutelage in basic math as it is essential for measuring accurately.

fractional hierarchy

With your ruler in hand once again, note that the longest vertical line in the measurement system is designated with a number to indicate the inch unit.

Each inch unit is then subdivided into groups of units of equal size. The next shortest measurement indicator line in the hierarchy is in the middle of the whole inch unit—indicating the two half units of the single inch (one-half inch or ½"). There is only one half-inch line because two halves equal one whole.

Shorter than the ½" line is the quarter inch measurement indicator line; there are two ¼" units. Refer back to Figure 3-3 for a visual explanation of the system of measurement on a steel ruler.

The next measurement indicator line in the hierarchy, shorter than ¼", is the ⅛" (one-eighth inch) indicator line. There are four ⅛" units.

On most simple standard rulers, the shortest measurement line indicator is the 1/16" (one-sixteenth inch) line. There are eight 1/16" units.

The first 1-inch unit of your ruler will usually *also* show 1/32" lines for the occasional case where you may need this tiny fractional measurement. Precision rulers, such as a Galaxy Gauge, provide 1/32" and 1/64" measurement indications along a 12" or 18" guide. There may be instances when such precision measurement is critical. Therefore, we suggest a precision ruler for your toolbox.

speed reading

If you are new to reading a ruler, it is likely you will find yourself counting lines *slowly*, which is a functional but inefficient method of finding the measurement needed. Instead of counting six lines to arrive at ⅜", practice recognizing the hierarchical lengths of vertical measurement indicator lines. Visually memorize the line lengths relative to the units of measurement they represent.

Use the ½" line as an anchor for remembering that ⅛" over the ½" line is ⅝"; or ⅛" below the ½" line is ⅜". It will take time but with practice you should easily recognize the measurements using only the hierarchy of measurement indicator lines on the ruler (instead of counting 1, 2, 3 . . . 16).

set dividers

If there is a linear series of measurement marks needed, use a set divider (tool) to speed the process.

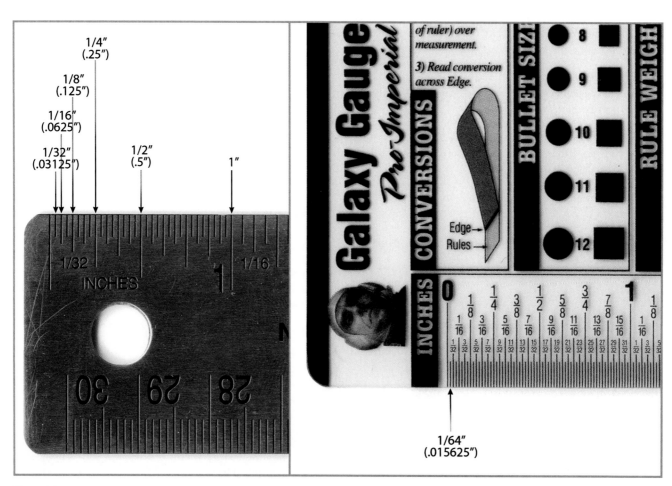

Figure 3-3
The rulers shown are *not* actual size. They are enlarged for ease of study.
Left to right:
Ruler with English/Imperial measurements (inches).
The precision ruler displays both ⅓₂" indicator lines and 1/64" indicator lines.

desired line of measurement. With a pencil, place a starting dot. Open the divider to the desired measurement and tighten (the top screw) to set the width. Place one point of the divider on the starting dot of measurement and the second point of the divider against the ruler (see Figure 3-4). Use the point of the divider to make a slight indent to mark the next unit of measure. Flip/turn the divider 180 degrees to demarcate the next point of measurement. Continue to turn the divider along the length of the ruler until all points of measurement are indicated. Note: Be aware to slightly indent the paper to mark the next measurement (do not make gaping holes).

Also use the set divider after marking the line of measurement to double-check for accuracy.

N.B. An old adage imparts this simple sage advice: *Measure twice. Cut once.*

measuring diameter and depth

Use a caliper for measuring thicknesses or distances between surfaces. For the purpose of creating comps, a caliper is particularly useful for measuring the exterior surfaces of three-dimensional objects such as a cylinder or a box. See Figure 3-5 for a visual example. A ruler may be insufficient and inaccurate for this purpose.

Using a set divider is easy: Tape the substrate to the surface of the worktable so it doesn't shift while measuring, or at least be aware of movement (which causes inaccuracies). Place a ruler along the

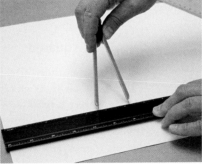

Figure 3-4
If there is a linear series of measurements needed, use a set divider (tool) to speed the process. Or use the set divider to double-check measurements to ensure accuracy.

Figure 3-5
Left to right:
For a precise measurement, use a caliper measuring the diameters of cylinders or a box top.
For desktop comps, using a caliper is the most accurate way to measure the size of the shape of a three-dimensional object in order to apply design matter to it.

Calipers are also useful for measuring depth such as the depth of the aforementioned cylinder. Another use would be to measure the thickness of paperboard or a collated stack of paper (to be used as book pages).

square off with a triangle (a.k.a. set square)

Do not fear. You will not need to study advanced geometry and trigonometry in order to fabricate a comprehensive mock-up of a design solution. But we will assume that you bring from your math studies a fundamental understanding of the measurement of angles.

As with a ruler, the measurements of angles needed for your graphic design solutions and subsequent comps can be calculated and indicated from within graphic design software programs while working on your computer. Within the software programs' command dialogue boxes, angle measurements can be set with the standard increments (90, 45, 30, 60 degrees) or with variations of those standards. Entering the desired measurements for the cut and/or fold lines of a design by using a computerized system is highly accurate.

Yet, there are some instances where a triangle tool is necessary. A triangle can assist in setting or checking the measuring angles,

act as a straightedge guide to cut angles accurately, and—most important in the context of your work with comps—provide essential "square insurance."

setting square

Square insurance (our term) refers to checking and adjusting, if necessary, all the right angles (90 degree) on a given substrate. This process is commonly known as **setting square**. A triangle has a precise 90-degree angle. When the triangle tool is aligned to correspond to the right-angle corner of the substrate, it can be used to determine if the paper (or other substrate of a given design project) is **squared**—that is, a precise 90 degrees.

If the substrate is not square (a.k.a. **off square**), then it will never be accurate or flush when cut and folded; see examples in Figure 3-6.

If you are working on a multiple-page comp, and even one section is slightly off square, it will cause problems (headaches) and the entire construction to be imprecise in alignment.

T-squared

The sturdy, steel T-square recommended for inclusion in your toolbox, as mentioned in Chapter 1, is not critical but can be very helpful.

The T-square can assist in drawing straight and square horizontal lines, and in conjunction with a triangle for drawing straight and square vertical lines.

Paper, foamcore, and paperboard are manufactured with precise 90-degree corner angles from which all measurements can be aligned. However, once cut by hand, the sheet of paper or other

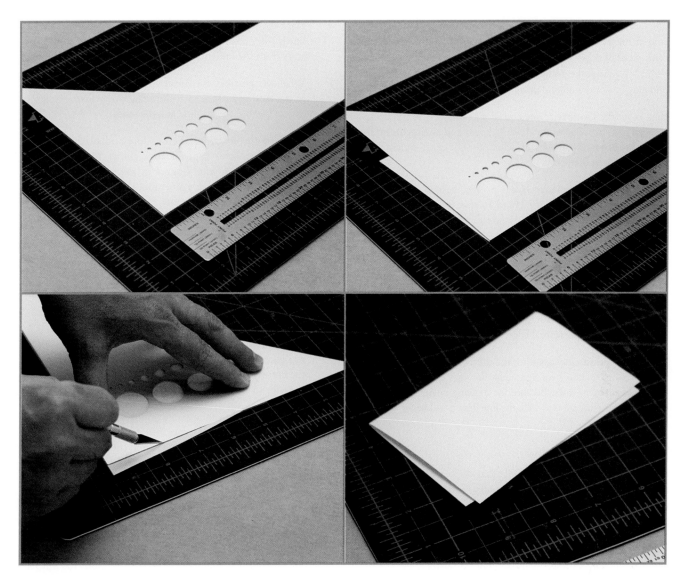

Figure 3-6

First row, left to right:

On square: Align the right-angle corner of a triangle along the 90-degree angle of a printed design or blank piece of paper. Note that the sides extending from the corner are exactly flush with the edges of the triangle.

Off square: Align the corner of the right-angle triangle along the 90-degree angle of the printed design. Note that one side of the substrate is not flush with the edge of the right triangle. The substrate is off square.

Second row, left to right:

Trim to make the substrate square.

When the page is not square, the folding will be misaligned.

substrate may have lost its manufactured precision if it was cut (by hand or machine) off square. Whether squaring up the corner of a blank piece of paper or the edge of an image, use a triangle with a T-square to check the accuracy of all desired 90-degree angles. The following is a brief guide to using a T-square:

- Note the crossbar at one end of a T-square. The bar is used to grab the edge of the drafting board and align with it. The edge becomes a track with which to slide the T-square vertically along the board.

- To use the T-square, place a printed design or a sheet of paper on your drawing board so that it is exactly parallel to the edge of the board. Secure the substrate to the board using drafting tape.

- Move the T-square to the desired horizontal location—use the edge of the board and the cross-T of the tool to fix it in position.

- Place the triangle with the 90-degree corner perpendicular to the T-square horizontal edge.

- Mark measurements and/or use the T-square (or a ruler) with a triangle to check for right-angle accuracy of existing edges or measurement lines. Because the drawing board is 90 degrees and the T-square is as well, the line drawn will be 90 degrees.

cut it out

For review and reinforcement, note that the blades of utility and craft knives should be sharp and remain sharp through the construction process. Change blades often—more so for thinner blades. Definitely replace the blade if the tip is broken.

You will notice that a dull blade can cut paper and cardboard or paperboard, but the result is usually not satisfactory; the cut line may be ragged or there may be resistance. A dull blade may snag in the process of cutting (it is not sharp enough to follow through) and tear the substrate. The abrupt resistance may also cause the blade to jump out of its track and cut your hand. Please exercise extreme caution when using cutting tools.

Scissors should also remain sharp—but do not trash dull scissors. When sharpened by a technician specializing in that purpose, scissors can last a lifetime.

Please read through the following guidelines before practicing.

practice cutting straight lines

A utility knife is the only tool recommended for cutting card/cover stock, heavy board, and foamcore (unless you have a knife for cutting foamcore). We recommend a utility knife for most substrates. The utility knife has a large handle that provides stability and therefore is usually safer than knives with thin handles. Note the following general steps needed for safe and successful cutting:

- Place the substrate or paper on a cutting surface so the cut line is *perpendicular* to your body. Stand slightly to the side, away from the knife.

- Whenever possible, the substrate should be within the edges of the cutting surface with the straightedge long enough to extend beyond the cut line at either end.

- Flush to the *inside* of the cut line and place the raised straightedge—this type of tool guides the cutting and helps to protect your fingers in the process. The index finger and thumb are vulnerable and thus the raised lip provides a barrier protection.

- Cutting too quickly may cause accidents despite the raised edge. Speed and force are not safe. *Cut slowly* and don't use too much pressure, which causes the blade to wobble. Let the blade accomplish the work, not your elbow. Be firm, not forceful.

- At the start of the cut line, push the blade into the full depth of the paper.

- With index finger, middle finger, and thumb, hold the straightedge steady. Pull the knife carefully and firmly along the cutting line. The blade should be flush to the edge. Use the edge to steady the blade.

- To cut through a long length, move your hand along the straightedge to keep it secure, but do *not* lift the blade out of the cut line. Continue to the end and cut cleanly through the edge of the substrate.

- After several uses, safely recycle the dulled blade.

N.B. For extra stability, use the raised-edge, heavy-duty bar of a mat cutter to cut deep substrates such as foamcore. See Figure 3-7 for a visual guide. Due to the thickness and strength of paperboard and bookboard, we recommend a guillotine cutter when available. You will need patience and many passes of a utility knife to cut paperboard by hand.

thin and lightweight substrates

The craft knife works well with lightweight substrates and is a good tool for cutting tight corners, cuts of a short length (several inches), and short curves.

Use as you would a utility knife; however, practice greater caution as this style of knife has a tendency to wobble more because of its thin, lightweight handle. Note that a raised-edge ruler is not necessary; see Figure 3-8. You can choose instead to use a flat steel ruler with a craft knife because less leverage is needed (the margin for wobbling and error is less). The cork backing of a flat ruler helps to keep the instrument from slipping; however, we prefer to remove the cork so the guiding edge is closer to the substrate.

Do not use a craft knife for foamcore, board, or other thick substrates; the tool is not strong enough. The ultrapointy tip of the craft knife

Figure 3-7
Left to right:
When the substrate is thick, start by pushing the knife partially through the thickness. Cut along the substrate once (approximately half the thickness). Remove the knife and keep the straightedge steady. Reinsert the knife and push through to the full thickness of the substrate and cut through.
If the substrate is quite thick, use a heavier straightedge for stability and cut with three or more passes of the knife. If you rush or use brute force instead of a sharp tool, it is likely the board will rip, fray, or tear instead of cutting through cleanly. Testing on scrap is always a good idea.

does the work, and its small size is not long enough or sturdy enough to cut through board or foamcore. In fact, when the tip breaks, the knife is spent. Throw it away and replace it with a new blade.

Please use caution; the blades of a craft knife are sharp and do not discriminate between fingertips and substrates. Keep the first aid kit handy just in case.

After several cuts have been made with a craft knife, dispose of spent blades in a safe container.

Figure 3-8
Use a craft knife for cutting lightweight paper. Place the cut line perpendicular to your body. Use a 6" or 12" ruler as a straightedge. This smaller size is easier to work with when cutting short lines. With index finger and thumb holding the straightedge ruler flat and flush to the line, push the tip of the knife into the paper to start the cut, then pull the knife carefully and firmly along the ruler. A sharp tool does not need pressure to make a smooth cut because the blade does the work.

safety note

Using a straightedge with a barrier is a safe way to use a utility or craft knife. However, only diligent focus and a wise sense of caution will fully prevent accidents. If there is a cutting accident, clean, disinfect locally, and bandage the wound immediately. See a doctor or nurse to ensure that there will be no infection.

Tip: Cover your exposed thumb and index finger with a self-sticking bandage prior to working for added protection.

cutting a refined angle

To cut the edge of a board at a 45-degree angle, a specialty tool known as a mat cutter does the job. The angle edge created by this cutting system has a refined visual appeal. See Figure 3-9 for an example.

Figure 3-9
Use a mat cutter for cutting the edge of a board at an angle (a beveled edge). The board angle has a refined visual finish (see inset).

scissors

A sturdy pair of metal scissors (and the larger metal shears) is helpful for quick cuts that do not require a precise measurement. Scissors can be used to cut away larger areas of excess paper before handling the final cutting edge or when a perfectly straight line is not necessary.

Serrated scissors are helpful for cutting thin sheets of metal or roughly textured paper.

Use precision scissors for cutting tiny curve lines (Figure 3-10) and for snipping away in tight corners.

As noted in Chapter 1, there are a great variety of scissors that have decorated edges. We don't recommend using anything other than perhaps pinking scissors or scalloped-edge scissors because decorative edging can easily appear amateurish and trite. Better to use your own cut edge design to ensure originality and relevance to a design concept.

cutting circles, ovals, and curves

Cutting accurate and perfect circles and ovals is not easy without a specialized knife and cutting templates (refer to Chapter 1 on tools for an image of a cutter of this type). Use a craft knife and great care if a template and fitted knife system is not available. See Figure 3-11 for a visual guide.

The recommended procedure for cutting with a circle template and fitted knife is noted in the following list:

◻ Proceed with safety in mind; the blades of these tools are scary sharp.

◻ Test the substrate before cutting the finished printed matter (practice using the tool).

◻ Fit the desired size template exactly on the circular or oval area to be cut.

◻ Place the tool in the track of the template. Press and guide the knife carefully around the circle or oval.

◻ Remove the cutter and template and carefully poke the shape out. If the circle is not completely cut through, use a craft knife to very carefully cut through any remaining uncut areas.

Figure 3-10
For cutting into small, tight corners, use precision scissors.

Figure 3-11
Cutting Circles and Ovals Step by Step

Left to right:
To manually cut circles, use a craft knife.

Do not lift the knife; rather, turn the paper.

Use very fine sandpaper to smooth any rough edges.

- If the line of the cut is nicked or slightly uneven, try using light sandpaper to smooth the edge. Proceed with the sandpaper using a light hand—be delicate in its application.

- If a half circle is desired, mark the end points and cut only to those points.

- The process is the same for using oval cutters.

hole punching

Use handheld tools to punch holes (one at a time) in paper and most lightweight substrates. If using heavy paperboard that does not cut through easily and you are seeking to have many holes punched in an accurate row, we suggest that you explore the cost of using a professional bookbinder or a local craftsman's book bindery for a one-off job of punching. You may find that the job can be done for a reasonable cost. See Figure 3-12 for a visual guide to hole punching. A guide to punching holes follows:

- To begin, measurements for the holes must be set to align with the center of the hole. Mark the right angle (or a crosshair) of the hole on the printed matter or blank substrate first before setting the punch. The demarcation can also be set on the computer. Remember that your hands are not as accurate as a computerized cutting machine. Allow that the hole may not be perfectly placed after cutting.

- For paper and other lightweight substrates, a Japanese-style (screw) hole punch works easily. Test your substrate and measurements on scrap before proceeding to the finish work.

- Align the punch at the point of measurement. Hold the handle of the punch firmly and press into the substrate. The hole/circle should cut cleanly with one "punch."

- For heavy substrates, use a bookbinder's punch and craft hammer. Refer back to Chapter 1 for an image of this tool. Test your substrate and measurements on scrap before proceeding to the finish work. The board may be too thick for the punch—in which case you will have to resort to a circle cutter or a craft knife, or have the holes punched by a professional (a bindery).

- Align the punch at the line of measurement. Hold the punch firmly in one hand. With the other hand, hit the top of the punch with one to three "bangs" of the hammer. The hole/circle should cut cleanly. If not, you will probably need to use a craft knife to cut through the many layers of the board.

- With a craft knife, carefully cut through the individual layers (or plies) of the paperboard; peel away each of the plies to make the hole. If the edge of the hole is rough, use lightweight sandpaper to smooth.

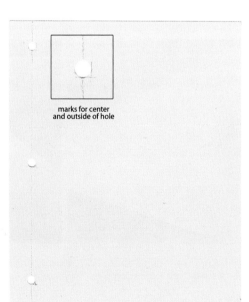

marks for center
and outside of hole

Figure 3-12
Left to right:
Hold the handle of the punch firmly and press into the substrate.
The hole/circle should cut cleanly with one "punch."

A close-up shows how the paper was accurately measured and marked for hole punching.

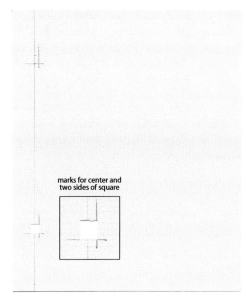

Figure 3-13
The reach of a decorative punch is limited to the edge and borders of the substrate, yet it can be helpful because it is at the ready and speeds the process.

A close-up shows how the paper was accurately measured and marked for hole punching.

square and circle punches and beyond

A single punch in the shape of a square, circle or other simple shape may be limited in use but can be helpful. The reach of the punch is restricted to the edge and borders of the substrate, yet it is at the ready and speeds the process. See Figure 3-13 for a brief visual guide.

We find the rounded corner punch particularly useful. It considerably speeds the process of cutting corners; see Figure 3-14.

score and fold

Folding is the action of laying one part over another part—to double. Preceding the action of folding, **scoring**—precisely denting, incising, or notching a line below the surface of the paper or other substrate—will assist in crafting an accurate and neat crease or fold.

Folding is necessary to build a comp that will guide a printer and/or binder and especially critical when the printed matter to be folded is complicated or custom in design. For comps, neatness and precision in alignment of the folding layers are critical in achieving a professional finish. To achieve this end, an understanding of the process of scoring and folding is necessary.

Once you learn the basic techniques for folding noted in the examples shown in this chapter, you can apply the techniques to

Figure 3-14
Insert and press. Use very light sandpaper to smooth the edge if necessary.

any number of fold configurations or formats. Although further discussion of folded formats is found in Chapter 5, at this point, we offer a basic overview of the process of scoring and folding.

begin with a plan

Planning and organizing the placement of the folds and the surface on which to score the substrate should become basic working procedure.

The planning stage of the comp begins with the blank substrate. The design and printed imagery will be planned in regard to the placement and number of the folds. Folds can be indicated using the digital ruler and/or measurement dialogue box of the computer software tools. Use a light grey hairline to indicate folds outside of the document. Measurement marks can also be indicated and checked with a ruler on the printed matter.

On both the desktop and the professional level, there are visual marks to indicate a particular type of cutting, scoring, folding, or gluing action on a diagram. Those marks are noted as follows (albeit not universally standard):

Cut lines are solid { ——— }.

Folding and scoring lines are indicated with a simple broken line { ------- }.

"Kiss cut" lines are indicated using a line with spaced dashes { - - - - - - }.

Perforated (cut through using tiny, spaced holes) lines are indicated with dots { ········ }.

Gluing areas are indicated as shaded areas { ///////// }.

all-important grain direction

The most important basic planning procedure involves organization of the folds relative to the grain of the paper. The tightest, neatest, most accurate fold is achieved when you score and fold the paper *parallel with the grain*.

Paper grain was first discussed in Chapter 2, and we put the knowledge gained to use here. See Figures 3-15 and 3-16 for a visual guide and diagrams of how to recognize the grain of the paper.

N.B. Do not proceed with scoring and folding unless you fully understand how to find the grain of the paper. A crease will not lay flat well unless it is folded *with* the grain. Reminder: Handmade paper does not have a grain, and ultra-lightweight paper will be less affected by the "pull" of the grain.

where to score

Does it matter which side of the substrate receives the score? Yes. We recommend placement of the score on the inside, or the "valley" of the fold. A fold (the result of the action of folding) can be oriented in two ways. Borrowing terms from Japanese *origami*, the folds created after scoring the paper are oriented or seen as a **mountain** (the outside of a fold) or a **valley** (the inside of the fold); see Figure 3-17. Using these terms will help with organizing, scoring, and implementing multiple folds.

how to score

It is nearly impossible to have a clean, precise, and neat fold without first scoring the line of the fold. For the best result, use a scoring tool to indent the line that is to be folded; see Figure 3-18. Without scoring, the substrate will bend or crack rather than crease; see Figure 3-19 for a visual example of the results of scoring versus substrates that were not scored.

Figure 3-15
Left to right:
You can feel tension and resistance of the paper curled *against* the grain.
The paper easily curls with the grain (little resistance).

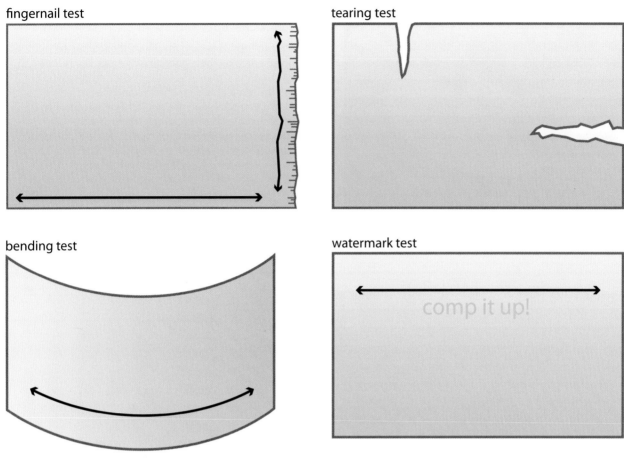

fingernail test

tearing test

bending test

watermark test

comp it up!

Figure 3-16
Grain direction diagrams.

Figure 3-17
Left to right:
Valley fold; mountain fold.
For the purposes of folding, the terms *valley* and *mountain* are borrowed from
the origami process and refer to the final intended orientation of the fold.

professional tip

With commercial folding machines, the scoring is implemented on the mountain of the fold. Our recommendation to score in the valley of the fold comes from both the result of our experiences and the procedure found in hand bookbinding and other handcraftsmanship techniques. We have simply found that the fold works best when scored in the valley. However, there are instances when the substrate may need to be scored on the mountain of the fold. Testing is necessary.

Figure 3-18
Score directly on the indicator line. Use a scoring tool for the best results.

Figure 3-19

First row, left to right:
Paper shown has been folded without scoring (dull, rounded crease).
Paper shown has been scored and then folded (sharp, flat crease).

Second row, left to right:
Duplex paper folded without scoring. The crease is cracked and ragged.
Duplex paper kiss-cut lightly to reveal color layers. Lightly cutting can be substituted for scoring when the paper is particularly thick or when using a duplex paper.

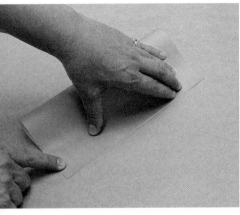 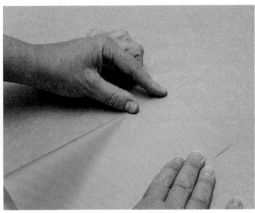 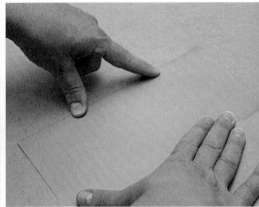

Figure 3-20
Basic Folding Step by Step
Prior to folding, the substrate is measured and scored if necessary—
lightweight paper such as 24# bond may not need scoring.

Left to right:
Align corners. Hold the corners steady; use fingers to lightly
crease.

Start and set the fold in the first inch; keep the right-angle corners
aligned.

Continue the crease and finish the fold.

Not pictured: Place a protective shield over the folded substrate.
Using the folding tool, burnish to tighten the crease.

As mentioned previously, there are instances when the substrate may need to be scored on the mountain or on both sides. The marks made for the score lines will need to be perfectly aligned and placed on both sides in order for the scoring lines to match on both the mountain and valley.

When using a duplex paper, the duplex should actually be cut lightly (but not through) with a craft knife on the mountain, rather than scored, in order to reveal the color of the opposite side; see also Figure 3-18. This type of light cutting is referred to as a **kiss cut**.

a perfect fold

The following list is notes for specifically implementing a fold. See also Figure 3-20 for a visual guide and Figure 3-21 for further instruction and practice.

◻ Assuming that the grain of the paper was determined, measurements marked, fold lines drawn, and scores implemented, folding can proceed.

◻ Pull the upper left corner of the substrate over the right corner; align precisely.

◻ Hold the two substrate corners in place. Using your fingers, lightly crease/fold along the scored line. If all measurements are accurate and the scores are precise, the folding should easily bend into place. If the alignment is slightly incorrect, you may be able to make very minor adjustments. If there is more than a $\frac{1}{16}$" problem, you may need to start over.

◻ Place a protective shield over the folded substrate (clean bond paper, vellum, or tracing paper).

◻ Using the folding tool, burnish the crease. Once the folding tool has been applied, it is impossible to make corrections.

 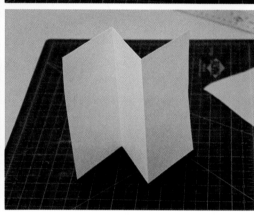

Figure 3-21

Score and Fold Step by Step

The primary fold should be parallel to the grain of the substrate. (Mark all measurements for three vertically oriented folds.)

First row, left to right:
Place a straightedge flush to the left of the fold line to be scored. Using even pressure throughout, carefully pull the scoring tool along the line from top to bottom.

Align and implement the folds.

Second row, left to right:
Cover with tracing paper for protection. Burnish (to tighten) the fold using a folding tool.

Finished folds—note the mountains and valleys.

practice scoring and folding

The following is a general checklist to use before scoring and folding. See also Figure 3-21 for a visual guide.

▢ Plan the fold:

The primary fold(s) should be parallel to the grain of the substrate.

Do not plan a fold to run through a thick layer of ink—the ink will crack.

Run a test on any substrate to determine its response.

▢ Mark all measurements (practice with three vertically oriented folds as shown in Figure 3-20).

▢ Scoring should usually be implemented in the valley of the fold. (For practice in planning the implementation of the scoring, fold the paper in a zigzag pattern.)

▢ Ready the scoring tool: The point of the scoring tool should not be as sharp as a cutting blade. It should be thin and sturdy enough to notch the fold line but without actually cutting through it.

We do at times use a craft knife for scoring or the blunt side of the craft knife blade, if the substrate is thick. If you choose this method, proceed with a light hand (be very careful not to cut through the substrate).

▢ Place a straightedge flush on the left side of the fold line.

▢ Place the scoring tool directly on the fold line and use the straightedge to steady the tool.

▢ Using even pressure throughout, carefully pull the scoring tool along the fold line from top to bottom.

▢ Align and implement the folds.

▢ Cover with tracing paper for protection; burnish (to tighten) the fold using a folding tool.

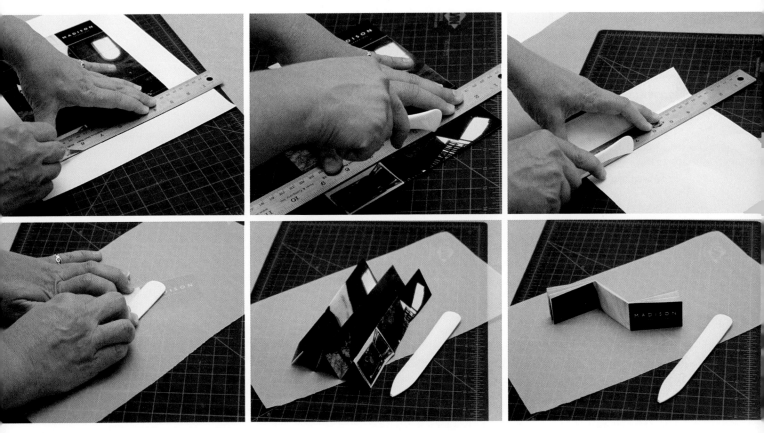

Figure 3-22
Folding Printed Matter Step by Step
First row, left to right:
Measure and place the score lines. Trim the image to its borders.

Score the valley fold lines.

Flip the paper to continue. Score the valley fold lines.

Second row, left to right:
Protect and burnish.

First round of folding.

Final folds are set at right angles to the main fold.

Student project: promotional.

When scoring *printed* matter, be aware of cutting through the ink with the tool. Test first to determine whether the printed substrate should be indented to score or kiss cut. With ink coverage, note that kiss cutting will reveal the inner layers of the substrate, which may or may not be desirable. Plan the printed matter to work with the fold lines—do not fold through critical areas of the design. See Figure 3-22 for an example of folding on printed matter.

no folding back

Okay, okay, if a fold *must* be undone, try lightly misting a blank side of the substrate with warm water. The water might loosen the fibers. While the substrate is *slightly* moist, try smoothing out the crease (still working on the blank side of the substrate) with a warm clothes-pressing iron. Alternatively, try burnishing the fold flat with the folding tool. Always protect the surface first. There is no guarantee that any of these methods would work, but we have had success at times. Be aware that relative factors such as paper thickness, ink coverage, and so on will affect the success of correcting a fold.

crafting the bond

As detailed in Chapter 1 concerning the contents of the toolbox, there are many formulas of adhesives available. Some comps can be accomplished without the use of adhesives, yet the construction of most books, booklets, pamphlets, brochures, packaging, tabletop signage, and so forth cannot hold together without glue.

Without proper use of the glue and application tools, adhering printed matter or boards or both can be a disastrous mess. Glue will certainly ruin the surface of printed matter, so be very organized, neat, and clean when using adhesives. If possible, have a gluing station separate from the construction area. If not, protect the surface of the construction table with a sturdy piece of paperboard. Definitely separate all printed matter from the glue and working tools.

First ready the gluing station with these supplies:

- ☐ Damp cloth and dry cloth for quick cleanup

- ☐ A measured pool of glue on a plate

- ☐ Waxed paper or parchment

- ☐ Brushes and board chips

- ☐ Clean newsprint or other scrap paper

- ☐ Substrate or other blank or printed matter to be glued

the glue to use

Liquid white glue (PVA) is our primary choice because it is reliable and strong—an all-purpose glue for creating comps. PVA white glue can be messy and a bit difficult to handle because it is lightly viscous. Without experience, it will take time and testing to learn how to apply exactly the right amount. Spread too much and the glue will ooze from between the glued substrates. Spread too little and the glue will dry before you can make the bond. Once it goes down, it usually never comes off. It stains too. Yet the strong bond it creates is indispensable. PVA white glue is best with heavy substrates such as text and cover stock, bookcloth, and paperboard. Use it with a brush for heavy substrates or spread it with a chip of paperboard for thinner substrates that may need less glue.

For lightweight papers and very thin substrates or unbacked fabric, we recommend glue stick for the simple reason that it doesn't ooze. Try the wrinkle-free formula for the strongest bond (relative to all types of glue sticks) or use the purple color formula that allows you to see the coverage in progress, guiding its application to ensure that all areas receive glue. Glue stick is uncomplicated, compact, self-applying, and easy to use but it doesn't have the permanent bonding power of liquid white glue.

Paste glue is yet another alternative for lighter-weight papers. Often, the choice is a matter of preference rather than purpose. Paste glue is thick. A paperboard chip is needed to spread it, yet it can be applied smoothly and evenly with relative ease because it doesn't run.

We also use a glue spreader that rolls on dots of very thin glue and creates a workable tacky surface. A glue spreader or, alternatively, glue transfer sheets work best with lightweight substrates. When a large area of coverage is needed, we usually turn to a glue spreader because it does not bond until the two substrates are burnished. The glue is somewhat workable in that it allows for slight shifting of alignment before burnishing. The bond is not as strong as the glues previously noted.

Figure 3-23 (right)
Simple Gluing Practice Step by Step

First row, left to right:
Set up a *clean* and ready glue area. Have several pieces of clean newsprint scrap paper as a working base, a holding plate with liquid white glue, tracing paper, a glue brush, a spatula or other flat tool to lift the substrate from the gluing surface, and a folding tool.

The paper that will *receive* the glued layer has been measured and marked and is at the ready. Set aside away from the glue.

Work quickly but carefully. Hold the substrate steady. Pick up glue from the plate, and begin applying a thin layer from the center of the substrate and radiating out to the corners. Too much glue will cause smearing, lumps, and buckling; too little will make for a weak and uneven bond.

Second row, left to right:
Hold the substrate in place with either a spatula or your fingernail; spread the glue and extend it beyond the edges of the substrate. Cover evenly. Remove the glued substrate and then the newsprint (fold into itself or let it dry for later use). At this point, you may need a quick wipe of the damp cloth to remove any traces of glue from your fingers.

Turn to the board holding the *receiving* substrate (clean area backed by newsprint), or place a clean sheet of newsprint on the existing work surface and place the *receiving* substrate on it. Place the *glued* substrate over the *receiving* substrate so that it aligns with the marks previously indicated.

Put a sheet of tracing paper over the glued area. Smooth lightly with your hand and fingers.

Third row, left to right:
From the center moving outward, *gently* burnish with a folding tool. Some glue may smear out from between the two gluing surfaces—be careful of this potential occurrence. If there is much smearing, you have used too much glue; remove it quickly with a lightly dampened cloth or use the spatula to gently scrape away the glue.

Finished result.

Finished comp; the glue needs to dry for a few minutes and will dry completely overnight.

Not pictured: A weight can be used on top of the glued item to keep it flat and assist with obtaining a complete and even bond.

Hot glue is essential for adhering small objects to a surface (for instance, placing a button onto paperboard). And, a dab of superglue might be the savior for the most stubborn surfaces. However, we can't recommend rubber cement because its solvent is toxic and so many other adhesives achieve the same results. Ditto for spray adhesive; if you are for some reason compelled to use spray, please apply in a well-ventilated area and use a face mask and spray box.

We offer several methods for gluing that can be adapted to a variety of substrates and projects. See Figures 3-23 through 3-25 for visual guides.

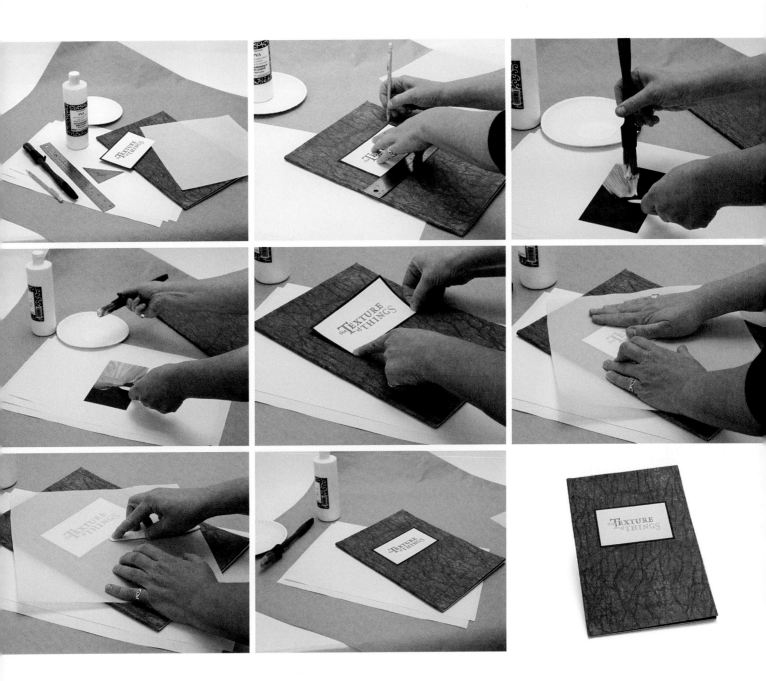

Figure 3-24 (left)
Figure 3-24 (left)
Simple Gluing (2) Step by Step
Gluing paperboard to Japanese printed paper or how to "wrap a paperboard."

First row, left to right:
The glue should be applied first to the object to be transferred.

In a radial pattern, brush on a thin layer of glue; work quickly and continuously so the glue does not dry in progress.

Nearing the end of the glue coverage, use a stylus or your fingernail to hold the substrate in place. Finish gluing. If you do not steady the substrate with a stylus, likely it will move and smudge the glue onto areas that need to remain clean.

Second row, left to right:
Lift the substrate with a flat tool.

Align and place the glued substrate onto the receiving substrate.

Press in place.

Third row, left to right:
Flip and cover with protective tracing paper. Using a folding tool, burnish to tighten the bond and smooth the substrates. Be aware of glue that might leak. Remove tracing paper, and remove stray glue with a spatula. Clean the spatula and fingers if necessary; replace the tracing paper and continue.

The edge of the paperboard may need additional glue (edges need glue too); apply glue to the edges of the paperboard with a small brush first. With a large brush (for quick work), apply glue to the paper—extending away from the paperboard. Work quickly because the glue dries fast.

Fold the corners of the flaps toward the center—on all four sides. *Not pictured:* With a folding tool, press in the paper at the edges of the board to adhere and make the corner flaps flat against the edges.

Fourth row, left to right:
Fold over the remaining flaps.

Remove stray overspill of glue. Cover with tracing paper and burnish.

Also burnish smooth and flatten the edges to ensure that the substrates are bonded.

The following are general notes for working with glue:

¤ Set up the work area with tools:

A supply of scrap paper ready as a quick, removable, and easily disposable gluing surface

A holding plate with glue, tracing paper, a glue brush, a spatula or other flat tool (such as stylus or butter knife) to lift the substrate from the gluing surface, and a folding tool

¤ Keep a lightly damp rag ready off to the side to clean fingers when necessary. Also, you can set up a clean area for working the substrate after gluing.

¤ Test substrates to determine the type of glue that works best.

¤ Place scrap paper on the surface of the gluing table; it should be large enough to extend several inches away from the substrate to be glued. Place the substrate to be glued on the scrap. (Use unprinted newsprint or whatever else is clear and clean.)

¤ Always place glue on the layer that is to be attached. Never place the glue on the receiving paper or substrate.

¤ Cover any glued surface with scrap paper or tracing paper and then burnish to tighten the bond.

¤ Allow the glue to dry completely before moving forward with the project.

keep practicing

Ready for another method and application? Right. Keep practicing. Learning to handle glue takes practice.

When applying glue to an important final stage of a design, be well organized before proceeding. Set up the glue area with tools. Have scrap paper as a working base, a holding plate with glue, tracing paper for protection while burnishing, paperboard chips, a spatula or other flat tool to lift the substrate from the gluing surface, and a folding tool.

See Figures 3-24 through 3-26 for covering cardboard with paper or fabric. Slightly different tools, materials, and procedures are used in each of the practice examples.

If you use plain fabric, use glue stick (liquid glue would ooze through the threads). If you use bookcloth fabric, liquid glue is preferable since it is a stronger and more permanent bond. In addition, bookcloth is backed with paper—preventing the liquid glue from oozing through.

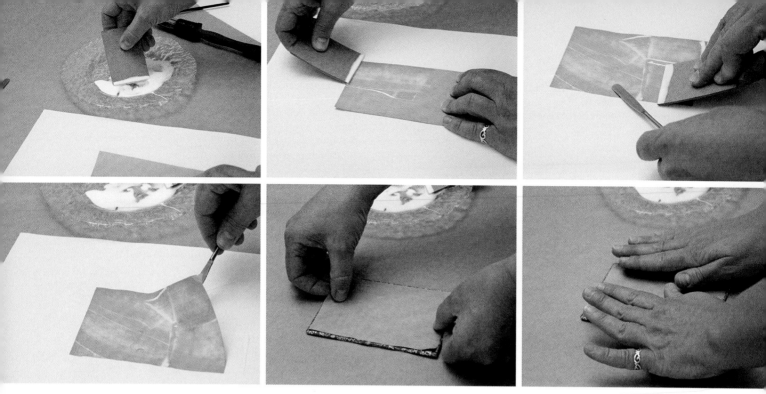

Figure 3-25
Simple Gluing (3) Step by Step
Liquid white glue application with a paperboard "chip" or how to glue without tearing the paper.

Use the paperboard chip on lightweight substrates. The board applicator helps to keep the thin paper steady.

First row, left to right:
Dip the board chip into the glue, taking on a small amount.

Apply the glue with quick sweeping strokes in one direction.

If necessary, hold the substrate in place with the spatula to finish gluing (the substrate should not move).

Second row, left to right:
Lift the glued substrate from the gluing surface. Remove the soiled gluing surface. Transfer to a clean area for working.

Align and place the glued substrate on the receiving substrate.

Lightly pat together to bond.

Not pictured: Cover with protective tracing paper and lightly burnish smooth.

Figure 3-26 (right)
Simple Gluing (4) Step by Step
Stick it together (how to adhere fabric and textured paper to paperboard).

Use glue stick on various lightweight substrates and especially for fabric. For the latter, white glue will ooze through the weave and make a mess of it.

Set up the glue area with tools. Have several pieces of scrap paper as a working base, a glue stick, tracing paper, a spatula or other flat tool (such as a stylus or butter knife) to lift the substrate from the gluing surface, a folding tool, and precision scissors to cut off any stray fabric fibers.

First row, left to right:
Hold the substrate in place at its edge and start gluing from the center.

Apply glue in a radial pattern.

Hold the board in place with a spatula to finish applying glue (do this to keep fingers free from the glue). There should be no gobs of glue. Remove stray glue gobs with the spatula or a craft knife. Make the surface as smooth as possible.

Second row, left to right:
Apply the glued board to the fabric; press into place.

Flip. Cover with tracing paper; burnish smooth to tighten the bond.

Flip. The edges of the exposed fabric and the board will receive glue. Press the soft glue stick into the edge of the board (for full coverage) and remove any stray gobs of glue.

Third row, left to right:
Fold over the four corners first.

Fold the remaining flaps up and over onto the board. *Not pictured:* Cover with tracing paper and burnish to tighten the bond with a folding tool.

Burnish the edges to flatten and tighten the bond.

Fourth row, left to right:
(Nearly) Finished.

Adhering textured paper—use liquid glue instead of glue stick to ensure that the glue fills the cavities of the textured paper; use a wide brush to assist in quick coverage of the textured surface. Place glued paper to receiving substrate; notice that the paper curls with liquid glue and will need burnishing to press the two pieces together and tighten the bond.

Cover with tracing paper to protect the surface. Burnish the entirety in a rotating motion.

Use precision scissors to trim stray extruding fibers.

Finished application (pictured: an invitation to a holiday party).

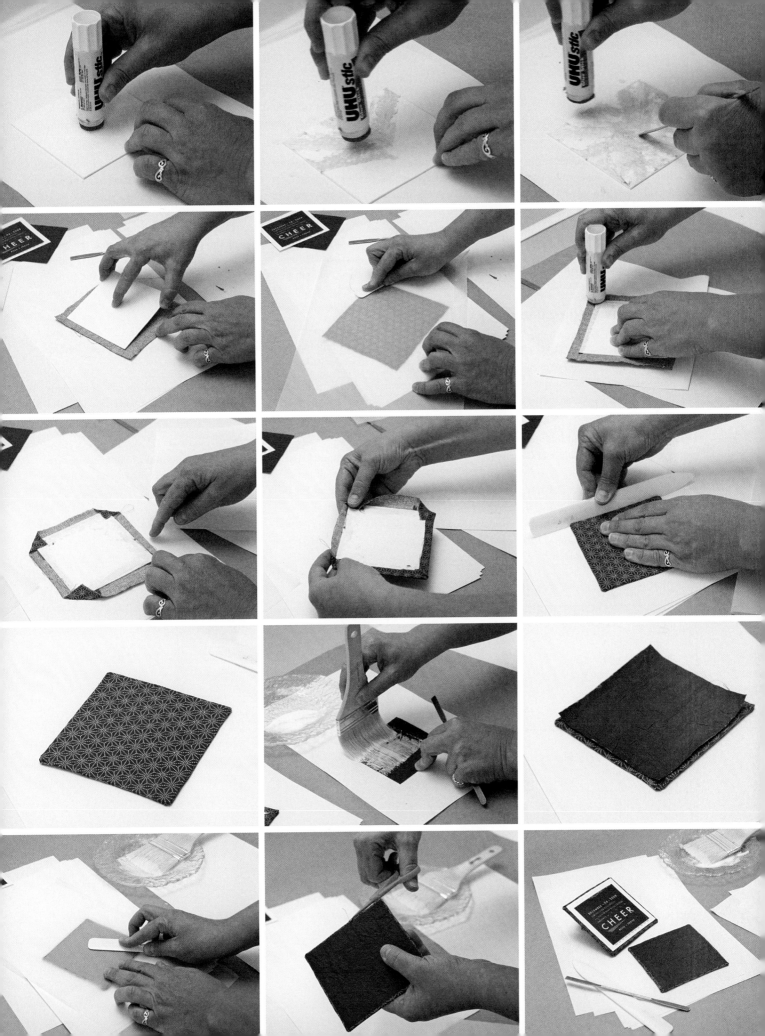

summary:
ready, set, practice

Understanding and practicing the fundamental techniques for handling the basic tools and materials needed for comps is the foundation for advanced work and the key to developing into a designer-craftsman.

Each project will bring its own set of problems to solve. Use the knowledge and techniques gained for organizing the work area, measuring, cutting, scoring, folding, and gluing, and apply these skills to most any type of design solution and its comprehensive mock-up.

exercise knowledge gained

The following exercises are simple projects that do not require implementation as finished design solutions (although the exercise projects could include type and images if you choose). The exercises are meant to fire up your creativity and guide practice that will hopefully lead to a better understanding of the various techniques covered in this chapter. Go ahead and score some for creativity.

Have a basic work area and tools ready according to the plan suggested and described previously in the chapter.

1. review

At this point, if you have not tried the step-by-step procedures for each basic technique, we suggest that you do so now. Knowledge and some skill in the techniques explained in the chapter are necessary for the following exercises.

2. single-sheet folded booklet

With this simple but rewarding exercise, practice measuring, checking for square, scoring, and folding. The final result is an interesting booklet; see Figures 3-27 and 3-28.

Suggested Substrate: 8.5" × 11" 40# (smooth) text stock or whatever else your creative heart desires—but not a paper that is heavier than text weight

Tools: Pencil, steel ruler, triangle, craft knife, scoring tool, folding tool

To begin, find the grain of the paper. We suggest that the grain parallel what will be the short folds (spine of the booklet) rather than the long fold that contains the cut line. Measure and lightly mark the fold lines and cut line on the practice substrate. Follow the diagram.

Cut where indicated and score the folds. Make all the folds and then unfold. This allows for more flexibility in the paper leading into final assembly.

Fold in half along the long length. Hold horizontally at the ends and push in toward the center; the cut should open to a diamond shape. Collapse the opening into itself and fold the left side over the right. It should form a little booklet.

Be inspired. Use imagery on the various units of the structure. On the blank test structure, write yourself notes directly on the paper to indicate the positions of the images.

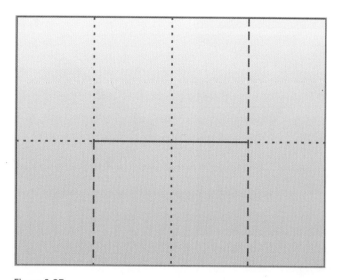

Figure 3-27
Note that in this particular case, the larger-spaced dotted lines indicate valley folds, and the more closely spaced dotted lines indicate mountain folds. Solid lines indicate cuts.

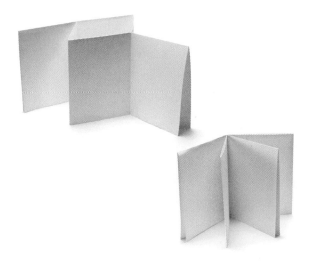

Figure 3-28
Left to right:
First-level folds. Fold as shown and continue to push together until the panels fold flat.

Final folded booklet.

3. origami inspirations

With this exercise, practice is gained in measuring, squaring off, cutting, scoring, folding, and constructing. It also allows for practice following a diagram and written directions; see Figure 3-29.

Suggested substrate: Decorative ultra-lightweight paper that will be easy to cut and fold; minimum of two colors (for ease of construction)

Suggested size of paper: 9" × 9"

Tools: Pencil, steel ruler, triangle, craft knife, folding tool

There is a great variety of diagrams for Japanese **origami** (actual meaning: fold/paper) projects available on the web. For this exercise, we suggest that you create a three-dimensional box with a lid. It allows for thought and practice in assembling parts to make a whole. The results can be quite attractive depending on the paper employed. As a bonus, a three-dimensional origami box requires no glue!

Yes, it is very easy to purchase precut origami paper for this exercise. However, you need practice in developing both good working habits and construction skills. Therefore, we ask that you start from scratch.

Begin by measuring, squaring off, and cutting four perfect 9" squares of decorative paper. Grain direction is not critical for this project. Follow directions on the diagram of choice. Scoring will not be necessary with the ultra-lightweight paper, but use knowledge gained in regard to folding. Sources for our origami inspirations include:

- *Origami Boxes* by John Montroll, Dover Publications, Inc.
- *Origami for the Enthusiast* by John Montroll, Dover Publications, Inc.
- *3D Puzzles to Cut and Construct & Solve* by Alan Robbins, Dell Trade Paperback.

Figure 3-29
The origami box such as the two pictured (top and lower left) will provide practice in the use of many of the basic tools as well as provide practice in folding. No adhesives were used for this project.

Folding boxes is a great exercise for enhancing construction skills and helpful in learning how to follow step-by-step directions. Pictured is an advanced-level box.

If boxes bore you, then fold a frog (lower right).

4. the magic pyramid (a three-dimensional puzzle)

This project was graciously given to us by our colleague, the all-around brilliant, charming, and funny Alan Robbins (www.alanrobbins.com).

> **Substrate**: Text weight paper
>
> **Tools**: Pencil, steel ruler, triangle, craft knife, folding tool, drafting tape, glue stick

The project provides continued practice in measuring, squaring off, cutting, scoring, folding, gluing, constructing, and following written directions (but no guarantee you won't pull your hair out trying to solve the puzzle). See also Figures 3-30 and 3-31 for the template and simple visual instructions.

ALAN'S DIRECTIONS

"[The Magic Pyramid] is a classic problem in solid geometry. A patent was issued for a version of the Magic Pyramid in 1940, but like most of the puzzles in [*3D Puzzles*], some variation of the basic idea had been around long before that.

The reason for its popularity is easy to understand. The puzzle's two disarmingly simple pieces create an intriguing challenge in spatial reasoning. It seems almost too simple. The solution is appealing, however, because the answer tends to come in a flash after a few moments of struggle.

[To make the pieces of the puzzle, see Figure 3-30 for the template.]

The two shapes that make up this puzzle are identical. Cut them out along the heavy outer line, then score all the thin lines using a ruler and the back edge of a razor or other dull edge.

Crease along these scored lines and follow the diagrams to fold the pieces into two identical wedge shapes. Glue tab A to the opposite edge to create a [wedge shaped] tube, then bring the side flaps up and glue the remaining tabs to the inside of the model.

If you want the pieces of your model to be completely white, with no lines showing, fold them so the lines end up inside the model. Either way, you should end up with two identical wedge shapes.

WORKING THE PUZZLE

All that's left now is the hard part . . . the solution. Just take the two pieces and try to put them together to form a pyramid."

Thank you, Alan.

5. hardcover folder

This exercise will focus on measuring, cutting, and gluing. Please use all knowledge gained in the chapter for this exercise. The result is a very useful folder for storing scraps of decorative papers or whatever!

> **Substrate**: Lightweight decorative paper (exterior of folder and for joinery), text weight or light cover weight paper (could have a textured finish) for the interior of the folder, writing grade or lighter, plain paper (unseen element for joinery), and 2- or 3-ply paperboard (In addition, grosgrain ribbon is an option to create a handle.)
>
> **Tools**: Pencil, ruler, triangle, utility knife, craft knife, PVA glue or paste glue, clean newsprint construction surfaces, general related supplies for cleanup and construction
>
> **Practice**: Measuring, squaring off, cutting, gluing, and constructing; learn to follow written directions along with photographic guides

Please first review the entirety of the written directions that follow and compare with the visual guide in Figure 3-32, because not all the steps are shown in the visual guide. Read all directions, and then proceed to practice.

We strongly suggest a trial run without glue to get a better understanding of the purpose of the paperboard, paper sizes, and the actions involved. Be very organized at the start in order for the working process to move along quickly and (hopefully) without problems.

General directions for constructing a wrapped paperboard folder:

- Prepare the pieces. Measure, square off, and cut two pieces of paperboard at 12" (vertical height) × 9" (horizontal width). The long measurement should be parallel with the grain of the board.

- Measure, square off, and cut one piece of decorative paper at 15" × 21.5". The grain should also be parallel with the longer measurement—if using milled paper. Reminder: Handmade paper does not have a grain.

- Cut a strip of the same decorative paper measuring 15" × 3" (long length with the grain). Set aside.

- Cut a strip of thin, lightweight paper measuring 14" × 3" (long length with the grain). Set aside.

- Cut two plain white (or color coordinated) sheets of paper at 11.5" × 8.5".

- All substrates should be ready for the next phase: construction.

- Draw a line down the vertical center of the large decorative paper.

- Glue the lightweight plain paper strip and adhere, straddled along the center line of the large decorative paper. This strip of paper reinforces the fold area.

- Align the two paperboards on the center of the back of the large sheet of decorative paper with approximately ½" space between the two boards.

- Draw a light line around the boards or mark the corners with points or draw cross-lines at the corners. The marks will guide placement of the boards upon gluing.

- Ready the glue and gluing area. Remove the boards from the decorative paper and bring to the gluing area.

Figure 3-30

The Magic Pyramid

Template diagram. When constructed three-dimensionally, these two disarmingly simple, flat shapes create an intriguing challenge in spatial reasoning. Diagram by Alan Robbins.

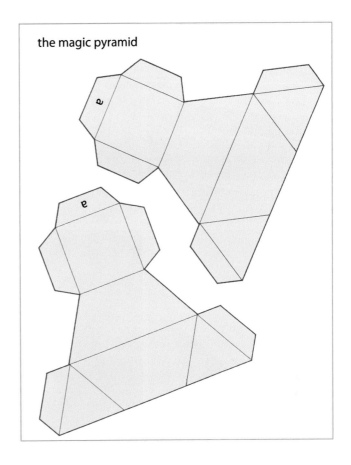

the magic pyramid

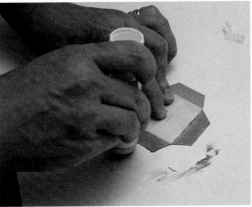

Figure 3-31

Magic Pyramid Step by Step

Left to right:

Cut out along the heavy outer line, and then score all the thin lines using a ruler and scoring tool.

Use drafting tape to mask out the interior of the box, exposing only the tabs. Use glue stick to bond the surfaces.

Finish with two identical five-sided, wedge-shaped forms. Now the hard part: Join the two wedges to form a single pyramid.

Figure 3-32 (left)
Hardcover Folder Step by Step

First row, left to right:
Sample materials; prepare all substrates in advance.

Be sure to check whether the boards are squared. Reinforce the center of the decorative cover paper. Center and place the paperboard over decorative paper; leave ½" space between boards. Mark alignment points.

Glue the boards, then adhere to the substrate of decorative paper. The drafting tape holds the board corners in place while the glue is drying. Remove tape before continuing.

Second row, left to right:
Glue the strip of corresponding decorative paper centered between the two boards. Using the folding tool, burnish into the center area (vertical).

Burnish to adhere the paper strip to the horizontal edges of the boards.

The remaining paper (flaps) should be glued and then folded over the corners of the paperboard, folded over the horizontal and vertical edges, and burnished flat.

Third row, left to right:
Optional: Use glue stick to adhere grosgrain ribbon to the boards (centered). Cover and burnish the ribbon.

Glue and adhere interior paper to the boards.

Finished folder.

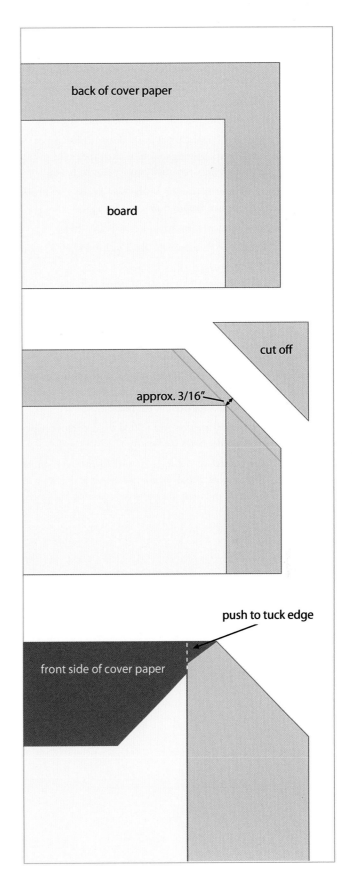

Note the diagrams (top to bottom at right) for an additional method for folding paper over corners.

Diagram of one corner of the board with cover paper below.

Leaving a measurement of approximately two boards thickness (about ³⁄₁₆") between the cut line and the corner point of the board, draw a 45-degree diagonal line (as a guide), and then cut the corner of the cover paper.

Fold the cover paper (flap) over the board. Using a folding tool, tuck the tiny folded overhang flush to the edge of the board. Repeat the process on the remaining three corners.

WORK SUPER QUICKLY AT THIS POINT

- Glue one board and return to the construction area. Quickly place the glued board within the pencil guidelines on the decorative paper. Press the board firmly and evenly into the decorative paper.
- Quickly repeat the glue procedure with the remaining board.
- Flip the paper and boards, cover with clean tracing paper or newsprint, and use the folding tool to tighten the bond and to burnish and smooth the decorative paper onto the board.
- Place a clean sheet of newsprint on the construction area with the uncovered/unglued boards exposed—facing up.
- Return to the gluing area (it should be clean and dry).
- Brush a thin layer of glue onto the back of the 14" × 3" strip of decorative paper.
- Glue the back of the decorative strip of paper and place, straddling the center space between the boards.
- Cover and burnish.

WORK QUICKLY AT THIS POINT

- Bring the covered boards to the gluing area. With the uncovered board side facing up, glue the back of the remaining, exposed decorative paper (the flaps beyond the board).
- Return to a clean construction area to fold the decorative paper flaps (corners and sides) over the boards.
- First, fold the corners of the flaps toward the center—on all four sides. With a folding tool, press in the paper at the edges of the board to adhere and make the corners flat against the edges.
- Fold the remaining horizontal and vertical flaps over all four sides.
- Cover the folded flaps and burnish lightly. Also burnish all of the edges.
- Place a clean sheet of newsprint between the boards and fold the boards together.
- Cover the top with tracing paper or newsprint and burnish to help smooth, flatten, and tighten the bond.
- Return to the open position.
- Move the covered boards (covered side down) to a clean construction surface.

  If you desire a string or ribbon closure, place a ribbon under the interior papers before gluing them to the board. The interior pages should be thick enough so as not to tear and so the ribbon doesn't show through.

- On a gluing surface, spread glue on the back of one 11.5" × 8.5" piece of the interior papers.
- Quickly return to the clean construction area and place and approximately center the glued paper on the exposed board. Be sure to clear away stray overspill of glue.
- Cover and burnish.
- Repeat.
- Place clean tracing paper or newsprint inside the folder; place some heavy books on it to flatten completely while drying. Let dry overnight. No peeking.

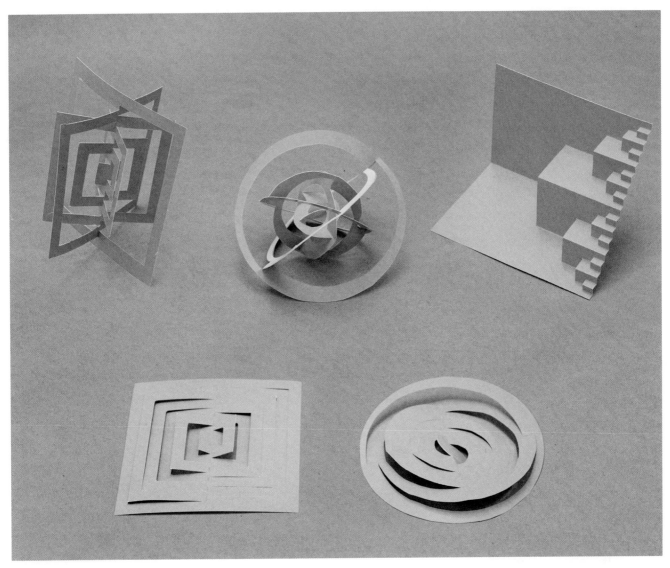

Figure 3-33
Kirigami structures.

6. extreme cutting

We finish with a suggestion for cutting practice and a relief from gluing.

Kirigami is a Japanese term (meaning: cut/paper) for the art of cutting paper. Kirigami makes for excellent practice in cutting intricate patterns and results in delightfully three-dimensional decorative structures. Search the web for kirigami (and origami) resources. For instance, you could look into the Origami Resource Center on the web. You can see the structure and pattern of cutting in Figure 3-33.

For further inspiration regarding artistic paper cutting, we suggest looking at the work of Marivi Garrido, Ingrid Siliaskus, and Joyce Aysta in their book *The Paper Architect: Fold-It-Yourself Buildings and Structures*. We also are intrigued by the art of Jen Stark, Béatrice Coron, Adam Fowler, and Ferry Staverman.

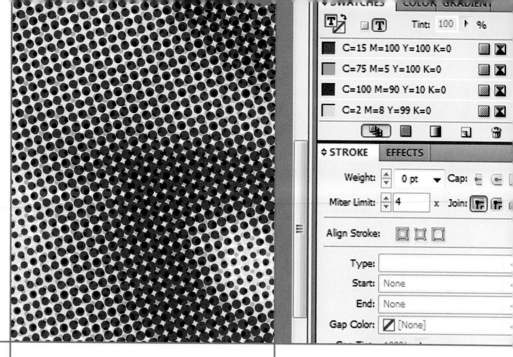
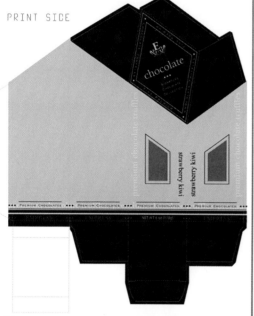

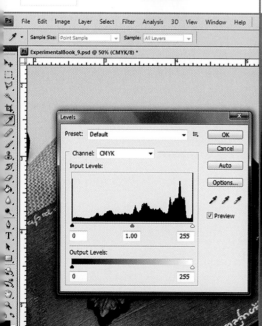
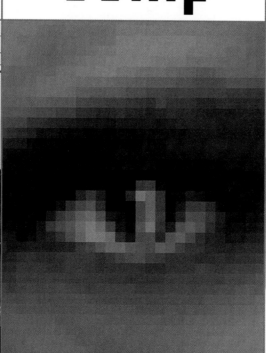

"If we accept graphic design's move into the digital realm, then we must champion new methodologies and theoretical approaches in establishing a history and appropriate critical discourses."
—*Dr. Teal Triggs, Professor of Graphic Design and Head of Research, School of Graphic Design, London College of Communication, University of the Arts London*

four
software basics

First row, left to right:
Vector graphic created in Adobe Illustrator.
Designer: Mike Boos

Close-up of CMYK color dots used in offset printing.

Screenshot of palettes in Adobe InDesign.

Second row, left to right:
Flat layout of package for chocolates (including lines designating die cuts).
Package: Empress Chocolates
Studio: Mark Weisz Design
Creative Director; Mark Weisz
Designer: Yael Miller
Copywriter: Yael Miller
Illustrator: Vinaya Prashanth

"Comp" icon created in Adobe Photoshop.

Brochure: from Cargo Magazine Radio-in-a-Can package
Studio: Gillespie Design, Inc.
Creative Director: Maureen Gillespie
Designer: Liz Schenekel
Copywriter: Ralph Allora
Printer: DJ Litho
Flat layout of accordion-fold brochure (including crop and registration marks).

Third row, left to right:
Screenshot of dialogue box in Adobe Photoshop.

Raster image (photograph) under high magnification to show individual pixels.

Vector graphic created in Adobe Illustrator.
Designer: Mike Boos

chapter four: software basics

learning objectives

- Gain an understanding of the appropriate use of software tools.
- Become aware of the various types of image file formats.
- Learn to use the image file formats appropriately.
- Become aware of the importance and use of color modes.
- Explore the potential of desktop digital printing.

into the cyberbox: software tools

More often than not, any given design solution will include some type of imagery that is created or produced digitally (on a computer) with software tools. Options for image creation include on-screen rendering, importing digital photography, and scanning and importing printed photographs, hand-rendered drawings, collages, paintings, and so on. In conjunction with excellence in handcraftsmanship, digital output skill is necessary for creating effective comps.

So that leaves the burning question: What are the best techniques for creating digital images for a design solution? Unfortunately, that is not a briefly or easily answered query. In fact, *creating* digital imagery is not the focus of this chapter. But relative to desktop craftsmanship for comprehensive mock-ups, the focus of this chapter is a brief but specific discussion relative to color, **image resolution** (measurement of the output quality of an image), and **image format** (a specific way in which information is encoded for storage in a digital file). Also included in this chapter is an overview and brief discussion of the use of desktop printers and desktop printing paper.

software appropriateness

One critical point in the study of design and craftsmanship must be remembered: Use of appropriate software is a must! For instance, when a **scalable** (varying size proportionately over a wide range) graphic is needed, digital drawing software is necessary. If a photograph needs to be edited, software specifically created for that purpose needs to be employed.

Efficient and best quality output to printers (or otherwise) will happen only when using the appropriate software. Each software tool has its appropriate purpose. First noted in Chapter 1 on hand-held tools and repeated here because the thought is also relevant to software, you can use a shoe to bang a nail into a wall, but there is a tool for the purpose that accomplishes the task most efficiently, swiftly, and correctly. Use the appropriate tool!

wwad? (what would adobe do?)

Although there are many software tools in use relative to design, the focus for the purpose of desktop comps is on what we like to call the "big three" from Adobe—Photoshop, Illustrator, and InDesign. Each of these software applications has its specific purpose and will eventually need to be mastered to be a viable designer. There are entire books devoted to discussing how to use the software, but our goal here is to overview the most fundamental and yet essential points necessary for successful comps.

Gleaning from the information provided on the Adobe website, the following descriptions summarize the use of the "big three" software tools. See Figure 4-1 for a screenshot of the workspace.

---

green idea

online delivery

Although this particular topic may not seem to have much bearing on the effort to "go green," there are several ways in which you can think green when dealing with software choice and computer use.

Many software companies—including Adobe—allow the purchase of software online, downloadable directly to your computer. With online delivery, there is no box, no paper manual, and no trash! Online delivery is a small green step, but every little bit helps.

Figure 4-1

Left to right:

Adobe Photoshop screenshot/workspace.

Adobe Illustrator screenshot/workspace.

Adobe InDesign screenshot/workspace.

Pictured are the basic digital workspaces for the essential digital toolbox. Adobe continues to streamline the interfaces of their various software applications, with the newest versions offering improved cross-integration. Although each application has its own specific tools and features, becoming familiar with the basic interface of one program will help in quickly learning the others. Learning the use of the three interfaces heightens overall usability and helps in creating a seamless cross-program workflow.

- **Adobe Photoshop** is a powerful photomanipulation and editing tool for photographers, graphic designers, and web designers.

- **Adobe Illustrator** is an image rendering tool that allows for the creation of sophisticated artwork for virtually any digital medium.

- **Adobe InDesign** is a page layout/composition software tool. Although it incorporates some drawing and photo-manipulation capabilities, InDesign primarily imports vector graphics and raster images to be composed with type into a single or multiple-page document. Built for demanding workflows, InDesign integrates smoothly with Adobe Photoshop, Illustrator, Acrobat, InCopy, and Dreamweaver software.

Although the Adobe Creative Suite also includes InCopy, Dreamweaver, and Acrobat (writer [distiller] and reader), instruction in the use of these software tools is not included in this book. However, a working knowledge of the software is necessary for success and viability in the field of design.

The following are brief descriptions of these tools:

- **Adobe InCopy** is a professional word processing software application built into InDesign.

- **Adobe Dreamweaver** is Adobe's web development application allowing designers to create web pages and other online content.

- **Adobe Acrobat** is a software tool that "encapsulates" the components of a document, including the text, fonts, and images—making a single new document format that is known as a **portable document format (PDF)**. A PDF is a file format that allows for easy document exchange from almost any application, on any computer system, resulting in the option to share it with almost anyone, anywhere. That is to say, PDF is used for representing on-screen documents in a manner independent of the application software, hardware, and operating system that created the documents.

you say you want a resolution

Correct and successful handling of the image resolution begins with an understanding of how the image was developed by the software. As Photoshop is a photomanipulation and photo editing application, the software specializes in handling and working with raster images. **Raster images** are also known as *tonal* or *continuous tone* images because of the smooth gradation of color values to create the forms depicted. A photograph is the primary example of a raster or continuous tone image. Paintings and other scanned or on-screen images can also be created by smoothly modulated gradations of color.

caveat designer

ppi versus dpi

Is there a difference between ppi and dpi? Some image editing software, as well as scanner software, use the terms interchangeably. Unfortunately, that's not accurate. Understanding the differences between ppi (pixels per inch) and **dpi** (dots per inch) is important. When referring to digital image resolution, the use of *ppi* is appropriate.

On the other hand, *dpi* is used when referring to printing resolution. Dots per inch, in terms of printing, is the smallest amount of ink that a given printer can print. The more dots that are applied per inch by a printer, the higher the resolution (and therefore quality of image reproduction) an imaging device can reproduce.

Figure 4-2

Left to right:

A close-up portion of the high-res image.

Here is the same close-up, but of the low-res version. It's easy to see the difference between the high-res and the poor quality low-res versions of the same image.

More technically specific, a raster image is any graphic that is composed of a fixed number of **pixels** (small squares/dots of color light) arranged on a screen-based grid that is commonly known as a **bitmap**. The visual quality of a raster image depends on several factors, foremost of which is its resolution (often abbreviated as **res**). Resolution is measured in **ppi** (pixels per inch). Because raster images are created with a fixed number of pixels, if they are upscaled (made larger in size) or printed at a higher resolution than they were intended or created (with a digital camera, scanned printed matter generated in Photoshop), the images will appear jagged or fuzzy; see Figure 4-2 for an example of high-resolution clarity versus unacceptable low-res images.

Without spending an entire book on raster image resolution (and by extension, its perceived visual quality), it's generally a good rule of thumb that any image intended for print output (as all images would be for comps) should be a relatively high resolution—that being a *minimum* of 300 ppi. A lower resolution (72 or 250 ppi for instance) is not sufficient to produce a crisp and sharp-edged printed image.

Overlooked more than it should be, both students and professionals often attempt to produce work for print with low-res, "pixelated" (jagged) images. However, there are few things more unprofessional than having a printed design solution with low-quality raster graphics. Do not use poor quality, low-res images. Images created for print must originate at 300 ppi and remain undistorted. See Figure 4-3 for an example of an image that despite its 300 ppi value, suffers from the poor quality of a low-res image.

image resizing (big problem, simple tip)

One of the biggest problems in developing printed comps concerns the struggle in obtaining proper image quality relative to size, particularly when a given image is one that is not of your own creation or a photograph created with a digital camera. Although cameras may seem essentially the same, image format or image characteristics are not necessarily the same from one camera to another. Images may be created in a low resolution (perhaps 72 or 144 ppi), but at very high **document dimensions** (height and width measurement—for our purposes, using inches).

Be aware of both the image ppi and document size. For instance, a camera may take photos in 144 ppi, at a size of 17.78" × 13.33" (or 2560 × 1920 pixels). A 17.78", 144 ppi image isn't really useful for the purposes of print work, so it's up to the designer to properly reformat the picture in an acceptable print resolution. As a reinforcing reminder: For the purpose of making comps, use 300 ppi as a base minimum resolution.

how to: proper image resizing

The following steps illustrate how to properly resize a raster image in Photoshop:

◻ Start with a 144 ppi image—perhaps a photograph from a digital camera. Transfer it to a computer.

◻ Open the image (*File > Open >* [select an image]) using Photoshop and navigate to *Image > Image Size.*

Figure 4-3

Left to right:

Even if an image is numerically high-res, use one of the best tools—your eyes—to verify quality. Is it jagged? Fuzzy?

The Photoshop dialogue box may state that the graphic on screen is 300 ppi. But the lack of quality (resolution in the image pictured) is usually painfully obvious. If you did not create the image and control its resolution, what may seem to be a high resolution posted in the dialogue box is most likely an improperly enlarged image (a "faked" 300 ppi).

Courtesy of Irish_Eyes, MorgueFile.com

¤ A dialogue box will open first, where all the various image settings (with entry boxes) can be seen, including height and width in pixel dimensions and document size, plus resolution.

You can not simply enter "300" in the resolution box to resize to an acceptable minimum resolution. The 144 ppi image might be mathematically reset to 300 ppi, but in actuality it is still only the quality of the original (144 ppi).By doing this, the software is in essence being asked to **interpolate** pixels— generate new pixels where there are none. An 800 × 800 pixel image has only the information for those 800 × 800 pixels. If it is upscaled, the software is generating new information— new pixels—by *estimating*. Allowing the software to fill in pixels or estimate pixel information (selecting colors) certainly leads to poor image quality.

¤ To resize properly, uncheck the box next to the words "Resample Image."

¤ At this point, the resolution can be changed and entered (using the minimum 300 ppi). Once the larger (reset) resolution is entered, the document size also changes. If the previous example of the 144 ppi, 17.78" × 13.33" is used, the original nearly 18", 144 ppi image has been reduced to approximately 8.5" × 6.4" and a workable and acceptable, *true* 300 ppi resolution; see Figure 4-4.

open with 300 ppi

Many single procedures and editing methods in Photoshop have alternatives to achieving the same end. Relative to resolution and sizing (and resizing) of an image, as an alternative to the previous example, the following method can be used:

¤ Start with a blank image in the appropriate 300 ppi resolution.

¤ Next, drag the low-res image (such as a photo transferred to the computer from a camera) into the newly created blank image. The size at which the dragged image appears in the new high-res image is its proper (and maximum) size at that resolution.

¤ Note that this "drag and drop" method may also involve additional steps such as cropping the border or changing the background color; see Figure 4-5.

Whichever method is selected, be sure the result is of high quality.

N.B. Under no circumstances should you upscale or enlarge the size of a raster image. If the image size originates at 2" × 2", it should never be any larger. Simply enlarging (scaling up) an image (*Edit > Transform > Scale* or *Image > Image Size* [enter a larger size]) will yield the same results—asking the software to interpolate and estimate. Generating new pixels results in a pixelated image.

resolution of raster versus vector

Whereas Adobe Photoshop specializes in manipulating and creating raster images (pixel based), Adobe Illustrator specializes in creating vector graphics. A **vector graphic** (also referred to as **vector art**) is different from a raster image in that it is composed of mathematically determined points, lines, or curves—not pixels. Being composed of points, lines, and curves gives a vector graphic

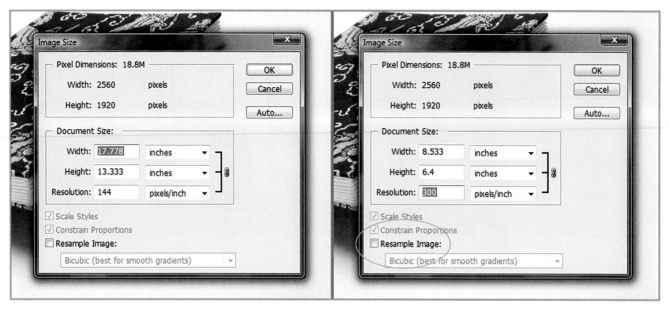

Figure 4-4
With the "Resample" box unchecked, the image is properly changed to
8.5" × 6.4" at 300 ppi.

Figure 4-5
The original image has been dragged and dropped into a 300 ppi image.
Adobe Photoshop's Crop Tool is used to cut the borders down to an
appropriate size.

the distinct advantage of being (within reason) infinitely scalable. For example, a vector graphic is suitable for use on a letterhead or business card, but can also be successfully enlarged for use in a banner or an outdoor board.

The most common example of a vector graphic is one that is used every day, but isn't always thought of as a graphic: the individual letters in a font. A letter generated as a vector graphic can be set at 6 points as well as at 600 points, and still be sharp edged and visually crisp. Diagrams, logos, pictographs, and **line art** (black-and-white images with no tonal variation) are other common examples of vector graphics. See Figure 4-6 for an example of a vector graphic and a rasterized version of the same graphic.

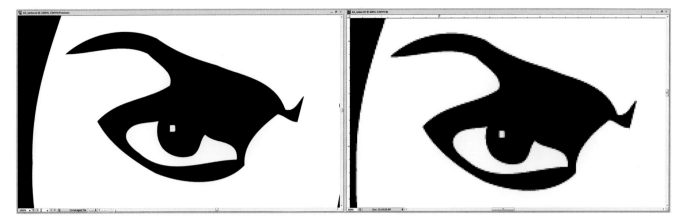

Figure 4-6

Left to right:

Pictured is a portion of a vector graphic shown under high magnification in Illustrator. Despite how small or how large the image is made, no clarity or sharpness is lost.

A rasterized version of the same image shows its pixels (and size limitations) when seen under high magnification in Photoshop.

vector graphic use

A vector graphic created in Adobe Illustrator is an appropriate way of designing a simple or complex shape or illustration; see Figures 4-7 and 4-8 for several examples. A logo, unlike many other images (such as a photograph), needs to be versatile—and to look sharp at any size, for any design to which it is applied. That is not to say that a logo cannot be hand drawn and scanned or created into a raster image or include a raster image as part of the design. However, the combination of raster and vector images is then subject to all the scaling issues of a raster image. Therefore, if you use a photograph or other raster image as part of a logo, always make sure the resolution and document dimensions are sufficient for print output.

in the mode for color?

Also critical to successful craftsmanship of a comp is the awareness and use of the screen color and its resulting output to print. Digital images can be created and saved in several different color modes, sometimes referred to as image modes. A **color mode** is a standardized method in which the software tool such as Photoshop organizes and handles the color of an image.

Although there are several color modes to choose from, the focus for the purpose of successfully producing comps is on CMYK or RGB modes. All images intended for print are always set in CMYK color mode. The **CMYK** mode includes the colors cyan, magenta, yellow, and black (the latter also known as keyline), which are the process colors of offset lithography—a commercial printing process briefly noted in Chapter 10.

Figure 4-7

An example of line art or "flat vector art." The color is solid and the quality is simple.

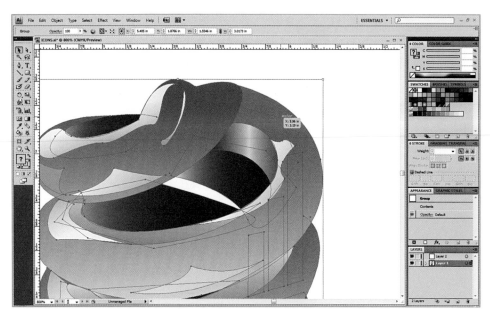

Figure 4-8
Vector graphics can also be significantly more complex and vibrant. Notice the smooth gradients and complex lines, bringing the look of this graphic closer to that of a raster image.

Images in **RGB** mode (red, green, blue—the primary colors of light) are specifically meant for on-screen applications such as the web or cell phones, but *not for print*. See Figure 4-9 for the Photoshop dialogue box that displays the notation on color modes.

N.B. Although it may seem simple, using the correct color mode is often overlooked. As much as true 300 ppi images are necessary for quality print output of images, professional practice demands that an image intended for print should be CMYK, not RGB color mode.

image is (almost) everything

Even through this brief exploration, you should understand that *quality* image use is a must for professional level design. Content selection and image composition are not in the scope of this textbook, yet they should be an important part of the study of graphic design. In this text, we focus on where to acquire images for your design solutions and the technical quality, rather than the idea or aesthetic quality.

You can acquire or import images from several sources:

- ❑ Take your own digital photos.

- ❑ Download images from a stock image website.

- ❑ Create and scan your own drawings, illustrations, collages, and paintings.

- ❑ Scan and import printed matter.

- ❑ Create a digital image/illustration completely on the computer.

shoot it yourself

One of the easiest ways to acquire an image is to take your own photos. It is relatively quick and easy to take photographs with a personal digital camera and it gives a designer control over all aspects of the photo. However, the art of photography takes a great deal of time to learn. In addition, access to the particular subject matter desired is usually limited, if not altogether inaccessible.

A camera that takes photos in a high resolution is essential to this process. A 10-megapixel (or higher) SLR (single lens reflex) camera is recommended. Even more important, however, is a good setup and lighting.

If you are untrained in photography, we recommend the "shoot it yourself" route *only* for simple, locally accessible subjects. Rather than risk an amateurish result, go instead to a professional source.

a myriad of stock imagery

A **stock image** provider is a website from which designers can download professionally created images of various types. There are dozens of stock image websites on the Internet, where a designer can acquire almost any kind of image, both professional and amateur. Some sites offer images for free, others charge a nominal fee, and yet others can be quite expensive based on the quality of content and the reputation of the photographer.

Specific needs and budget will dictate where the image is acquired (the site source) and the cost of the image. There is one important caveat: Be sure to read and understand the usage

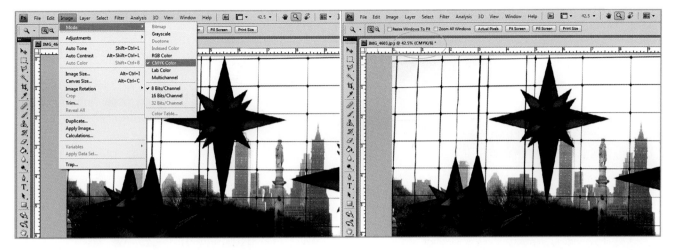

Figure 4-9

Left to right:

The color mode of an image can be checked or changed in Photoshop. Navigate to *Image > Mode,* and pick the appropriate mode.

Additionally, the color mode can be seen on the title bar of the open image.

Photo courtesy of Milijana Dukovic

contracts on the stock image site. While many comps may be student work or for demonstration purposes, if an image goes into actual production (commercially printed), designers may be required to pay additional fees to use an image. No two sites are identical in their usage stipulations, and within a given site, the various images may each have their own rules and restrictions of use. If you abide by the contracts, you will avoid negative consequences.

The following are a few recommended stock image websites, listed alphabetically:

- ¤   Big Stock Photo
- ¤   Dreamstime
- ¤   Getty Images
- ¤   iStockphoto
- ¤   Morguefile
- ¤   Photos.com (Jupiter Images)
- ¤   Shutterstock

create the image yourself

Perhaps some of the best images come completely from the designer and a few clicks of a mouse. Some graphics are born out of a designer's imagination and skill using the appropriate imaging software. Often, a logo may start as a sketch on paper and then get scanned and refined—an admirable start. Or, the first point of *digital* contact may not be from a scanner or camera, but directly on the blank digital canvas. Photoshop and Illustrator are not only powerful *manipulation* programs, but powerful graphics *creation* tools; see Figure 4-10 for two examples.

green idea

Working on a computer (especially when dealing with photos and images) can use a significant amount of electrical energy. There are numerous electronic components in contemporary systems, and each one is increasingly power-hungry. Fortunately, like so many software companies, hardware manufacturers are also attempting to go green with their products. Newer processors, while more powerful in terms of computational strength, have become more energy efficient. Likewise, the major electronic components (such as motherboards) often have power-saver functions built in.

Most computer systems can be set to energy-saver modes, and some feature additional power conservation settings. Monitors and hard drives can be set to shut down when there is no user activity. Set the system to sleep or hibernate when it's not in use.

These may be small steps, but if everyone is more mindful of individual power consumption, the cumulative result can make a great difference!

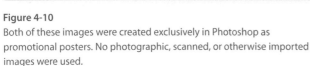

Figure 4-10
Both of these images were created exclusively in Photoshop as promotional posters. No photographic, scanned, or otherwise imported images were used.

scan master

Another way to acquire an image is to use a flatbed scanner. Essentially, if the object can fit onto a scanner bed, it can be scanned. This applies not only to flat items and existing printed matter, but to any three-dimensional objects as well.

Some designers have created quite a niche for themselves by creating "scanner art," which is creative use of a scanner to import anything and everything into a graphics editing program. As discussed earlier, always make sure an image is scanned in a high resolution for print output.

As you would with a stock image selection from the web, select the image for both aesthetic value and appropriateness and technical quality.

scanning a printed image

Scanning a printed image can be problematic. As found in magazines and books, printed images are composed of numerous colored dots (a result of the offset lithographic process).

Scanners use a similar imaging process— interpreting the image as a composition of dots (per inch). Unfortunately, the dots of a printed image almost never match those of the scanner. The two processes clash, resulting in an image imposed with a **moiré** pattern (a patterned distortion).

Because of the mismatch, scanning a printed image will yield a grainy image, even if scanned at extremely high resolutions. Remember that the scanned image will only be as good as the source. See Figures 4-11 through 4-13 for analysis of a scanned image from a printed source.

There are a few ways to compensate for the mismatched processes and moiré pattern, but often the final result still might not be of the best quality. Some scanners have built-in software to remove the moiré pattern during the scanning process; the software is sometimes called a **descreener**. Every software package has its own conventions and capabilities, so there is a need to explore and understand all the features of the software included with the scanner. See Figure 4-14 for an example of a built-in descreening function.

Figure 4-11

Comic book cover: The Art Directors Club of New Jersey

Studio: The Design Studio @ Kean University

Creative Direction: Steven Brower

Designers: The Design Studio team

Pencils: Ian Dorian

Inks: Ian Dorian, Janna Brower

Colorist: Christopher J. Navetta

Copywriter: Christopher J. Navetta

Printing and finishing: CMYK Printing

Client: Art Directors Club of New Jersey

An image scanned from a printed source. When reproduced in a very small size, little distortion is visible.

Figure 4-12

When shown larger, however, the dot (moiré) pattern becomes visible, making for a grainier image.

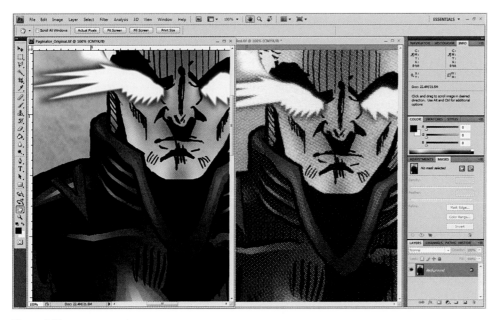

Figure 4-13

A comparison screenshot in Photoshop also shows the difference between the original image (left) and the scan of the printed image (right).

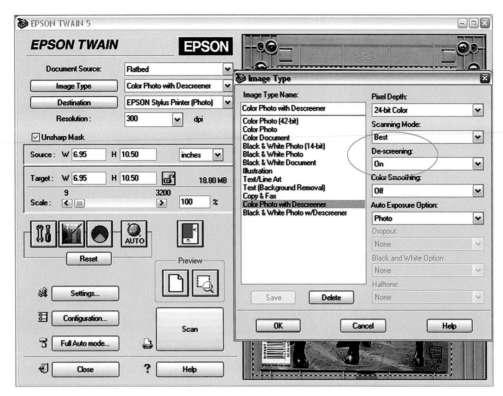

Figure 4-14

A scanner software's option to remove (or at least minimize) a moiré pattern when scanning a printed image.

In addition, creative use of native (originally built-in) Photoshop filters can help remove the unwanted moiré pattern. Use of the Despeckle filter is a good first step, but if the results are not satisfactory, combine with a Gaussian Blur and Sharpen/Unsharp Mask filters to potentially improve the results. See Figures 4-15 and 4-16 for a brief visual guide to the process.

Finally, there are many types of third-party (non-Adobe) filters specifically meant to remove moiré patterns. Each offers a particular set of features and user controls and each has a certain degree of effectiveness. As with other Photoshop techniques, there are numerous paths to the same end. The way to find out what works best is to experiment!

which image format is best?

Although there are numerous formats in which a digital image can be saved, a select few are most commonly used for professional graphics work, which is the focus here. Knowing which format to use—or not use—can make the difference between a clear, sharp image versus a fuzzy, distorted one. Understanding and selection could impact the ability of external printers or service providers to print a given design application.

Presented here is a list of popular image file formats and a brief explanation of their use:

◻ *TIF or TIFF (Tagged-Image File Format)*—A TIFF is a bitmapped image (raster/continuous tone) format. As with all raster images, it is resolution-dependent—it was created with a specific set number of pixels and should *not* be enlarged. TIFFs should be high (print quality) resolution, a minimum of 300 ppi. Scaling up a lower-resolution file will result in image degradation and a loss of quality. For further explanation, see the previous section in this chapter on scaling raster images. TIFFs can be saved without any compression, which will result in no loss of image quality—particularly important for images intended for print. TIFF is widely accepted as a raster image standard in the printing industry.

◻ *PSD (Adobe Photoshop Document)*—A PSD is Adobe's proprietary raster image format used in Photoshop. This file format has the advantage of being able to contain multiple layers within one image, any of which may contain Photoshop layer effects, masks, and so forth. This makes the image significantly more versatile when manipulating. Supplying layered PSDs for print output can sometimes be problematic, however, as some features of the layers may be dependent on the version of Photoshop in which they were saved. Multiple layers can also increase file size (measured in megabytes on a computer). Use of PSDs for printing by an external service provider is recommended only if that provider has given approval.

Figure 4-15

Left to right:

The Despeckle filter in Photoshop.

Gaussian Blur filter dialogue box.

Unsharp Mask can also be used.

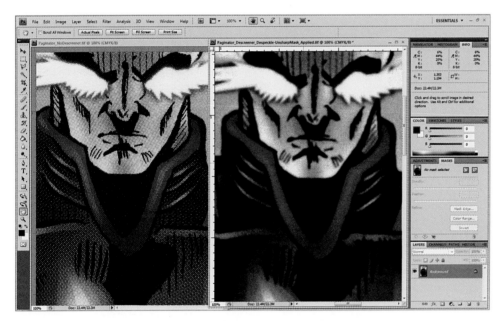

Figure 4-16

Before and after the attempt to remove the dot pattern. In this particular example, there is some improvement over the unaltered scanned image, but much of the moiré pattern still remains. Completely removing the pattern is impossible. The scanned image will never be as clear as the original, completely digital image.

¤ *JPEG or JPG (Joint Photographic Experts Group)*—JPEG is in most cases what is considered a "lossy" format. That is, JPEGs use compression to limit the size of an image—which can sometimes result in noticeable loss of visual quality (blurring or distortion of the image). That quality loss is also cumulative. Every time a JPEG is saved, it recompresses the image, resulting in continued degradation.

Most digital cameras can save images in the JPEG format, and JPEG is often a format used by stock photo suppliers. Always evaluate any JPEG for image fidelity and save it in a "lossless" format (such as TIFF) before printing.

¤ *EPS (Encapsulated PostScript)*—An EPS file can contain both vector and bitmap graphics. If the image was created as a vector using Illustrator, it has all the qualities of a resolution-independent vector image. If the image was created using Photoshop, however (whether imported from a digital camera or scanned or otherwise created from scratch), it has all the qualities of a raster image, and is resolution-dependent. Always be mindful of what is contained in any EPS file.

□ *AI (Adobe Illustrator)*—AI is Adobe's proprietary file format for saving vector graphics. Like PSDs, however, AIs can sometimes be software version-dependent. That is, an AI saved in Illustrator *version X* may not necessarily be accessible in earlier versions of Illustrator. For this reason, it is often best to save vector images in the EPS format.

As with all file formats, it is necessary to understand the capabilities and limitations of external sources (such as service providers) before supplying the files for print output.

laying it on the line

The final of the "big three" software tools discussed in this chapter is Adobe InDesign. Particularly among those just beginning their study of graphic design, InDesign is the most misused—or *unused*—software. Quite often, students compose the entire design solution using Photoshop or Illustrator. This instance can make a teacher or professional designer cringe. Just as Photoshop and Illustrator specialize in their respective uses, InDesign specializes in page composition—also known as **layout**—which is the arrangement (or composing) of graphics and **text**—arrangements of type set at 11 points or less (a.k.a. body copy), headlines/subheads (over 11 points), captions, and so on. InDesign can also handle large-scale graphics such as posters or exhibition signage.

Once the graphics are created in Photoshop or Illustrator, they are imported into InDesign and designed in relation to the text (body copy or otherwise). The final, whole composition can then be prepared for print.

just prior to print

Also use InDesign to compose text; this software tool features text editing tools for pinpoint control over every letter, word, and line of type placed on a page. See Figure 4-17 for a sample of the InDesign document setup dialogue box. Text design using InDesign is infinitely (and easily) editable and can quickly facilitate any necessary content or design changes. If type is composed in a graphics program (particularly if it is rasterized or converted to outlines), it is significantly more difficult to change in any way.

InDesign is the last point of contact before the design goes to print by an external provider (or on another computer). **Preflighting** and **packaging**—that is, organizing a document with all requirements and settings—is necessary for the output provider. "Preflight" is a feature of InDesign that searches the document and lists all its components, including (but not limited to) fonts, images, and colors. The preflight dialogue box displays any potential problems, such as images in an incorrect color mode or missing fonts, and provides necessary

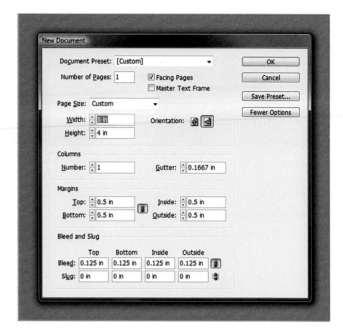

Figure 4-17

The Document Setup dialogue box in InDesign allows you to set the basic parameters for composing a document, including number of pages, page size, margin width, column widths and spacing, and bleed (extension of an image beyond the borders of the substrate). Working with the output provider—even if the provider is yourself and your desktop printer—is crucial at this step.

information such as image resolutions. Preflight can be considered the last line of defense before a document is packaged and sent off for print. By preflighting and packaging a document, InDesign creates a new folder with all necessary components of that document, including images and fonts as well as the InDesign layout (file) itself.

print it up or out

Once the design is complete, how does it get from the screen to paper? For output to paper and other substrates, printers do the job. The term *printer* can have several meanings.

A printer (such as an inkjet or a laser) can be the physical device that sits on the desktop and generates an image. A printer (often referred to as a **service provider** or **output provider**) is also a person or establishment who provides that same function, usually on a much larger scale. Building a solid relationship with these people is a must in every designer's career. A printer can be the savior of a designer's project . . . or perhaps, at times, the bane of his or her existence. (Beware that the feeling may be mutual.)

providing for print

One of the most important steps in creating a **document** (a file containing images and text intended for print output) using InDesign is understanding the requirements of the output provider.

If a provider (and the equipment in use) requires a document in a specific size with specific bleeds and a specific type of graphics, those requirements must be strictly adhered to, or there will be problems in the printing process. Put simply, the design won't get printed.

Fortunately, in the process of constructing a comp, designers (particularly students) are often their own output providers. Printing is usually accomplished on a desktop **inkjet printer** or **color laser printer**. An inkjet propels liquid inks in droplets of various sizes onto paper to create images. A laser uses dry pigment powders (known as **toner**) in conjunction with a laser to adhere the colored toner to paper. Both are suitable for a comp.

Whichever type of printer is selected, it is essential to know all the capabilities and limitations of the printer before a document is configured. If something is designed in a size that the printer can't handle, the piece won't get printed.

For the purposes of constructing a comp, designers often focus primarily on being their own output providers and working with desktop printing equipment.

desktop technology

Inkjet printers work with a wide variety of papers and other media to produce high-quality, vibrant colors and prints that are as good looking as some digital "professional" output methods.

Just as images are defined in Photoshop using a CMYK color mode, a printer works in a corresponding way, using a combination of cyan, magenta, yellow, and black inks to produce images.

Some inkjets even feature "light cyan," "light magenta," and "light black" cartridges. The thought behind these is that in order to produce a lighter shade of a color, fewer dots of that color are applied to a substrate. If the color is very light, that small amount of dots could result in a grainier image. With a lighter variation of the ink, more dots can be applied, yielding more consistent (and less grainy) coverage and a crisper overall image. Some inkjets even feature a swappable matte or standard black cartridge, which can be used to achieve various finishing effects on your paper.

The choice of a personal inkjet might seem somewhat daunting at first, but note a few key features as a guide to the selection process:

- *Image Quality*—Overriding almost all other considerations, the general technical quality of the image is the most important factor. Choose a printer that has excellent output by comparing print matter in-store when purchasing. Read online reviews from professionals that will help with image quality analysis.

- *Color/Inks*—Some printers work in the standard CMYK, and others work in CcMmYKk, utilizing the available "light" variants of the inks.

- *Paper Handling*—Always choose a printer that will work effectively on a wide array of printing papers relative to grade, finish, thickness, size, and use of sheets and rolls.

- *Size*—Although the standard is 8.5" × 11", it is highly recommended that larger-format models—those capable of printing at 11" × 17" or 13" × 19"—be considered. Not every project will fit conveniently on an 8.5" × 11" substrate (paper or otherwise). Spend the extra money and opt for the larger format. Particularly for the purposes of a comp, it will likely be one of the most convenient, flexible, and time-saving purchases a design student will make in regard to desktop printing.

- *Special Substrates*—Many printers can work with vellum, transparencies/plastics, foils, fabrics, and even rigid media like inkjet-printable CDs and DVDs. If you want any of these options, be sure to discover if the printer can handle the specialty substrates.

Whichever model printer you purchase, get to know it well. Explore all the settings and options that are part of the corresponding software. Factory (default) settings often don't yield the best output; a bit of tinkering and tweaking is necessary to get the best possible results. The more you know about the hardware, the greater the potential for highest-quality results and the easier it will be to avoid or troubleshoot problems.

the paper's the thing

See Chapter 2 for information on paper and other media used with desktop printing equipment.

beyond the desktop: external service providers

Fortunately, access to fast, digital printing can make working with an external service provider relatively easy. Using an external provider opens the possibility of outputting work on larger, professional quality machines. See Figures 4-18 and 4-19 for examples (and magnitude) of professional printing presses. For the purposes of making individual comps, however, such small printing is usually costly compared to the desktop and, therefore, may leave fewer options when choosing the service provider.

Figure 4-18
Offset press.

© Moreno Soppelsa | Dreamstime.com

beware of copy centers

The biggest mistake design students tend to make when choosing an appropriate service provider is to select a "copy center."

Although there is nothing wrong with the service of a copy center, they provide little more than the name states—a place for copies. The equipment and capabilities at copy centers are usually limited to color copiers, color laser printers, and a small number of secondary machines such as spiral binders or laminators.

Perhaps the prints generated from the printers at the copy center may be better than those of your desktop inkjet. The limitations still may not be worth the cost or quality.

Such establishments are often staffed with employees who are (by no fault of their own) not trained to provide the professional attention of a commercial printer. They are employed to make copies of an existing document, not print one-of-a-kind, precious design solutions.

Figure 4-19
Photograph: *Digital printing—wide format.*
An example of a digital press (in this particular case, a wide-format digital printer, used for large applications such as signs or banners).

© Moreno Soppelsa | Dreamstime.com

Countless are the printed projects that students have submitted with the complaint, "My work was supposed to look better, but the guy at the copy place messed it up."

Our retort: Be responsible for your own setup and printing needs.

online digital printers

As an alternative to retail storefront copy centers, there are online digital printing services. The digital prints provided through online sources are usually of higher quality than a copy center, and most online printers have a trained staff that can help with color adjustments and other technical issues.

Many online printing services also offer printing on more than just paper, including apparel (shirts, hats, jackets, shoes, etc.), housewares (mugs, glasses), and more specialized items such as bags, buttons/pins, stickers, keychains, clocks, umbrellas, and USB drives.

Note that the online service is not instant. As with copy centers, substrate choices are limited, and no two offer exactly the same services or turnaround time. Planning is necessary to allow enough time for adjustments, returns, and shipping.

We recommend and have had good results with the following online printers:

- Café Press
- Vistaprint
- Zazzle
- Overnight Prints
- ArtsCow

professional value

The best professional practice beyond the desktop is to build a relationship and rapport with a reputable, professional printer. As noted earlier, a printer can be either a savior or a destroyer of a design. Early and constant communication with a printer when working on any project is paramount. If you don't know the output specifications and needs, how can you possibly set up files properly?

Moreover, with an ever-changing industry such as print, it is necessary to always be in touch and in tune with the latest advances and changes. Having a printer that you can easily talk with and learn from is the best way to keep abreast of printing technologies.

life, the universe, and prepress

Jean-Marie Navetta

Designer, Production Specialist, and Princess

No matter how you're looking at it, being good at production skills is not sexy.

Nope. It's unlikely that you'll ever hear a thrilling story about converting picas right down to the perfect point. I've yet to meet someone who can talk about the thrill of the press check. And no matter how hard I've tried, there aren't groupies for the designer who knows how to get the image across a gatefold to match without a flaw.

So in a world where good designers are approaching fame similar to that of rock stars (and Chip Kidd, this would be you), where's the appeal to getting good at production?

Three reasons: it will keep you employed, clients will love you, and . . . it will keep you employed. (Seriously, none of us are in this for the thrill of the chase. The rent is due and fontography isn't paying the rent these days.)

Allow me to illustrate with a story.

Upon graduating from college, I had two skills that I could talk about. The first was existing for more than 48 hours on two cans of Coke and Cheez Doodles. The second was knowing how to lay out and get a newspaper printed. The first skill didn't fit a resume well; the second kept me from living in my parents' basement for too long and got me on the right track to good design jobs.

This marketable skill landed me a job at a publishing company where I'm certain that it was my ability to create foolproof style sheets and templates that any freelancer could file—and not my surly disaffected post-college personality—that kept me employed and moving up the food chain. And while finding the perfect layout for explaining polymerase chain reactions wasn't my life's goal, it got me some real-world experience and enough pieces in my portfolio to look for the next big thing.

And from there, the rest is history. The production skills I built up at that first job helped me move to the second where I got to spend a little more time designing. And my hours doing press checks on my creations there helped me into the next position, where I realized that not only did production give me some job security over the other designers who couldn't preflight themselves out of a PageMaker document, but it helped me find solutions to creative dilemmas based in production.

For example, finding the perfect paper for a high-profile development booklet was proving to be an impossible dream. Hundreds of swatches had gone by and we were still nowhere. But knowing that I could create my own tinted matte varnish and then bump up the contrast by covering photos with a crystal varnish made the project perfect. The lead designer and I had a weird yin-yang thing going on with our skills, and it worked. Sure, it isn't as exciting to hear about as redefining a brand, but it made the client happy . . . and helped them make some serious money.

Over the course of my journey through production geekdom, I realized that the most ridiculed among creatives are the clueless who think that production is beneath them. The designer who created her masterpiece using forty-five spot colors. The creative who developed his piece d'resistance using only images culled from the web at 72 ppi. The artist who decided that the most effective promotion would use materials that jacked up the per piece cost to $15 . . . for something that would be disposed of within an hour. (He, too, was disposed of shortly thereafter by the client.)

I eventually became a creative director and discovered the harsh truth: I'm not a great designer (a reality almost as crushing as knowing I would not grow up to be a princess), but I know what works. And when it comes to making something work that stays within budget and gets done on time, my production skills have served me well. It's kept me working. When no one else can solve the press dilemma, I'm the kind of person a company can call in.

These days, I'm a client—the very person that I feared so much in my days pre-Quark, pre-InDesign—and I'm maybe the scariest client of all, because I know when the designer's proposal is going to break my budget, when the folds that they've suggested won't be possible on any machine and require a horde of manual labor, and when the mistakes made before the project goes to prepress are going to cost me more than they should. In other words, now I'm the person who hires and fires because she knows better . . . and it's all thanks to the production years.

So what's my advice to impart to the student dragging through that production class? That one's easy: learn how to love it. Know that you'll only be as good as what you can make real. All of your brilliant ideas aren't worth the Cougar Opaque that you've sketched them on if they can't happen to spec and on budget. Suffer through the production skills class. Develop Jedi-like mastery over your styles, master pages, binding, and folds. Revel in the free paper samples that come your way. Find joy in the perfect varnish.

In the same way that cracking the perfect design is a puzzle, so is production. If you can master both sides of the process, you'll be unbeatable—and, more importantly, in an age that expects designers to master a multitude of disciplines—you'll be infinitely employable.

And in the end, isn't that what we all want?

—Jean-Marie Navetta

summary:
ready image; print

Understanding and eventually becoming fluent in the Adobe Creative Suite is essential for success and viability as a designer. Realizing which software module (Illustrator, Photoshop, InDesign, etc.) is the correct digital tool for the task is the best professional and student (desktop) practice.

On the desktop for use in crafting comps, it is most important to become adept at image formatting, handling (high resolution is a must for print), and setup of the correct color modes for print output. Having your own desktop printer that allows output in a variety of sizes onto various types of paper and specialty substrates is essential in order to make a design solution tangible. If a desktop printer is not available, a digital print service provider (in-store or online) is an alternative.

exercise knowledge gained

Spend some quality time with your computer and the software from the good people at Adobe. Again, this entire book could be spent on Photoshop examples and exercises, and the rest of your natural life could be spent experimenting and practicing in all the various graphic production software. That's not our focus. There are millions upon millions (that's a lot) of very basic exercises; we offer a few short exercises and several application projects that can provide a start and basis for honing your skills.

1. mine this chapter

If you haven't attempted the exercises mentioned previously in this chapter, do so now. Take photographs with your digital camera, check the resolution, and resize if necessary. Scan an image from a book or magazine; manipulate the image quality to eliminate any moiré pattern. Scan several three-dimensional objects and note the results.

2. stock library

Using any of the stock photo websites, start a photo library. Store the images on your computer hard drive for future use. Always browse those sites for the newest and best images. And definitely take advantage of when stock photo sites offer free images!

3. creative filtration

One of the most useful features of Photoshop is its vast array of graphical filters. These filters can also be one of Photoshop's most abused features—or at least one of the most *telling*, as poor implementation or overuse of filters smacks of rank amateurism and thoughtlessly cheap-looking design.

The only way to move beyond amateur use is to learn to combine filters to achieve fresh and exciting effects (rather than the tired and clichéd imagery instantly recognizable as a particular filter—such as Craquelure).

This particular exercise might involve the feedback of a fellow student designer, as his or her perception may ultimately determine if you've successfully completed the following tasks:

- Select a photograph with the knowledge that a filter or filters will be applied in at least a half dozen ways.
- Test each of the Photoshop built-in filters to determine their character.
- Be creative: Layer and combine filters to achieve fresh visual results that go beyond the recognizable and generic single filter.
- Compose at least six distinctly different creations.
- Show these new images to an objective judge (a peer or instructor or pro designer). If he or she can name (within reason) exactly those filters you've employed, then you haven't succeeded. Keep working until you've essentially "stumped" your judge. See Figure 4-20 for a student example.

4. join a photoshop challenge

Play at the exercises as listed above, but also go online and join in on a similar challenge. Find groups such as the National Association of Photoshop Professionals online, which have several challenges posted for fun and for the purpose of developing skill.

Figure 4-20
Can you tell which filters—or combinations of filters—were used? If so, your job's not done yet! (The center image is the original, unaltered photo.)

There are online communities and forums that are populated by designers of all skill levels sharing their knowledge or expertise, and by those seeking those virtues from others. Search around sites such as the Adobe Design Center to find one that sparks your interest and become an active community member.

5. do the evolution

As has been said numerous times, there's infinitely more you can do with the digital tools than what has been briefly covered in this chapter. And the field of digital techniques is ever-changing and evolving. Keeping up with developments is a challenge (who has the time?), but do muster to the challenge and stay relevant.

In order to keep learning, subscribe to a publication specific to the software. Magazines such as *Photoshop User* and *Layers*—only two examples—are excellent in that capacity. They provide news and information and useful articles. In addition, the magazines include specific exercises that can keep creative juices flowing. Subscribe and read. Complete all the "how-tos." Do the work. Don't stagnate. Never neglect your education!

6. extra! extra! reenact history!

Hey, we're living in the twenty-first century, right? There is much history behind us, and there are many ways to learn about our history. In the field of visual communications (particularly print), one of the most era-defining examples is the newspaper (at least for the last couple of hundred years). Newspapers are a showcase of the work of graphic designers and typographers. Designing a newspaper—or simply a front page—gives you the opportunity to develop skill using raster and vector graphics, and to develop skill in typography and page composition.

To begin: Pick a world-changing event in history (or one of less overall global importance), and design a newspaper front page for that day. The page should be composed using InDesign, with the inclusion of appropriate graphics created in Photoshop and Illustrator.

Include at least the following:

- A masthead or nameplate—This should include the name of the newspaper and its logo/type treatment, and all the additional information that might appear along the top of the front page (weather, index, features, etc.). Use Illustrator for the masthead and any vector graphics (pictograms for the weather, perhaps), use photos that illustrate the event, and compose all elements using InDesign.

- Photographs—Of course, there will be pictures. Find some! Edit! Photomanipulate! Think of how they can be made to look as realistic as possible relative to the application of the newspaper. Although the image quality of many contemporary newspapers is far improved from its history, use Photoshop filters to create the grainy effect of the historic date selected.

- Illustrations—Whether a graph, a chart, or a table (information graphics), add vector art. Remember to use the best tool for the job—work some Illustrator magic!

- Text—There should be a lot of copy. Pay particular attention to how actual newspapers compose the body copy. Note the number of columns. How large is the text size? What typefaces are in use? How many styles and sizes? Are there captions to the photos? Rules or borders to separate sections? How wide are the margins?

- Reference existing papers as a guide, and let your creativity take over.

This project involves use of the three basic software tools discussed in the chapter and helps develop proficiency. Once the practice newspaper is composed, if possible and available, print the design solution on newsprint. See Figure 4-21 for a student example.

Figure 4-21
Student project: *London Times* (*War of the Worlds*) re-creation.

After all the design is done, some additional photography of the printed piece plus some subsequent creative filtration make for an interesting visual—even if the event depicted isn't historically accurate . . . or real!

7. let's go to hollywood

Everyone loves the movies (at least everyone we know). One of the most creative and potentially exciting visual communication applications is the ubiquitous movie poster. Movie posters are a challenging design exercise as well as a conceptual exercise because they encapsulate an entire story—sometimes one of epic proportions—in a single composition.

Do research. Choose a popular film, one that many people know so that a critique of your results has a base from which it can be evaluated.

Begin by brainstorming and sketching a concept for the movie poster. Once you have your basic idea, it will be time to go digital. Set the size of your poster to 24" × 40". Printing at this size will be noted at the end of the instructions for this project.

Include and practice the following:

- Use Photoshop to import and manipulate the imagery. If appropriate, create special effects. Is the film a sci-fi blockbuster? (Do you need to render something like a rotoscoped lightsaber effect or some sort of laser blast?) Or is it maybe a *noir* thriller? Perhaps manipulate the color and shadows of a photograph to properly convey the shadowy feel.

- Use Illustrator to create the type treatment (logo) for the title of your film, plus any movie studio logos, and so on.

What does the logo say about the subject or tone of the film? What sort of typeface is appropriate, and how can you manipulate the type so it is conceptually appropriate and exciting? How prominently should the title be featured on the poster? Size the vector graphic based on the necessary visual hierarchy.

- Compose the poster using InDesign. Don't sacrifice any authenticity. Movie posters often feature large amounts of credits, studio information, copyrights, and indicia. Include and design all secondary information. Some of the text can be challenging to compose in a clear hierarchy (not to distract the viewer from the main image).

- Critique with peers or an instructor. Make the edits (there is no great design; there is only great redesign).

- Are you up to the challenge? Print the poster (either in sections or—if available—on a large-format printer). InDesign will allow for the "tiling" of the document so that it can be printed in sections on smaller sheets of paper. (Again, knowledge of your desktop printer's software is necessary in this case.) Once each section is printed, trim (if necessary) and adhere each piece in order to a large substrate. Alternatively, the piece can be printed at its full size (and in one piece) by one of the service providers that were discussed earlier in the chapter.

part two:
application of basic skills

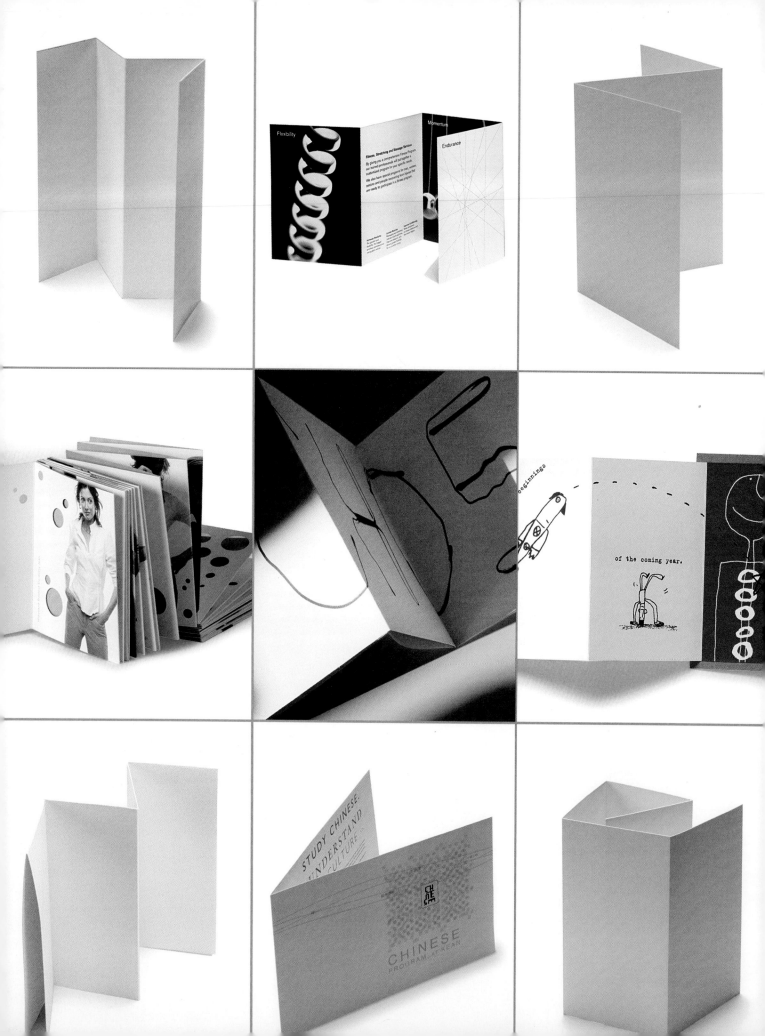

"Ideas and creativity come from what you know. A designer's role is to be aware of everything. You can pull out of your head only what is in there."
—*Kris Clemons, Gerhardt & Clemons (from an interview with Mark Oldach).*

First row, left to right:
Blank folding comp.

Sales Brochure: Executive Fitness
Studio: And Partners
Creative Director: David Schimmel
Art Director: Susan Brozozowski
Photographer: Photonica
Client: Executive Fitness

Blank folding comp.

Second row, left to right:
Continuous fold poster brochure (detail).
Studio: Design Ranch
Creative Directors: Michelle Sonderegger, Ingred Sidie
Copywriter: Jeff Mueller
Photographer: Michael Haber
Designer: Brynn Johnson
Printer: M-Press
Bindery: M-Press
Client: Lee Jeans

Poster/invitation: Madame Chose (detail)
Studio: Paprika
Creative Director: Louis Gagnon
Art Directors: David Guarnieri, Louis Gagnon
Designer: David Guarnieri
Copywriter: Pierre Laramee
Printer: Art-Seri
Client: Commissaires

Holiday Card: Nike (detail)
Creative Directors: Michelle Sonderegger, Ingred Sidie
Copywriter: Gordan MacKenzie
Illustrator: Meg Cundiff
Printer: Hammerpress
Studio: Design Ranch
Client: Nike

Third row, left to right:
Blank folding comp.

Brochure: Study Chinese
Art Direction and Design: Erin Smith
Studio: Media and Publications, Kean University
Client: Chinese Program

Blank folding comp.

five
a folded finish

chapter five: a folded finish

learning objectives

- Gain a basic understanding of the post-printing "finishing" process of folding.
- Realize the basic and practical uses of folds and how the reader experiences the unfolding.
- Learn the basic "anatomy" and styles of folded formats.
- Gain awareness of the range of mechanical standards and custom-folded formats.
- Develop skill in comping a variety of folded formats.
- Explore the creative potential of folded formats.

fold it!

The final stage of the professional production of a design involves **finishing** the work—in the situation discussed herein, *folding*.

The design solution is cut down from the full sheet of paper on which it was printed. The full sheet is known as the **print sheet** or **press sheet**. The resulting cut piece is bent and creased to lay over itself—**folded**—and perhaps combined with other pieces. The resulting final size, shape (square, vertical rectangle, etc.), and arrangement or **folding format** is one that has been specified or created by the designer at the start of the conceptualization process. See Figure 5-1 for a professionally designed, simple folded format applied to an informational and promotional brochure.

For cost-effectiveness, ease of distribution, and ease of reading, the information in this brochure was folded to a compact size. The use of alternating black and white panels dramatically coordinates with the folded format and helps to organize and highlight the information presented.

Unless there is a unique post-printing technique, cutting, or folding element involved, finishing of a standard folded format is usually part of the overall cost of printing. As stated by Robert Ryan, owner of CMYK printing in Saddle Brook, New Jersey, the cost of finishing is usually one-third of the overall fee.

If the design solution can be accomplished using a standard paper size and format, the overall cost could be kept down. Complicated folding (such as seen in Figure 5-2), flaps, pockets, and any variety of unusual combinations of folds will add to the cost of production. Yet, there are many justifiable purposes for thinking creatively such as differentiating the design from others in order to make it uniquely expressive, distinctive, and memorable.

A professional will balance creativity and cost. Working with the printer should start at the beginning of the design ideation and concept development to ensure that a great idea can happen within the budget set by the client. As a student, be aware that the best professional practices also apply on the studio desktop.

green idea

Perhaps folded formats may pass into history in the future. For the present, folded formats are still in widespread use relative to design and printed matter. To "think green," design creatively but not frivolously—respect both the client's budget and the impact of design on the environment.

Figure 5-1
Sales Brochure: Executive Fitness
Studio: And Partners
Creative Director: David Schimmel
Art Director: Susan Brozozowski
Photographer: Photonica
Client: Executive Fitness
This example shows a simple folded format applied to an informational and promotional brochure.

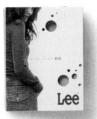

Figure 5-2
Studio: Design Ranch
Creative Directors: Michelle Sonderegger, Ingred Sidie
Copywriter: Jeff Mueller
Photographer: Michael Haber
Designer: Brynn Johnson
Printer: M-Press
Bindery: M-Press
Client: Lee Jeans
For this Lee Jeans promotional brochure, the designers used a continuous fold format that reads as a brochure or unfolds to create a large poster-like piece. A complicated folded format will cost more than a simple one, but creative and smart design also has the potential to drive profits up. There is purpose to this creativity—to differentiate and make memorable. The folded format in this design solution is also known as a snake or meander fold.

Figure 5-3
Folded direct mailer and related collateral: ADCNJ Award Show
Studio: The Design Studio @ Kean University
Creative Direction: Steven Brower
Designers: The Design Studio team
Pencils: Ian Dorian
Inks: Ian Dorian, George Rodriguez, Christopher J. Navetta, Ori S.
Colorist: Christopher J. Navetta
Copywriter: Christopher J. Navetta
Printing and finishing: CMYK Printing
Client: Art Directors Club of New Jersey
The nine panels of this direct mail "call for entries" were carefully designed to coordinate the unfolding plot with the folded format. Much time was given to the comp to ensure that the reader could unfold the piece in the proper sequence. The printer also needed a comp to fully understand the design.

The story ended triumphantly (for the superhero designers) and with an entry form for the readers (on the reverse side).

when is folding necessary?

For printed matter, folded formats are ubiquitous and, generally speaking, necessary for designing a large amount of information on an easy-to-read and compact format.

A design solution that has a significant amount of information needs to be easy to read and compact for two general reasons:

¤ **A comfortable reading experience**

When a great amount of information needs to be presented in an economic manner, folding is a good solution. A person cannot read a large amount of information on a flat piece of 40-inch paper that stretches beyond arm's length—the design must unfold neatly, fit comfortably in the hands of the reader, and follow a logical progression to allow for ease of reading.

Turning the pages of a book or unfolding the information of a folded brochure or direct mail application can be either an easy and comfortable experience or a stressful experience for the reader, depending on how well the designer has considered the folding in relationship to the hierarchy of information and ease of progression of reading/looking.

The format should only be a puzzle or mystery if it enhances the concept of the design and communication. Otherwise, the format and layout of information should function smoothly. If the reader is frustrated because the information is difficult to follow (in its layout and format), it is not likely the information will be absorbed or acted upon.

A reader's clear understanding of the informational *content* is usually the responsibility of the copywriter. However, success is best achieved when the designer and copywriter work as a team to develop the design and copy nearly simultaneously. See Figure 5-3 for an example of a format unfolding to tell a story.

The printed design is often mailed. Therefore, a folded format is cost-effective because it can be made compact and sized to fit standard mailing envelopes and postage (both save on cost).

A folded format can also be a self-mailer where the address is printed directly onto the piece. This makes an envelope unnecessary, again saving on cost. Envelopes are discussed in Chapter 6.

Yes, we know what you are thinking: A stapled booklet can also be self-mailing. However, the standard stapled booklet usually costs more than a standard folded self-mailer. In addition, a standard folded format usually is less expensive than a bound booklet or book because there may be no need to use glue, staples, or other mechanical parts. Albeit, when you venture into complicated folds, the cost of production rises.

Design costs are a relative adventure. Beware that costs fluctuate wildly depending on the paper used, the printing techniques involved, and the three-dimensional format.

N.B. You can always wish for clients willing to spend more for a meaningfully creative design, or you can stop wishing and learn how to truthfully communicate your ideas with depth and a convincing rationale.

be aware of printing industry standards

Yes, there are standard (a.k.a. basic or common) folds and folded formats. Becoming aware of standards in the industry is part of the responsibility of a designer. Standard folds and folded formats often coincide with envelope standards and standards in mailing conventions. Also be aware that there are international sizes and standards that differ from those in the United States. The conventions for the differences in standards were touched upon in Chapter 2 on paper.

And, yes we know, *standard, basic,* and *common* are not usually exciting words for a designer. Creativity in design and standardization within the printing industry may be seen as opposing or even warring forces. What designer doesn't like the creative freedom of unrestricted budgets? The reality is that most design work must be completed within a reasonable amount of time (the client ordered the design today and wants it today) and within a limited budget (how much does a folded format cost?).

Standard paper sizes and styles, and standard folds and formats should not be the death knell of creativity—on the contrary, a limited budget often calls for a greater amount of creativity and is certainly a creative challenge. Big budgets don't always coincide with great ideas. An unlimited budget helps, but it doesn't automatically increase creativity either—bad taste, empty ideas, and mediocrity happen with any amount of money.

manufacturing the fold

Printing companies vary in the range of printing and finishing capabilities that can be performed under one roof. These companies can range from small-scale offset lithography and/or digital printing in small quantities to giant-scale and massive production through finishing that would include printing, bindery, folding, special effects, wrapping, and shipping.

There are companies that specialize in finishing, including folding and binding. Most printers, even the smallest scale or individualized techniques, will usually have some folding and binding capabilities. There are printing and binding specialists for both standard and customized work.

industrial folding machines

Industrial folds are implemented through a *mechanical* production process; the paper passes through metal rollers that exert relative, calibrated pressure to create the fold.

A comp will never have the sharpness of a **mechanical fold**—which forces an ultrasharp crease that virtually eliminates the natural flatness of the paper. Yet, on the studio desktop, a mechanical fold is well simulated using a folding tool.

Get your folding tool at this point and "dog-ear" the upper right corner of this page, first with your finger pad and then with a folding tool (as described in Chapter 3). You now have a literal and irreversible bookmark for this chapter. Creative, yes?

To further your study in regard to mechanical folding, visit the North American Sappi paper website. On the main menu, click on *Education and Support > Professional Bookshelf > Technical Publications,* then scroll down to find the .pdf document on "Folding and Creasing." Guaranteed interesting? Let us just say that this document will considerably augment technical and practical knowledge.

folded by hand

When a custom-designed fold is needed, beyond the capabilities of folding machines, hand techniques can be employed. However, this significantly increases the cost. A hand-folded piece would make sense for small quantities for special events.

caveat designer

The vocabulary used to describe folding and folded formats may vary from printer to printer within the industry and within the profession of design. We have tried to use the terms most commonly found in the industry of printing and binding.

anatomy of folds and folded formats

As with growing your understanding of mechanical processes, becoming aware of the basic features, styles and categories of folds and formats can contribute to an understanding of what is possible (both on the desktop and at the professional level). Therefore, you potentially expand your creative capacity while adding to your practical knowledge.

distinguishing features

Panels, pages, spreads, and flaps are basic features of a folded format. The **panels** are the two-sided sections of the folded format. A **page** is a single side. **Flaps** are shortened panels. **Spreads** are two or more pages meant to be seen or read as a whole. For a visual explanation of panels, pages, spreads, and flaps, see Figure 5-4.

flat measure and finished size

In preparing to set up a folded format for design and later for printing, measurements are calculated both in the unfolded state (**flat size**) and folded state (**finished size**); see diagrams in Figure 5-5. The flat size does not include **bleed allowances**—the printed area beyond the dimensions of the design that are cut away in order for the image to be flush with the edge of the paper. Bleed allowances are noted for printing purposes but not in regard to flat and finish size of the fold.

A folded format is first designed as a flat single sheet. The design is produced and measurements are calculated in the unfolded state. The flat measurement includes **fold compensation**— use of a fractional measurement necessary for shortening one dimension of a panel in order to fold multiple panels of one format into each other (expanded notes on fold compensation are in the next section).

The process of folding from start to finish is frequently referred to as **folding down.** After the folding is completed, the overall height and width make up the finished size.

Figure 5-4

First row, left to right:
Two panels consist of four pages.
Three panels have six pages.
Second row, left to right:
Spreads are two adjacent pages and usually meant to be seen as a whole.
Flaps are shortened panels.

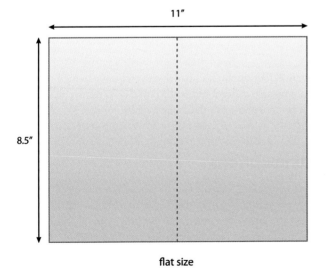

flat size

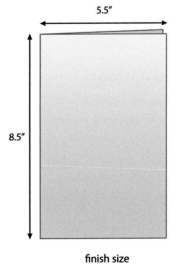

finish size

Figure 5-5
Folded format measurements are calculated both in the flat size and finished size.

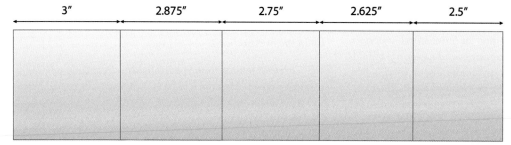

| 3" | 2.875" | 2.75" | 2.625" | 2.5" |

Figure 5-6
Fold compensation could include *approximately* 1/16" to 3/32" (or more) for each panel in the folding sequence. If the format has many panels, the compensation will increase progressively.

more on compensation

When a panel is designed to fold in, it should be slightly smaller in measurement to the previous panel relative to the sequence of the folding; see Figure 5-6. If there are multiple panels in one long row to fold in, the panels will be progressively smaller as they fold into themselves. Without the compensation in measurement, the finished format will buckle—that is, the paper will not fold in neatly and lay flat but will instead have a wrinkled or possibly rounded appearance.

The designer is responsible for including measurement compensation in the design. A comp of the actual paper is needed to ensure that the folding can be accomplished and to show the printer (or instructor). Without a comp, the bindery will go ahead and execute the folds as they see fit. If the measurements are not correct, the layout will be compromised.

> **professional note**
>
> A blank comp of the folded format is also called a **folding dummy**, a **paper dummy**, or a **sequence folding dummy**.

orientation and shape options

The orientation of the folded format can be placed in the following four categories. See the examples in Figure 5-7 for a visual reference.

- ▢ *Standard or Basic Upright* (also referred to as booklet)— finished height will be more than ¾" greater than the width.

- ▢ *Oblong*—finished width will be more than ¾" greater than the finished height.

- ▢ *Narrow*—finished height will be at least twice the finished width.

- ▢ *Square*—finished dimension equilateral (albeit it may have as much as + or – ¾").

Figure 5-7
Orientation categories of folded formats.
Left to right:
Standard, Oblong, Narrow, Square

Be practical. For instance, square shapes cost more to mail than the standard upright. Always realize the postal costs relative to size and weight before selecting or designing a folded format.

folding options

Folding and folded formats can be generally categorized to help digest and organize the information regarding the standards. Once you have the knowledge stored, you can pull it out of your brain or your resource binder (virtual or printed) when needed.

N.B. Relative factors affecting the success of the folding and folded formats include weight, thickness, and finish of the paper or substrate, and the number of folds involved.

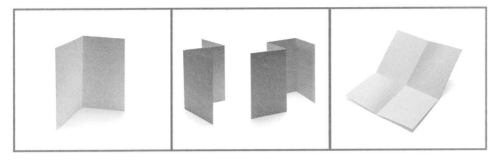

Figure 5-8
Left to right:
Single fold.
Parallel folds with three panels and with four panels.
A right-angle fold is creased perpendicular to a parallel fold or folds.

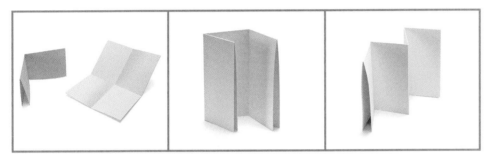

Figure 5-9
Left to right:
Four-panel broadside standard fold.
Six-panel broadside letter fold.
Eight-panel broadside accordion fold.

The basic folds in the following list can *usually* be created in any of the format orientations noted previously. See also Figure 5-8 for visual examples of basic folds.

◻ **Single fold:** one fold dividing the paper or substrate in half; also known as a standard or a half fold

◻ **Parallel fold:** a fold made in the same direction (parallel) to the previous fold

◻ **Right angle:** a fold made at a right angle to a previous fold

broadsides and short folds

A **broadside** is a folding option in which a sheet of paper is first folded in half *before* implementing a specific folding style. Implementing a broadside doubles the amount of panels and pages. See Figure 5-9 for examples of several styles of broadsides.

When half of the panels of a broadside are shortened, the result is called a **short fold**. See Figure 5-10.

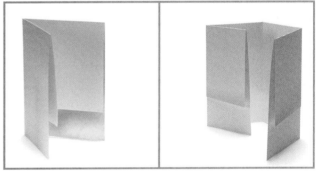

Figure 5-10
Left to right:
Four-panel broadside with inside short fold.
Eight-panel broadside with outside short fold.

folding format styles

There are standard format styles that can be accomplished on most folding machines. These folding format styles can be employed for a variety of design ideas relative to presenting a hierarchy of information. There are essentially eight categories of standard folding formats (note you may find that in the field, there are variations in naming conventions) and a separate

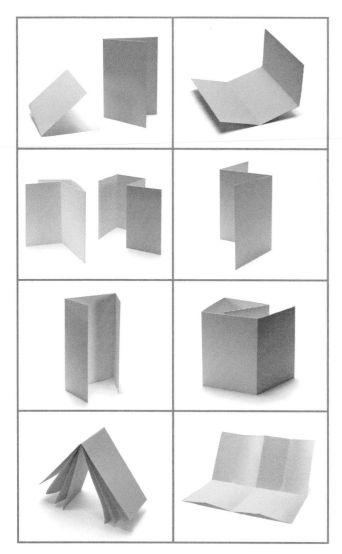

Figure 5-11
Categories of folding format styles.
First row, left to right:
Basic/standard: two panels, four pages.
Letter: three panels, six pages.

Second row, left to right:
Parallel: four panels, eight pages.
Note: The four-panel parallel is known as a double parallel.
Accordion: three panels, six pages.

Third row, left to right:
Gate: three panels, six pages.
Roll: five panels, ten pages.

Fourth row, left to right:
Map: panels, twenty-four pages; lightweight paper required.
Poster: eight panels, sixteen pages; lightweight paper required.

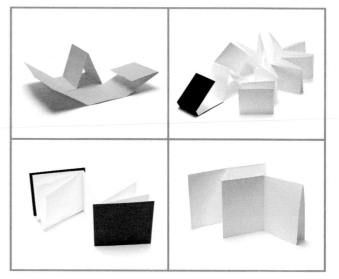

Figure 5-12
First row, left to right:
Two variations on a meander/snake fold with closing wrap.

Second row, left to right:
Z-fold map. Broadside, tricky parallel (this one folds down into a booklet—see also Chapter 3, Figure 3-28).

category for those styles that go beyond the standards. See Figure 5-11 for examples of the eight categories of standard folding format styles.

Any format that does not fit neatly into the standard categories would be considered a specialty or exotic fold; see Figure 5-12 for examples.

The categories of folding format styles are listed as follows with a brief description:

¤ **Basic/standard:** This folding format style has a single fold (horizontally or vertically) with two panels and four pages. A vertical orientation is known as a standard upright. A horizontal orientation is known as a basic landscape.

¤ **Letter:** This folding format style has two parallel folds resulting in three panels and six pages. The folding configuration consists of having the left and right panels fold over the center panel. The letter fold is likely to be familiar. It is commonly used for business correspondence. But don't stop with stationery letterheads; the style can be easily used for simple brochures. This can also be known as a C-fold, business letter, or 3-panel parallel. A letter fold with one short panel is also known as a church fold.

¤ **Parallels:** This folding style has four or more panels that remain parallel throughout the format. The style ranges from the simple double parallel pictured in Figure 5-11 to more complex styles such as a broadside triple parallel.

- **Accordions:** This style is a common and popular style with a zigzag folding configuration. It is likely common because all panels are equal in size, therefore eliminating the stress of calculating the measurement compensation (easy for us!). In addition, accordions are good for brochures, and this style can be adapted to handle as though it were a bound book. We love accordions for their versatility. This can also be known as a concertina or Z-fold—the latter having three panels.

- **Gates:** This fold is characterized by its centralized symmetry. Basically, two panels fold evenly into the center from opposite sides. This folding style requires a specific machine (or attachment) to accomplish and therefore may be costly to produce. Yet, we like this format because the gate can be designed as a "grand entrance" or portal into the information and imagery.

- **Rolls:** This style contains at least four panels that consecutively fold into each other. The fold compensation is tricky—it should allow for each panel to be progressively smaller so that they fold into each other without buckling. This format works well when a suspenseful unfolding of information is desired. The reader slowly unrolls one panel at a time to reveal the message. This can also be known as a barrel fold.

- **Maps:** A map fold is a multiple-panel accordion finished with a right-angle fold and set in a tall or narrow orientation. It is commonly designed to open completely rather than to be read as individual panels or spreads. Its usual purpose is as its name—for maps. It can be adapted for use as a brochure or other graphic design applications. Only lightweight paper works for map folding. We like using the map format with two opposing right-angle folds (z-shaped) because much information can fit on this very compact format; see Figure 5-12.

- **Posters:** This style is a broadside parallel or broadside accordion configuration (can also include a right angle fold) with a variety of sequencing possibilities. It is usually meant to open and remain flat. Because of the many panels involved, usually a lighter-weight paper is necessary.

  We have found that poster folds frequently succumb to our creative urges and lead to customization of the configuration. When does a poster fold become an exotic?

- **Specialties (or exotics):** These are formats that do not fit the categories listed above but may start with one or more of the standard styles. When the budget is available, we love designing specialties and exotics for creative fun.

  Some constructions are quite popular and thus have become familiar and worthy of their own category. Specialty folding and formats are noted further along in this chapter.

folding sequences

Folding formats can be oriented and configured—designated with a specific **folding** (and unfolding) **sequence**—in a variety of ways.

Consider the following:

- The format can potentially be oriented as an upright, oblong, narrow, or square.

- Panels can be shortened into flaps (inside hidden or on the outside).

- Broadsides can be implemented .

- One half of the broadside can be made into a short fold.

- Some formats can finish with a right-angle fold.

- The format can open from left to right or right to left. See Figure 5-13 for a basic folding sequence variation.

- Many folding styles can be combined.

A variety of folding sequences is possible for standard and specialty format styles. You need your analytical brain and your imagination working together to further realize all the variations. In Figure 5-14, we offer several simple variations on the standard folding formats. Or, turn to the Fold Factory website, where for a fee you will find the templates (that include compensation measurements) for hundreds of formats and folding sequences.

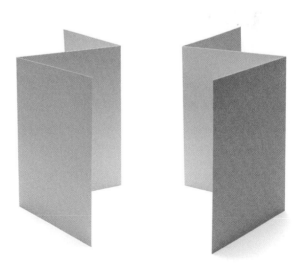

Figure 5-13

Variations in sequence: accordion opening from left side and accordion opening from right side.

In addition, if the intention is to mail the format stuffed in an envelope or designed as a self-mailer, there are again relative factors affecting success. For instance, accordion folds often cause problems when mechanically stuffed into envelopes and usually need to be secured closed for self-mailing using **wafer seals**—adhesive paper circles (or other simple shape) applied at the center along one side to cinch all panels closed.

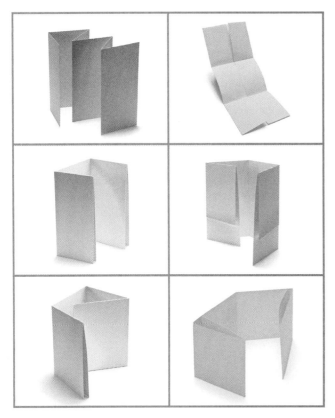

Figure 5-14

First row, left to right:
Upright, accordion with a wraparound parallel.
Gate and letter (could be a poster).

Second row, left to right:
Upright, broadside letter.
Upright, broadside gate with short outside.

Third row, left to right:
Square, broadside roll.
Square double gate.

selecting a folded format

Although selecting and designing a folded format is usually a contributing element of a design concept, instruction on conceptualization and layout of type and images is not the focus of this book. In-depth instruction can be found through additional course work and in several books, including *Graphic Design Solutions* by Robin Landa. Yet, a brief overview is in order at this point to get your brain cranked up and give some purpose to practice comps.

a folded idea

First, be creative up front. The folded format should be thoughtfully considered at the start of ideation. The format can be as important as any of the design elements (color, type, textures, images, etc.). It could contribute to the design concept, and it should function well; see Figure 5-15 for a professional example of a creative and well-executed specialty folded format. Refer back to Figure 5-2 for a closed version of the format pictured in Figure 5-15.

A fold can literally contribute to the design concept (either in a serious, mysterious, or humorous way) or metaphorically contribute. However the format works, there should be a rationale for the design.

Second, be practical. To help determine which folded format to choose, consider that a folded format involves *unfolding*. Think of your design as having an unfolding plot: a beginning, the middle, and an ending. Create a folded format that coincides with and enhances the unfolding plot of your design; see Figure 5-16 for a professional example. The story intrigue starts with the headline or title at the beginning on the front panel, the reader unfolds in a specified progression to engage in the visuals and narrative, and finally at the end, the reader is given a summary and an exit—perhaps contact information or a brand logo.

Or, simply use the unfolding to order the information for the reader. A folded format should assist in the hierarchical display of text and images; see Figure 5-17 for a professional example.

being creative

Beyond the standard mechanical folds is the realm of creative specialty, custom, or exotic folded formats, such as mentioned and seen previously regarding the categories of folding formats. To assist with the production of specialty folding ideas, machines can be adjusted to accommodate customized folds. Or a specialty format can be created by *hand* to produce an out-of-the-ordinary fold.

If the design calls for a custom solution and the budget is available, the printer will accommodate. There are also service companies that specialize in custom-folded and three-dimensional constructions such as Structural Graphics.

Creativity is at times allowed to push past printing industry standards. Designers seem to be drawn to the mysterious impulse within to create in a unique (or at least unusual) way—for visual impact (capture attention), to stand apart from the masses (differentiate), and for the smart fun of it (engage)!

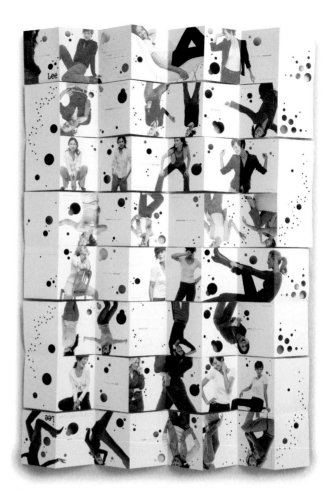

Figure 5-15
Studio: Design Ranch
Creative Directors: Michelle Sonderegger, Ingred Sidie
Copywriter: Jeff Mueller
Photographer: Michael Haber
Designer: Brynn Johnson
Printer: M-Press
Bindery: M-Press
Client: Lee Jeans
When the budget allows, a specialty fold can thoughtfully and creatively add fun. The format pictured is a meandering accordion, also known as a snake or a meander fold. It is pictured open to its flat size. The flat size folds into an easy-to-use and compact book-like format (refer back to Figure 5-2 for the finish size of this design).

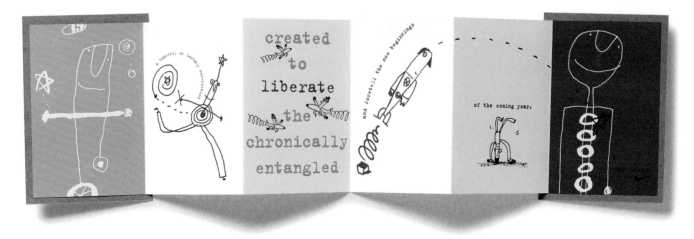

Figure 5-16
Studio: Design Ranch
Creative Directors: Michelle Sonderegger, Ingred Sidie
Copywriter: Gordan MacKenzie
Illustrator: Meg Cundiff
Paper selection: French
Printer: Hammerpress (letterpress)
Client: Nike
Accordion folded format. The format moves the story line along in this unfolding holiday card.

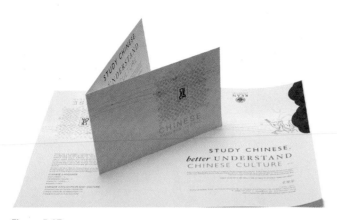

Figure 5-17
Brochure: Study Chinese
Studio: Media and Publications at Kean University
Art Director and Designer: Erin Smith
Client: Chinese Language Program at Kean University
For this informational brochure, the designer employed a single-fold broadside to organize information in a visual and unfolding hierarchy.

Figure 5-18
Direct Mail: ATT Sweet Dreams
Art Direction and Design: Michael Sickinger
Studio: Marra Advertising
The playful paper folding puzzle seen in these images is called a Swiss Cross flexagon. The folding and refolding design tells a story in four parts and engages the viewer interactively.

reminder: contributing to the design solution

If you have a deep budget (and even if you don't), a clever, smart, and custom-designed creative use of folds (folded into the concept of the design project) can contribute to and heighten the *physical presence* and *punch* of the printed design. The folded format needs to meet the following criteria:

- Is integral to the concept
- Enhances the audience experience
- Differentiates from competitors
- Makes the content memorable
- Is within budget

If the specialty folded format and the exotic folding involved do not answer to the criteria listed, then they are likely to be meaningless and wasteful extras. We urge you to be *thoughtfully* creative and nonconformist. Great design is creative, smart, thoughtful, on strategy with marketing needs, and within budget.

trademarks on folded formats

Some specialty or custom-engineered folded formats have been so successful that the design is *patented* or has a *trademark*. A designer using or adapting the folded format with a trademark would need to pay a fee for the template. Custom-designed folds are constantly being "engineered" (with great names such as MagnaPop, Book-Cube, and Four-window Pull). See the Structural Graphics website for information on these patented folds. See Figure 5-18 for a professional design using, for a fee, a patented folding format.

screen-based competition

Okay, we know that an interactive website, a television commercial, and an outdoor e-board can have live animation, backlit color, and sound. A printed design may seem to shrink in comparison to the awesome attention-grabbing power of live movement and interactivity. However, using thought-provoking folded formats can potentially capture the reader by creating a strong physical presence, adding interactivity, interest, surprise, drama, intrigue, or simply *fun*; see Figure 5-19. People love to touch and unfold paper. You can confirm this through simple observation.

A folded direct mail document might go into recycling, but in comparison think how equally easy it is to turn off your TV or click out of a website. Every designer is competing for a piece of attention in our overstuffed visually inundated world. We trust the touch factor as much as animation for a potential powerful design experience.

Even though we have seen websites that animate folding and simulate the turning page of a book, what does a folded, printed design have that a website will never have? Paper can actually *stimulate* our sense of touch—touché to that, web design.

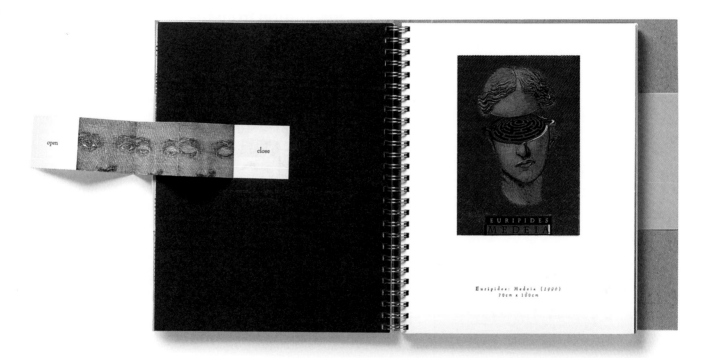

Figure 5-19
Istvan Orosz book
Studio: Design Ranch
Creative Directors: Ingred Sidie and Michelle Sonderegger
Illustrator: Istvan Orosz
Paper selection: Various French Paper Co. and vellum
Printer: Hammerpress (all hand letterpress)
Client: Istvan Orosz
An accordion fold placed within a book to create a sense of surprise and delight, and interactivity.

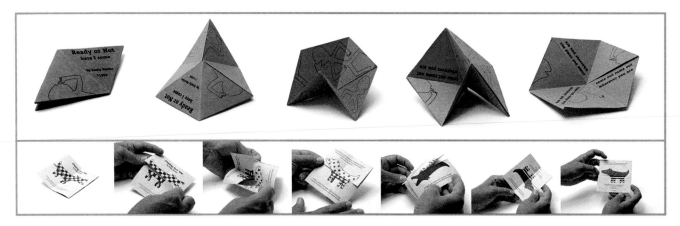

Figure 5-20
Two folded delights by artist Emily Martin, Naughty Dog Press.
First row:
Hexaflexagon.
Title: *Ready or Not Here I Come.*
Second row:
Square flexagon.
Title: *Chasing Your Tale.*

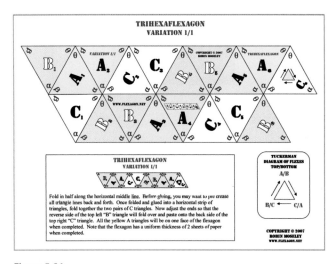

Figure 5-21
Flexagon template.
Artist/mathematician: Robin Mosley
Trihexaflexagon.

inspiration from the fine arts and mathematics

For centuries, fine artists have been folding and creating artwork in various formats (printed or otherwise), searching for creative ways to express their thoughts. Both historic and contemporary **book arts** (art that specializes in the book and folded formats) are a crucible for new and exciting visual directions for folding and bookbinding (discussed in Chapter 7).

See Figure 5-20 for two examples of folding fun from book artist, Emily Martin. Obviously, there are hundreds (thousands?) more artists, fine arts resources, and book arts centers, such as Pyramid Atlantic, Minnesota Center for the Book Arts, Keith Smith Books, Dieu Donné, The San Francisco Center for the Book, and Seattle Center for Book Arts.

We also reach into the intriguing world of mathematics for games and puzzles that can be translated into design formats. See Figure 5-21 for a template example generously supplied by Robin C. Mosley at www.flexagon.net where you can explore more folded math puzzles.

Some of the handmade artists' formats and mathematical puzzles can be adapted to mass production or custom production; refer back to Figure 5-18 (the Flapper pictured is a simple Swiss Cross flexagon).

Some traditional and contemporary artist folds and mathematical puzzles that we find creatively playful include meander fold and pamphlet fold (refer back to Figure 5-15), or a Magic Wallet or Jacob's Ladder. Be aware that while searching the web for more information or templates, the names of these artist folds may vary.

comp it up! folded formats

As discussed in the introduction of this book and noted here in regard to folded formats, whether at a student level or professional, a comprehensive mock-up must be created to determine the look and functionality of a fold and the finished format.

The comp is created for practical reasons in order to test the functional aspects of the design in regard to the user or reader of the product. Can the reader unfold the format easily and follow the hierarchy of information? There should also be a complete comp of the design to test the flow of the text and the success of the hierarchy of information.

If images are used, do they work with the structure of the format? And certainly, a comp is necessary to see how and if the folding will work properly relative to measurements and to the paper stock selected.

A comp also helps in developing the design on an aesthetic level—what might seem intriguing or beautiful in the designer's mind might not translate into a physical form. The designer and copywriter have the greatest possibility of success when all aspects of a design are put through testing from the very start of concept development.

Finally, the printer isn't a mind reader; a comp is essential as a visual guide to folding sequence and finished appearance. Most considerations in the industry are also found on the studio desktop during the comprehensive mock-up process of a standard or custom format, and need to be addressed in order to make a successful comp. Review Chapters 2 and 3 on paper and basic techniques and make sure the knowledge and skills gained are applied to comping folded formats.

general procedure

Consider the practice guide that follows as a checklist for folding:

- *Make ready*
  The work area should be neat, organized, and clean. Hands should be washed and dry. Materials should be cool and dry and all at the ready.

- *Paper stock*
  For aesthetic purposes, select paper that is appropriate to the design concept; however, practical and functional aspects should also be considered.

  The weight, thickness, and finish will affect the success of the fold—that is, whether the folding can be implemented without significantly cracking the substrate.

  Rule of thumb: As the number of folds increase, the weight and thickness of the paper should decrease. Testing is always necessary.

- *Print planning*
  Be aware that printing across a fold may also affect the success of implementation. Folding across heavy ink coverage may cause the ink to crack. Avoid heavy and/or dark ink coverage across a fold.

  Also review instructions from Chapter 3 on adhering two printed pages together before folding. A quick reminder here: There will be stretching and "pulling" of two adhered sheets of paper as the folding proceeds; therefore, scoring is critical. Or, print on only one side of the sheet of paper. Fold, then unfold; follow with adhering individual pages on the unprinted side of the format.

- *Paper grain*
  Design, score, and fold parallel to the paper grain. When a format calls for folding in more than one direction, the main fold or primary folding direction should follow the grain.

- *Measure with precision*
  Double-check all measurements for spacing accuracy. Make sure all edges and folds are set square.

- *Fold compensation*
  Keep in mind fold compensation when designing folded formats. Generally speaking, consider that any panel that is designed to fold into another needs to be shortened by 3/32" or more, depending on the weight, thickness, and finish of the paper and the total number of folds. If using a broadside or a right-angle fold, you may need to have additional compensation due to the doubling of the paper.

- *Scoring review*
  For the tightest fold, we recommend to always score the fold. The depth of the score will be relative to the thickness of the paper.

  Generally speaking, for desktop comps, we recommend that you score in the valley of the fold. There are instances (such as when using thick paper or a fancy finish) when you will need to score on both the front and the back of the fold line. Scoring on both sides is tricky; take time and measure twice to ensure accuracy.

N.B. Note that in the professional field, scoring is done on the mountain of the fold.

- *Fold*
  Begin the fold with your hands; protect the surface of the format. Use a folding tool to tighten and finish the fold.

- *Assess*
  Plan on multiple comps before you reach the final version. All materials, measurements, and the design of information need to be tested, assessed for success, and re-created if necessary.

See Figures 5-22 through 5-29 for samples of several levels of student work.

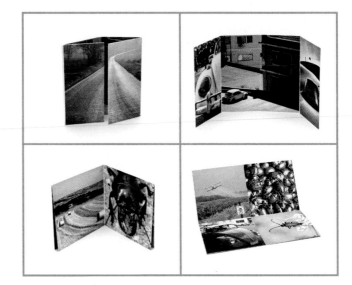

Figure 5-22
Second-level project: image research, editing, and composition.
Folding formats: gate (first row) and simple right-angle fold (second row).
Student designer: Alexander D'Angelo

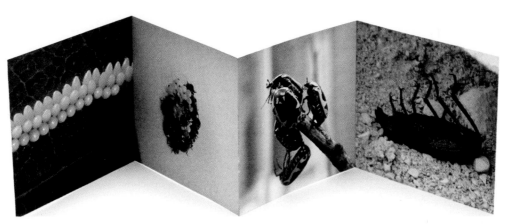

Figure 5-23
Second-level project: image research and storytelling.
Folding format: accordion.
Student designer: Alexander D'Angelo

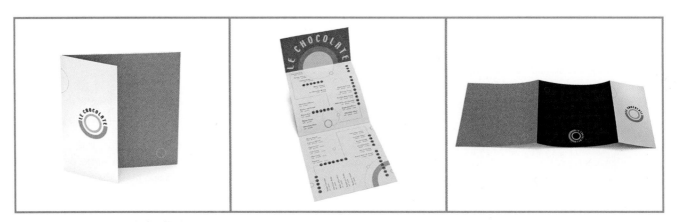

Figure 5-24
Third-level student project: menu design.
Folded format: letter with short outside panel.
Student designer: Sylvia Miller

Figure 5-25
Fourth-level student project: announcement for a cooking competition.
Folded format: specialty with gate.
Student designer: Jamie Maimone

Figure 5-26
Fourth-level student project: promotional brochure.
Folded format: specialty accordion gate.
Student designer: Michael Boos

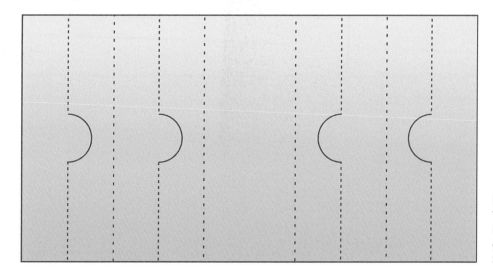

Figure 5-27
Template used for Figure 5-26.
Folded format: specialty accordion
gate template.
Student designer: Michael Boos

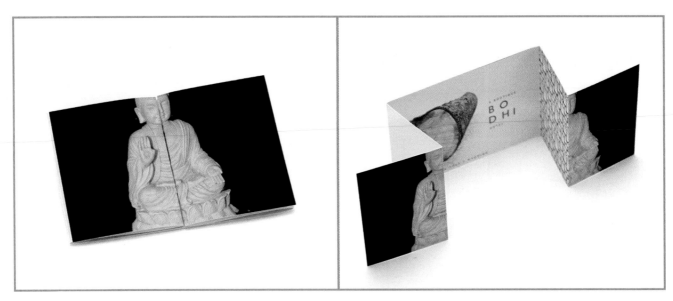

Figure 5-28
Student project: invitation.
Folded format: reverse gate.

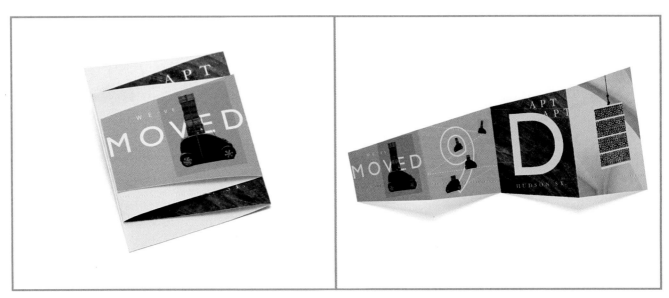

Figure 5-29
Student project: moving announcement.
Folded format: specialty accordion.

summary:
ready, fold over, and away

Once you've gained an understanding of the post-printing "finishing" process of folding, and realize the basic and practical uses of folded formats and their "unfolding experience," integrate them creatively into your design solutions. Remember that smart design is on-target and respectful of limitations (budget or otherwise). Explore all folded formats and experiment to increase both creativity and craftsmanship skill.

exercise knowledge gained

Trish Wikowski, the professional folding fanatic at the Fold Factory, has this piece of sage advice to avoid problems in the final folded product: "think finishing first."

We concur and add our own advice for acquiring superior craftsmanship skill: practice.

Go on now and fold.

1. Folded Format Toolbox

Start your own folded format toolbox. Create samples of all standard folds and formats using different weights of paper. Start with plain paper, 60# text and 80# cover. From there, begin experimenting using the same folds with different paper types and weights. Discover how the substrate affects each fold—compare how two (or more) different substrates react. Keep these samples, labeled, in a pocket folder inside a three-ring binder and use them for reference and inspiration.

2. Unfold the Visual Story

A folded format should contribute to the overall concept of a design and assist with visual hierarchy in regard to information.

Using a roll fold format, design a visual story or progressive visual sequence of some sort. For instance, the format should start with a panel that is yellow in color and unfolds to reveal all the colors of the spectrum in order. Or, tell a story by having each panel display the unfolding of a sequence of events such as a Frisbee flying through the air, ultimately caught in the mouth of a dog.

When an extra long accordion is needed to tell a story or display information, two sections may need to be joined to accommodate the design. To join, one set of panels needs to also have a short flap (½") to which glue is applied. If the joint seam is undesirable, two full-size panels can be glued together to join the two sections; see Figure 5-30 for the relative diagram.

3. Make It a Big Picture

Repeat your visual story or sequence, but in this instance, the plot or hierarchy of information should unfold into a large format such as a 9- to 12-panel poster format. See Figure 5-31 for an example of an unfolding story into a poster format.

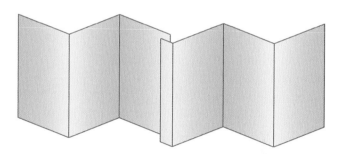

Figure 5-30
Diagram for joining two sections of an accordion folding format.

Figure 5-31
Student project: promotional.
Folded format: poster.

4. Custom Templates Toolbox Resource

Gather existing pieces that creatively or inventively use folds. Using them as a reference, reverse-engineer them and create your own templates that can then be used for future projects. Keep both the originals and your templates with the rest of your samples in your binder. Remember to note the source of each template. Be aware and responsible in regard to possible copyright and patent issues if you intend to use these for professionally printed work.

5. Flexagons!

There is much to learn about the fascinating mathematical paper-folding, brain-teasing games called flexagons. Visit www.flexagon.net, a portal to a nonprofit community of mathematicians and aficionados. As noted on the website:

"Flexagon.net was created to provide a place for all those interested in flexagons to share their ideas, templates, or anything related to flexagons. Here is what you will find:

1. Original flexagon templates—For some of the templates, each triangle or polygon unit is separately labeled and every corner coded. This allows one to more easily discover all the combinations of faces and rotations of the polygons.

2. Information on technical aspects of flexagons and on creating flexagons."

Use the template in Figure 5-21 provided by Robin Mosley or visit the website to download additional templates. There are also videos on how to manipulate the folds on these wonderful constructions.

There is a fascinating world of mathematical structures that can be adapted for use in graphic design and more than one source to explain them to you.

6. Engineer a Folded Format

Start by referencing the custom-folded formats noted in the chapter, and work from there. For example, after experimentation with asymmetrical folds, create your own variation and see how you can change the shape of a format, its amount of faces/pages, and ultimately the overall presentation.

To further this assignment, create it as a graphic design application such as an invitation to a sales meeting or a business partnership announcement.

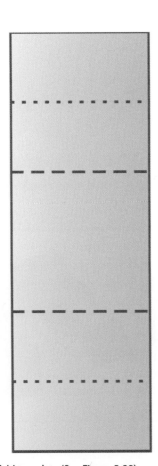

A. Reverse gate fold template (See Figure 5-28).

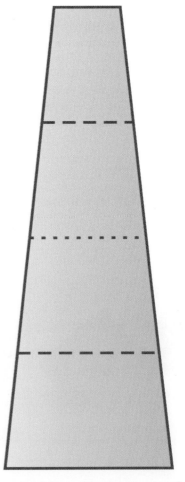

B. Graduated accordion fold template (See Figure 5-29).

C. Poster fold template (See Figure 5-30).

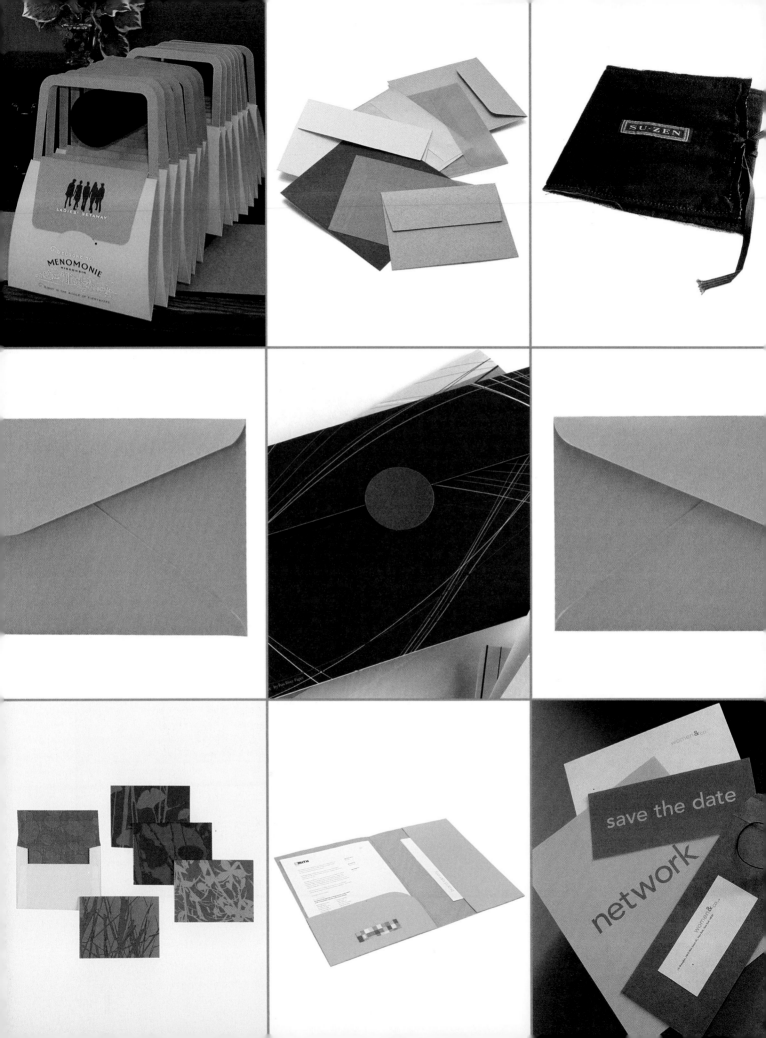

"We create solutions in response to problems, the more specific the definition of the problem, the more directed the efforts at solving it. Constraints are not your enemy, but your friend."
— *Rick Eiber, World Trademarks: 100 Years*

First row, left to right:
Promotional matter: Ladies' Getaway purse
Studio: DBD International, Ltd.
Creative Director: David Brier
Art Director and Designer: David Brier
Copywriter: David Brier
Printing and bindery: Rooney Printing
Client: Menomonie Area Chamber of Commerce
As stated by the designer: "The 'purse' was designed to specifically appeal . . . to the ladies of the Ladies' Getaway who would have this piece as a keepsake plus it served to have their itinerary on the inside when they arrived."

Manufactured envelopes.

Booklet/folder: Su-Zen
Studio: Mucca Design Corporation
Creative Director: Matteo Bologna
Art Director and Designer: Matteo Bologna
Photographer: Steven Gross
Client: Su-Zen

Second row, left to right:
Commercial/official envelope comp, stage right.

Stationery: Starwhite
Studio: Arketype
Creative Director: Jim Rivett
Art Director: Jim Rivett
Designers: Laura Treichel, DeGaull Vang, Luis Avalos, Robb Mommaerts
Copywriter: Fox River Paper Company
Photographer: 44 inc.
Printer: Independent, Inc.
Client: Fox River Paper Company (now Neenah Paper)

Commercial/official envelope comp, stage left.

Third row, left to right:
Letterhead, notecards, and envelopes: Bennett Schneider
Studio: Design Ranch
Creative Directors: Michelle Sonderegger, Ingred Sidie
Designer: Tad Carpenter, Rachel Karaca
Illustrator: Tad Carpenter
Paper selection: Mohawk Options
Printer: M-Press
Client: Bennett Schneider
Self-promotional matter: Smith Design
Studio: Smith Design, Glen Ridge, NJ
Creative Director: James Smith
Client: Smith Design

Stationery: Women & Co.
Studio: And Partners, NY
Creative Director: David Schimmel
Art Director and Designer: David Schimmel
Paper selection: Mohawk Superfine
Printer: Dickson's Inc.
Client: Women & Co./Brinsights

six
within: envelopes and folders

learning objectives

- Acquire knowledge of standard styles of envelopes and folders.
- Become aware of specialty and/or custom envelopes and folders.
- Learn the basics in constructing envelopes and folders.
- Explore the creative and expressive potential of envelopes and folders.

envelop the message

A creative envelope, or folder, could speak volumes about its contents and the identity of the source (the client's product, service, or other offering) when the design concept determines it so. An envelope does not have to be merely a container of information but rather it can be a compelling visual and tactile object (see Figure 6-1), the first and personal point of contact made with the reader, and/or the potential start (or opening) of a design concept.

Like an envelope, a design-integrated folder can also be an expressive receptacle containing information that is engaging enough to open, read its contents, perhaps discover or learn something new, and consequently be moved to action. See Figure 6-2 for a professional example.

Figure 6-2
Promotional matter: Ladies' Getaway purse
Studio: DBD International Ltd.
Creative Director: David Brier
Art Director and Designer: David Brier
Copywriter: David Brier
Client: Greater Menomonie Area Chamber of Commerce
As noted by the designer, the brochure and other parts of the design were "all printed full color plus a custom 5th color mix and flood dull aqueous coating. The Ladies' Getaway Die Cut Purse [is made of] 120# McCoy Silk Cover [Mohawk Paper]. Envelopes [are made of] Chromatica Translucent Mango."

Figure 6-1
Catalog: Su-Zen
Studio: Mucca Design
Creative Director: Matteo Bologna
Art Director and Designer: Matteo Bologna
Photographer: Steven Gross
Client: Su-Zen
The fabric and texture of this folder is both conceptually appropriate and compelling. A folder or envelope may be the first point of entry into the design concept and should be as carefully considered as all the additional elements of the design solution.

professional note

A design that is a short-lived gimmick is never as effective as a "smart" design that is an original *and* thoughtfully integrated aspect of the design solution. If the task of visual communication can be accomplished digitally (to reach the largest audience, to save postage and paper) then by all means, pursue a digital solution. If a digital solution is not the best route, then learn as much as possible in regard to paper alternatives. Reminder: You cannot access the options if you are not aware of them.

Yet, in this digital and web world in which designers do thrive, one might ask: Is there truly a need to contain information in a physical, material-based envelope or folder? Why put a design solution through "snail mail" when the consumer or reader can be reached by e-mail so much faster? There are many occasions when well-conceived and designed printed matter received into the reader's hands creates a dramatic physical and tactile impact, beyond what's possible on a screen. See Figures 6-3 and 6-4 for examples of creative envelopes and folders at work within identity applications.

Yes, smart e-mail messages can and do work well. Digital direct mail is also effective when thoughtfully designed. But because of the great amount of them received so frequently, e-mails may feel impersonal in their approach. For a truly personal and direct connection, place the information in the reader's hand.

We applaud the conscious effort to reduce paper waste, and we ourselves engage in the use of services such as automatic bill-paying systems to reduce the use of envelopes. However, there are still occasions when you will find the need to contain a body of complex information for presentation and transport—to meetings, for instance, or for direct mail applications. Gather the papers and additional materials in a folder or an envelope to make it personal and desirable to open and read, such as the folder/envelope seen in Figure 6-5.

Figure 6-3
Personal stationery product: *Natura Naturata*
Studio: slover [AND] company, New York, NY
Creative Director: Susan Slover
Designers: Marianna Hardy, So Hong, Saskia Hoppe, Amy Gorrek, and Jennifer Teixeira
Copywriter: Rosemary Kuropat
Photographer: Thomas Bricker
Client: Chronicle Books, Giftworks Division, San Francisco, CA
Noted by the designers: "*Natura Naturata* is manufactured from mixed substrates such as: natural and beater-dyed chipboards, unbleached newsprint, Baltic pine wood, vellum SBS boxboard, Wire-O bindings, bungee cords and straps.

Figure 6-4
Brochure: Webster House
Studio: Design Ranch, Kansas City, MO
Creative Directors: Ingred Sidie, Michelle Sonderegger
Designer: Rachel Karaca
Copywriter: Kerri Conan
Photographer: Gabe Hopkins
Printer: M-Press

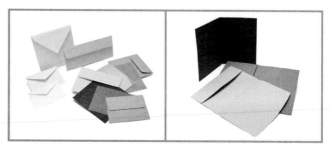

Figure 6-5
Direct mail: Every Mile Counts in the Drive to Cure Breast Cancer
Studio: Ritta & Associates, Englewood, NJ
Creative Director: Kay Ritta
Art Director: Cesar Rubin
Designer: Cesar Rubin
Client: BMW

standard envelopes and folders

A designer has the responsibility to explore all of the possibilities, whether creating envelopes or folders or additional format substrates. And a *conscientious* designer must also weigh the factors of beauty and creativity versus printing and assembly cost, mailing, and practical use. To that end, the established standard sizes and configurations of envelopes and folders should be weighed against the custom-designed or off-standard and experimental possibilities. A designer can stay within the standards and still be creative—by knowing all the options and then manipulating and using them with imagination. See Figure 6-6 for a small group of industry-made, interesting, standard envelopes and folders.

envelopes inside and out

Did you think envelopes came in two standard sizes—one for personal letters and one for business? Okay, maybe you also have seen metal clasp envelopes for holding a flat sheet of 8.5" × 11" paper or loose pieces of information. Keep thinking and learning—there are many standard, commercially produced envelope colors, textures, shapes, and sizes. And there is much to learn about the practical and creative use of them.

We give you some starting points and suggest that you further your awareness by researching envelope supply companies, printers, and **converters** (manufacturers of envelopes). And, there are paper mills that manufacture envelopes or those that have connections with envelope manufacturers.

Figure 6-6
Left to right:
Standard doesn't necessarily mean without options. Industrially manufactured envelopes come in a variety of substrates, colors, textures, and styles.
Pictured are several examples of manufactured folders. Use the standards to help guide function and expand on the basic styles to contribute to a design solution.

For further technical information and an extensive list of standard sizes, Central Lewmar (paper distributor), in conjunction with Marquardt & Company Fine Papers, has an excellent book (*YES! Your Envelope Sourcebook*) filled with a copious amount of information on paper suitable for envelope construction, envelope sizes and use, printing tips for envelopes, and mailing standards and resources. If the *YES!* book is not available in your area, search the web. National Envelope/Williamhouse and Neenah Paper as well as other paper mills have information on both standard envelopes and folders. The experienced representatives at paper distributors, paper mills, printers, and other manufacturers have information on cost, availability, and envelope styles and sizes. Distributors and manufacturers usually have a large inventory of envelopes ready for labels or printing and sampling.

envelope anatomy

Seam envelopes are essentially the most standard style in use in the United States (there are also international sizes and styles). Regardless of its size or specific style name, the anatomy (elements of construction) of a seam envelope has the same parts. Seams may also vary slightly in size, placement, curvature, or shape in the various styles, but the basic anatomy always includes the top flap, adhesive or other type of seal, throat, shoulder, seams, side flaps, back or bottom flap, front or face, and back; see Figure 6-7 for diagrams of the anatomy.

From these, variations in design can be created. And remember that the type, size, shape, color, texture, and style of envelope employed should contribute to the design concept and meet the needs and requirements of the design solution.

> **tech tip**
>
> In the United States, sizes are listed in inches with the shortest dimension first. Orient an envelope with the flap at the top when making measurements or reading or ordering a particular size.

general seam styles

Seam envelopes can be divided into two general types: open end and open side; see Figure 6-8 for comps of the standard types of seam envelopes and their anatomy.

Open-end (OE) envelopes have an opening on the *short* dimension. For instance, a 6" × 9" OE envelope would have an opening on the 6" dimension. Open-end envelopes are suited to hand insertion of contents. Larger-size OE envelopes are also called "catalogs." Parts of this envelope include the top flap, adhesive seal, adhesive overlay area, throat, side flaps, and back or bottom flap; refer back to Figure 6-7.

Open-side (OS) envelopes have an opening on the *long* dimension; refer back to Figure 6-8. For instance, a 6" × 9" OE envelope would have an opening on the 9" dimension. According to envelope manufacturers, open-side envelopes are best for automatic (machine) insertion of contents and can be used for hand insertion of contents as well. OS envelopes are also at times called "booklets."

seam styles

There are four types of seam styles. They can be found in a variety of sizes and shapes. Flap shapes will also vary. Flap styles are discussed further along in this chapter. Seam styles are as follows:

- ¤   Center seam
- ¤   Single side
- ¤   Double side
- ¤   Diagonal

Diagonal seam envelopes have seams that run diagonal from the bottom corners upward toward the center of the envelope; see Figure 6-9. In addition, the top flap is a diagonal that runs from the upper corners toward the center.

The diagonal seam is by far the most common construction and commonly employed envelope style. According to envelope manufacturers, diagonal-seam construction works well with mechanical insertion equipment, postal machines, and laser printing. Yet, a professional designer will always test the paper of the envelope and its construction before ordering (and paying) in bulk. Specific shapes and sizes of diagonal-seam envelopes include commercial/business correspondence (some styles with windows), wallet flap, first-class and airmail, Monarch, Baronial, and Lee (also noted further along in this chapter).

Figure 6-7

Flat template (unfolded), assembled envelope, and envelope anatomy diagram.

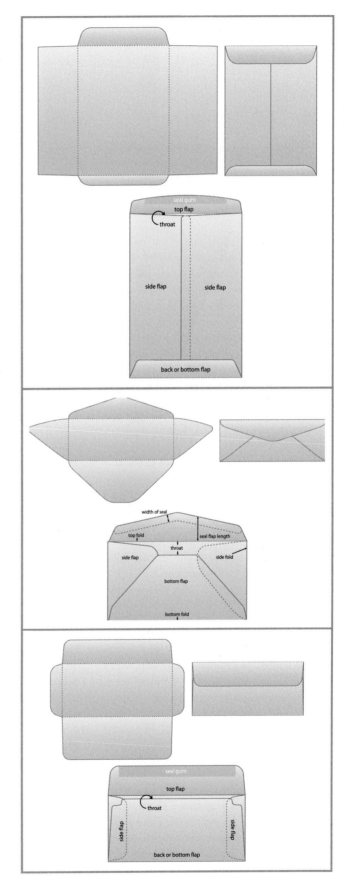

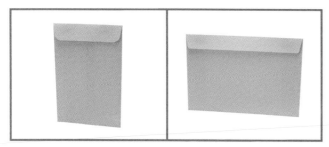

Figure 6-8
Left to right:
Open-end envelope.
Open-side envelope.

Double side seams run nearly parallel to the side folds. These envelopes are also known as square seam, square flap, or side seam. The side seam construction works well for printing on an uninterrupted area both on the front and back of the envelope. Some envelopes of this style can work with laser printing, but at a professional level or for the desktop always test before purchasing a bulk amount. Specific shapes and sizes of double side seam envelope include booklet, A-style announcement (or simply, announcement), squares or square flap, commercial square flap, Monarch square flap, remittance, two-way remittance (a.k.a. hitchhiker), and adhesive flaps (a.k.a. Peel & Seel, Flip-N-Stic, or Simple Seal).

The single side seam is parallel with and near to the edge of the envelope. This style of seam is most often found on open-end envelopes. As with the double side seam, the large unobstructed area works well for interrupted printing. According to envelope manufacturers, although this style accommodates printing well, it is not best suited for automatic insertion machines. Manual insertion is best for this style. Specific shapes and sizes of sideseam envelopes include catalog and jumbo side seam.

Located in the center of the envelope, the center seam style provides added strength for holding heavyweight contents. However, according to envelope manufacturers, this style of seam is usually not best suited for use with automatic insertion or postal machines. In addition, always work with a printer in regard to suitability for laser or other printing techniques because the substrate employed for the construction of the envelope will affect the success of printing.

flap styles

Did you ever take notice of the flap on the back of an envelope? The shape of the flap is governed by convention (there are standards), but within the basic styles industrially produced, design choices still must be made concerning both shape and printing. See Figure 6-10 for flap styles and Figures 6-11 and 6-12 for two examples in professional application.

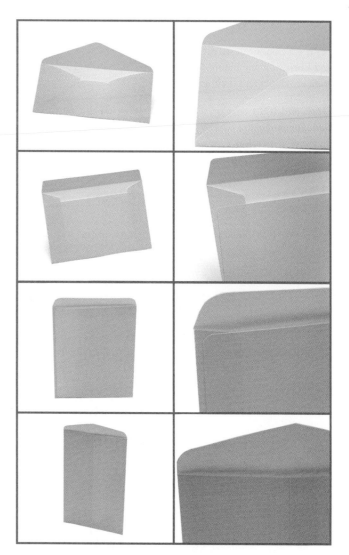

Figure 6-9
Seam styles.
First row, left to right:
Diagonal seam envelope and detail.
Second row, left to right:
Double side seam envelope and detail.
Third row, left to right:
Side seam envelope and detail.
Fourth row, left to right:
Center seam envelope and detail.

variations within seams and flaps

There are specific styles—shapes, sizes, and names—of center seam, side seam, and diagonal seam envelopes,. Standard shapes and corresponding sizes were created based on function. To further awareness of styles mentioned previously, see the following list. Noted are those in most common use with their popular sizes. In addition, see Figure 6-13 for diagrams and flat templates of the common styles.

Figure 6-10
Flap styles.
First row, left to right:
Commercial point.
Mail point.
Second row, left to right:
Wallet.
Point.
Square.

Figure 6-11
Packaging system detail: D. Porthault
Studio: slover [AND] company
Creative Director: Susan Slover
Designer: Jennifer Teixeira
Photographer: Thomas Bricker
Envelope with pointed flap.

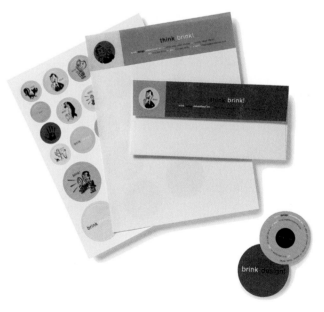

Figure 6-12
Stationery: Brink (letterhead, envelope, and accessories)
Studio name: Design Ranch
Creative Directors: Michelle Sonderegger, Ingred Sidie
Copywriter: Mara Friedman
Photographer: Tim Pott
Paper selection: Newsprint
Printer: Sedalia Democrat Newspaper

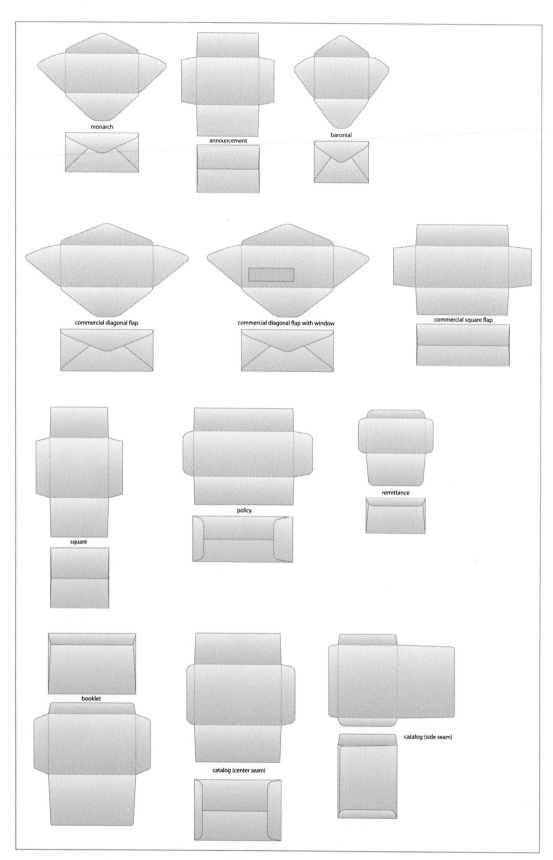

Figure 6-13
Standard envelope styles shown assembled and as flat templates.

Envelope *Styles* (United States) are noted by category, name, style variations, and the popular sizes.

- **Social and commercial/business announcements** (diagonal and side seam). Commonly used for invitations, announcements, and other social and/or business announcements and invitations. Text weight paper is most commonly employed.

  A-style announcements (double side seam, square flap):

A-2:	4⅜" × 5¾"
A-6:	4¾" × 6½"
A-7:	5¼" × 7¼"

- **Baronial/pointed flap** (diagonal seam), also called announcement/pointed flap:

5 Baronial:	4⅛" × 5½"
5 ½ Baronial:	4⅜" × 5¾"
6 Baronial:	4¾" × 6½"
Lee:	5¼" × 7¼"

- **Commercial and official business correspondence (diagonal seam).**

  Commonly produced in a variety of writing and text weight paper grades. Most used for letterheads, letters, invoices, and other business forms and correspondence.

  Diagonal seam, commercial point flap, wallet flap (includes window styles):

6 ¾:	3⅝" × 6½"
10:	4⅛" × 9½"

  Monarch, diagonal seam, commercial point flap:

9:	3⅞" × 8⅞"
10:	4⅛" × 9½"

  Side seam, commercial point flap:

6 3/4 :	3⅝" × 6½"
9:	3⅞" × 8⅞"
10:	4⅛" × 9½"

  Square flap, side seam type (includes window styles):

10:	4⅛" × 9½"

- **Policy** (open end, center seam, square flap).

  Commonly used for business correspondence. Open on the short side of the envelope.

10 Policy:	4⅛" × 9½"

- **Catalog** (open end, single side seam or open end, center seam, mail point flap).

  Commonly made of kraft paper although a variety of paper grades can be found. Meant for holding catalogs and flat sheets of paper or a variety of printed matter.

1 Catalog:	6" × 9"
10 ½ Catalog:	9" × 12"
12 ½ Catalog:	9½" × 12½"
13 Catalog:	10" × 13"

  In this category additional styles include clasp envelopes (No. 55: 6" × 9"), glove (7: 4" × 6⅜"), and scarf (1: 4⁵/₁₆" × 6¾"). First class is notable for its green printed, half-diamond border (10½: 9" × 12"). At times, policy envelopes are categorized under catalog. The styles were noted with their base size.

- **Booklet** (open side, side seam, wallet flap, includes window styles).

  Once commonly in kraft paper, now produced in a variety of colors and paper grades. Good for mail applications such as annual reports (while they are still in print), brochures, sales information, or any variety of printed matter. Also available as a printed first class.

6½ Booklet:	6" × 9"
9½ Booklet:	9" × 12"
10 Booklet:	9½" × 12⅝"
13 Booklet:	10" × 13"

- **Square** (double side seam, square flap)

  Less common and more costly to mail. Used for announcements, invitations, booklets, and promotions.

5:	5" × 5"
7:	7" × 7"
9:	9" × 9"

- **Remittance** (double side seam, wallet flap).

  A collection envelope with a large printing surface. Good for mail order and general remittance applications. A two-way remittance (a.k.a. hitchhiker) has a perforation along the edge of the top flap—used to detach the printed mail and allow for return mail reuse (6½: 3½" × 6¼").

6¼:	3½" × 6"
6¾:	3⅝" × 6½"
9:	3⅞" × 8⅞"

A selection of additional styles to consider (not illustrated but listed with base or popular size):

- **Coin** (center seam): a small size envelope; used for coins and small parts (2¼" × 3½")
- **Jumbo** (open-side wallet flap, open-end square type flap, 12½" × 18½" and 9" × 16", respectively)
- **Expansion**: noticeable for its gussets that allow for expansion; produced with Bristol and kraft papers (4" × 9½" × 2" or largest: 12" × 6" × 2")
- **Interoffice** (catalog or commercial): produced using kraft paper that has been printed with specific office names and route listing; commonly with button and string closure or without a glue seal. Not meant for mailing (10" × 13" and 11: 4½" × 10⅜")
- **Drug and pay** (diagonal seam usually with half-oval flap): tiny open-side envelopes used by florists and pharmacists (1¾" × 2⅞")

considerations in and out

Envelope selection should start with knowledge of the available styles, the overall budget for the project, including accompanying cost of mailing (first class, nonprofit, bulk, etc.), and any other limitations that may be imposed by the budget.

As a reminder: While working within a budget, selecting an envelope design and printing should be considered relative to the design concept.

Also consider the amount of content to be included in the envelope; the size of the envelope that will be needed; the shape, texture/paper, and color of the envelope and its seal; whether an additional response envelope is required; and any printing or special effects.

capacity envelopes and folders

The discussion thus far has focused on flat envelopes. In addition, an envelope can have depth (albeit very shallow before it turns into a box). An envelope or folder that has depth is referred to as a **capacity** envelope or folder. See Figure 6-14 for a diagram (anatomy) of a capacity envelope.

manufacturing and printing

All envelopes are die-cut (see Chapter 10) with as many as possible fit to a single sheet of paper or other substrate. The style and size will determine the quantity that fits. The envelope templates are set up on the sheet of paper either long side (straight) with the grain or set up diagonal to the grain—the latter following the diagonal shape of the side flaps.

Working with paper mills or printers, envelopes are manufactured by what is known as a printer/converter. At the converter the envelopes are cut, folded, glued, and assembled. The envelopes are primarily made from writing and text grades of paper (in conjunction with a specific paper mill) or they are custom made from paper that has been preprinted (see Chapter 10 for printing processes).

seal styles

Not all envelopes need to seal with adhesive placed under the flap, but most do. The official closing seal (such as the wax version used by the historic monarchs of England) could be on the *outside* of the flap. These seals could also be employed for mailing purposes to keep a folded brochure or a booklet from falling open.

There are several ways that a seal can be accomplished. See the professional examples in Figure 6-15 for a blank string and button envelope, Figure 6-16 for a wafer seal, and Figure 6-17 for a standard remoistenable seal. The standards are listed as follows:

- **Remoistenable** seal gum: The glue is activated by moistening the gummed area of the flap.

- **Peel & Seel**: A tape liner covers a resin-based adhesive; when the liner is removed and the flap is pressed down, a bond is created without moisture. To comp this seal, use double-stick tape covered with wax paper strips.

- **Metal clasp**: A double-prong light metal clasp is used for security; this envelope seal cannot be fed through automatic processors.

- **String and button**: A string tie closure is designed for flexibility and repeated use. It cannot be run through automatic processors.

- **Wafer**: An adhesive-backed, small paper or plastic shape (usually a circle) is used as a functional seal for folded paper not in an envelope, or it is used decoratively with an envelope.

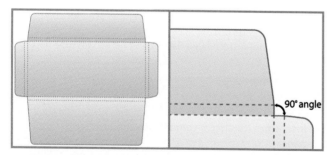

Figure 6-14
Left to right:
Diagram of capacity envelope; note the slightly tapering flap angles as would be found in a flat envelope.
The inside corner angles, however, are set at 90 degrees in order to have them meet flush and create the capacity pocket.

Figure 6-15
String and button style closure for an envelope made with specialty milled paper.

Figure 6-16
Stationery system: Starwhite
Studio: Arketype
Creative Director: Jim Rivett
Art Director: Jim Rivett
Designers: Laura Treichel, DeGaull Vang, Luis Avalos, Robb Mommaerts
Copywriter: Fox River Paper Company
Photographer: 44 inc.
Printer: Independent, Inc.
Client: Fox River Paper Company (now Neenah Paper)
A decorative wafer seal closure was used for this formal
announcement.

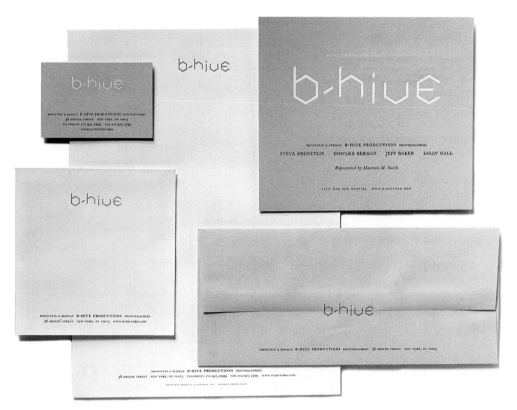

Figure 6-17
Stationery: B-Hive
Studio: And Partners
Creative Director: David Schimmel
Art Director: David Schimmel
Client: B-Hive
Remoistenable seal gum closure.

postal regulations

Although you don't actually mail a comp, postal regulations should be a part of a professional designer's knowledge bank. The US Postal Service provides the bulk of information on their website and in printed form. Or you can simply walk up to the clerk in a post office and ask for help.

Some postal regulations should be considered at the desktop comp level as well (comp it up as actual as possible):

▫ The delivery point must appear on the second line from the bottom, directly above the name of the city.

▫ Addresses should be at least 1" from the left and right edge of the envelope.

▫ The bottom last line of the address should be no more than 2¼" up from the bottom edge of the envelope and at least ⅝" up from the bottom edge of the envelope.

▫ The insert seen through a window envelope should show only the address with at least ¼" between the address and all four of its edges.

▫ The lower right half of the envelope should be free of printing and symbols.

▫ Square or other nonstandard envelopes will cost more (relative to size) than a standard commercial envelope. To avoid the surcharges to current costs on nonstandard sizes, select and/or design envelopes within these limits:

➤ Thickness of letter size cannot be more than ¼".

➤ Envelopes that are ¼" thick or less must be rectangular, at least 5" long, and at least 3½" high.

➤ Envelopes that are smaller than 3½" high and 5" long are prohibited from the mails.

➤ Maximum size is 15" long, 12" high, and ¾" thick.

➤ Pieces must be at least 0.007" thick and weigh not more than 70 pounds and be no more than 108" in combined length and girth.

comp it up! envelopes

For standard envelopes, we suggest that you simply purchase one and use it as a template. To do so, carefully open the seams (use a letter opener or a knife but keep safety in mind), unfold the envelope, and lay it flat. The unfolded envelope can then be placed on the paper and traced or scanned to create a template. Or, place the unfolded envelope directly on the substrate selected or the printed matter for your envelope comp and trace along the edges to mark guides for cutting and folding (beware of the front-to-back relationship). Use bond or text weight paper for envelopes and cover weight paper for capacity envelopes.

For the most thoughtful approach, we encourage the construction of original work for your design solutions, yet you do not necessarily need to make your own *standard* envelope from scratch for every comp. There are many interesting standard envelopes that can be manipulated in other ways (printed upon or hole punched, for instance) to elevate the mundane to the thoughtful and innovative.

You can easily purchase standard envelopes at stores that sell stationery, art supplies, printing paper, and craft supplies. On the web, there are many sources to purchase envelopes; however, you can't touch the actual envelope and will not know if the paper, texture, and color are what you need for your design.

Do not compromise your concept and its design with a standard envelope that is merely an afterthought to the whole project. It is most admirable to have a design concept that is thoughtfully on target in its solution and original in its execution. Consider all aspects of the design.

general procedure

At this point, we assume that your design concept and solution has been reviewed and approved. Several stages of comps are needed in working out a successful solution; therefore, the following guide includes the first through final stages of the crafting process. Read the entire list carefully before you start. Adjust the list relative to the stage at which you are working. See Figure 6-18 for a visual guide to creating a capacity envelope comp.

Figure 6-18

Capacity Envelope Step by Step

First row, left to right:

After printing the envelope template and cutting the outer edges, assembly begins. Kiss cut (score) the fold lines—in this case, paper printed on both sides best receives the score on the mountain fold.

Fold and test-assemble the envelope.

Insert scrap paper to hold the shape of the envelope steady; draw a light line around the bottom flap (onto the side flap) to indicate the area to receive glue. Unfold the bottom flap.

Second row, left to right:

Protective scrap paper remains under the side flaps. With a small flat brush, lightly glue the indicated areas—do not glue beyond the pencil line because the extra glue may seal the pocket of the envelope as well. Glue both side flaps.

Remove the soiled scrap and insert a clean scrap paper. Adhere the bottom flap to the side flaps and smooth to tighten the bond.

Finished comp.

The following are some of the steps needed to create successful and functional standard envelopes:

☐ *Plan*

Yes, do plan—on multiple comps before you reach the final version.

All materials and measurements need to be tested. Select and test the paper or other substrate for its suitability to printing, scoring, and folding.

Plan for folding with the grain of paper. Open-end envelopes should have the grain running from top flap to bottom flap. Open-side envelopes should have the grain running from side flap to side flap.

When an image is used on the envelope, plan the image placement with thought to the folds and seams. Create a digital template to guide the color and image composition while designing on the computer. Organize digital files so that folds and scores are indicated with dotted hairlines in light grey. Or, pencil in the fold lines lightly after printing. You will need some kind of guideline to fold precisely.

Avoid folding through dark colors, dark images, or heavily inked areas as they have a tendency to crack.

Catalog or booklet envelopes usually need to be designed in several pieces unless you have access to a large-format printer.

Double-check measurements and fold lines for accuracy. See Figure 6-19 for a practice diagram/template.

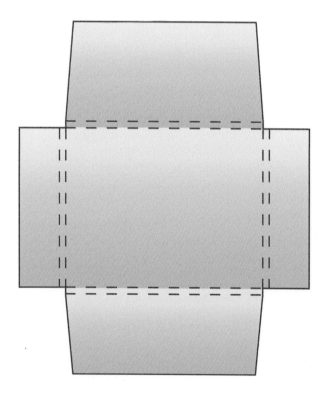

☐ *Prepare*

The work area should be neat, organized, and clean.

Hands should be washed and dry. Keep a damp and dry towel at the work station for convenient and quick spot-cleaning of surfaces and hands.

Tools should be ready.

Materials should be cool and dry and all at the ready.

☐ *Proceed*

Place the envelope template over a printed substrate and trace the outer edges with a light pencil. Or, create the shape of the flat envelope directly on the computer and print it out for cutting. Use a straightedge to cut straight lines. Turn the template and knife to cut curves, but try not to lift the knife until the curve is finished.

Use light sandpaper to smooth slightly rough edges.

Use a metal straightedge to assist in scoring and folding accurately; test and then score the fold line before folding—in the illustration, we use a kiss cut due to the heavy paper and ink.

Assemble and insert scrap paper to hold and protect the shape of the pocket.

Gluing: Indicate in light pencil the edge of the bottom flap (each side) to mark the boundaries of the area to receive glue.

Unfold; work quickly to brush glue (PVA) on the indicated glue areas. Be sure not to place glue beyond the width of the overlay area!

Remove scrap and replace with clean scrap paper.

Assemble the envelope and carefully press to bond the glued flaps. Use a folding tool to burnish the seams of flat envelopes. Capacity envelope flaps can be burnished, but a stiff paperboard insert will be needed to keep the edges from being crushed.

Let dry completely before use.

Figure 6-19
Capacity envelope template.
The depth of a capacity envelope depends on what you plan to enclose.
The width of the capacity envelope should be the measurement of the width of the contents plus 1/16" for a comfortable fit.

stationery gallery

Learning the anatomy and creative standard variation for envelopes is essential for any study of design; see Figures 6-20 through 6-23 for professional examples of envelopes in application.

Once the basic anatomy of an envelope is well understood, it is possible to expand into custom designs. You can be creative with awareness—think outside the envelope. See Figure 6-24 for two templates and see Figures 6-25 and 6-26 for professional examples of custom-designed envelopes.

Figure 6-20
Stationery: Women & Co.
Studio: And Partners, NY
Creative Director: David Schimmel
Art Director and Designer: David Schimmel
Client: Women & Co.
Button and string policy envelope with sticker labels produced with Mohawk Superfine paper.

Figure 6-21
Studio name: Design Ranch
Creative Directors: Michelle Sonderegger, Ingred Sidie
Copywriter: Kerri Conan
Illustrator: Michelle Sonderegger
Paper selection: French
Printer: Hammerpress (letterpress)
Client: Fervere

The soft and earthy color palette and tiny patterns give this bakery shop stationery system homey warmth. The policy envelope is less formal than a diagonal-seam commercial flap, thus communicating the personal nature of the business.

Figure 6-22
Stationery: Bennett Schneider
Studio: Design Ranch
Creative Directors: Michelle Sonderegger, Ingred Sidie
Designers: Tad Carpenter, Rachel Karaca
Illustrator: Tad Carpenter
Paper selection: Mohawk Options
Printer: M-Press
The envelopes in this fancy stationery system were printed with
saturated color and a bold pattern on the inside to give the stationery a
surprise and rich visual appeal.

Figure 6-23
Invitation: American Express
Studio: And Partners, NY
Creative Director: David Schimmel
Art Direction and Design: David Schimmel
Client: American Express
A Baronial-style envelope was employed for this formal invitation.

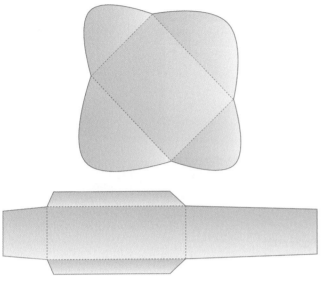

Figure 6-24
Custom envelope templates.
Assemble without adhesives; close with wafer seals.

Figure 6-25
Stationery: Nara Japanese Robata
Studio: Design Ranch
Creative Directors: Michelle Sonderegger, Ingred Sidie
Designer: Tad Carpenter
Illustrator: Tad Carpenter
Printer: M-Press
Client: Nara

Figure 6-26
Invitation: J & J 50th Wedding Anniversary Party
Art Direction: Rose Gonnella and Joseph Konopka
Design and Assembly: Joseph Konopka
Client: Josephine and Joseph Gonnella
A handmade cover stock, square envelope with a faux wax seal
(thermography—see Chapter 10); handmade peel-and-seal strips were
necessary to prepare for mailing and implementation.

about folders

Although there are companies that specialize in manufacturing and keeping a stock of their particular group of common and standard size folder styles, the systematic breakdown of styles is general rather than highly categorized as with envelopes.

Pocket folders are by far the most common style in use, although not all folders need to have two pockets. Regardless of variations in its overall shape, the anatomy of a pocket folder contains the following basic parts: front panel, back panel, pocket flaps, spine (for capacity folders), and usually contains glue tabs. In addition, many folders include slits and tabs on the pocket for separating and holding items such as business cards and other printed matter.

Folders can be a flat, noncapacity (with a single fold at the spine) or a capacity folder (with two folds creating the spine). For professional examples of pocket folders, refer back to Figures 6-1, 6-3, and 6-4, and see Figures 6-27 and 6-28.

Folders need to be made of a heavier weight of paper stock (cover or Bristol is recommended by manufacturers) than do envelopes because they need to hold more and weightier content than an envelope. Alternative substrates such as handmade paper, metal, and wood can expand one's creative repertoire with folders.

The basic anatomy of a folder can be realized through the study of the common styles. See Figure 6-29 for the diagram of an anatomy of standard folders (flat and capacity). For variations in pocket styles, see the diagrams in Figure 6-30.

comp it up! folders

As noted for standard envelopes, we suggest that standard folders can be made using a commercially manufactured example as a template. To do so, carefully open the seams of the folder (use a letter opener or a knife but keep safety in mind), unfold, and lay flat. The unfolded folder can then be scanned and saved digitally for use as a template while designing with the computer. Or, it can be placed on the paper stock or other substrate that you have selected and traced along the edges to mark guides for cutting and folding (beware of the front-to-back relationship).

Once the template is traced, you can then alter the shapes of the corners and pockets to add an effect that contributes to your design concept.

We have included here several folder templates for you to follow to make practice comps; see Figure 6-31. The templates can be enlarged to a standard size such as 9" × 12". See also Figure 6-32 for business card holder styles that could be placed inside a folder.

As we have stated previously and reinforce here, we encourage the construction of original work for your design solutions. In the case of folders, we suggest that each one is made from scratch.

Figure 6-27
Stationery and promotional material: DERMAdoctor
Studio: Design Ranch
Creative Directors: Michelle Sonderegger, Ingred Sidie
Copywriter: Kerri Conan
Illustrator: Tom Patrick
Client: DERMAdoctor
The folder in this stationery and promotional matter has two asymmetrical pockets and a business card slot. The color and illustration add customized distinction.

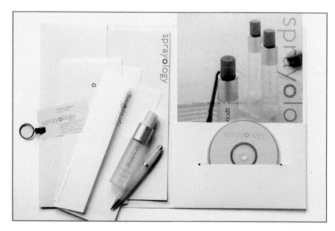

Figure 6-28
Print collateral and stationery: Sprayology
Studio: slover [AND] company
Creative Director: Susan Slover
Designer: Karen Yen
Copywriter: Rosemary Kuropat
Photographer: Greg Delves
Paper selection: 130 pt. Carolina Board/C2S
Printer and bindery: Masterpiece Printers/New York
Client: Sprayology, California
This folder is well configured to hold a CD plus a variety of informational matter.

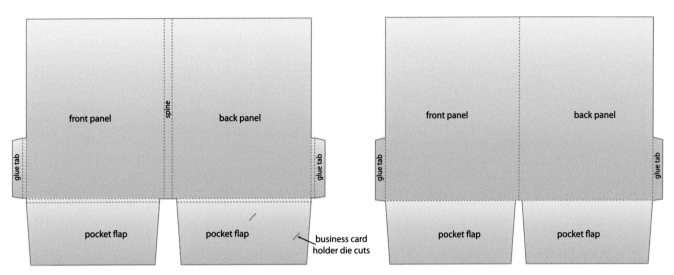

Figure 6-29
Anatomy of the inside of a capacity folder and the anatomy of a flat folder. Both folders have glue tabs on the body of the folder.

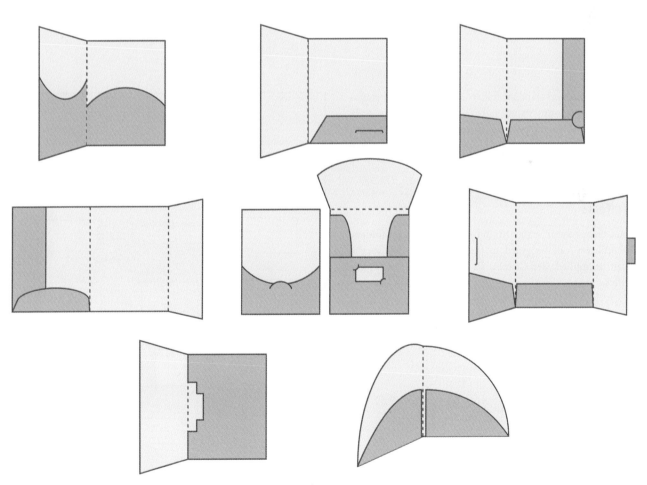

Figure 6-30
Diagrams of folders with various custom pocket configurations.

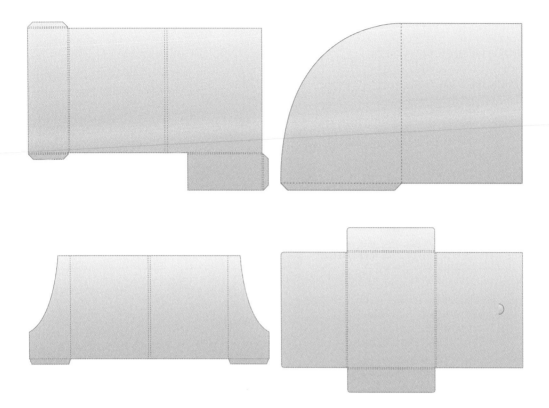

Figure 6-31
Folder templates.

You can easily purchase standard folders at stores that sell stationery, art supplies, printing paper, and craft supplies. On the web, there are many sources to purchase folders. With either source, use the samples as templates and points of departure for your own design solution.

folder effects

To expand creatively on standard, industrially produced folders, text and imagery can be glued to the panels or other special effects can be applied. See Chapter 10 on special effects for the possibilities.

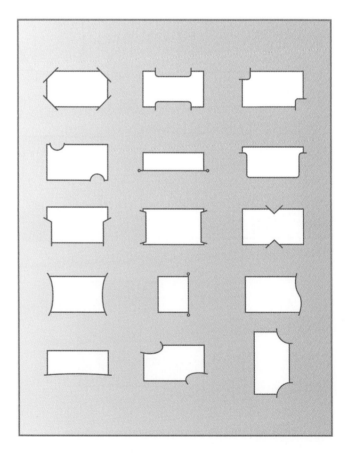

Figure 6-32
Business card holder styles.

tips for procedure

At this point, we assume that your design concept and solution has been reviewed and approved. Several stages of comps are needed in working out a successful solution. Therefore, the following list includes steps for the first through final stages of the construction process. The procedure list is nearly the same as the crafting of envelopes with several adjustments—particularly the use of cover stock. We repeat the working list here as a reminder and for convenience.

The following are some of the steps needed to create successful and functional comps of folders:

◻ *Plan*

Multiple comps are necessary before you reach the final version.

All materials and measurements need to be tested.

Select and test the paper or other substrate for its suitability to printing, scoring, and folding. Cover stock is needed to give the folder its holding strength and durability.

Plan for folding the long dimension of the folder with the grain of paper. The spine should be folded with the grain.

When an image is used on the inside of the folder, plan the image placement with thought to the pockets. Create a digital template to guide your composition while designing on the computer.

When an image wraps around the outside of the folder, plan the image placement with thought to spine width.

Organize digital files so that folds and scores are indicated with dotted hairlines in light grey. Or, pencil in the fold lines lightly after printing. You will need some kind of guideline to fold precisely.

Avoid folding through dark colors, dark images, or heavily inked areas as they have a tendency to crack.

Double-check measurements and fold lines for accuracy.

◻ ***Prepare*** as noted previously for envelopes.

◻ *Proceed*

Cut out the outer edges of the panels, pockets, and tabs.

Use a metal straightedge to assist in scoring and folding accurately.

Test and score fold lines on the substrate before folding. A kiss cut may be necessary if the substrate is thick.

Before using a folding tool, cover the substrate with a scrap of vellum or tracing paper to protect the surface.

Use a folding tool for sharp, tight creases. For a capacity folder, do *not* use a folding tool on the pockets as it might cause you to flatten them in error.

First fold the side flaps toward the front center and then fold the bottom flap up toward the throat.

Unfold flat. Place scrap paper to protect the panels and surface while gluing.

Using liquid white glue (PVA), cover the inside of both glue tabs (whether the pocket tabs or the body tabs).

Remove the soiled scrap paper and replace with clean scrap to protect the panels while adhering the tabs to the panels.

With scrap paper in place, fold the glue tabs over, bring the pocket flap on top of the tabs, and press to bond.

Allow the glue to dry before use.

summary: select, ready, hold

Envelopes do not have to merely contain information or act as a vehicle for mailing. Rather, envelopes can be engaging visual and tactile design elements. A creative envelope or folder can be the entry point of a design solution and can speak volumes about the contents and the identity of the client and their product, service, or other offering.

Any study of design includes the development of awareness of envelope and folder standards and creative options—in order to successfully operate on a functional level and to fulfill creative potential. Work within the boundaries and standards for practical purposes but also play with the boundaries to thoughtfully differentiate the design solution.

exercise knowledge gained

We begin as usual by suggesting that you gather templates for creative inspiration—you can't store every idea variation in your head.

In practice and for comps, use standard formats when possible but think creatively too. The exercises that follow are simple projects that do not require finished design solutions to implement (although the exercise projects could include type and graphics if you choose). The exercises are meant to enhance creativity and guide practice that will hopefully lead to bettering your overall craftsmanship skill.

1. envelope library

Gather a library of commercially made envelopes for your resource binder, noting the source of each individual piece. Nothing is worse than having a sample and not remembering where it came from. These envelopes can act as templates for your own creative design. In addition, you will grow accustomed to the various standard shapes and can design on a practical level and expand to a creative level.

2. specialty envelopes

Using the templates provided in Figure 6-24, create samples of the specialty envelopes. Remember the primary folds are with the grain of the paper. Try using exotic handmade papers (no grain) or printed papers for this project. Once the practice is complete, try designing and constructing a unique shape of your own. See Figures 6-33 and 6-34.

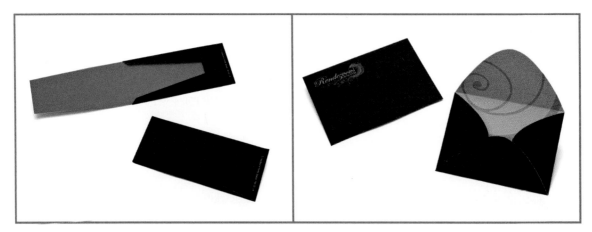

Figure 6-33
Custom envelope designs.
Student designer: Michael Boos

Figure 6-34
Invitation to a black tie dinner.
Student designer: lee Ling Yee

3. folder library

Folders may be a bit bulky to store. However, we recommend that you make note of the various parts of a folder, sketch potential configurations, and keep them in a resource binder for practical reference and inspiration. If you have the storage space, gather and establish a library of industrially produced folders noting the source of each individual piece. The folders can act as templates for your own creative design. In addition, you will grow accustomed to the various standard shapes and configurations and can design on both a practical level and a creative level.

4. folders and envelope partners

Practice creating the folders using the templates provided in Figure 6-31. Once practice is complete, try creating your own folders for use in a stationery system application. See Figure 6-35 for a student example.

5. ideas with alternative substrates

Using substrates other than paper, design an envelope or folder for use in a promotional design application. See Figure 6-36 for a student design using a fuzzy alternative to paper.

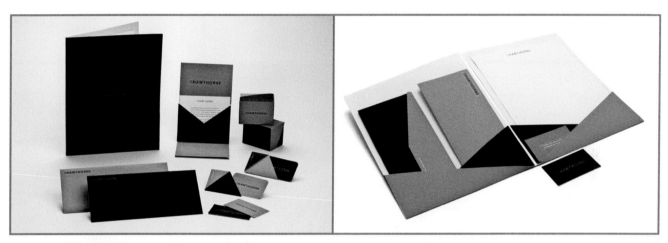

Figure 6-35
Hotel stationery system.
Student designer: Allison Grow

Figure 6-36
Vegetarian restaurant promotion (The Screaming Carrot).
Student designer: Ryan Herbison

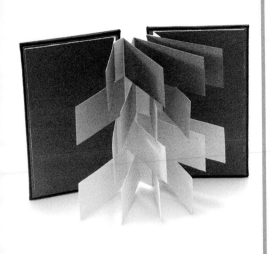

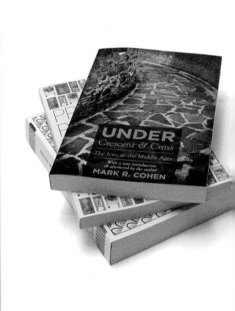

"I am glad of all details, whether they seem to you to be relevant or not."
— *Sir Arthur Conan Doyle, stated by Sherlock Holmes in* The Adventure of the Copper Beeches

First row, left to right:
"Flag" binding practice blank.

Book: Istvan Orosz
Studio: Design Ranch
Creative Directors: Ingred Sidie, Michelle Sonderegger
Illustrator: Istvan Orosz
Paper selection: Various French and vellum
Printer: Hammerpress (all hand letterpress)
Client: Istvan Orosz

Coptic binding using board covers wrapped with
Chiyogami paper.

Second row, left to right:
Booklet: Three Typefaces
Studio: The Design Studio at Kean University
Creative Director: Martin Holloway
Designers: Jason Alejandro and Neil Adelantar
Client: Office of Research and Sponsored Programs,
Kean University

Brochure: Delta Asset Management
Studio: And Partners
Creative Director: David Schimmel
Designer: Amy Sealfon Eng
Photography: Vincent Ricardel (Executive Photography)
Illustrator: Photonica (Stock)
Paper stock: Mohawk Superfine; Canson satin
Printer: Dickson's Inc.
Client: Delta Asset Management

Book: *Under Crescent and Cross*
Studio: Princeton University Press
Creative Director/Designer: Jason Alejandro
Client: Princeton University Press

Third row, left to right:
Comp of a Z-fold binding.

Magazine: POL Oxygen Stretch
Studio: Frost Design
Creative Director: Vince Frost
Design Manager: Laura Richardson
Printer: Everbest Printing, China
Client: POL Oxygen

Comp of a meander fold binding.

seven
binding together

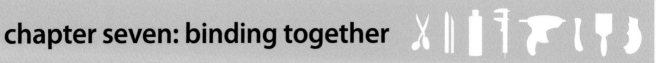

learning objectives

- Gain a basic understanding of industrial binding processes.
- Learn the basic anatomy of books.
- Develop practical knowledge regarding styles and use of bindings.
- Learn to comp a variety of bindings.
- Explore the creative potential of standard and custom bindings.

get it together

How is a book held together? What sort of binding is appropriate for a product catalogue, an elegant brochure for a fine art exhibit, or a view book for a philanthropic organization? Whether the book or a smaller-size booklet is held together with glue, thread, metal wires, clasps, or a combination thereof, the method or style of **binding** is a critical functional factor and could potentially be a conceptual factor as well. See Figure 7-1 for a variety of bindings in professionally designed books and pamphlets.

Numerous types of adhesive, mechanical, and creative custom bindings are possible when a book is manufactured through a company (called a **bindery**) that specializes in machine and hand-binding processes or through a printing company that has bindery capabilities.

Figure 7-1
Industrial bindings.
Bottom to top:
Case bound (bookcloth cover), perfect bound, side stitch (wire), stab, comb, side stitch (Singer sewn), Wire-O, sewn and glued ("deconstructed"/exposed spine), screw and post, saddle stitch (wire), grommet, spiral/coil, grommet and chain, saddle binding with hand-tied string, and miniature meander fold book.

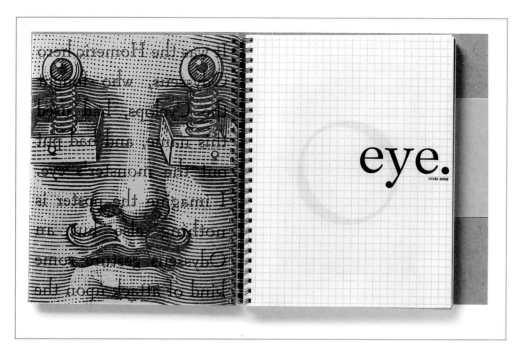

Figure 7-2
Book: Istvan Orosz
Studio: Design Ranch
Creative Directors: Ingred Sidie, Michelle Sonderegger
Illustrator: Istvan Orosz
Paper selection: Various French and vellum
Printer: Hammerpress (all hand letterpress)
Client: Istvan Orosz

Specialty bindings and the use of unusual materials that require handcraftsmanship are usually accomplished through professionals and craftsmen at a bindery. The good news is that most bindings are possible to simulate on the desktop for comps or for personal self-expression (and fun).

creativity starts with practical knowledge

In order to factor bindings into a design, you will need to first become aware of the options and functions of standard binding techniques. Once you establish a foundation of knowledge, you can develop and discover what is creatively possible within the standard techniques and then move beyond when appropriate and if the budget allows.

You will need to become aware of the benefits and limitations of adhesive bindings and the various forms of mechanical binding using staples or wires (the latter seen in Figure 7-2) in regard to both their *use* and *construction*. Employing multiple techniques is also possible. For instance, a collection of hand-sewn pages can be stapled or combined with the use of tapes to make a larger and more stable binding.

Keep in mind that unusual and custom bindings can distinguish a design solution. They should be functional, integral to the design solution, and at times, appropriately decorative, as seen in Figure 7-3.

Figure 7-3
Brochure: Webster House
Studio: Design Ranch
Creative Directors: Ingred Sidie, Michelle Sonderegger
Designer: Rachel Karaca
Copywriter: Kerri Conan
Photographer: Gabe Hopkins
Client: Webster House
For this simply bound booklet, the addition of a hole threaded with ribbon softens the mechanical and industrial character of the stapled binding.

Figure 7-4
Brochure: Lee Jeans
Client: Lee Jeans
Studio: Design Ranch
Creative Directors: Michelle Sonderegger, Ingred Sidie
Copywriter: Jeff Mueller
Photographer: Michael Haber
Printer: M-Press
The designers selected an accordion folded format and transformed it into a book by adding board covers to the first and last panel. This type of binding is sometimes called a "flutter" book.

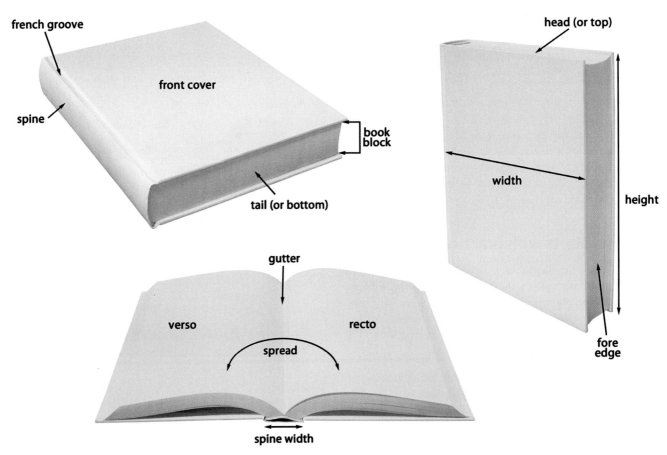

Figure 7-5
Anatomy of a hardcover (casebound) book.
Books

© Tamer Yazici | Dreamstime.com

Accordion fold books and booklets (Figure 7-4) are of a distinctive type that can potentially distinguish a design solution. There are more. Read on.

anatomy of a book

Every journey has a first step, and for bookbinding, that first step is learning basic terminology for the various parts of a book or booklet. Yes, the anatomy of a book may seem fairly simple. And yes, some of the terms are rather self-explanatory, but others might be a bit new. With added knowledge, your visual vocabulary will grow as will your ability to communicate thoughts and ideas into practical and creative realities. See the following list for the terms describing the anatomy of a book and its binding elements. See also Figure 7-5 for a visual guide to the anatomy of a hardcover book and Figure 7-6 for the anatomy of a stapled booklet.

¤ **Spine:** The portion of a book where all the pages are gathered and bound, and where the pages and covers hinge. In the culture of Europe and the United States, spines are traditionally on the left side in books; in Japan and China, the spine is traditionally on the right. But in actual practice, the spine can be on any side of the book.

¤ **Spine width:** The thickness of the spine.

¤ **Head/top:** The upper edge of a book, perpendicular to the spine.

¤ **Tail/bottom:** The lower edge of a book, perpendicular to the spine.

¤ **Width:** The measurement from spine to fore edge.

¤ **Height:** The measurement from the top edge to the bottom edge of the cover.

¤ **Front cover:** The outer facing of a book.

¤ **Back cover:** The reverse of the front cover; the rear facing of a book.

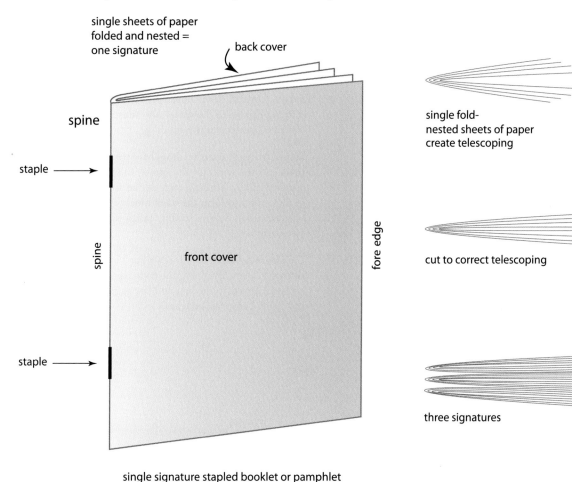

single sheets of paper
folded and nested =
one signature

back cover

spine

staple

spine

front cover

staple

fore edge

single fold-
nested sheets of paper
create telescoping

cut to correct telescoping

three signatures

single signature stapled booklet or pamphlet

Figure 7-6
Anatomy of a booklet and cross-section diagrams showing a single signature, stacked signatures, and the telescoping problem of a single signature of nested pages.

- **Hinge joint:** An indented groove located parallel to the spine edge on the front and back cover of the book; the distance of the hinge joint from the spine is relative to the thickness of the book block.

- **French groove:** The hinge joint of a casebound book. The French groove is not indented into the cover, but rather it is the space between the border area and the cover board.

- **Border area:** The space between the spine and the hinge joint.

- **Book block:** The collection and thickness of pages of a book.

- **Fore edge:** The outer facing of the text block; the edge opposite the spine.

- **Gutter:** Within the text block, the space where two pages meet at the binding.

- **Spread:** Two adjacent or facing pages (at times designed to be seen as a whole).

- **Endpapers:** A sheet (spread) of paper on the inside facing of the front and back covers.

- **Leaf/folio:** A complete page (front and back):

  - **Recto:** The left side of a leaf in an open book.

  - **Verso:** The right side of a leaf in an open book.

- **Signature:** One section of pages folded down (in half) into a nested group. A signature or signatures can be stapled, glued, sewn, or otherwise bound together; a book can have a single signature or multiple signatures.

- **French fold:** A single page that has been folded in half before inserting into the spine with the fold exposed along the fore edge.

bound by duty

Before you can begin to explore the creative potential, you need to understand something of how books are bound and the many types of bindery therein.

When designing, consider the budget, and consider what kind of binding is appropriate for a particular design solution. The most commonly found commercial bindings are listed as follows (and most are noted in Figure 7-7) with brief practical information included. We have used the most frequently employed terms in regard to binding; however, due to variations in vocabulary that occur between binderies, we suggest a bit of research on the web to cross-reference the information. We suggest research into industrial and fine bookbinding companies such as L.B. Bookbindery LLC and Muscle Bound Bindery. Or, research fine bookbinders/craftsmen such as Cardoza-James and Brewer-Cantelmo. There are many binderies. Standard bindings are listed below in the two following categories: adhesive and mechanical.

Adhesive bindings

- **Perfect** binding is an all-purpose, fairly inexpensive, and therefore ubiquitous adhesive binding. It is not so perfect according to some professional bookbinders due to its tendency to crack at the spine. In addition, a perfect binding does not allow the book or booklet to lie flat when open. When the budget can accommodate, several higher-quality alternatives are available such as one of the following.

- **Layflat binding** uses a detached spine that allows books to lay flatter than perfect binding.

- **Euro binding** uses a cloth lining that allows the cover to lay completely flat.

- **PUR binding** is a highly durable polyurethane adhesive that is flexible and will lay virtually flat.

- **Notch binding (a.k.a burst)** incorporates cutting parallel grooves into the spine perpendicular to the binding edge to allow the adhesive glue to seep into the spine and strengthen the bond. This method negates the need for grind-off at the spine. Grind-off is noted in the sidebar (further along in this chapter).

- **Tape** bindings employ a strong (heat-activated) adhesive tape.

- **Singer (thread) sewn** bindings have a column of stitches running parallel to the spine. An industrial sewing machine is used to implement this binding.

- **Smyth (thread) sewn** bindings have parallel rows of stitches that cross the width of the spine. The threads are sewn in a linked chain, binding each of the individual signatures to each other to form the book block. A specialty machine is needed for Smyth sewing (a.k.a signature sewing or section sewing).

- **Case binding** uses a Smyth-sewn book block that is attached to board covers. By gluing the endpapers of the inside front and back covers to the first and last page of the book block, the casing boards are attached.

Figure 7-7 (right)
Types of binding.
First row, left to right:
Casebound, Perfect, Saddle stitch (stapled).
Second row, left to right:
Wire-O, Comb, Spiral.
Third row, left to right:
Grommet, Screw and post, Stab (also includes glue).
Fourth row, left to right:
Tape, Rubber band, Side stitch (stapled).

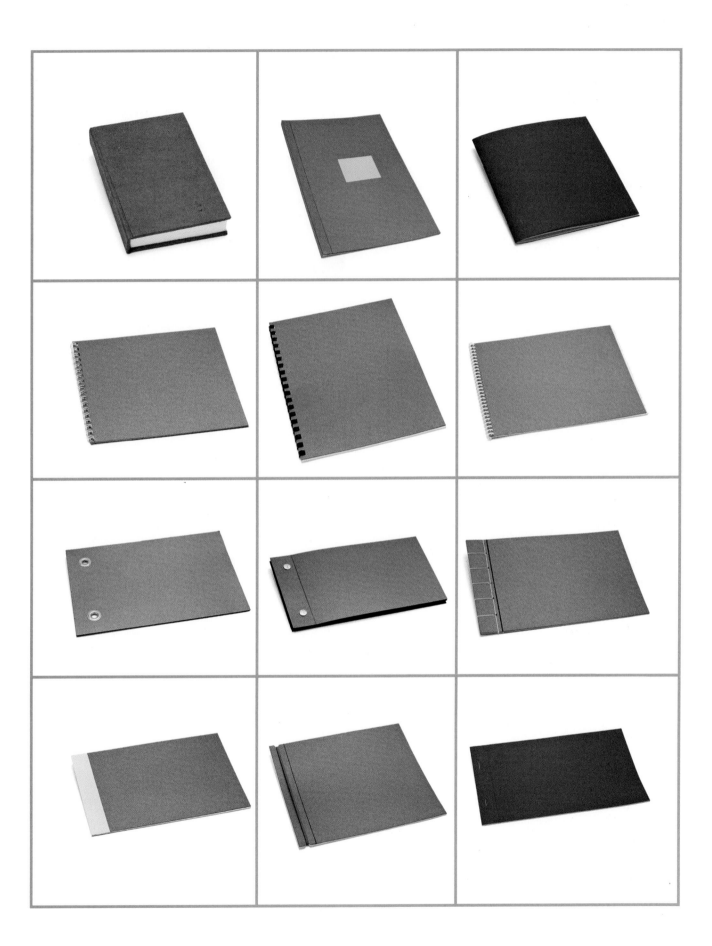

Mechanical bindings

Bindings in this category use metal staples, wire, screws, rivets, grommets, or plastic clasps and coils.

- ▢ **Saddle-stitch binding** has one signature clamped with wire (staples) along the spine.

- ▢ **Side-stitch** binding uses wire (staples) applied to the front of the book in the area known as the border area (between the hinge joint and the edge of the spine). Alternatives to staples include rivets, grommets, screw and posts, rubber bands, or thread and glue (the latter being an exception to this category in that it uses an adhesive along with a mechanical part).

- ▢ **Wire-O** or **double-loop Wire-O** uses metal wire looped through prepunched holes, which are then clamped to tighten (into the shape of the letter O). The advantage of a Wire-O binding is that it lies completely flat. The disadvantage perhaps is the visibility of the wire along the spine and in the gutter of the booklet.

- ▢ **Spiral** wire, spiral coil, or simply "spiral" binding uses a wire or plastic spiral coil threaded through prepunched holes. This binding also allows for the book to lie flat. As with Wire-O, the coil is visible along the spine and in the gutter.

- ▢ **Velo** binding uses plastic straps, clamped into prepunched holes along the border area. This is an inexpensive method employed for reports and other simple word-processed documents.

- ▢ **Plastic comb** binding uses a plastic clasp hooked onto prepunched holes and clamped. This method is most inexpensive, but it looks it (cheap). It is used for quick turnaround (most copy centers or office service stores such as Staples will have a comb-binding machine). It lies flat but not comfortably. Like Velo, it is employed for reports and other word-processed documents.

bound for glory (but first get practical)

We wish we could cover all the world bindings for you, but binding is a wonderfully huge area of exploration that makes for its own book. The *foundation* of binding is explored in this text with the hope that it will provide basic skills and inspire further development, exploration, and growth.

bind 'em up!

Most of the standard machine-made and professionally handmade bindings can be simulated (comped) on the desktop to look nearly commercially made. Those that can be easily simulated are discussed further along in the chapter.

The many considerations in the industry may also be found on the studio desktop during the comprehensive mock-up process and need to be addressed in order to make a successful comp.

Figure 7-8
Enlarged, close-up view of the foot and fore edge of the book block that has been inked (also known as *staining*). To comp this effect, use a watercolor marker. Test the paper and marker to see whether the marker ink bleeds (spreads randomly into the book block). We recommend coated papers—this type may bleed less than uncoated papers. If the ink is quickly applied, the bleeding is reduced.

Please review Chapters 2 (paper) and 3 (basic craftsmanship techniques) and make certain the knowledge and skills gained are applied to practice bindings.

inside adhesive bindings

Industrially and on the desktop, adhesive bindings are a versatile and practical binding method for a wide variety of books and booklets. With adhesive binding methods, there is the potential to include foldouts, half-pages, hard (board) covers, special printing and postprinting effects (see Chapter 9), a back cover pocket, a slip jacket or wrapper, an inked fore edge, and much more—when appropriate and if the budget allows. See Figure 7-8 for a close-up view of a book with an inked (a.k.a. stained) edge.

With proper planning, basic adhesive binding is also one of the more economical binding methods available. All is relative regarding professional design, printing, and bindery. Go ahead and add the "triple summersault" roll fold and see what happens to the cost. See Figure 7-9 for a professional example of perfect binding.

perfect construction and beyond

Perfect binding relies on glue to keep individual sheets (or leaves) of paper together. During manufacture of a perfect bind, the signatures are stacked and **jogged** (vibrated to help ensure that all of the sheets are perfectly aligned and ready for further processing) to meet flush at the spine. The spine width is then slightly ground down (the process is known as **grind-off**) to make the spine flat and to create a pitted texture that will assist in absorbing the glue. A flexible adhesive, whether cool or heated (thermal glue is more common on mechanical perfect bindings), is applied to the spine, and then the cover is attached. Finally, the book is trimmed on the remaining three sides to make each edge perfectly smooth and flush.

In the professional field, *always* discuss bindery issues and processes with the printer or bindery representative to determine the feasibility relative to cost and to ensure there are no errors or surprises in the final product. For instance, the thickness of a book is an issue in regard to the type of binding that can be performed. Perfect-bound books have an approximate range of spine widths, from ⅛" to 1¾" thick. The number of minimum and maximum pages varies *greatly* depending on the thickness and finish of paper. Answer? Solution? Have the printer/bindery make a blank comp of the bound book with the paper stock selected for the design solution.

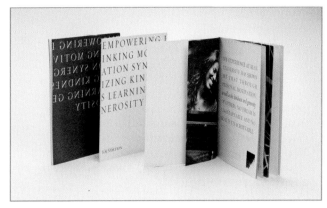

Figure 7-9
Annual report: The Kean Foundation
Studio: Cinquino & Co.
Creative Director: Ania Murray
Art Director and Designer: Erin Smith
Client: The Kean Foundation
The same perfect-bound book photographed from left to right: showing fore edge, spine, and open to a spread with a half-page.

why grind?

The construction of industrially bound books and booklets begins with a single sheet of printing paper. The pages of a book are not printed one at a time per page, but rather they are printed on a single sheet of paper as a *group* of pages. The configuration of type and images (pages) on the printing paper is called **page imposition** (see Chapter 9 for more information on printing). For speed and economy, groups of pages are configured to get as many pages printed as possible on a single sheet. For speed, economy, *and* physical fabrication, the printed sheet of pages is then folded down and nested into a unit called a signature (refer back to Figure 7-6 for a diagram of a nested group of folded paper).

A signature has a slightly rounded spine edge and consists of an even number of pages (commonly the count is 8, 16, or 32 pages). The number of pages that can be folded comfortably into a single signature is determined relative to the size and weight of the paper in use. If a book has more than 16 pages of text weight paper, multiple signatures are used rather than one huge signature so that the single signature is fairly flush at the fore edge of the book. Too many pages in a single signature may cause severe **telescoping** (a.k.a. **page creep**)—a condition where the inner pages of the signature are much longer than those folded on top of each other. Although the top, bottom, and fore edge of the book are eventually trimmed flush after binding, it is best to be aware of telescoping so that the amount of trimming is minimal.

For a book with multiple signatures, the process of grinding off at the spine of the book is necessary to create a rough surface that will best absorb the binding glue and also to slightly flatten the rounded edges of the stacked signatures. Instead of grinding off, the notch binding method uses several parallel grooves cut at a perpendicular angle to the spine to assist with adhesion.

To get the best visual of the stacked and glued signatures, look at either the top or bottom of the book where the spine meets the book block. With a thinner (small number of pages) book, the spines of the signatures may have been ground off completely. Usually, it is possible to see the multiple signatures of a larger book.

Enlarged, close-up view of the cross-section of multiple signatures in a perfect-bound book. The glue is dark in color (the pages are white). Notice the ragged edge created by the grind-off. Perfect-bound books are not archival and have a tendency to crack at the spine when the glue becomes aged and brittle.

Page imposition, signature configurations, and so on are the business of the printer and binder. Yet, the knowledge thereof is important practical information for a designer. However, as you will see further along in this section, folding down to signatures for glued binding is not necessary for creating comps on the desktop.

On the desktop also test thickness. If perfect is the binding choice, we recommend the booklet should be at least 3/16"; any smaller and the book is likely to warp from too much glue.

A simulated perfect bind is not implemented exactly as it would be at a commercial bindery. There is no need to make signatures or grind off, yet you will need to plan for a hinge joint and possibly trim the top, fore edge, and bottom of the book.

Although perfect-bound books can be simulated, the layflat binding, Euro binding, PUR binding, and notch binding require a specialty glue and/or equipment and are simply not necessary (or possible) to implement on the desktop.

comp it up! (almost perfect)

Perfect-bound books are easy and quick to comp. In fact, there are desktop, hot glue machines available for this purpose (see perfect-binding machines at online sources such as BindingStuff, General Graphic, or MyBinding). For handmade desktop comps, this simple bind can become a mess if you're not careful and neat with the use of glue. Too much adhesive can easily creep in between pages and glue them to each other instead of the spine. We recommend light and thin coats of white or paste glue to be used with care and awareness.

general procedure for bookbinding

Practice begins with a blank comp whether on the desktop or at a bindery. A blank comp is recommended so that the type and image design of the pages can be planned and composed in an actual three-dimensional format with successes and problems noted. It is difficult to anticipate problems in page layout; therefore, the blank book can assist in the process of layout and help to avoid waste (of time and paper) in the long run. All materials, measurements, and the design of information (relative to how and where it falls in the sequence of pages or **pagination**) need to be tested.

Don't expect to anticipate all problems and results simply by reading. Fabricating a blank comp is a necessary start for learning and understanding what is involved in a binding technique. The following list is a general outline for practice binding. Use it for perfect-bound simulations and adapt the guide for mechanical bindings and beyond.

▫ *Plan*

As you plan the size and thickness of the book block (blank or with a design), remember that a perfect-bound book comp will not lay flat. If forced flat, the spine will crack and the pages will loosen and fall out of the text block or fall away from the cover. Note that 1/4" to 1" of the spine side of a page will be "lost" or "swallowed" into the gutter of the book. The thicker the book block, the greater the loss of image area to the gutter, especially toward the center of the book. A similar situation holds true for a side-stitch or side-bound book. Wire-O and coil bindings must accommodate punched holes in the gutter that extend approximately 1/2" to 1" into the page.

An upright or landscape orientation is recommended for a perfect-bound book and for most bindings due to the least amount of adjustments for the gutter and most economical use of paper. An oblong format is recommended for side-stitch booklets because this format compensates for the significant amount of area lost to the binding. Narrow formats and square formats can also be employed; however, just be aware of the image area lost to the gutter and layflat capabilities.

Select and test the paper. The cover should be of cover weight; the book block can be writing or text weight. Plan for the spine to be parallel with the grain of the paper.

Work *with* the paper grain and *not against* it. In order for the book to lie flat, the grain of the paper (both for the cover and interior pages) must run from the head/top to the foot/bottom of the book.

A perfect-bound desktop comp should be *at least* 10 pages and probably *not more than* 16 pages. Since comps are simulations, we don't anticipate your books to have much more than 20 pages.

The spine of a perfect-bound book should be about 3/8" to 1/2" thick because the glue needs to have enough of a platform for receiving the glue. In addition, the book block should be trimmed flush and flat at the spine. The top, fore edge, and bottom can be trimmed at this point as well, or wait until the book is glued; the glue must be completely dry before trimming.

The cover will have a spine equal to the thickness of the book block. The cover of the book should be scored and folded, ready to fit over the book block. Also plan and score the hinge joint. Score from the spine edge into the book at approximately the same thickness as the spine. For instance, if the spine thickness is 1/4", score the pages and the cover 1/4" from the edge of the spine (parallel to the spine).

Figure 7-10
Perfect Step by Step
First row, left to right:
All pages are cut to size and the cover is cut to size, folded, and scored at the hinge joint. For each page of the book block, measure a ¼" to ½" border from the spine edge; this border will receive the glue.

Align the second page over the first glued page.

Burnish the glued pages; continue to glue and apply each page until all are finished in turn.

Second row, left to right:
Score the hinge joint on the front and back of the cover before gluing to the book block; the hinge should be the same width from the spine edge as the glued pages. Apply glue to the spine and the border on the front and back of the book block. Attach the cover (this one has a simulated die cut).

Finished comp; place a weight on the entire book and let the glue dry.

◻ *Get organized*
The blank book block should be jogged, cut, clamped, and set at the ready. Also, ready the cover.

The work areas (one for glue and one for construction) should be neat, organized, and clean with all tools at the ready (brushes, board chips, spatula, folding tool, craft knife, pencil, stapler, other mechanical parts, etc.).

Place PVA glue or paste glue on a flat, glass plate adjacent to the gluing surface. Ready a glue brush or board chips for spreading the glue.

Have a stack of blank newsprint or other clean scrap ready on the gluing surface for quick cleanup and disposal of glue spillover. Have a damp rag and dry cloth for keeping hands clean.

◻ *Proceed*
Place the book block on the gluing surface, but let the spine slightly overhang the table. Hold firmly. Brush a thin layer of glue along the spine. Let dry. Repeat.

For the cover, brush a thin layer of glue onto the spine of the book block as well as the spine border on the front and back. Adhere to the book block. Allow the glue to dry completely.

Alternatively, the spine border of *each page* can be glued together with a thin amount of glue. Be sure to clean the gluing surface in between each application of glue. See Figure 7-10 for a brief visual guide for simulating an adhesive (perfect) binding.

After initial practice of the blank perfect-bind comp, you may have discovered some problems. Perhaps the pages are not holding together (the book may be too thick) or perhaps the glue is seeping into the book block (the paper may be too thin). We have some alternative methods and possible solutions.

Figure 7-11

A student design solution was used as the model for this practice. The recommended weight of paper is no more than 20# text but it does work with heavier paper. Testing is necessary.

Left to right:
After folding the pages in half, glue the pages back to back using stick glue or a glue spreader (pictured). Be aware that liquid glue may cause warping. Cover the page and burnish to adhere.

Detail of the bottom of the finished comp with dust jacket covering.

First alternative: *Staple* the book block pages together along the joint area with a heavy-duty *cinch* stapler (the staples are flat and will lay flat). Brush one light layer of glue on the spine. Finally, glue on the cover as noted previously. The staples should be hidden and the binding will look almost the same as a perfect bind—remember this is a comp, not an actual perfect binding.

Second alternative: With this method (known as Professor Martin Hollway's back-to-back technique) you do not have to worry about crossover problems. However, the book will be much thicker than a book created using the methods previously described because the pages will be double thickness. Refer to Figure 7-11 for a brief guide to the process. Also, refer ahead to Figure 7-60 for a student example in a finished form.

Figure 7-12
Limited edition book: John Hennessy Poems
Studio: Kean University
Art Director and Designer: Erin Smith
Client: The Kean Review (speculative project)
A tape binding can be both economical and aesthetically attractive.

ultimate alternative

The online (on-demand) publishing companies produce actual perfect-bound books one at a time. In addition, many other types of binding can be selected from online sources. Upload your files, pay a small fee for setup and one book (or more), and the work is done for you—not a comp, an actual perfect-bound book.

Does the "one-off" solution seem too good to be true? There are limitations and problems with any image crossover, time restraints, and quality relative to cost. Research and testing is necessary when dealing with an on-demand publisher, such as Lulu, Scribble Press Gallery Books, or Blurb.

Figure 7-13
Tape Bindings Step by Step
First row, left to right:
Measure the book thickness with a caliper to determine the width of the spine; use the spine measurement to determine the width of the tape that is needed.

Draw a line to be used for aligning the tape; the distance from the spine to the edge of the tape should be at least 3/4″ (better 1″) on both front and back; the tape should be wide enough to accommodate the spine.

Apply a thin bead of glue to the spine to assist with adhesion (not pictured). Align and apply the tape; wrap the tape around the spine to the back cover. Press to implement the bond.

Second row, left to right:
Trim the excess at the ends with a sharp craft knife.

Burnish the spine to tighten the bond and ensure that all the pages adhere to the spine.

Finished comp.

tape binding

Similar in application to perfect binding are tape bindings. Individual signatures are stacked and jogged for alignment, the spine is ground flat, and glue is applied to the spine. A flexible strip, usually cloth or cloth-like, is then applied over the spine (with a small overhang onto the covers) and pressed into place. The book is trimmed on the remaining three sides. There is a limit to the thickness of the book block relative to tape binding; consultation with the service provider is necessary to determine the limit. On the desktop, most book block comps are thin enough to allow for tape binding; however, avoid using tape exclusively on books more than ⅜″ of spine width.

On a desktop comp, tape can be applied for added strength and perhaps a visual element to glued bindings. We do not trust the strength of tape alone—add glue to the spine and/or the pages as well.

For the comp, we recommend bookbinders linen tape or a combination of bookbinders tape and another tape (the latter perhaps for design purposes). The tape should extend 1″ beyond the spine edge on both the front and back covers. The cover is then glued over the tape, or the tape is incorporated as a design element. See Figure 7-12 for a professional example and Figure 7-13 for a visual guide to applying a tape to the spine.

Figure 7-14
Promotional booklet: Puppet Hands
Studio: Square Melon, Westfield, NJ
Creative Directors: Robert Nicol and Deborah Rivera
Art Director: Robert Nicol
Designer: Robert Nicol
Illustrator: Robert Nicol
Copywriter: Robert Nicol
Paper Selection: Mohawk Smooth
Printer: Print Pelican
Saddle stitch with staples; the spine is shown at the top, and the inside front cover is shown at the bottom.

saddle stitching

Often found on brochures, magazines, comic books, catalogues, and a variety of promotional and informational booklets, a saddle stitch utilizes a wire (staple) to bind pages together. Pages are stacked, jogged, and then folded (at the spine) into a single signature. The staple or "stitch" is then applied along the spine fold. The number of staples can vary depending on the size (height) and thickness of the book block. After stapling, the remaining three sides are then trimmed. See Figure 7-14 for a professional example of a saddle-stitch booklet.

Saddle stitching is very simple and can be easily achieved by machine or hand. Special staplers with extra-deep capacities (and a page-depth measurement gauge) can be used on the small scale to saddle stitch by hand. Saddle-stitched books can vary in strength depending on the paper stock and the amount/type of staples used. Alternatively, and for design purposes, strong thread or string can be used instead of a metal staple, giving a bit more of a literal meaning to the "stitch" in saddle stitch.

saddle up!

Saddle-stitch binding is nearly a cinch. The most difficult part of binding with saddle stitch is making sure the staples align exactly with the spine fold. Staples that are applied and result in a misalignment on the front or back cover of a book are not acceptable.

A saddle-stitch book will have a single signature book block. Test the stapler on a stack of scrap paper the same weight (of paper) and thickness of the book block. We recommend a long-handle, standard stapler for this purpose. A cinch stapler will crush the spine. See Figure 7-15 for a brief visual guide to the process. There are

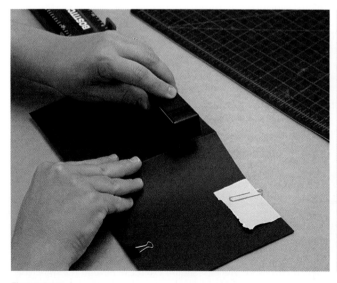

Figure 7-15
Saddle stitch sample.
Left to right:
Secure the book block with clasps or clips; align the spine of the book to the stapler and execute.
Finished comp.

actual desktop "saddle" staplers, but they are small and significantly limited in use. Therefore, the long-handle stapler is preferable for its wider range of coverage.

creative variations

A creative variation on a saddle binding would be to cut tiny holes in the spine using a circle punch or a bookbinder's awl (tool selected is relative to the thickness of the paper) and then thread a string through the holes to bind the signature. Refer back to Figure 7-1 for a professional example and Figure 7-16 for a diagram to implement binding with string along the spine.

The spine could also be completely sewn in a straight stitch. To accomplish the latter, you will need a sewing machine fitted with a presser foot and some sewing skill. Trim the booklet to size while closed. Open the booklet flat and run it through the sewing machine, making a straight stitch along the spine.

A double spine is also possible using saddle and/or perfect binding. In bookbinding terminology, a double spine (one at left, one at right) is called **dos-à-dos**.

Further creative direction could include the use of cover weight paper for the panel that forms the cover; use a variety of papers within the book block such as vellum, writing, or text weight textured paper. The center spread of a saddle stitch can be a gate

fold, a single foldout left or right, or a roll fold. But do test to discover if the stapler in use can accommodate the paper stock and thickness of the book block. When using a foldout within a booklet, remove the foldout spread, trim the fore edge to correct telescoping, and reinsert the foldout before stapling.

N.B. When a creative binding variation is selected, be sure that it contributes to the design concept rather than being merely decorative.

side stitch

Another method using staples or "sewn" stitches is the side-stitch binding. As opposed to being stapled or sewn along the spine as in the previous saddle method, side-stitch bindings are performed on the face (or cover) of the book along the border area. See Figures 7-17 and 7-18 for professional examples of a side-stitch Singer-sewn binding and a side-stitch stapled binding.

comp it on the side

For a desktop side-stitch comp, the printed pages should be cut, stacked, jogged (trimmed again if necessary), and clamped before implementing the binding. Also, use a cinch stapler for a desktop comp because cinch staples lie flat.

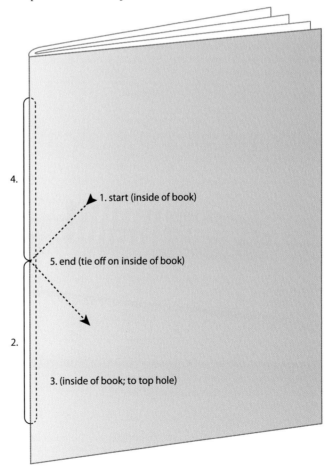

Figure 7-16
Diagram for sewing a saddle with thread (known as a pamphlet stitch).

Figure 7-17
Book: Crown Vantage
Studio: HvA Design
Creative Director: Henk Van Assen
Client: Crown Vantage
The binding pictured is known as side-stitch sewn. The color of the
thread can be contrasted with the cover paper to emphasize the binding.
The leaf shape on the cover is a cutout (a special postprinting process
noted in Chapter 10).

Figure 7-18
Promotional catalogue: Yannus Furzon Saberworks Summer MMIX Catalogue
Creative Director: Christopher J. Navetta
Designers: Christopher J. Navetta and Gregg Iveson
Client: Yannus Furzon Saberworks
A side-stapled booklet.
The staples are left exposed because they complement the industrial
nature of the subject matter pictured.

Figure 7-19
Side-Stitch Stapling Step by Step
First row, left to right:
The book block is ready; clamp and score the hinge joint.

Measure the position of the staples.

Position the cinch stapler and implement.

Second row, left to right:
Cover the stapled area by gluing on a contrasting back cover, spine, and joint area cover.

The cover over the joint area hides the staples.

Finished comp without cover over the staples and with cover over the staples.

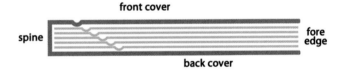

Figure 7-20
The diagram shows a cross-section of graduated scoring of pages of the book block. Each page is scored approximately ½₂" or one page thickness (further toward the fore edge) than the previous score. Proportions are exaggerated to more clearly illustrate the score lines.

We recommend an oblong format for side-bound booklets since so much of the image area is lost in the gutter with this method. In addition, a hinge joint is usually necessary on the cover. When heavier weight paper is used for the book block, consider scoring each page as well. Score on the first page below the hinge joint, and then each consecutive page will be scored in graduation—that is, an additional page thickness further away from the previous score line. See Figure 7-19 for a visual guide to stapling the border area of a book. See also the diagram in Figure 7-20 for a cross-section illustration of graduated scoring of pages. Scoring the individual pages of a comp assists with ease of opening and turning the pages of the booklet.

creative thinking

There are many creative ways of approaching a side-stitch bound booklet. A side-stitch binding can be performed with various size staples or flat metal straps or sewn with thread, cord, or ribbon.

If you don't like the appearance of the staples, a wraparound cover can be applied to hide the staples. Or the staples can be left exposed for budgetary or aesthetic purposes.

As in the industry, a dust jacket can be added to hide the wires. Alternatively, the staples can be hidden by a whole or partial cover—apply glue to the border area to attach a prefolded cover.

Special printing or nonprinting effects can be applied to the cover (see Chapter 10), staples can be painted (with paint formulated for metal), or decorative staples can be applied. Refer back to Chapter 1 on tools for a reference to various staplers. In addition, a variety of paper can be used in the book block, and folded formats can be added.

Side-stitch bindings (and other mechanical bindings) on the desktop also lend well to the use of French fold pages; see Figure 7-21 for a professional example of French fold pages.

To construct French fold pages, first fold the paper in half and then stack with the fold at the fore edge. Since this method essentially doubles the amount of paper in the book block, be sure to have good reason for its use. Doubling the pages gives them both added strength and elegance. The pages can be printed on both sides, for instance with the inner side of the fold having a solid color or "hidden" images.

We also encourage the use of a board cover or a board case to replace the standard cover weight paper. For a simple hard cover, glue a board (front and back) to the first right facing page of the book block from the hinge joint to the fore edge (do not cover the staples).

Covering the entire book in a case (hard covers and spine) is discussed further along in the chapter.

variations on the side

Beyond staples, variations on side bindings can involve the use of metal or plastic strips, rubber bands, or thread stitches. See Figures 7-22 through 7-24 for professional examples of variations for side-bound booklets.

comp the variations

To simulate industrial Singer-sewn binding, you will need a sewing machine fitted with a presser foot or a leather foot—an element for sewing thick fabrics (or in this case, paper). If you have a sewing machine and some skill, do consider using it for binding. Be aware, however, that sewing will likely be most successful with thin, lightweight paper. If you don't have a machine, hand sewing is an option. Protect your fingers; use a thimble.

For a side-bound book that uses a rubber band binding, we have included in Figure 7-25 images of the comp and a model diagram (both for a single page of the comp and the cover of the booklet). For student design solutions, a rubber band binding is both forgiving and flexible because it can be disassembled and reassembled with ease. Also, this binding easily lends itself to French fold pages.

Figure 7-21
Book: Step Rd
Studio: Voice
Creative Director: Scott Carslake
Designer: Scott Carslake
Paper selection: PhoeniXmotion
Printer: Finsbury Green Printing
Bindery: Finsbury Green Printing
Client: Step Rd Wines
French folding pages.

Figure 7-22
Gift books: Natura Naturata
Studio: slover [AND] company
Creative Director: Susan Slover
Designers: Susanna Koh, Karen Yen, and David Allegra
Copywriter: Rosemary Kuropat
Photographer: Raeanne Giovanni
Client: Chronicle Books GiftWorks Division, San Francisco, CA
Metal strips that penetrate the entire book block and cover are folded down and secured to create this functional and unusual variation on a side binding.

stab binding

The industrial binding previously shown in Figure 7-23 is actually a simulation of a historic method (originating in Asia) of hand binding. The side-stitch sewn binding is known as stab binding. The industrial method, however, is essentially a variation on perfect-bound books. After gluing, the perfect book is punched with holes and sent through a machine that creates the stitches. The stitches are decorative and do not actually bind the book. The glue binds the book.

The traditional method uses stitching alone, but the book is indeed perfectly bound if well crafted. We have asked Neil Adelantar—our friend, colleague, and an origami and hand bookbinding enthusiast—to demonstrate the traditional stab binding technique. See Neil's hands in action in his feature article.

Figure 7-23
Annual report: "The Impact of One on Many"
Studio: KPMG
Creative Director: Donna Bonavita
Art Director: Donna Bonavita
Client: KPMG Foundation
Pictured is a glued, punched, and stab binding. The red thread is an echo of the doctorial robe worn by the figure in the photograph. More importantly, the specialty stab binding contributes to the distinction and importance communicated in the cover image.

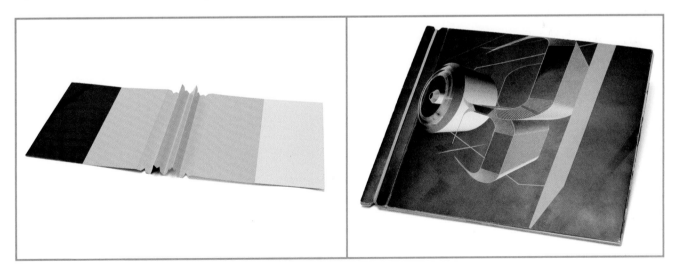

Figure 7-24
Side-bound book using rubber bands. Shown in the photograph is a sample of the inside folded cover (with end flaps); insert pages into the center fold; join the cover to the book block with a rubber band.

The booklet shown is the self-promotional portfolio of Cesar Rubin and Alejandro Medina.

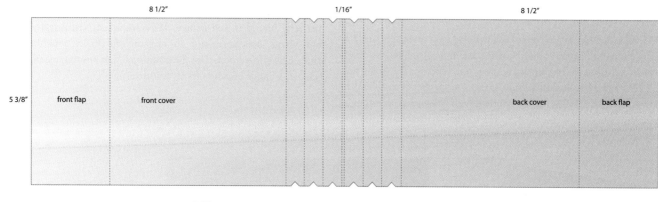

8 1/2" 1/16" 8 1/2"

5 3/8" front flap front cover back cover back flap

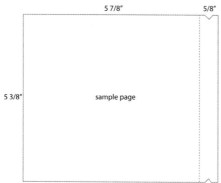

5 7/8" 5/8"

5 3/8" sample page

Figure 7-25
Diagrams of a single page and the cover. The folds will create an accordion fold. Fit the book block into the center valley. Bind with a rubber band.

screw and post binding, grommets, and rings

Screw and post binding, grommet binding, and grommet and ring (or chain) binding are also side bindings because of the mechanical element applied to the spine border on the front and back of the book. For professional examples of these binding methods, see Figures 7-26 and 7-27.

comp it up: screw and post

The screw and post method of binding places a screw and elongated nut (the "post") in a hole or holes drilled through the pages of the cover and book block (the post is inserted into the back of the book; the screw is inserted into the post at the front of the book). The length of the screws and/or posts will vary depending on the amount of pages to be bound.

This method can also be used in conjunction with a rigid strip on the back and front (along the spine border) in order to provide more strength for the binding by better distributing the compression. One or multiple screw and post sets can be used with an upright, square, or oblong format. A hinge joint is usually necessary as well. Screw and post bindings have the virtue of being removable and allow for pages to be added or taken away from the book easily.

To make a comp of a screw and post binding, you will need to punch a hole through the cover and all the pages of the book block; see Figure 7-28 for a brief visual guide. Screw and post sets can be purchased through a craft supply store that stocks bookbinding elements and tools.

grommets

To make a comp of a grommet side binding, you will need to punch holes through the cover and all the pages of the book block using a hole punch; the grommets are pressed into the holes using a grommet punch (a specialty tool noted in Chapter 1). See Figure 7-29 for a brief visual guide.

In conjunction with grommets and often seen on applications such as the ubiquitous "three-ring binder," a ring binding uses one or more series of locking metal rings to keep the pages of a book together. The number of the rings will vary depending on the size of the book. Many variations of this very simple binding are possible, with materials from metals, plastics, and even cord/string/ribbon used to form the rings, or a chain can be substituted for the metal ring. To comp: Punch a hole in the pages of the book block, implement a grommet, and add the ring or chain.

Figure 7-26
Sales promotions: Microsoft Mac Office v. 10
Studio: Hornall Anderson Design Works, LLC
Creative Director: Jack Anderson
Art Director: Bruce Stigler
Designers: Bruce Stigler, Holly Craven, Elmer dela Cruz, Don Stayner, Sonja Max, Belinda Bowling, Jon Graeff
Copywriter: Amy Bosch
Metal ring binding through a grommet. Beaded chain threaded through a grommet.

Figure 7-27
Direct mail collateral: BMW X3 SAV
Studio: Ritta & Associates, Englewood, NJ
Creative Director: Jonathan Hom
Designer: Cesar Rubin
Client: BMW, North America, LLC
Screw and post binding.

stab binding by hand

Neil Adelantar is an art director and graphic designer as well as a folding and binding enthusiast.

Considered a type of side stitch in the industry, stab binding is actually an ancient and traditional method of hand binding books without adhesives.

To hand bind using the stab method, stack the pages and align at the spine; the sewing is implemented along the border area. A hinge joint can be placed just beyond the threading or flush with the edge of the thread.

Depending on the cover material and the number of pages, threading holes are either drilled into the book or punched before sewing.

The number of holes (and by extension, the pattern of the stitching) can vary. Once the basic (five hole) stab stitch is accomplished, it can be varied to produce other types of decorative configurations known as hemp-leaf, tortoise-shell, or *Kangai*.

Like side-stitch bound books, stab-bound books will not open flat. Likewise, scoring can be used to help pages open. An oblong format is suggested to avoid having to score pages. A stab binding can have a hard cover as well. The cover board can be placed over the first page, leaving the spine border exposed.

If a board cover is desired instead of a more flexible (and able to be scored) cover material, the boards will need to be cut in two pieces—the spine border and the cover area (from hinge to fore edge). The two pieces of board can be covered and made into one continuous piece (with a French groove hinge).

See the accompanying figures for a diagram of the sewing procedure and a brief visual guide.

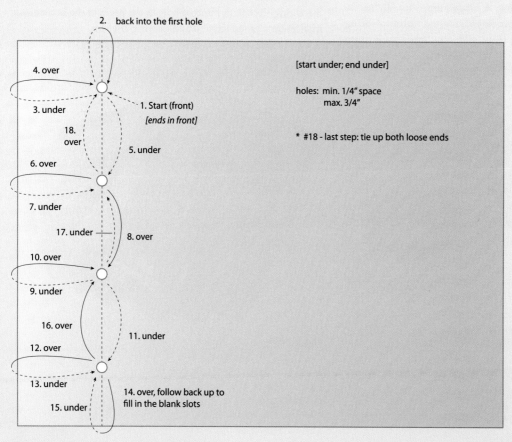

Diagram of the procedure for stab binding.

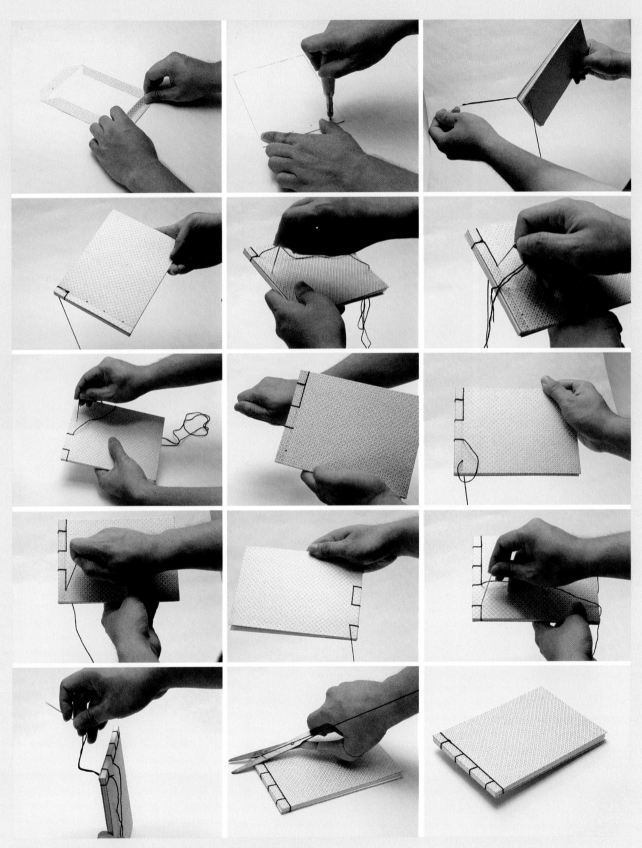

Shown are several procedural steps in the process of stab binding.
Follow the diagram for the complete steps needed to finish.

Figure 7-28

Screw and Post Binding Step by Step

First row, left to right:

Measure the placement and drill holes (of corresponding size to the screw and post) in the book block. Insert the post into the hole from the back of the book. Thread the screw into the post.

Score the hinge joint.

After the cover is scored, use a steel ruler placed along the hinge joint to assist in making the fold.

Second row, left to right:

Fold back the cover and score the first page of the book. Fold back the second page and score the page. Continue folding back the pages and scoring each. The result will be that the score on each page will be graduated away from the hinge joint. Scoring assists in opening the book.

Finished comp with two screws and posts.

Finished comp with one screw and post; scoring not necessary.

Figure 7-29

Grommet Binding Step by Step

First row, left to right:

Grommet loaded into the prepunched hole. The tool in the picture is called a Crop-A-Dile. It is made specifically for punching holes and pressing grommets.

Two hands (or one strong one) are needed to crimp the grommet.

The back view of the pressed grommet.

Second row, left to right:

Finished comp.

When thicker substrates or a bigger hole and grommet are desired, use a punch with a hammer and anvil to implement the grommet. Pictured is a hole punch and hammer.

Place the male grommet on the anvil and place the substrate with the hole over the grommet.

Third row, left to right:

Place the female grommet over the substrate and male grommet.

Using a grommet punch, hammer the grommet to crimp.

Finished comp.

Figure 7-30
Spiral Binding Step by Step
First row, left to right:
Tools and punched pages for spiral binding.

Threading the plastic coil.

Cut excess with a serrated scissors.

Second row, left to right:
Crimp the ends with needle-nose pliers.

Finished comp.

spiral binding

Spiral or coil bound books have a series of evenly spaced, circular holes punched along the spine border. After the holes are punched, a spiral-shaped wire is threaded through the holes. The ends of the spiral are crimped or bent to prevent the ends from dethreading and sliding out of the holes. Spiral bindings are relatively inexpensive and simple with the chief advantage of allowing the book block to open easily and lay flat. Refer back to Figure 7-1 for an example.

To make a comp of a spiral binding, you will need the coil element and a proprietary machine. We do not recommend punching the holes by hand—the effort and result are not worth the time spent. Refer to Chapter 1 for information on a spiral binding machine. See Figure 7-30 for a brief visual guide to spiral binding on the desktop. Spiral binding can also be accomplished at an office supply store.

wire-o

Very similar to the spiral binding, Wire-O binding employs a metal wire laced through prepunched holes of a book block. The holes are square as opposed to the round ones for spiral binds. Once the holes are punched, the wire—which looks like a contiguous series of connected "double-Cs"—is then hooked into the holes. The entire book is then placed spine-first into a clamp that provides even pressure throughout the length of the book. The double-C shape of the individual units of the wire is then compressed into the shape of an "O." Excess wire can be clipped and clamped, and the three remaining sides of the book are trimmed. Refer back to Figures 7-1 and 7-2 for professional examples.

To comp a Wire-O binding, you must have the wire element plus a proprietary machine to punch the holes through which the binding elements will be clamped. As with spiral binding, the most pressing concern is the alignment of the holes. We recommend testing on the substrate that will actually be put into use for the final comp to determine the placement of the holes. See Figure 7-31 for a visual guide. Alternatively, Wire-O binding is available at most retail office supply stores.

creative wire variations

Creative variations on Wire-O bindings abound. Since the wire spine prohibits any printing on the spine, the book is often wrapped with a cover. The cover can be wrapped around the spine to cover the wire and allow for printing on the spine. The detached cover of this method may need a "belly band" or sleeve to keep it closed. An alternative method of spine wrapping is called Canadian bind. The Canadian bind method keeps the spine attached so that the cover doesn't flop open.

French fold pages can work well with Wire-O binding, or add a foldout page. For the latter, be certain to trim the folding page panel away from the gutter so it will not get caught in the wire. A wrapped wire, a Canadian bind, and a double spine are shown in Figure 7-32.

comb binding

Similar in application to the Wire-O binding is comb binding. The comb-binding method uses square holes but then features plastic tubing with one side cut into tines like those on a comb. Pages of the book block are cut to size, holes are punched, the plastic comb is inserted, and it is clamped closed. A comb binding can be accomplished on the desktop with a proprietary machine or inexpensively accomplished at a copy center or office supply retail store.

smyth sewn and case bound

Smyth-sewn bindings employ glue and thread. The process was invented in 1878 by David McConnell Smyth (1833–1907). On an industrial level, to ready for Smyth sewing (also known as section sewn or signature sewn) a book block is created of stacked signatures (no grind-off); the signatures are each sewn to the next along the *width* of the spine—forming rows of chained thread. The spine is further strengthened using adhesive and tape over the stitching. Smyth-sewn books lay completely flat and are durable. Either cover weight paper or paperboard can be used as coverings for Smyth-sewn book blocks. An aesthetic trend recently has been to leave the sewing exposed—making the construction visible.

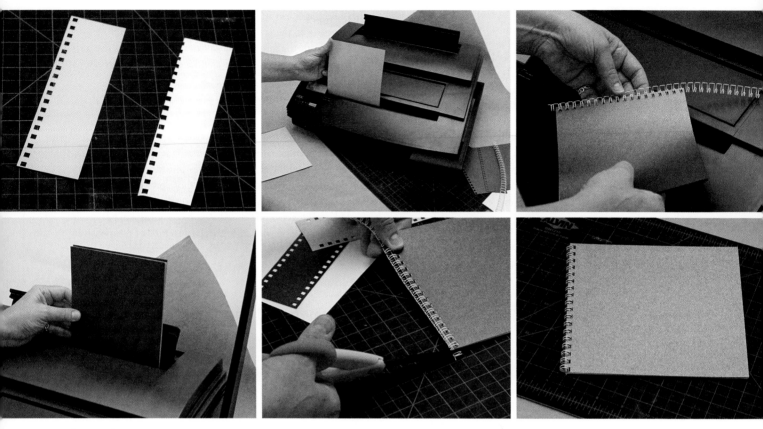

Figure 7-31

Wire-O Binding Step by Step

First row, left to right:

Cut scrap paper to the size of the page and insert in the machine to test hole alignment. (On the left, the holes are correctly aligned. On the right, the holes are askew. Since the latter is potentially destructive to your comp, the testing is a necessary step.)

With the test successful, insert the page into the machine and punch the holes. Repeat for each page and the cover.

Thread the wire through the punched holes of the cover and entire book block.

Second row, left to right:

Place the threaded book block into the machine to compress the wire and clamp closed.

Cut the excess with serrated scissors or a wire cutter.

Finished comp.

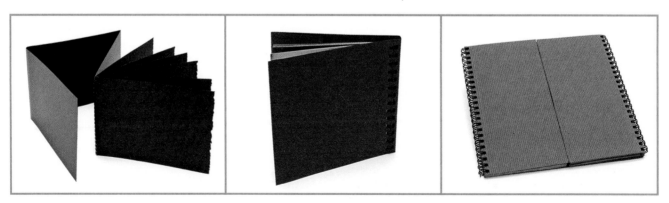

Figure 7-32

Left to right:

Blank comp of a wrapped cover used to hide the wire binding.

Blank comp of Canadian binding.

Blank comp of double-spine Wire-O.

Figure 7-33

Book: French by Damien Pignolet
Studio: Frost Design
Creative Director: Vince Frost
Designer: Jacqueline Molony
Photographer: Earl Carter
Illustrator: Michael Fitzjames
Printer: 1010 Printing International Ltd., China
Client: Penguin & French
First row, left to right:
Cover (closed book)—embedded ribbon bookmark.

Inside spread (image at left and text at right page).

Second row, left to right:
Inside spread with image crossover.

Endpaper (using an image).

Coptic Binding

Shown in this image is a finished, handbound *Coptic* binding (an ancient sewn bookbinding technique). Japanese *Chiyogami* paper is used on the cover. Note the detail of signatures and threading. Binding crafted by Neil Adelantar.

Industrial Smyth sewing (exposed spine and glued). If hand-sewn bookbinding is of interest, we suggest research into Coptic binding techniques.

A casebound book is one that has been Smyth sewn and then attached to rigid front and back cover boards and a board spine. The spine can be flat or round, or there are times when the spine is left without a board. The boards are joined prior to attaching to the Smyth-sewn book block. To join the boards—thus creating a case—paper, library buckram (bookcloth), leather, vinyl, or other substrate is glued and wrapped around the boards (gift wrapped in a way). Finally, the book block and case are joined together by attaching the endpapers to the inside front and back cover and the first and last page of the book block. See Figure 7-33 for a professional example of a Smyth-sewn casebound book and Figure 7-34 for a detail of a casebound book that has a bookcloth covering.

Figure 7-34
Catalog: The Mall at Short Hills
Studio: Brogan Tennyson Group Inc.
Creative Director: Jen Battle
Designer/Production Artist: Laura Menza
Client: The Mall at Short Hills
Binding details.
The full book can be seen in Chapter 2, Figure 2-30. Pictured here are two details of the corner of the book and the spine of the book showing the French groove.

Industrial versions employ materials and a process that simulate the traditional but are significantly less expensive and time consuming. Sewn by hand using a variety of stitching techniques, traditional case bindings are accomplished by highly skilled professionals and artisans for limited edition specialty books and/or repairs and conservation of antique books. For more information on the traditional techniques of hand-sewn and cased bindings, we recommend any of the books written by master bookbinder, Keith Smith.

simulated casebound books

As noted previously, much has been written and practiced concerning hand-sewn and handmade cased books. For the purpose of a comprehensive mock-up for a student design solution, we are not recommending that you pursue the complexity of this type of desktop bookbinding. However, we have some tips for shortcuts to avoid sewing and for simulating a casebound book.

Simulated casebound books can be of high quality but are not actual or archival—remembering that our pursuit here is for comps, not for posterity. See Figures 7-35 and 7-36 for a step-by-step visual guide to comping a casebound book.

variations on case bindings

Since imaginations know no bounds, so go the potential variations on case bindings. A few common additions and adjustments include slip jackets, interior half pages, foldouts, inked or stained edges, shaped covers, and punctured covers. The case covering can also be whole or in part made of bookcloth, the boards can be exposed and left without covering, and/or a slip case can house the book. See Figures 7-37 through 7-39 for professional examples and Figure 7-40 for student-generated comps using variations on case binding.

Figure 7-35 (right)
Case Bound Step by Step
Please read the entirety of the written instructions and visual guide before attempting the process.

First row, left to right:
Ready the work area. For a blank comp you will need the following materials and tools:

- One book block (pictured: multiple-signature book block glued and taped at the spine).

- Two endpapers (for the inside front and back of the book).

- Three boards: front, spine, and back covers; we recommend using a specialty substrate for the purpose, aptly named bookboard.

- Cover substrate for wrapping around the boards.

- Tools and additional materials for construction include scrap paper, triangle, folding tool, PVA glue, glass dish, brush, spatula, embossing stylus, small flat brush, precision scissors, and white pencil.

Mark the position of the boards on the cover paper.
Mark the cut line of the corners using a board chip (the width of the board allows for the proper spacing between the book cover corner and the cut line).

Second row, left to right:
Cut the corners of the cover paper.

Spread glue in a radial pattern on the boards. Hold the board in place with a stylus or spatula.
Place glued boards into place on the cover paper.

Third row, left to right:
Flip; place protective tracing paper over the cover boards and burnish to tighten the bond.
Test and prepare the corner tucks while the cover paper is dry; pull up the remaining flap of cover paper and press in the corner toward the board. Repeat on the remaining three sides and unfold.
Apply the glue to two flaps, quickly tuck in the corners, and fold up. Repeat.

Fourth row, left to right:
Burnish all edges to smooth and tighten the bond.
Place scrap paper inside the case; close the book and lightly burnish the French groove.
Apply glue to the spine of the book block.

Fifth row, left to right:
Press or burnish the spine to tighten the bond; pick off stray glue with a dull craft knife.
Place a scrap under the first page of the book; apply glue to fully cover the first page.
Remove soiled scrap paper and replace with clean scrap; align the right panel of the endpaper over the first page to glue the endpaper to the first page.

Step by step continued in Figure 7-36.

Figure 7-36

Case Bound Step by Step

First row, left to right:

Use a folding tool to burnish the endpaper onto the first page and then use the folding tool to tuck the endpaper into the spine.

Using clean scrap below, glue the back of the remaining (left) panel of the endpaper.

Adhere the glued endpaper to the board cover. Burnish and tuck the spine edge again.

Second row, left to right:

Place a clean scrap between the endpapers; close the book and press to assist with tightening the bond.

If there is excess endpaper overhang, trim with precision scissors.

Finished comp opened to the inside. Refer back to Figure 7-7 for an image of the finished comp in a closed position.

Figure 7-37

Book: Sabiduras
Studio: HvA Design
Creative Director: Henk Van Assen
Designers: Henk Van Assen, Amanda Bowers
Paper selection: Mohawk Superfine
Printer: Chas. P. Young
Client: Museum of Fine Arts, Houston, Gego Foundation, Caracas, Venezuela
As noted by the designers, "The linen [cloth] cover features a blind embossed reproduction of one of the artist's prints and is supplemented with a bilingual belly-band."

Figure 7-38
Book: Lee Voyages
Studio: Design Ranch
Creative Directors: Ingred Sidie, Michelle Sonderegger
Designer: Tad Carpenter, Brynn Johnson
Copywriter: Jeff Mueller
Photographer: Jeff Bark
Printer: M-Press
Case bound with black bookcloth and exposed board covers.
The exposed board is debossed and printed with clear varnish.

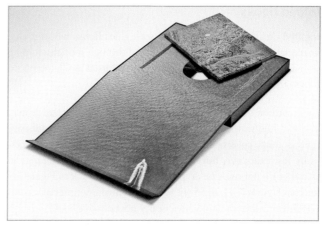

Figure 7-39
Book: Coral Island
Studio: Kinetic, Singapore
Creative Director: Roy Poh
Client: Coral Island Residences
Standard casebound book inside a sensational clamshell box
(magnetic closure).

Figure 7-40

First row, left to right:

Accordion fold book block attached to the case.

Bookcloth-covered, casebound book with window cut out on the front cover. Designed and crafted by Patrick Morrison.

Board covers and spine exposed over the endpaper (a rubber substrate) with embedded bookmark ribbon.

Second row, left to right:

Case bound with bookcloth cover (raised shape embossing—see Chapter 10).

Bookcloth and Japanese paper casebound book housed in a clamshell box. Designed and crafted by Gordon Brown.

Online published casebound book. Designed by Alan Robbins.

folded books

Limited on time? Rather not deal with glue? Books without glue or mechanical parts can be accomplished through specialty folding formats (some of which were previously discussed in Chapter 5 on folded formats).

An accordion fold format is most like a book. Or, a broadside map fold can fold down into a book-like format with a little adhesive used to attach covers perhaps. Nonadhesive bindings are not necessarily less expensive, but certainly they have a time advantage in that they do not use glue or use little glue. Refer back to Figure 7-3 and see Figures 7-41 and 7-42 for professional examples of a completely nonadhesive book and a nearly nonadhesive book.

creative thinking with folded formats

We all learn by doing and by seeing. There are countless variations using folded formats for book blocks. See Figures 7-43 through 7-46 for two of our favorite variations with templates.

miscellaneous variations on various bindings

We can never get enough of interesting bindings. Two more examples of professional design solutions are included here for inspiration. See Figures 7-47 and 7-48.

Figure 7-41
Poster and booklet: Yale Undergraduate Senior Exhibition
Studio: HvA Design
Creative Director: Henk Van Assen
Client: Yale University School of Art
From the designers: "With a small budget, both a poster and booklet had to be produced. By using a folding system that employs a single central cut, the flattened poster becomes a small [eight] page booklet."

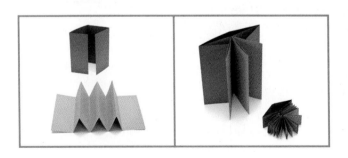

Figure 7-42
Newsletter: Fítfréttir
Studio: Ó!
Art Director: Einar Gylfason
Designer: Einar Gylfason
Client: FIT, Association of Icelandic Graphic Designers
Left to right:
A Z-fold map folding format that uses cover weight paper covers transforms the folded paper into a small booklet.
A close-up of the folded format.

Figure 7-43
Left to right:
Separate components of an accordion fold book block with blue dust jacket.

Assembled accordion fold book block with blue dust jacket. Shown is an upright narrow format and a square, miniature format.

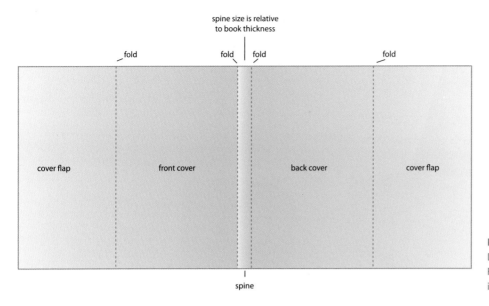

spine size is relative
to book thickness

fold fold fold fold

cover flap front cover back cover cover flap

spine

Figure 7-44
Diagram for a dust jacket. Refer back to
Figure 7-43 for an example of the jacket
in application.

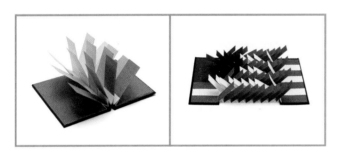

Figure 7-45
Student projects.
Left to right:
Flag book using accordion fold spine with alternating tab pages
and board covers.
Flag book variation.

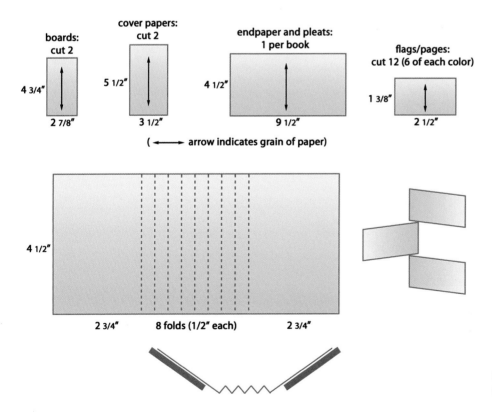

boards:
cut 2

4 3/4"

2 7/8"

cover papers:
cut 2

5 1/2"

3 1/2"

endpaper and pleats:
1 per book

4 1/2"

9 1/2"

flags/pages:
cut 12 (6 of each color)

1 3/8"

2 1/2"

(⟷ **arrow indicates grain of paper)**

4 1/2"

2 3/4"   **8 folds (1/2" each)**   2 3/4"

Figure 7-46
Diagram for flag book binding.

Figure 7-48
Booklet: Su-Zen
Studio: Mucca Design Corp.
Creative Director: Matteo Bologna
Art Director and Designer: Matteo Bologna
Photographer: Steven Gross
Client: Su-Zen

Figure 7-47
Stationery gift items: Natura Naturata
Studio: slover [AND] company
Creative Director: Susan Slover
Designers: Susanna Koh, Karen Yen, and David Allegra
Copywriter: Rosemary Kuropat
Photographer: Raeanne Giovanni
Client: Chronicle Books GiftWorks Division, San Francisco, CA

book arts are boundless!

As a medium for personal expression, book arts are in their own category. Part sculpture, part image making, part writing and authorship, and of course all bound using handcrafted bookbinding, book arts may be an ideal creative venue for graphic designers (and students) who practice typography and visual storytelling almost daily.

Although bookbinding has a history of techniques that are still practiced today as an art (and adapted for commercial use), the elements of what constitutes a bound book are vast. Artists and designers use tradition and their imaginations for creative adaptation of traditional techniques with seemingly endless innovation. See Figures 7-49 through 7-51 for professional-level books created by artists and designers. See Figures 7-52 and 7-53 for an example and diagram for a meander fold book.

We are truly grateful to our editors for allowing a small side trip and crossover into the book arts in this chapter. Using everything you have learned in this chapter and previous chapters, adapt the materials and techniques to book arts projects for personally expressive reasons.

Figure 7-49
Handmade books.

Artist: Jody Williams
All books are in the private collection of Rose Gonnella.

Figure 7-50
Artists of the books clockwise from lower left: Sarah Longworthy, Peter
and Donna Thomas, Zach Pearl, Jocelyn Chase, Sally Boyd, Sara Witty,
Ellan Spitzer, Cathy Ryan, Erin Smith.
All books are in the private collection of Rose Gonnella.

Figure 7-51
The Chronicle of the Rohirrim.

Designer/craftsman: Christopher J. Navetta

Figure 7-52
Comp of a meander fold book.

Crafted by Richard Arnold.

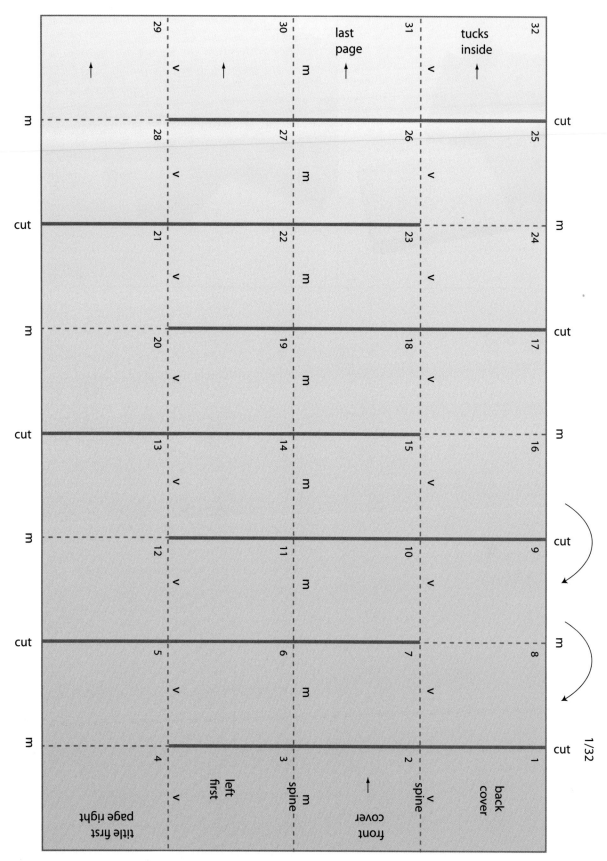

Figure 7-53
Diagram for a meander fold.

214

summary: set up and bind

Once you develop practical knowledge in regard to types and uses of industrial bindings, implement the bindings for both functional and aesthetic purposes. Adapt the industrial method for desktop comps in order to visually display the knowledge you gained and its appropriate application.

Once the lessons of bookbinding are absorbed, and the business of design study accomplished for a time, you may find that exploring and creating books is personally rewarding. Write a story. Make a book to tell it with words, images, textures, paper, and its binding.

Learn by doing. As we have clearly seen in this chapter, there are many options of bookbinding. It may be simple to choose the best functional binding or challenging to incorporate the binding method into a conceptual element. Whichever the case, choose the binding carefully and keep both concept and budget in mind. Figures 7-54 through 7-62 display student-crafted books using various methods of desktop binding.

Figure 7-54
Perfect-bound book titled *The Nature of Poetry* and detail of spine.

Student designer: Lisa Doolittle

Figure 7-55
Stab binding with handmade pillow cover.

Student designer: Michael DelSordi

Figure 7-56
Nonadhesive, accordion fold book with dust jacket.

Student designer: Nicole Santiago

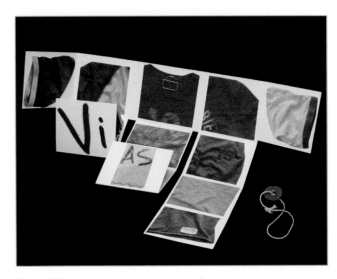

Figure 7-57
T-shirt foldout book.

Student designer: Marc Grill

Figure 7-58
Wire-O booklet with graduated short pages.

Student designer: Alex D'Angelo

Figure 7-59
Wire-O bound with glued cover.

Student designer: Milijana Dukovic

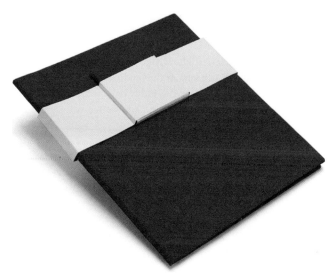

Figure 7-61
Two casebound books, the larger using a pocket belly band to contain the smaller version.

Student designer: Patrick Morrison

Figure 7-60
Casebound covered book with suede and bookcloth (title printed on paper glued to the fabric).

Student designer: Michael Boos

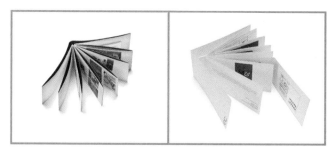

Figure 7-62
Left to right:
Accordion format booklet.
Student designer: Ryan Guijo
Side stitch and cover wrap (with page foldout).
Student designer: Yingyos Charubusapayon

exercise knowledge gained

The knowledge gained in this chapter can be put to use far beyond desktop comps for design solutions. Creating your own books can be a lifelong pursuit. Practice now to gain skill and apply to enhance your creativity in regard to design solutions; continue exploring, recording, and binding your own view of the world. Keep books alive.

1. Shopping and Scavenging

As with the previous chapters, gather a collection of professional examples of the kind of work that inspires and ultimately teaches you. Look anywhere you can for books of any shape, size, and subject—with particular focus on the paper and how they are covered and bound.

The more you see in practical and creative application, the better you will understand. Although the mall and bookstore are good starting points, you may be presented with limited options there.

Everything is new and expensive! So find those antique shops and flea markets and continue your hunt. You may just find the more unusual and perhaps more interesting books and booklets there. You never know what you might uncover. Keep as many as possible for a reference or at least keep photographs of your finds in a digital library. Bonus: A used book can be recycled for comps and personal projects.

2. Return and Bind

If you have not completed all the practice bindings we have noted in this chapter, return to the text and complete each binding technique using a blank book block. Completing the blank comps should raise your awareness of the process (and problems) as well as sharpen handcraftsmanship skill.

Directions in the chapter include the following bindings:

- Perfect
- Tape
- Saddle stitch, single signature
- Side stapled
- Side stapled with French fold pages
- Singer sewn
- Stab
- Screw and post
- Grommet
- Spiral (machine needed)
- Wire-O (machine needed)
- Case bound
- Folded books: accordion with jacket and meander

3. On Demand

We suggest that you explore a simple perfect-bound book using one of the on-demand publishers.

You can design a book that displays your personal photography, drawings, or illustrations. Or, select a commonly found nature object such as rocks, leaves, or clouds. Photograph the object exploring the many variations of the object in context. Take the opportunity to sharpen skills in observation and resulting composition.

4. Exploring Perception and Reality

For this project we suggest an oblong, side-stitch booklet using foldout pages.

To begin, you will need to select a subject matter. We suggest choosing one of the following creatures from the animal kingdom: wolves, dragonflies, doves, frogs, any fish, or lizards.

Find photographic imagery of the select subject in its natural environment. The images will need to be available at high resolution. Next, find images of the subject as it is interpreted or perceived by artists. Search for drawings, illustrations, paintings, sculpture, mosaics, jewelry, and other images of the subject.

Review your collection of images and pair one photographic image with one artist's interpreted image. Pair images so they are similar in composition.

The title of your booklet is *Perception versus Reality.*

Each page will have two images and a folded tab or foldout. To make a foldout, extend a single page one-half length more than the desired length of the booklet. For instance if the book is to be 4" in height by 8" in width, then make the page 4" × 12". At the fore edge, fold back 4" of the page onto itself.

On the top of the foldout, fit flush to the edges of the page and print (or glue on) the artistic image of the subject. On the area below this (top) image (not directly on the foldout area), print the photographic image of the subject. The artistic image on the top of the foldout page should completely hide the realistic image below. The point of the image pairing: a visual exploration of how nature is perceived versus its reality. What is perceived hides the true reality.

Optionally, a page can fold out, fold down, or fold up. Also consider incorporating a roll fold into the booklet. Tell an unfolding story about perception versus reality.

Foldouts can be accomplished in commercial binding but will considerably increase the cost of the process and product. Even if the budget allows, use creative extras only when they are conceptually indispensable.

5. Personal Book Projects in Multimedia

We know what you're thinking: In this age, *multimedia* usually holds some sort of audiovisual connotation, but in this particular case, it refers to the physical media (the substrates) used for book construction. You've accomplished the basics, using papers and maybe some boards and even some fabrics. But how can these media—or more unusual ones not always associated with contemporary books such as those in wood or plastics or vinyl—alter your approach to bookbinding? Experiment on a personal level with no particular design problem in mind. See Figure 7-63 for a student example. In brainstorming your own project, perhaps keep the following ideas and approaches in mind:

- Make the spine and covers of a book out of thin wood.
- Create a completely soft cover/spine out of fabric or plastic. With a soft medium such as fabric, you can easily puncture it with a needle for sewing or punch holes in it for screw posts.
- Design a book with no paper at all! Can you make an entire book—pages, covers, and spine—with no paper?

Figure 7-63
Heavy Reading.

Student designer: Jon Dorieux

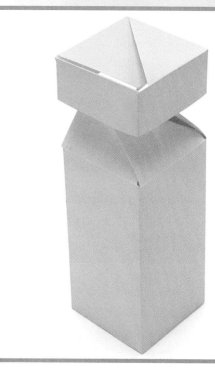

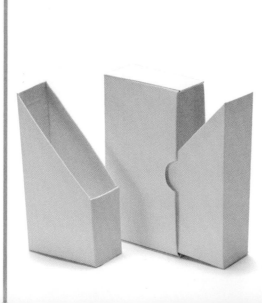

"Packaging is an essential component in our culture. More than a container, a bag, a box, a bottle, it tells stories . . . It presents and promotes, informs, and instructs."
— *Steven DuPuis and John Silva, from* Package Design Workshop

First row, left to right:
Food packaging: Le Grande Luxe (soft cheese [*brie*])
Studio: Smith Design
Creative Director: Glenn Hagen
Designer: Glenn Hagen
Client: Joan of Arc Le Grande Luxe

Comp of a hendecagonal box.

Shopping bags: Sant Ambroeus
Studio: Mucca Design Corporation
Creative Director: Matteo Bologna
Designer: Andrea Brown
Client: Sant Ambroeus (Italian-style cafe)

Second row, left to right:
Comp of a cushion-top carton.

Premium body care product packaging: Monde Sensuelle
Studio: slover [AND] company
Creative Director: Susan Slover
Designers: Marianna Hardy, Sol Hong, Saskia Hoppe, Amy Gorrek, and Jennifer Teixeira
Copywriter: Rosemary Kuropat
Photographer: Thomas Bricker
Client: Bath and Body Works

Comp of a twist-top box.

Third row, left to right:
Gourmet food packaging: Grapeseed Oil, California Grapeseed Co.
Studio: Louise Fili Ltd., New York, NY
Creative Director: Louise Fili
Designers: Louise Fili and Mary Jane Callister
Client: Jean-Georges Vongerichten

Comp of a slipcase box.

Gift box: Bathazar
Studio: Mucca Design Corporation
Creative Director: Matteo Bologna
Designers: Matteo Bologna, Christine Celic Strohl
Photographer: Luca Pioltelli
Client: Keith McNally (restaurateur)

eight

packaging all around

learning objectives

- Explore packaging formats.
- Examine the range of materials used in packaging applications.
- Learn basic techniques for packaging comps.
- Explore the creative and expressive potential of packaging.

pack it in

A package is not just a container. Packaging forms and overlying graphics communicate visually and with words to define the specific content of the package (food, electronics, clothing, etc.). In addition, a package may also communicate corresponding emotions, ideas, and the experience of the content.

Packaging is a design specialty. Producing a single box or bottle or a packaging system is complex mingling of research and marketing, branding, industrial design, and graphic design. As a reminder, the content of this textbook does not delve into concept development due to the vast depth and breadth of the proprietary study needed to design packaging. Instead, we place the focus on becoming aware of physical packaging options, resources for expanding knowledge of the field, and guidance for creating comprehensive mock-ups on the desktop.

Consider your student work in creating packaging comps a small starting point. Producing packaging comps is such an essential and critical aspect of the professional field that craft artists, specialty designers, and large companies exist whose sole purpose is to fabricate packaging comps. Given the enormous (and daunting) amount of packaging on retail shelves, there are certainly many "comp houses" and freelancers working in the field. We suggest web research on several of these specialists such as Comp24 or Creative Comps. Packaging design studios may also have in-house operations for fabricating comps such as the studio led by the typographically brilliant and charming creative director, Gregg Lukasiewicz. The three-word directive that the Lukasiewicz Design team uses to guide their thinking is one that all design students should consider embracing. See Figure 8-1 for the Luke Design business model and Figure 8-2 for an example of packaging from Luke Design.

Figure 8-1
Studio: Luke Design
Creative Director: Gregg Lukasiewicz
Client: Self

Vision
By itself vision is the ability to recognize and champion the development of an idea . . .
but without technical skill and enthusiasm, vision remains just a dream.

Artistry
Interpretation of an idea with a level of skill and expertise requires artistry . . .
but without enthusiasm and a great concept, this skill is senseless.

Passion
Passion is great . . .
but without a visible way to express yourself, passion remains just an emotion.

The team at Luke Design, as an "off-duty" exercise to visualize their business and collaborative philosophy, designed and fabricated this tower of boxes.

Figure 8-2
Perfume packaging: Healing Garden
Studio: Luke Design
Creative Director: Gregg Lukasiewicz
Client: Healing Garden
The elegant glass bottles and graphics of the Healing Garden packaging communicate a feeling of luxury and premium quality.

materials and formats

Study begins with the standards of packaging materials and formats. Knowledge of these brings with it the potential for creative use. Being aware of and knowing the visual vocabulary (both in shape and substance) of packaging expands the possibilities for visual communication and experimentation beyond the standards. For example, as a designer, you may know that a glass bottle is necessary to contain perfume. But what shape will best express the identity of that fragrance? Should clear or color glass be used? What size should the bottle be? Perhaps glass is not the only option. Or perhaps the standard can be extrapolated. See Figure 8-3 for professional examples.

paper or recycled plastic?

Contemporary product packaging is constructed from a wide variety of materials and many combinations of those varied substrates. Traditional materials such as glass, wood, and metal have been in use to contain, transport, and store products of all kinds for centuries. See Figure 8-4 for a historic and visually compelling container.

Paper and its many forms (paperboard, cardboard, etc.) have been used for packaging since the late nineteenth/early twentieth century. Plastics followed shortly thereafter. Recently, knowledge plus awareness of the environment has led the way to greener and less bulky packaging (going green can also be healthy for the bottom line). Refinements and reinvention of packaging materials have abounded since their inception. As technology changes, so does packaging and its capabilities. See Figures 8-5 through 8-7 for professional examples of packaging in a variety of substrates.

paper all around

Paper (in its rigid form known as paperboard) and plastic may be the most ubiquitous materials in which to contain, wrap, or box a product. Metal and glass are plentiful as well. In less use, due to cost and accessibility, are materials such as fabric, ceramics, wood, and cork. All are up for grabs on the desktop. Obviously though, volumetric objects made of glass, metal, wood, plastic, and so forth will not fit in a desktop printer and neither will the flat and rigid paperboard and plastic that is the stuff of packaging.

Since direct printing onto a true packaging substrate is not possible on desktop inkjet printers, instruction and construction on packaging comps primarily involve paper—adhered to existing three-dimensional objects such as paperboard boxes and glass or plastic bottles. Not to disappoint, we do have tips and techniques for working with glass, metal, and some forms of plastic.

Figure 8-3
Premium body care product packaging: Monde Sensuelle
Studio: slover [AND] company
Creative Director: Susan Slover
Designers: Marianna Hardy, Sol Hong, Saskia Hoppe, Amy Gorrek, and Jennifer Teixeira
Copywriter: Rosemary Kuropat
Photographer: Thomas Bricker
Client: Bath and Body Works
The designers address the packaging design contribution: "The collection [of bath products] was based upon three related fragrances, *Orchidée Noir, Fleurs Sauvage, and Rose Sauvage* that were blended into seven different kinds of products. Each product was then captured in an artisanal bottle shape that gave the collection an historical air. A labeling system that mixed modern typestyling with handwritten calligraphy made each product form a collectible, purchased as much as an object to grace the bath or boudoir as for its fragrant interior."

Before a discussion of the forms and formats of standard packaging, we have a bit more information on several particular basic substrates, including:

¤   Paper/paperboard

¤   Glass

¤   Plastic

¤   Metal

¤   Miscellaneous

Paperboard (cardboard) and paper are among the most common materials used for packaging. Paperboard and paper packages are relatively versatile. They can vary in size and weight, accommodating

Figure 8-4
Amphora.

© Openko Dmtytro | Dreamstime.com

Figure 8-5
Gourmet food packaging system: Vong
Studio: Louise Fili Ltd. New York, NY
Art Directors: Louise Fili and Mary Jane Callister
Client: Jean-Georges Vongerichten

Figure 8-7
Snack food packaging: Jubes
Studio: Kinetic
Creative Director: Roy Poh
Client: Jubes

Figure 8-6
Gift stationery packaging: *Natura Naturata*
Studio: slover [AND] company
Creative Director: Susan Slover
Designers: Susanna Koh, Karen Yen, and David Allegra
Copywriter: Rosemary Kuropat
Photographer: Raeanne Giovanni
Client: Chronicle Books, GiftWorks Division

virtually any dry substance or contents. Multiple layers and configurations (such as **corrugation**—the shaping into folds or parallel and alternating ridges and grooves) can significantly increase strength. When mixed or coated with other materials (wax, for example), paperboard containers can be adapted to hold liquids. Being a pliable substrate, paperboard packages are relatively easy and flexible to print and fabricate. Either the paperboard is printed or paper

is printed and wrapped on and around the paperboard. Panels of paper and paperboard can be glued together, making size, configuration, and design of a package nearly limitless. From soft, lightweight paper bags to the thick and rigid cardboards, the malleability of the substrate makes it a preferred choice for many applications. If properly treated, most paper is recyclable, usually making paper-based packages an ecological choice. See Figure 8-8 for a professional example of paper and paperboard packaging.

the beauty of glass

Packages constructed from glass are usually created for their strength and beauty. Glass bottles and jars are practical for a number of applications, particularly for the containment of liquids. Glass may also carry a distinct feeling of being sturdier, cleaner, more impressive, and more important than some of its packaging counterparts. Although many plastics can do the same job as a container made out of glass, using glass can potentially elevate the stature of a product. Success, however, is relative to many factors in the market, only one of which is design. See Figure 8-9 for an example of fancy glass.

On a practical level, glass can be direct-printed, using silk screening or a similar process (silk-screen printing is noted in Chapter 10). Glass is also used in conjunction with paper or plastic labels. Like paper, glass is largely recyclable.

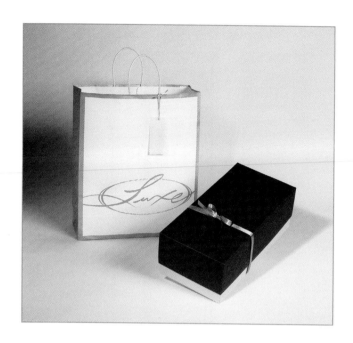

Figure 8-8
Stationery packaging: Luxe
Studio: Archetype, Green Bay, WI
Creative Director: Jim Rivett
Art Director: Jim Rivett
Designers: Jason Davis, Robb Mommaerts, DeGaull Vang, Tami Anundsen, and Ann King-Larson
Copywriter: Carol Cassel/Word*play
Photographer: 44 inc.
Client: Fox River Paper Company (now Neenah Paper)
Printers: Independent Inc., Wright Brothers Paper Box Company, Pack America Corp., Print Craft
Pictured are examples of a paper shopping bag and paperboard box for stationery packaging identity.

The extended paper choices explained by the designers: "This creative sales kit for Fox River Paper Company was sent to packaging designers and paper converters to create top-of-mind awareness for its luxury packaging papers. The kit sampled the finest papers for luxury bags, boxes, gift wraps, hang tags and labels in the company's top seven favorite paper lines. The kit also included helpful spec information on basis weights and sizes, performance and process production notes, and features and benefits of using these papers."

Figure 8-9
Perfume packaging: Bond no. 9
Studio: Luke Design
Creative Director: Gregg Lukasiewicz
Client: Bond no. 9
Because of its long history and an inherent feeling of importance, glass is the preferred substrate to contain elegant or high-quality perfume. The bottle format pictured was custom designed to create a unique and distinctive visual form that would specifically identify the perfume.

one word: plastics

Plastic exists in many forms. DuPont created **cellophane** (a type of plastic film) in 1928, which was quickly followed by polyvinyl chloride (PVC) by B.F. Goodrich and polystyrene by Dow in 1930. Many variations of polyethylene, first introduced by Standard Oil of Indiana and Phillips Petroleum, soon followed. Dow again made a breakthrough in 1944 with the invention of Styrofoam (a substance that for ecological reasons now needs to be totally retired from use).

Plastics are in use for a great variety of content and in a host of shapes, sizes, thickness, permeability, and strength. Foodstuffs particularly benefit from the use of plastic packaging, as it can be virtually impermeable and keeps contents fresh for an extended period of time. Electronics packaged in plastic are safely protected. Plastics can be molded, extruded, or otherwise sculpted in essentially any form. Usually lighter in weight than glass, plastic is therefore lower in cost to ship.

Plastics are often used in conjunction with paper (for labels, like many glass containers) or paperboards on applications such as blister packs (a specific format noted further along in this chapter) or to make plastic film "windows" in boxes. Many plastics are also recyclable. For the future, we hope more technological developments arise that protect the environment from the adverse effects of plastic. In the meantime, please use sparingly and recycle. See Figure 8-10 for a professional example of packaging that uses plastic substrates.

show me the metal and more

Although metal packaging has largely been replaced by plastic, many metal packages are found on the supermarket shelves containing products such as beverages or vegetables. Tin was once a common packaging material, but it was eventually surpassed by aluminum and steel. Metals are used primarily for strength and longevity, but much like glass, the metal itself has the potential to define the identity and stature of a package. Although metal can be direct-printed, the graphic detail and color are not of the fine quality as those achieved on paper. The color of the metal needs to be reckoned with too, yet the limitations should not be a deterrent to excellent graphic design. See Figure 8-11 for a professional example of metal packaging.

Figure 8-10
Body care product packaging: Tahitian Noni
Studio: Hornell Anderson Design
Creative Director: Lisa Cerveny
Art Director: Sonja Max
Designers: Sonja Max, Belinda Bowling, Ensi Mofasser, Kathy Saito, Beth Grimm, Julie Jacobson
Illustrators: Don Demer, Francis Livingston
Client: Tahitian Noni, Int'l.

Figure 8-11
Beverage packaging: Hiro
Studio: Hornell Anderson Design
Creative Director: Lisa Cerveny
Art Director: Sonja Max
Designers: Sonja Max, Belinda Bowling, Ensi Mofasser, Kathy Saito, Beth Grimm, Julie Jacobson
Illustrators: Don Demer, Francis Livingston
Client: Tahitian Noni, Int'l.
For practical purposes regarding containment and storage of effervescent beverages, aluminum cans are a preferred choice. Graphics can be direct-printed on metal.

Figure 8-12
Jewelry packaging: David Yurman
Studio: Luke Design
Creative Director: Gregg Lukasiewicz

Beyond the basics of paper, glass, plastic, and metal, you can find packaging substrates that are made of fabric, wood, ceramic, cork, or combinations thereof. Refer back to previous examples and see also Figure 8-12 for a majestic package for jewelry made of board covered in fabric.

common formats, forms, and functions

Now that we have considered materials, we move on to formats (the general shape) and forms (the specific shape). Packages can be found in all the basic and generic shapes: oval, round, square, rectangle, and triangular. Freeform or custom-designed shapes are also possible. The shapes can be oriented upright, oblong, or narrow.

Within the common shapes and orientations, there are the basic formats of packages such as the following:

- Bottles and jars
- Cans
- Boxes and cartons
- Bags
- Blister packs
- Clamshells
- Wrappers

See also Figure 8-13 for corresponding blank packaging examples.

Within each of the formats there are a variety of forms (round, oval, tall, etc.), and there also may be properly named forms (such as the Boston Round bottle) for specific content such as body care products. Refer back to Figure 8-10 for an example of a Boston Round bottle.

form follows function

You will find that skill developing graphic design is not all that is involved in the work. Packaging design needs to be physically functional as well. Before work begins on the aesthetic design of a package, and before the format and form of the package and the material are selected, a determination of the package's function is necessary. Once functionality is grasped, the corresponding appropriate and cost-effective form or shape can be thoughtfully selected from existing industrial designs or custom designed.

Functionality can be roughly broken into several categories, and many packages fall into more than one. Basic *functional* package variations abound—far too varied in name and far too many to name them all. We offer our own sampling of package function categories by subject: food (wet and dry), beverage, medical, chemical, and household. See the sidebox in this chapter for a list of the purpose and general function of containers. To further understanding, note that bottle and jar categories can be categorized by a specific form that relates to a physical function such as containers with handles, a "drum," a wide-mouth container, a sprayer, or a dropper bottle. See Figure 8-14 for several bottle forms that have a specific physical function.

Figure 8-13 (right)
First row:
Bottles, jars.
Second row:
Cans and boxes.
Third row:
Bags and blister packs.
Fourth row:
Clamshells and wrappers.

working creatively within standards

A few package formats require designers to follow specific standard sizes or configurations. It is up to the designer to follow the standards when appropriate. For example, unless you are designing a completely custom package for the discs, CD jewel case inserts and liner notes should be a specific size in order to properly fit in the prefabricated plastic cases. Standard DVD cases are similar in application. You cannot create a DVD insert or sleeve of an arbitrary size. Standard sizes save money and time. But like other restrictions in regard to envelopes, folders, and folded formats, experimentation and variations within the standards are possible. See Figure 8-15 for a creative solution using a standard functional spray bottle.

Additional standardized types might fall within a company's own (not necessarily within industry-wide) constraints or standards—at times with a copyright and/or patent. For example, Coca-Cola uses a very specific bottle shape for their products that is an integral part of Coca-Cola's image. Proprietary standards should be understood before the design process. Be aware not to use a patented package form or design without permission.

Figure 8-15
Spray bottles: Calgon
Studio: Luke Design
Creative Director: Gregg Lukasiewicz
Within a standard form, brilliant ideas are obvious.

---

caveat designer

Our discussion is limited to general tips and techniques. With guidance, our goal is to provide a *foundation* for further (self-motivated) development, not a comprehensive coverage of each and every type of package.

packaging with a purpose

- **Contain (or Bind) and Carry:** Products need to be delivered to the individual consumer, in other words, contained for movement from manufacturer to user. Boxes, jars, cans, bags, and so forth all serve to contain. Some objects, by their very nature, demand containment. Grains, granules, powders, and liquids, for example, must be contained. Other products that are containers in themselves such as a smart phone or an audio disc need to be further contained for delivery (and marketing) to the consumer.

- **Protect and Store:** Items inside a package need to be protected in some way. This protection can be from movement or breakage (shock, crushing, etc.). Contents may also need to be protected from the elements, including water, air, or dust/dirt. The former requires the package to cushion or cradle the contents. The latter requires the package to have a seal of some sort.

- **Safety:** While similar in definition to protection, safety is also an independent concern for packaged items, as it refers more to the consumer than the item itself. Foods and drugs, for example, need their safety guaranteed. If the package is tampered with or compromised in any way, the contents can lead directly to bodily harm to the consumer. Tamper-proof seals and authentication devices are examples of safety devices. Packaging also includes informational functionality—for example, listing ingredients, posting warnings, and delineating operating instructions.

- **Security:** This term is often used interchangeably with the previous two categories of protection and safety, but security more often refers to concerns of theft or illegal sale to inappropriate consumers. To combat theft, electronic security devices can be used, from simple in-store tags to more complicated radio frequency identification (RFID) devices.

- **Sales/Marketing:** Although it might not be a physical function such as the categories listed previously, the critical function of many packages is to sell the product within. Packaging is the direct and immediate point of contact with the consumer. It can be a powerful element in shaping a consumer's decision to purchase.

See the accompanying figures for professional examples of various functions.

Bakery carry packaging (handle box): Balthazar Bakery
Studio: Mucca Design Corporation
Creative Director: Matteo Bologna
Designers: Matteo Bologna, Christine Celic Strohl
Photographer: Luca Pioltelli
Client: Keith McNally
Pictured at left rear, a box with a built-in handle specifically for carrying food.

Food packaging: *Tahitea Chai*
Studio: Hornall Anderson Design Works LLC
Studio: Hornall Anderson Design
Creative Director: Lisa Cerveny
Art Director: Sonja Max
Designers: Sonja Max, Belinda Bowling, Ensi Mofasser, Kathy Saito, Beth Grimm, Julie Jacobson
Illustrators: Don Demer, Francis Livingston
Client: Tahitian Noni, Int'l.
The designers lend some insight into the design and function of the packaging: "For this new . . . product, we wanted to give the packaging an international flair to reflect the origin of *Chai* tea. Borrowing from the architecture of the *Taj Mahal*, we were able to use this well-known historical landmark as an immediate flavor indicator, as its very presence seems to conjure images of exotic spices and flavors. . . . Subtle colors and illustrations on the additional *Tahitea* flavors also reflect the culture and quality of the product. Reusable tins lend sustainability to the entire line of packaging."

Food packaging: Bella Cucina Dolci
Studio: Louise Fili Ltd., New York, NY
Art Director: Louise Fili
Designers: Louise Fili and Mary Jane Callister
Client: Bella Cucina
Marketing to "old world" taste. The packaging for *Bella Cucina* products echoes traditional European cake and cookie boxes. The reference is to the wholesome, delicious baking of traditional European style and is a signal that the taste and quality of the contemporary product are also traditional, reliable, and good.

James Smith.
Founding Partner and Creative
Director, Smith Design

q & a with james smith,

founding partner
and creative director,
smith design

Do you have industry standards in mind when designing a package? For example, can you look at a product and know that it will fit in "X" box size or "X" bottle? How often do you use a custom size or shape box?

Everything is custom. We seldom begin a package design without a die for that particular package. We must know the top from the bottom, left side from right side—not so evident on a blank die. Most dies are supplied by the client's vendor (printer). If a die isn't supplied, sometimes just the dimensions are supplied; we will create our own "working" die. The "real" die later replaces this working die and the design is altered, usually slightly, to match.

What are the most common materials used in your packaging, and how do you choose which material is appropriate for a project?

Paperboard is the most common substrate. Material for the packages we design is usually dictated by the client's budget. Most package design projects do *not* give the designer the choice of package stock. Now though, we are pitching "green" and reminding clients that there are different ways to package a product. Also, regardless of the design, artwork must be created to meet the needs of that particular package material whether paperboard, glass, or aluminum.

How often do the designers at Smith have to create a physical comp of the package in working process?

Whether the client requests one or not, we make one. We cannot get approved a six-sided package looking at a flat proof. Most of the time, the clients will need the dimensional packages, comps, for research and presentations to sales teams.

What is the quality of those comps? How do they help you and/or the client with the project? (What are the benefits of having a physical comp as opposed to just delivering digital files?)

The quality of the comp depends on everyone's needs. Usually it is printed from our Cannon printer and mounted on lightweight board. Sometimes we mount it on a dummy box(es) of the actual stock in which the product will be packaged. If the design will be printed using the four color [process] plus PMS colors (many packages are five or six colors) and an accurate representation is needed, we send it out to a "comp" house (Comp 24, Kaleidoscope, etc.). If it is for a TV commercial, then a color-corrected comp needs to be done. A comp or package dummy is the best and only way to be sure all the panels face in the correct direction and orientation and work together correctly.

What are some of the design and production (including a comp) considerations at the start of the working process?

Of course, cost is most important, since we are in a business. But physically, the most important thing is building a schedule to get the project done within the established time frame, including being aware ahead of time what difficulties we may run into at the eleventh hour.

The size/shape of a package depends on the cost of the product in the package as well as the package itself. The design is also determined by the shelf size and how many packages will fit on the shelf facing the consumer. It is the job of the designer to study the category of the package/product. It is okay to be different [from the other packages in the category], but not so different that the consumer can't find it. Or the product won't stand up [right] on the shelf. Or the way the package was designed causes it to get damaged in shipping.

Whatever category, the product should be photographed in the store/supermarket. A photo should be scanned; then place the newly designed package into the "photo" of the category and see how it holds up to the competition. Clients can't afford gimmicks. Don't bring them more problems—just solutions.

Our job is to communicate a message. We can't lose sight of that.

Top to bottom:
Food packaging: Rosa's
Studio: Smith Design
Creative Director: James C. Smith
Designer: Glenn Hagen
Illustrator: Angel Souto
Client: Rosa's
Health and beauty bath line packaging: Clie
Creative Director: James C. Smith
Designer: Angel Souto
Illustrator: Angel Souto
Client: Clie

crafting your own

With the formats, forms, materials, and functions taken into consideration, the question remains: How do you craft a comprehensive mock-up for any and all the numerous packaging configurations?

First, please review Chapters 1 through 4 for the basic tools, materials, and knowledge that can assist with and be adapted for packaging comps. Second, review and glean as much as possible from Chapter 5 (folding formats), Chapter 6 (envelopes and folders), and Chapter 7 (binding) for various constructed techniques. Adapt the knowledge and formats in each of these chapters to packaging. For instance, a capacity envelope or folder is a type of box, after all. Or, the process for fabricating a case-bound book, noted in Chapter 7, can be adapted for packaging. And once Chapter 10 is covered, combine the specialty printing effects learned with packaging.

In this chapter, we have separated our guidance on craftsmanship into categories based on the materials and basic forms of packaging. The orientation, function, and specific format of the package and its graphic design are yours to consider.

In general, there are two places to start—designing a package based on a standard or traditional existing model with original graphics *or* customizing the package. See Figures 8-16 and 8-17 for professional examples of common forms and custom formats.

ready-mades

It is possible to purchase both flat and assembled packages (ready-made), including boxes, bags, bottles, and jars—made of paper, plastic, glass, metal, wood, and so on. Ready-made objects are particularly useful for round or odd shaped boxes, extra-large boxes, and of course glass and plastic bottles, jars, and other containers that cannot be fabricated on the desktop.

The blank, ready-made package can then be affixed with labels or painted and accoutrements added. Refer back to Figures 8-13 and 8-14 for ready-made containers.

We have our favorite sources for blank package forms, including craft retailers, the dumpsters behind Luke Design, and our local dollar store where many useful items can be had inexpensively. Or, you can buy a package off the retail shelves, transfer the content to another source, and reuse the container for student portfolio purposes.

simulating textures

Blank packages come in a variety of colors and a limited variety of substrates. To customize color and simulate textures, the object can be painted with specialty paints (spray or brush-on versions). Due to the toxic chemicals found in craft paint sprays, you may decide to forgo their use. If you decide to use spray paint or liquid paints, look for formulas that are the least toxic. Wear a mask for safety

Figure 8-16
Left to right:
"Body Guard" cream in a plastic tube.
"Calm Cool and Corrected" cream in a wide-mouth glass cosmetics jar.
"Total Nonscents" antiperspirant spray in a plastic canister.
Body care product packaging: DERMADoctor
Studio: Design Ranch
Creative Directors: Michelle Sonderegger, Ingred Sidie
Copywriter: Kerri Conan
Illustrator: Tom Patrick
Client: DERMADoctor
Clever and charming graphics transform common containers into uncommon ones.

Figure 8-17
Clothing packaging: Cintamani
Studio: Ó!
Art Director: Örn Smári Gíslason
Designer: Örn Smári Gíslason
Copywriter: Thoromar Jonsson
Client: Cintamani
The unusual and creative hexagonal box contains T-shirts. The custom box is appropriate for a custom clothing design.

when spraying, and always apply paint in a well-ventilated area or place the object within a ventilated spray box. See Figure 8-18 for samples of ready-made packages that have been painted to simulate a variety of colors and textures.

anatomy of a box

Construction of boxes begins with an understanding of the parts that make a whole. Knowing the anatomy of a box assists with clarifying and directing the function and sequence of the construction of the parts. See Figure 8-19 for a diagram of the anatomy of a simple, standard box template.

die lines

In the field or on the desktop, a designer needs a model or guideline of the package in order to place graphics and direct construction. The flat guideline is known in the industry as a **die line.** A die line includes solid cutting lines, score and fold lines, bleed areas, and glue indications (and whatever else is needed). After the die line is complete, it guides the manufacture of the physical object known as the **die** (sometimes referred to as the **cutting die**)—a machine-fabricated and fitted cutting tool in the shape of the die line. The die cuts the printed substrate into the specified form.

See Figure 8-20 for a professional example of a die line with the cutting lines, score and fold lines, bleed lines, sizes of panels, notes from the designer, and the graphics (the die line pictured here is a scan of a printed original). See Figure 8-21 for the resulting paperboard box; also pictured are bags that are based on a die line and cut from paper.

Figure 8-18

Left to right:
Ready-made containers before painting.
Painted containers:

First column:
Sandstone texture paint on paperboard square box, clear varnish on a wooden canister, translucent blue paint on a glass bottle, translucent (frosted) paint on a glass bottle.

Second column:
Metallic blue paint on a paperboard box, rough stone paint on a circular paperboard box, gloss purple enamel paint on a circular wooden box.

Third column:
Terra-cotta texture paint on an oval paperboard box, hammered metal charcoal-colored paint with brushed silver enamel paint on a hexagonal paperboard box, black chalkboard paint on a paperboard box.
Plastic, three-drawer container painted with hammered metal texture paint (specially formulated to bond well to plastics).

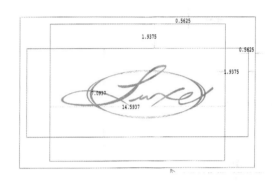

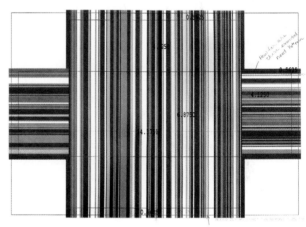

Figure 8-20
Die lines: Luxe
Studio: Archetype, Green Bay, WI
Creative Director: Jim Rivett
Art Director: Jim Rivett
Designers: Jason Davis, Robb Mommaerts, DeGaull Vang, Tami Anundsen, and Ann King-Larson
Copywriter: Carol Cassel/Word*play
Photographer: 44 inc.
Client: Fox River Paper Company (now Neenah Paper)
Printers: Independent Inc., Wright Brothers Paper Box Company, Pack America Corp., Print Craft

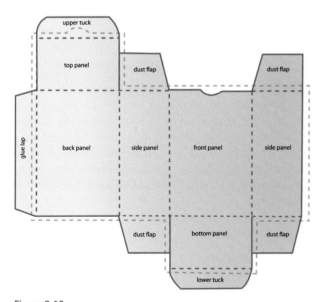

Figure 8-19
Basic anatomy of a simple box.

Figure 8-21
Stationery Packaging: Luxe
Studio: Archetype, Green Bay, WI
Creative Director: Jim Rivett
Art Director: Jim Rivett
Designers: Jason Davis, Robb Mommaerts, DeGaull Vang, Tami Anundsen, and Ann King-Larson
Copywriter: Carol Cassel/Word*play
Photographer: 44 inc.
Client: Fox River Paper Company (now Neenah Paper)
Printers: Independent Inc., Wright Brothers Paper Box Company, Pack America Corp., Print Craft

remake a box

With a paperboard ready-made in hand, use it as a model to make a die line. To make a die line and see how it works, carefully pull the package or box apart and flatten. Yes, that might seem counter-intuitive or counterproductive. But you have to remember that in the process of designing a three-dimensional object, we also work "flat." Even a simple square or rectangular box can prove intriguing (and confusing) in its variations on folds, closures, and detachable parts. So carefully open the box, flatten it, trace the outline, and take note of the parts; see Figure 8-22 for an example of a disassembled and resulting die line.

To reinforce the value of creatively tearing up a package, we recommend viewing the talk given by movie director J.J. Abrams (on the mystery box) online at the TED (Technology, Entertainment, Design) website.

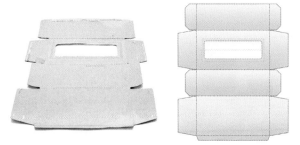

Figure 8-22
Left to right:
Disassembled box.
Resulting die line.
Rip! Tear! Learn! Learn how the package works. Learn why it works. What is the folding sequence? Are the tabs glued? Do they interlock? Is it the paper cover stock or board? The more you are aware of all the parts and folding mechanisms, the better start you will have in fabricating your own package.

ready die lines

Exploring die lines leads us to the good news for boxing comps—there are hundreds of die lines available from which to guide construction or place your own on a ready-made. See Figures 8-23 and 8-24 for a few samples of packaging (simple and complex) and the simple flat guidelines (die lines) for making them.

We encourage custom and creative work, but there is no need to reinvent a die line for an existing box or other containers; see Figure 8-25 for a professional example.

Designing the form of the box is fun, but engineering the form is surprisingly difficult with no training or industrial design knowledge. In fact, some of the die lines we have found on the web and in various books have been incorrect—the errors discovered when assembled. Therefore, testing is necessary when working with an existing package design die line. Test the engineering of the guide. Test the paper for folding flexibility and strength. Test your skill with assembly.

Figure 8-23
First row, left to right:
Arc-top carton die line.
Arc-top carton blank comp (closed and open).
Second row, left to right:
Cushion-top carry carton die line.
Cushion-top carry carton blank comp (closed and open).
Third row, left to right:
Basic pillow pack die line.
Basic pillow pack blank comp.

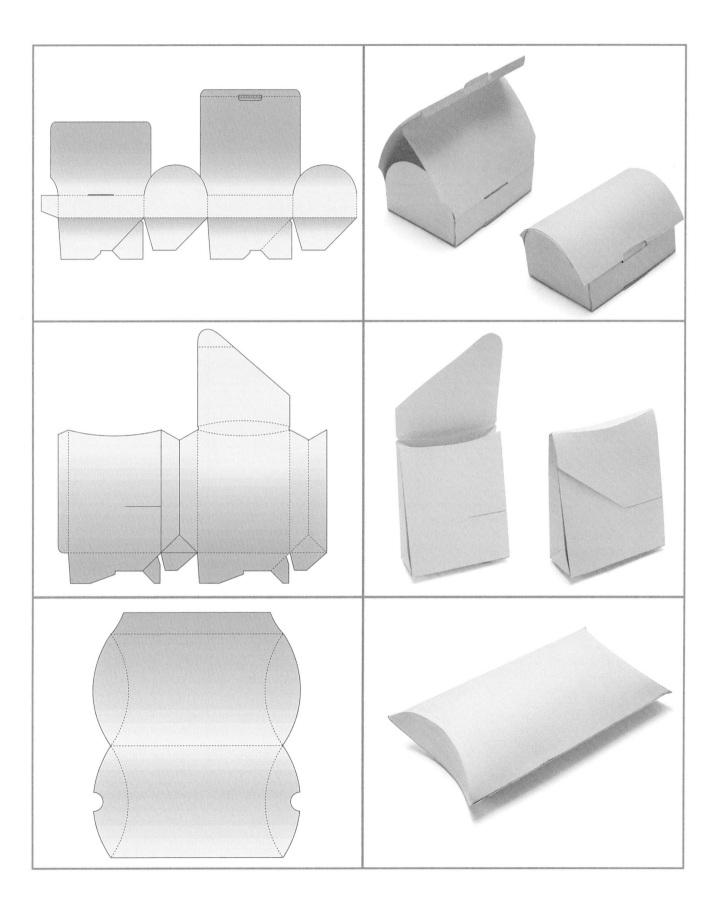

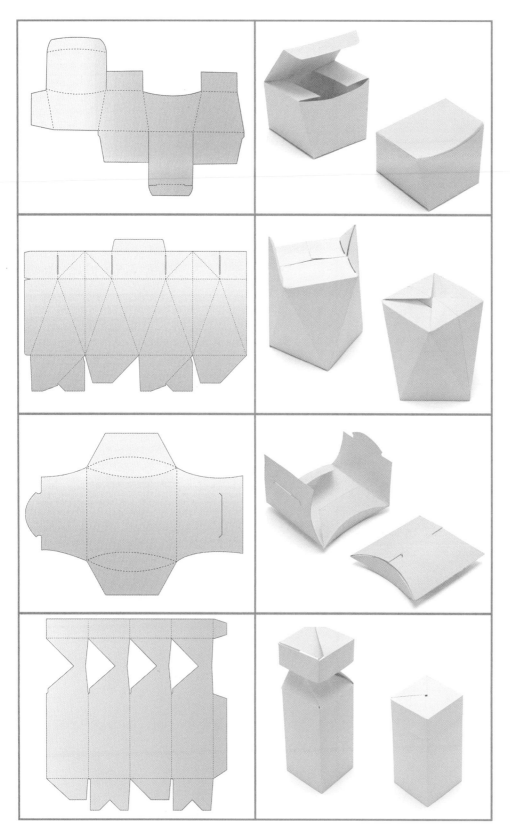

Figure 8-24

First row, left to right:

Reverse-tuck carton die line.

Reverse-tuck carton blank comp (closed and open).

Second row, left to right:

Eleven-sided (hendecagon) box die line.

Eleven-sided box blank comp (two views).

Third row, left to right:

Top-opening pillow pack die line.

Top-opening pillow pack blank comp (closed and open).

Fourth row, left to right:

Pop-up lid box die line.

Pop-up lid box blank comp (closed and open).

Figure 8-25
Food packaging: Carolina Sausage
Studio: Habitat Visual Communications
Creative Director: Al Montagna
Designer: Brian Buttavacuole
Client: Arnold Foods
Standard package formats need not be a limitation on creativity. A smart and conceptually based use of graphics raises a standard packaging form to a creative one.

comp the box

We suggest practice comps on four box variations, including those known as one-piece folder, two-part tray and lid, tray and sleeve, and slash box and slipcase. See Figure 8-26 for die lines and samples of the corresponding assembled comps. See Figure 8-27 for a professional box tray and sleeve. For more information on basic forms, search the web for companies that specifically manufacture boxes (or other packaging forms) such as the Taylor Box Company or Pack for America.

Enlarge and use the provided flat guides. Enlargements may distort the guide, so be aware that you may need to make adjustments. Use knowledge gained thus far with folded formats, envelopes, and folders. Remember, solid lines indicate cutting, broken lines (dashes) indicate scoring and folding, and diagonal slashes indicate where to apply glue. Tabs will need to be glued, so call upon gained skills for the process. Carefully read both the simple start-up guide in the following list and the brief visual guide provided in Figure 8-28 before attempting your packaging comps.

Start-Up Guide

- Use cover weight paper (80#–100#). Test fold for grain and cracking.

- The grain of the substrate should follow the longest direction of the form. Some folds will be against the grain.

- The fold lines must be scored. Use a scoring tool. Depending on the weight and thickness of the substrate, a wide indentation (or a kiss cut) may be necessary. For a wide score, cut two lines, flush—side by side.

- Implement the folds in both directions (mountain and valley). The folded line should be flexible. Burnish the folds.

- Assemble the flat template without glue. Test construction. Disassemble.

- Note problems and make adjustments. If the substrate is too thick, it will not hold its folded form. If the substrate is too thin, the box will flop over and fall apart.

- Several gluing options are suggested. Glue stick and double-stick tape will suffice for this practice. White glue, paste glue, or superglue gel is recommended for a more permanent bond.

- Glue the tabs and adhere to the large panels.

- Hands should be cleaned of any stray glue before final assembly.

Figure 8-27
Stationery packaging: *Natura Naturata*
Studio: slover [AND] company
Creative Director: Susan Slover
Designers: Susanna Koh, Karen Yen, and David Allegra
Copywriter: Rosemary Kuropat
Photographer: Raeanne Giovanni
Client: Chronicle Books, GiftWorks Division

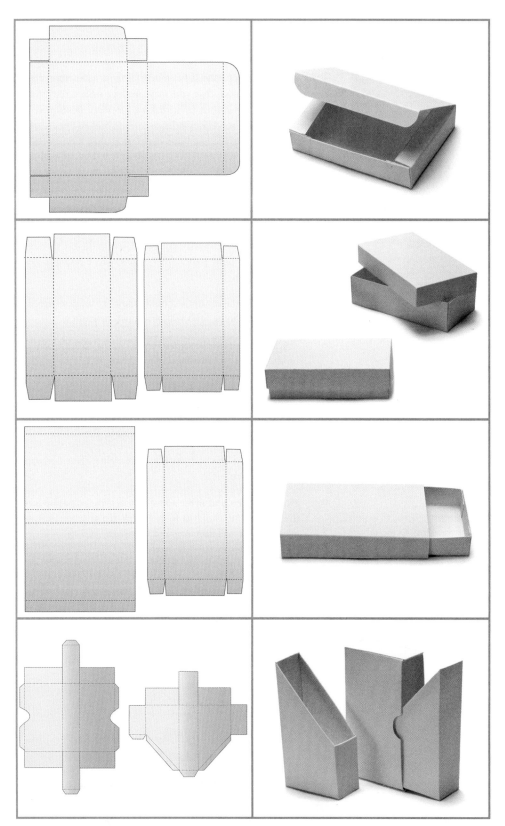

Figure 8-26

First row, left to right:
One-piece folder box die line.
One-piece folder box blank comp.
Second row, left to right:
Tray and lid box die line.
Tray and lid box blank comp.

Third row, left to right:
Tray and sleeve box die line.
Tray and sleeve box blank comp.
Fourth row, left to right:
Slash box and slipcase die line.
Slash box and slipcase blank comp.

Figure 8-28
Comp of a Simple Box Step by Step

First row, left to right:
Draw the die line onto the substrate and cut it out.

Score the fold lines. Protect the substrate and burnish with a folding tool. If a heavyweight paper substrate is in use, kiss cutting may be necessary or use a wide score (two side-by-side passes of the tool). Implement the folds in both directions (mountain and valley). The folded line should be flexible. To test, assemble the flat template without glue.

Apply double-stick tape to the tabs.

Second row, left to right:
Cut off excess tape.

Assemble the box (tabs are adhered to the panels of the box).

Finished comp (note type of closure).

graphically design

After completing several practice comps on blank substrates, continue practice using printed templates. Or, adhere printed panels to the blank comp.

◻ *Start with a blank comp.* Select a template. Assemble. Test construction. Construct as many folding comps as necessary, both out of plain paper and then out of the actual printing paper you will use to construct the package. Set aside.

◻ *Sketch.* Take time to sketch the graphics directly on the template to see where and how the shapes should be oriented. Test assemble and determine if the orientation is correct.

◻ *Plan* the design with the edges in mind. Placement of imagery needs to be exact. Allow for 1/16" score and fold lines. Heavy ink coverage at the fold lines may cause cracking.

◻ *Digitize.* With the die line on screen, place the graphics.

◻ *Print* the die line, cut, glue, and assemble.

plastic box comps

To comp a plastic box, you will need rigid plastic (it has no grain), which you can purchase at a craft or art supply store. Proceed as stated for a cover weight paper box. But for plastic, the scoring should possibly be *carefully* kiss cut. You can also use a folding tool to burnish, but protect the surface as usual. See Figure 8-29 for a comp of a plastic box.

Some types of plastic can be printed on the desktop. However, using plastic acetate that is not compatible with your inkjet printer may be a disaster. Find a plastic sheet that is compatible for your desktop printer and proceed as noted previously. See Figure 8-30 for a comp that uses a printed sheet of plastic.

If the plastic is not compatible with your desktop printer, it may damage the printer beyond repair. To avoid problems altogether, some alternatives to direct printing are suggested in the following list:

◻ Print on adhesive-backed plastic sheets and adhere to the rigid plastic. Drawback: The adhesive-backed acetate sheets may not be clear. They might have a "frosted" appearance.

◻ Print on paper and insert into the box or adhere to the box.

◻ Create a partial, printed paper "sleeve" and place over the box.

See also Figures 8-31 through 8-34 for examples and several step-by-step tips for alternatives to printing on plastic sheets.

bottles and jars

For comps of bottles, jars, and tubes, you will need ready-made forms. Making a comp of a bottle (etc.) is a simple matter of adhering paper or plastic film labels. However, we do have several suggestions for placing the labels. Refer back to Figure 8-34 for several examples of labeling.

Figure 8-29
Plastic box assembled at left. The die line can be seen below the plastic sheet; double-stick tape or gel superglue is necessary for assembly when using plastic.

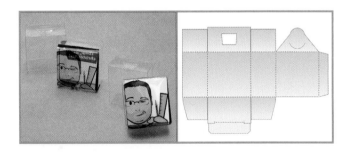

Figure 8-30
Left to right:
A box constructed from a printed, clear plastic sheet; the same box with white paper inserted (the image is more visible).
Die line for the box.

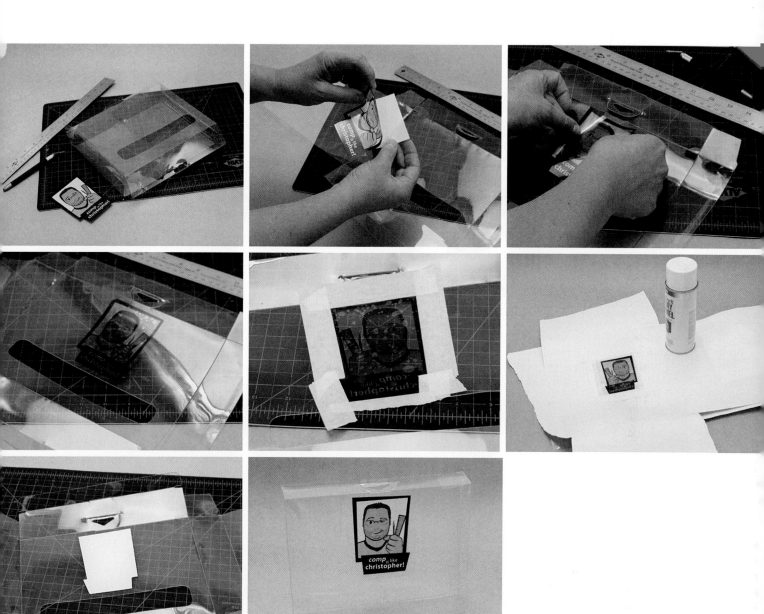

Figure 8-31
Printed Plastic Alternatives Step by Step

First row, left to right:
Ready-made package with printed adhesive-backed graphic.
(Print on adhesive-backed plastic sheets to adhere to rigid plastic.)

Peel graphic from the adhesive sheet.

Adhere to the package.

Second row, left to right:
Graphic applied; the image needs to be opaque in order to increase its visibility.

Flatten box; mask the graphic area.

Use scrap paper to cover the remaining exposed areas of the box. In a well-ventilated area, spray the exposed area with paint (white in this case).

Third row, left to right:
Mask removed to reveal the finished white backing.
Finished comp.

Figure 8-32
Left to right:
Ready-made clamshell box, printed panel; assembled box.
Print on paper and insert into the box or adhere to the box.

Figure 8-33
Create a full or partial, printed paper "sleeve" and slide over the box.

Figure 8-34
Left to right:
Paper wrapped around the form (and glued at the back), opaque adhesive sticker paper applied on glass, clear adhesive sticker paper on a plastic jar.

shopping bags

Use ready-made shopping bags and flatten to make your own template. Be aware that handles can be fabricated from a variety of materials as seen in Figure 8-35.

So many shopping bags (and containers) and so little time! See Figures 8-36 and 8-37 for professional examples of bags.

To comp a bag, either preprint before folding or place labels on ready-made bags. Iron-on transfer paper can be used for fabric substrates such as canvas. Be aware of the texture of the fabric—it may interfere with the graphics and transfer of ink. Always follow the iron-on transfer paper manufacturer's instructions for the proper practice of ironing images onto fabric.

Figure 8-35
Types of shopping bag handles.
Back row:
Built-in handle (cut out of the paper).
Center row:
Braided fabric cord, grosgrain ribbon.
Front row:
Plastic tube, raffia.

Figure 8-36
Food packaging: New York Times—Coffee and Tea
Studio: Gillespie Design Inc.
Creative Director: Maureen Gillespie
Designer: Kate Aiello
Illustrator: Isabelle Dervaux
Client: The New York Times

Figure 8-37
Carryout paper sack: Washington Square
Studio: Mucca Design Corporation
Creative Director: Matteo Bologna
Designer: Christine Celic Strohl
Photographer: Luca Pioltelli
Client: Washington Square (restaurant)

green thought

A three-dimensional object can be built solely on screen using CAD software or more simply by drawing the object in Illustrator and Photoshop. If you are concerned about the overuse of ink and paper and the use of plastic, make the comp only when necessary or desired. Follow green practices as much as possible.

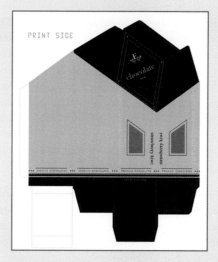

Die line.

Specialty food packaging: Empress Chocolates
Studio: Mark Weisz Design
Creative Director: Mark Weisz
Designer: Yael Miller
Copywriter: Yael Miller
Illustrator: Vinaya Prashanth
Client: Empress Chocolates

Digital comp.

Specialty food packaging: Empress Chocolates

soft substrates and rigid objects: go digital

As mentioned previously, there are digital alternatives to physical comps. Digital comps are especially useful for three-dimensional objects of custom design that do not have handy ready-made versions and for large-scale objects such as environmental graphics (outdoor boards, banners, signage, etc.).

Adapt the instructions in the step-by-step guides (see Figure 8-38) for use on a variety of "soft goods" such as T-shirts, tote bags, and large-scale objects such as outdoor banners, bus shelter banners, and other environmental graphics. These objects are certainly pertinent to the study of design concepts and applications. Do continue study of Photoshop techniques in order to successfully create digital comps. We suggest a subscription to publications such as *Photoshop User* or *Layers* magazines, published by the Kelby Media Group, where you will find information on special techniques in every issue.

In addition, several online sources will direct print graphics onto fabric and ready-made objects such as tote bags, pins, pens, cups, and so on. Be aware that the inventory of objects will be limited. We suggest Café Press, Zazzle, and ArtsCow. Remember that you are the designer of the graphics not the object itself.

Figure 8-38 (right)
Digital Graphic Application on Ready-Made Messenger Bag
Step by Step

First row, left to right:
Start off with your two images—the image you want to place (in this case, a logo) and a photo of the object on which you want it placed (in this case, a messenger bag). Drag (or copy and paste) the logo into the image of the bag, which will place it on its own new layer.

From the *Edit* menu, select *Transform > Distort*. This will place a box around the logo and allow you to manipulate it from any one of several points placed around the logo.

Maneuver the four corners to (as closely as possible) match the angle and shape of the bag. The logo is now roughly in the correct spot (and appears to be on the same plane as the bag), but it is still flat.

Second row, left to right:
Return to the *Edit* menu and select *Transform > Warp*.

This will lay a grid and series of points over the logo.

By "pushing and pulling" the various cells and points of the grid, manipulate the logo to follow the contours of the bag. In the model here, the word *thinking* falls over the biggest indentation in the bag's surface, so it receives the most warping.

Third row, left to right:
The logo has conformed to the shape of the bag, but it is still stark, solid red and white, and therefore it doesn't look like part of the bag itself. To accomplish a more realistic look, changing the *Layer Blending Mode* can often help. On the *Layers Palette*, change the mode from *Normal* to *Overlay*. (This may not always produce the desired effect depending on the underlying image, so again, experimentation is necessary.) When *Overlay* is selected, the logo picks up the textured surface of the bag.

To better match the look of the photo of the bag, the edges of the logo need to be softened slightly—it's still too "hard-edged" to look like it's really a part of the original photo. From the *Filter* menu, select *Blur > Gaussian Blur*. Enter a very small number—this is only to give a slight softening effect and not distort the logo too much. (In this case, a 1-pixel radius was used.)

To make the logo conform to wrinkles of the bag, use the *Dodge* and *Burn* tools to lighten highlights or darken shadows, respectively. Some areas of the logo might require fine-tuning to match the bag's surface even better. The bottom right corner, for example, was distorted again using the *Warp* tool to better wrap around a wrinkle.

Figure 8-39
Finished *digital* comp.
"Thinking Creatively" conference logo designed by Steven Brower. Other layer blending modes, changing opacity of the logo, and additional warping/distortion of specific sections of the logo might be necessary to make the effect more realistic. Experiment! Every situation is different.

An alternative for this effect involves the creation of a *displacement map,* a method that might work better if the surface is more wrinkled than the bag used here. As we've mentioned many times, this book is not intended to be a Photoshop tutorial, so we highly recommend that you consult your favorite Photoshop books or magazines or search online to learn more.

photoshop it up

There are numerous ways to go about most tasks in Photoshop. The following two examples are quick methods to achieve reasonably convincing effects for packaging comps. See Figure 8-38 for a step-by-step visual guide to digitally placing a graphic on a soft, fabric object. Figure 8-39 shows the finished digital comp. See Figure 8-40 for a step-by-step guide to placing a graphic on a rigid object, and see Figure 8-41 for the finished digital comp. They are by no means the only methods to reaching the desired end. However, these methods are a good starting point for exploring the use of Photoshop in creating the illusion of graphics on actual objects.

extending packaging techniques

On a creative note, consider extending the use of packaging and its comps into additional promotional applications such as direct mail marketing, sales kits, and invitations to special events. See Figures 8-42 and 8-43 for professional examples of extending the duty of packaging.

Figure 8-40
Digital Graphic Application on a Ballpoint Pen Step by Step

First row, left to right:
Again, start with two images—the image you want to place (in this case, the same logo) and a photo of the object on which you want it placed (in this case, a pen). The original version of this logo appeared on a yellow background, so a pen that features a yellow body was chosen. Drag (or copy and paste) the logo into the image of the bag, which will place it on its own new layer.

Scale the logo to fit over the body of the pen by going to *Edit > Transform > Scale*. Remember to hold down the [Shift] key when scaling, otherwise the proportions of the logo will be distorted.

Because the body of the pen flares slightly, use *Distort* to match the outer shape.

Second row, left to right:
Select *Edit > Transform > Warp*. Again, the grid and points appear.

Manipulate the logo to match the curvature of the pen's body. Because the surface is cylindrical, the closer to the top and bottom the logo lies, the more distorted it would be. By selecting increasingly smaller segments of the top of the logo, use *Edit > Transform > Skew* to achieve the desired effect.

Third row, left to right:
Repeat this for the bottom of the logo.

As in the previous example (soft bag), a *Gaussian Blur* is used to soften the logo slightly.

Use the *Dodge* and *Burn* tools to match the highlights and shadows of the pen, respectively.

Figure 8-41
Finished *digital* comp.
"Thinking Creatively" conference logo designed by Steven Brower.
Pen.

© Eliasgomez | Dreamstime.com

Figure 8-42
Invitation: Mjólka dairy production grand opening
Studio: Ó!
Creative Director: Örn Smári Gíslason
Designer: Örn Smári Gíslason
Client: Mjólka

Figure 8-43
Direct Mail: Cargo Magazine (Perfect Frequency)
Studio: Gillespie Design Inc.
Creative Director: Maureen Gillespie
Designer: Liz Schenekel
Copywriter: Ralph Allora
Client: Cargo Magazine
Gillespie on the use of packaging for direct mail:
"Cargo Magazine needed a high-impact way to reach media buyers to announce their launch and generate ad sales. To break through the clutter of in-boxes, a three-dimensional mailing vehicle was used. The pop-top type can when opened, reveals a radio with an LED screen continuously scrolling Cargo's tagline. If you have an idea for a unique mailing vehicle, check with your local postmaster to get permission. You can mail more things than you think. I've heard of floor tiles and coconuts being mailed without extra packaging!"

summary: pack it up and go

There is much more to explore relative to packaging formats, forms, and materials. Using the information presented as a guide, continue your research of packaging design specialists, industrial packaging fabricators, and print converters to learn more about formats, forms, and materials. Keep aware of "green" developments as well. Once you have absorbed the lessons, exercise the knowledge gained through design projects, and perhaps flex your newly attained skills for personal, expressive projects as well.

exercise knowledge gained

1. you're collecting again

First, hunt and gather. As with gaining knowledge of any aspect of design, expose yourself to as many good examples of packaging as possible. This component of your samples collection may take up a bit more space than the others—but there's also a lot of fun to be had in the collection! Make sure you get samples from many different types of products and packages: boxes, bags, tins, paper, board, plastic, wood, metal, and combinations therein. Use them for ready-made substrates or to make your own die lines. Read about what works and what doesn't. Understand how the constructions work. Understand *why* they work. Learn from great professional examples.

2. go one step further

Using a favorite film or piece of music (or perhaps explore the unknown to learn something new), design a CD/DVD package and incorporate a booklet, folder, or other folded format. Take an existing CD/DVD apart and use it as a die line, purchase a blank ready-made, or design your own custom-shaped box. In addition, use the knowledge you gained from the chapters on folded formats and bookbinding to create a complementary booklet or folded format for the CD/DVD. Be sure the packaging helps to enhance the overall design concept. See Figures 8-44 and 8-45 for two student examples of custom packaging.

3. focus on one thing

Before getting into designing multiple packages at once (a packaging system), study packaging design with a focus on *one* item such as one specialty food, a sporting supply, a small electronic device, or a personal care product. Fabricate the comps or practice the use of Photoshop skills for the latter. Think about the form of the package in relation to the subject matter and the design concept. "Marry" conceptual form and function into a synergistic whole. Use materials (metal, paper, plastic) both functionally and conceptually. See Figures 8-46 through 8-48 for student examples.

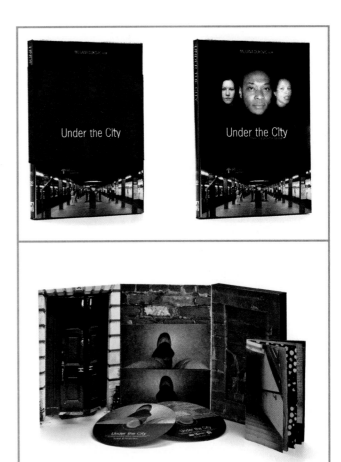

Figure 8-44
Student project: *Under the City* DVD.

Student designer and photographer: Milijana Dukovic
The DVD is packaged in a completely custom box, fitted with a creatively appropriate torn paper sleeve (belly band). Inside the box are pocket slots to hold the discs and a box inset for a booklet that is saddle-stitch bound. The discs are direct-printed.

Figure 8-45
Student project: CD packaging.

Student designer and photographer: Luis Guillen
This CD package is composed of paperboard, a ready-made plastic CD hub, and a poster fold insert.

Figure 8-46
Student project: Cupcake gift food packaging.

Student designer: Lindsay Perrina

Figure 8-48
Finished comp for "Jayde Gardens" student comp.

Student designer: Michael Boos

Figure 8-49
Student project: "Teaism," an intimate café for tea drinkers.

Student designer: Michael DelSordi

Figure 8-47
Student project: "Gube" (specialty golf balls) packaging.

4. identity and corresponding packaging

Now get complicated. Establish an identity for a specialty store or a food service and extend the identity to as many applications as time allows. We know the temptation is to fill the packaging system with custom, specialty forms. Specialty packaging is fun to design and we encourage it—but only selectively. Overall, we suggest the use of standard forms and sizes for the practice packaging system. Yet, to satisfy any zany creative urges while remaining a realistic, functioning designer, include just one specialty package.

Perhaps the custom package is a gift box or a holiday special, a unique item in the system, or for use as a one-time promotion. See Figures 8-49 and 8-50 for student examples of packaging systems.

5. more application mixers

Continue to explore identity applications extending into applications including soft goods and merchandise creation and packaging. The packaging project could explore one of the following basic categories of packaging: fashion and apparel, beauty and personal health care, food and beverages, domestics, or technology.

See Figure 8-51 for a student example.

Figure 8-50
Student project: "Lingerie de Chocolat," a chocolate and feminine womenswear store combination.

Student designer: Megan Falb

6. personal explorations

Instead of a graphic design project, we urge you to explore your inner creative self through a construction or sculpture project that doesn't have a client *per se*. For instance, we love to make our own inspired versions of movie and theater props. Projects like this are excellent opportunities to explore the use of materials and media that might not always be utilized in the more standard types of packaging. Craft it yourself now—whatever it is that toots your flute. See Figure 8-52 for an example.

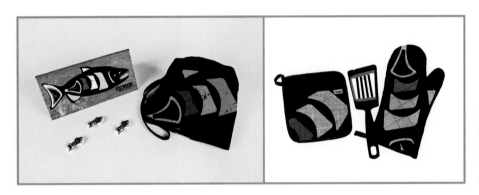

Figure 8-51
Student project: "Chinook Cook Shack," seafood restaurant identity and merchandise.

Student designer: Lindsay Perrina

Figure 8-52
Personal project: Ressikan Flute (prop replica) and packaging
Designer: Christopher J. Navetta
Left to right:
Pictured is the finished box with tools and materials: poplar wood, enamel and stone texture spray paint, household spackle (applied over the wood before painting), wood glue, hammer and brads, corner clamps, crushed velour (foam underneath), ready-made tinwhistle (painted gold, then brushed with brown and silver model enamel), aluminum tape, and handmade satin string tassel.

The finished prop (flute) in the open box, and the box closed.

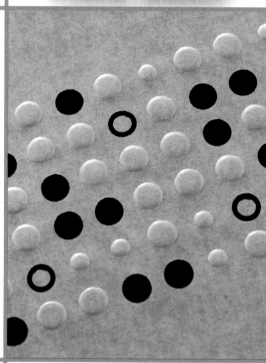

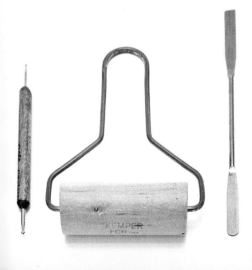

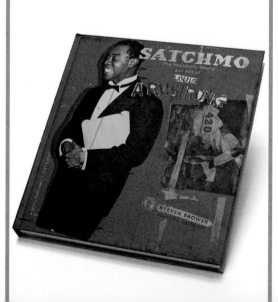

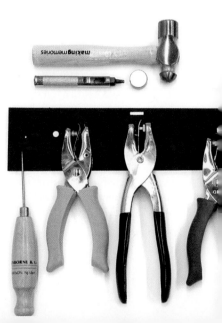

> "Fun begets quality."
> —Michael Lebowitz, Principal, Big Spaceship

First row, left to right:
Thermography powder.

Packaging: Skin care product
Creative Directors: Michelle Sonderegger, Ingred Sidie
Copywriter: Kerry Conan
Illustrator: Tom Patrick
Studio: Design Ranch
Client: DERMAdoctor
Materials and techniques: Plastic canister with frosted metallic paint;
flexographic printing

Brushes and applicators for gluing.

Second row, left to right:
Promotional brochure: Dartmouth College
Creative Director: David Schimmel
Designer: Charisse Gibilisco
Studio: And Partners, NY
Client: Dartmouth College
Printer: Hemlock Printers
Materials and techniques: Mohawk Options paper, clear foil stamping
(on cover), glued (perfect) binding, conventional offset printing

Folder cover (detail): Fibermark Paper
Creative Director: David Schimmel
Designer: David Schimmel
Studio: And Partners, NY
Client: Broadform
Printer: Dickson's
Materials and techniques: Fibermark Paper, "bind" embossing,
conventional printing

Promotional book with clamshell case: Coral Island Exclusive
Waterfront Villas
Creative Director: Roy Poh
Studio: Kinetic, Singapore
Client: Ho Bee Group
Materials and techniques: Vinyl covered board, conventional and
specialty flexographic printing

Third row, left to right:
Embossing tools, brayer, spatula.

Book cover: *Satchmo: The Wonderful World and Art of Louis Armstrong*
Creative Director: Steven Brower
Designer (and author): Steven Brower
Studio: Steven Brower Design
Client: Abrams
Materials and techniques: Conventional offset printing, thermography
(title), and spot varnish (subtitle)

Various hole punchers.

nine
specialty printing and
postpress special effects

chapter nine: specialty printing and postpress special effects

learning objectives

- Gain a basic understanding of specialty printing and postpress special effects.
- Develop skill in simulating a variety of specialty printing and postpress special effects.
- Explore the creative potential of specialty printing and special effects.

special occasions

Specialty printing processes and postpress special effects are meant to create tactile and physically compelling surfaces that excite and draw the viewer into the design and composition but can also truly enhance and/or drive the design concept; see Figure 9-1 for a design solution that successfully incorporates a specialty, postpress process.

Certainly, no special effect (printed or otherwise) will improve a poor design concept; however, inclusion of an elegant or playful, mysterious, or just plain fun visual effect used with intelligence or wit can transport a good design into a texturally and literally outstanding one.

Yet, nothing diminishes the professional level of a design more than abuse and overuse of specialty printing or other postpress special effects—glitzy eye-candy that has no conceptual backbone. Any effect—whether a fold, a binding, a specialty substrate, or a printing technique—should be an element among many that is interacting in conjunction with the whole to deliver the design solution and be budget smart.

By no means can we explore all the types of printing and special effects that can be accomplished. Technology plus human imaginations are powerful engines that are constantly inventing new things. Rather, think of our discussion as a foundation in the area. The industry is a dynamic and fluid one, so count on lifelong learning. We believe you will have fun playing in this chapter.

why make a comp? a review

In the professional field, designers rely on samples from the manufacturer, or they might use their own past work to show the client how a special effect looks. This is the professional practice because usually there isn't time or need to create a handmade comp of a special effect. In these cases, the client understands or will accept the generic sample.

Figure 9-1
Invitation: Kean University holiday party
Art Direction and Design: Erin Smith
Studio: Cinquino & Co.
Client: Kean University Foundation
Materials: Cardstock paper, laser cutting, conventional offset printing with metallic ink
The delicate and lace-like character of laser cutting is perfectly suited to the subject matter of this invitation to a winter holiday celebration.

So why comp specialty printing or a postpress special effect? For a student, one or two design solutions (in the overall portfolio) that display a smart use of specialty printing or special effects would speak of that individual's awareness of what is possible in the professional field. In addition, handcraftsmanship skill is displayed.

Designing appropriately and with intelligence is our advice for the use of special effects. But we do urge our students to explore, to wander creatively, to be inventive, to be zany at times, and to otherwise create to their heart's content.

To prove a point, look around. There are professional designers creating all those spectacular visual effects. Therefore, we want our students to reach for smart creativity too. Yes, explore the beautiful, the elegant, the mysterious, and fun—and go for the zaniness when possible!

With the encouraging words come a caveat. It is not always possible to comp a refined or complex special effect. Yet, some effects can be accomplished to a degree—enough to land on the basic look and feel of the printing or special effect. We touch upon as many effects as possible within the limits of this book and guide you further with links to resources.

Supply outlets include all those mentioned in Chapter 1 on basic tools. Additional resources are noted throughout this chapter.

sampling the specials

Beyond the printing basics, a wide variety of specialty printing processes and postpress visual effects are performed with special printing inks and varnishes, without ink, or in combination; see Figure 9-2 for a design solution using several appropriately fancy visual effects.

Because of the crazy, powerful creative drive of designers, it seems that there are no limits on what can be physically achieved with printing and postpress special effects. (Okay, maybe there are some—the client's budget and a few technical limitations as well.)

The specialty printing listed is a group most often seen in use but by last count not the limit of what can be produced. We limited

Figure 9-2
Invitation: Art Directors Club of New Jersey award show
Creative Director: Keith Rizzi
Designer: Keith Rizzi
Copywriter: Debra Rizzi
Studio: Rizco Design
The invitation and envelope created for the Art Directors Club of New Jersey award show displays a variety of printing techniques, including conventional lithography, metallic ink, die cuts, and burnished engraving—suitably fancy relative to the event.

our discussion to those that could be fairly easily simulated on the desktop: varnishes, spot color, thermography, foil stamping, and silkscreen.

In addition, we note those printing processes that are almost impossible or not at all possible to simulate on the desktop, but any designer should be aware of them and therefore they are also included: *engraving* and *letterpress* and contemporary novelty processes such as *lenticular* printing and *anaglyphs.* These processes are discussed further along in this chapter.

desktop specialty printing

There are many specialty printing processes. Challenge a printer and just see what develops, but be aware of the rising costs of production revolving around specialty printing. Specialty print processes add to the cost of production, yet the physical and tactile surface created may be worth the extra money in order to differentiate the design solution from among the massive amount of printed matter produced.

The following are several basic specialty printing and postpress processes that can be simulated on the desktop:

¤   Varnishes

¤   Spot color

¤   Thermography

¤   Sculptural printing

¤   Silkscreen

¤   Foil stamping

make it shiny or matte

A **varnish** is a clear oil-based coating applied to a printed substrate, usually over an existing printed image, that is intended to protect the surface or create a surface finish (both in look and feel) different from the areas around it.

"Green" coatings such as nonvolatile **UV** (dried or cured by ultraviolet light) or **aqueous** (water-based) are applied over the entire surface of a brochure cover, for instance, to heighten shine, deepen color, and/or protect the surface. Aqueous coating provides a protective finish that is claimed to exceed the quality of varnish. Aqueous dries quickly and is resistant to smudges and fingerprints. It is ideal to protect heavy ink coverage and is available in dull or gloss finish. See Figure 9-3 for an example of allover coating.

Figure 9-3
Book: *The Kean Review*
Creative Editor: Rose Gonnella
Art Direction: Erin Smith
Design: Erin Smith, Allison Grow, Jason Alejandro, Matt Senna, Neil Adelantar
Client: The Kean Review
The deep color and heavy ink coverage on this journal cover called for an aqueous coating to protect it from fingerprint smudges.

Alternatively, varnishes and UV coatings can be applied to a discrete or isolated *spot* on the page. Isolating the application is referred to as **spot varnish** (or spot UV). See Figure 9-4 for a professional design solution effectively using spot varnish.

The spot varnish finish can be glossy (reflects light) or matte (absorbs light). There are also levels in between such as semigloss, satin, and "luster." Varnishes are usually smooth to the touch, but can be applied for a rougher textural effect as well.

Professionally implemented, spot varnishing can be performed either during or after the standard printing process, depending on the equipment used. In addition, varnishes can be combined with other special effects such as embossing (discussed further along in this chapter).

N.B. Only the manufacturer, the printer, or postpress specialty company representatives can determine if the effect you have in mind can be technically accomplished. Learn what is possible and open communication with the technicians who can accomplish the effect—there can be no surprise errors on the professional level.

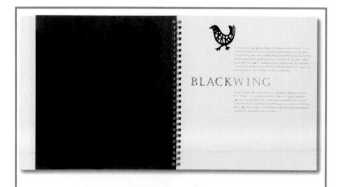

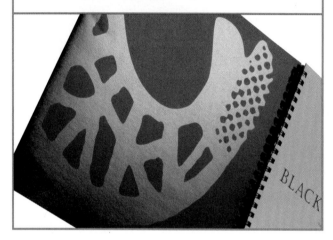

Figure 9-4
Top to bottom:
Book: *Step Rd*
Creative Director: Scott Carslake
Designer: Scott Carslake
Copywriter: Step Rd Wines
Studio: Voice
Client: Step Rd Wines
Printer and Bindery: Finsbury Green Printing
Materials: Paper—PhoeniXmotion, conventional offset printing
and spot varnish
Close-up of varnish effect. Spot varnishing can have a compelling visual
effect on a printed piece, at times making colors more vibrant or making
a particular part of a design appear to "pop out" from the surface or
recede into it. According to the designer, "Step Rd is printed on a very
high quality stock; we wanted whiteness, the right texture and a stock
that would allow spot varnishes to perform."

comp it up! the varnished truth

Methods for simulating spot varnishes include:

- Use of special printing paper
- Frisket film application
- Clear gloss, self-adhesive, printable inkjet sheets
- Gloss spray and frisket film mask

Simulating a spot varnish and incorporating it into a comp can prove to be somewhat of a tricky process. There are several methods, but truthfully, none can reproduce a surface as *fine* as the professionally created application. Desktop simulations are good for comps and personal projects. However, nothing substitutes for superior professional quality.

specialized desktop printing paper

If a simulation of a full-page varnish is desired, we recommend simply using gloss, luster, satin, or other specialized desktop printing paper. The surfaces of these papers yield the appearance of a varnish or a UV coating.

For *spot* varnish, we recommend printing the spot area on glossy, luster, or satin inkjet paper and *gluing* it onto a matte surface. There may be a ridge where the glossy paper meets the matte paper, but the contrast is the point. See Figures 9-5 and 9-6 for a student design solution and the simple steps to produce a comp of a booklet cover with a simulated full-bleed varnish.

Figure 9-5
Student project: Promotional brochure/biking company
Designer: Michael Boos
Production: Michael Boos and Rose Gonnella
Simulated spot varnish was used to contrast the landscape image (inkjet printed on matte paper) with the image of the compass (gloss paper) and the binding material (*faux* suede).

Figure 9-6
Spot Varnish Using Gloss Paper Step by Step
Left to right:
The book was constructed in pieces and assembled without the final image that was to receive the simulation of a spot varnish.

The compass image was printed on Epson glossy photo paper and then adhered to the blank substrate (two layered for strength).

When held in hand, the glossy image seems to project forward while the landscape image recedes—thus appropriately enhancing the depth of field. The three finishes and variety of materials combine to enhance the earthy qualities.

printable gloss paper method

A second method to simulate spot varnish employs either clear adhesive sheets such as **frisket** (airbrush masking film) or self-adhesive, peel and stick, printable clear gloss paper. The clear sheets (a.k.a. label paper) and frisket film can be cut to virtually any size and shape by hand and then adhered to the design in the appropriate spot location.

The drawback is that the possible formation of unsightly air bubbles below the frisket or clear sheets will make the "varnished" spot look as though it's blistering. Prevent this from happening by working slowly and lightly burnishing if necessary.

Another possible drawback is that the adhesive on frisket is made to be temporary, and your clear sheet may therefore eventually peel off. Comps, however, are not meant to be archival.

Simulating a spot varnish with frisket film and clear sheets can have superb results in many cases and so we recommend this clean and simple route. See Figure 9-7 for brief instruction in the use of frisket for spot varnish simulations.

two spray methods

The third and fourth methods for simulating spot varnish involve the use of *clear spray paints*. There are a wide variety of clear finish paints including shiny high-gloss to the dullest mattes and even "frosted" finishes.

N.B. Spray paint may have fumes that can be toxic. Handle properly. Use a respirator and apply any spray in a well-ventilated room or use a spray box (a box that helps to contain the particles rather than letting them escape into the air of the room and your nostrils).

To use the spray, apply frisket film or paper mask around the area to be coated (to protect it from the spray), keep the mask and the substrate perfectly flat, and then apply the spray. See Figures 9-8 and 9-9 for two methods using clear spray.

Be aware, this method also has its drawbacks. Many papers won't hold sprayed liquids very well—the coatings may bleed into the paper, leaving the image edge blurry. If spraying over a printed image, the ink may also bleed and obviously destroy the printed image. Testing is mandatory.

Desktop printing papers that already have a coating will take to the spray method significantly better than matte papers, but that is not to say that the ink on the paper itself won't be affected. As per usual, testing for suitability is a must. We suggest that you keep the spot small.

color spots

The frisket mask method can also be employed to simulate a spot color. It can also work for a spot of metallic or flat opaque color. Briefly, a flat area of **spot color** is printed in addition, at extra cost, and along with standard lithographic printing. A spot color is incorporated into designs for various conceptual, visual, and technical purposes—to differentiate, to add color richness or a discrete "punch" of color, or to print onto dark paper or fabrics.

To simulate a spot color for a comp, proceed as you would with the spray paint and frisket method but switch from the "varnish" (clear spray) to metallic or otherwise opaque paint. See Figure 9-10 for a step-by-step example of spot color—silver on brown paper.

Figure 9-7
Spot Varnish Using Clear Adhesive Paper Step by Step
Not pictured: Print design solution and set aside.

Separately print the shape to receive the spot varnish on an
adhesive-backed, clear printing paper.

First row, left to right:
Cut the shape from adhesive sheets.

Peel the backing to expose the adhesive and carefully lower the shape
into place on the preprinted substrate.

Second row, left to right:
Burnish carefully to remove air bubbles.

Finish and detail of result.

Figure 9-8
Stencil and Clear Spray Spot Varnish Step by Step
The image composition for this example was designed by
Christopher J. Navetta (Steven Brower, Creative Director).

Not pictured: First, print image.

Separately, print the outline of the subject image on the stencil material
(index weight paper).

First row, left to right:
Cut out the stencil.

Use double-stick tape that has been "detacked" (first stick to fabric such
as your shirt—this decreases the tackiness of the glue on the tape) on
the reverse side of the stencil and adhere in place to the printed image.
Not pictured: Spray the clear gloss evenly over the exposed image area.
Be sure to spray in a well-ventilated area and/or outdoors and please
use a face mask for safety.

Second row, left to right:
Original design without varnish in comparison to the finished shiny
result. Yes! You can create a spot varnish on the desktop.

Figure 9-9

Spray with Frisket Mask Step by Step

The image composition for this example was designed by Christopher J. Navetta; illustrated by Ian Dorian; colored by Christopher J. Navetta (Steven Brower, creative director).

Print full image. Place frisket over the design and trace the image onto the frisket.

First row, left to right:

Cut out the image area to be masked (and test fit the mask).

Test-fit the mask over the area to be protected from the spray.

Peel the backing.

Second row, left to right:

Carefully adhere the frisket mask to the printed image area.

Not pictured: In a well-ventilated area or outdoors, spray the clear gloss onto the image. Let dry.

Each spray varies in dry time, so follow directions on the can.

Carefully remove the frisket only after the paint has dried.

Held in hand, it is easy to see how varnish reflects light.

Third row, left to right:

Finished comp.

Seen in comparison, the varnish enhances the depth of the color and provides contrast.

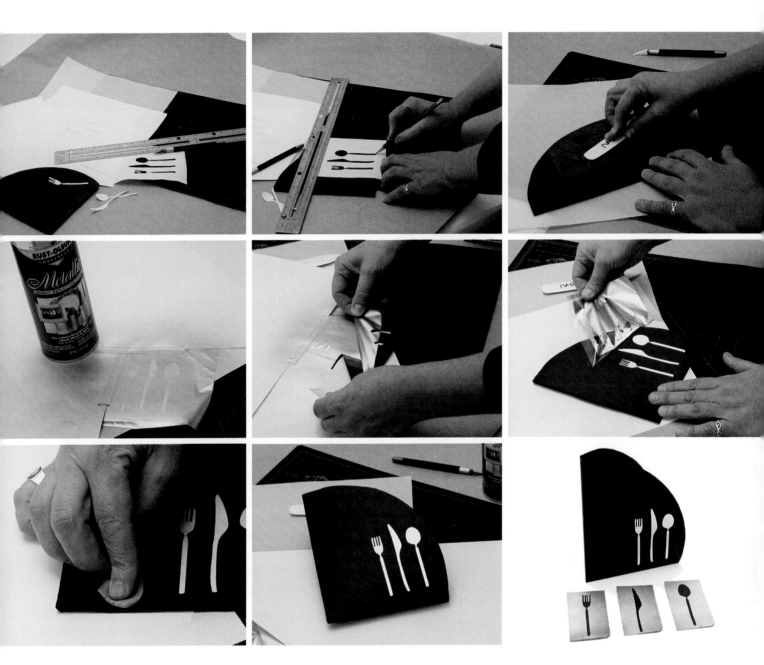

Figure 9-10

Spray and Frisket Mask Method for Spot Metallic Step by Step

Begin with a design concept and composition that is appropriate relative to the technique of metallic spot color.

Print the full image.

First row, left to right:

Place the frisket over the design and trace the image onto the frisket (complete). Cut out the image area to be masked.

Peel the backing and test fit the mask; use a soft pencil to mark placement of the mask.

Carefully adhere the frisket mask to the printed image area and burnish to adhere the large coverage of frisket. Additional masking material (scrap paper) covers the entire surface (anything that does not receive the color).

Not pictured: In a well-ventilated area or outdoors, spray the metallic paint onto the image area.

Second row, left to right:

Let dry. Each paint varies in dry time, so follow directions on the can.

Carefully remove the frisket only after the paint has dried.

Third row, left to right:

Clean up any overspray particles with a kneaded eraser—press lightly and pull up with the eraser; do not rub.

Finished result.

In this image, note that the simulated business cards have been sprayed with the same metallic paint. The image mask is the "positive" shape instead of the "negative" shapes that were used to mask the images for the folder.

The image composition for this example was designed by Christopher J. Navetta. The folder and cards were designed and crafted by Rich Arnold.

Figure 9-11
Sculptural Printing Step by Step
Left to right:
Begin with a design concept and composition that is appropriate relative to the technique of sculptural printing. Print the design and print test alternatives (always test).

With a steady hand, apply the paint to the image area.

It is best to get the paint applied correctly in the first place. You can try to fix holes or lumps but results vary in success.

Photographs used in design: *Hot Dog in a Bun*

© Digital Food | Dreamstime.com

Hot Dogs & Baseballs on an American Flag
Dreamstime © Creativestock | Dreamstime.com
Home plate and chalk lines on a baseball diamond

© Papabear | Dreamstime.com

sculptural printing

Sculptural printing is a process by which liquid polyurethane is applied over a printed image to give it a rounded, raised, or domed effect. The coating can be applied manually (as from a syringe-like device) or, for larger jobs, by specialized machines. The polyurethane can be applied over virtually any printed matter, such as lithography or digitally printed. Dome or raised printing is most commonly seen in application on labels or stickers, giving them a three-dimensional feel without having to print on alternative (usually more expensive) substrates. Obviously, this is not a "green" print process—such as foil stamping has become—but it may be someday.

See Figures 9-11 and 9-12 for a step-by-step procedure where the mustard pictured on an image of a hot dog is made sculpturally golden. You will need sculptural paint or three-dimensional paint, or foam, puff, or texture paint, which can be found at craft supply stores. You will also need a steady hand.

a stamp of approval

Foil stamping is technically a specialty *postpress* process that provides for the "printing" on substrates that do not take well or at all to the full-color printing provided by offset lithography, digital, or desktop inkjets. For instance, foil stamping can be employed for use on color paper and textured paper; see Figure 9-13.

Stamping involves *impressing* color film (the foil) onto the surface rather than using ink as with offset lithography. The process yields a tactile quality given that the stamping creates a slightly impressed surface. The process is also known as block print, foil emboss, hot stamp, and heat stamping.

The word *foil* does not necessarily mean that the stamping result will be of *metallic* foil as you may expect, although it can be; see Figure 9-14 for metallic foil. Rather, the process involves a film (this is the foil) that could be matte and opaque, clear, metallic, prismatic/holographic, or textured (refer back to Figure 9-13 for opaque foil stamping).

Foil stamping implemented industrially uses a **die** (a metal form that has been fabricated into a specific image shape or typeface). The die presses the film/foil into a substrate with the aid of heat, resulting in the image adhering to the paper.

desktop stamping

On the desktop, foil stamping can be roughly simulated. Rather than using foil, proceed using a rubber die and ink. Standard pigment, foam inkpads are available in many colors and a variety of finishes. The various inks available are suited to a variety of substrates. Some inks will take to any type of surface, and others are more specialized for glossy papers or nonpaper surfaces like plastics or acetate. Inks can be quick drying; others take a bit longer, allowing you to use multiple stamps and blend colors.

Figure 9-12
Book design: *Golden Recipes from the Ballpark*
Designer: Christopher J. Navetta
Photograph used in design: *Hot Dog in a Bun*

© Digital Food | Dreamstime.com

Figure 9-13
Book cover: *Summer Nantucket Drawings*
Art Direction and Design: Russell Hassell
Illustration: Rose Gonnella
Studio: Russell Hassell
Printer: Studley Press, MA
Client: Rose Gonnella
The title of the book was created using an opaque stamping over warm green, textured Strathmore cover weight paper. The ink is conceptually appropriate for the "summery" subject matter as well as solving the technical problem of printing on a textured, color stock with light ink.

Figure 9-14
Promotional brochure: The Tate Residences
Creative Director: Roy Poh
Studio: Kinetic, Singapore
Client: Hong Leong Holdings Ltd.
Left to right:
The metallic ink of foil stamping creates a texturally impressive surface and functions well on a dark substrate.

A foil stamped image can also cover a large image area for dramatic results.

Figure 9-15

Manufactured Stamp and Hand Printing Step by Step

First row, left to right:

This stamp was fabricated industrially to the (student) designer's specifications (cost: $25).

White ink was selected in order to print over dark paper. Grey ink was added to the stamp pad to cut the brightness of the white.

Not pictured: Measure placement of the image on the surface. Use the boundaries of the stamp (not the image itself) to set the placement points. Once the stamping is complete, use a soft pencil so that the marks can be easily erased with a gum eraser.

Apply ink to the stamp.

Test on a scrap of the substrate or a similar one. Note coverage and compensate with more or less ink for the final. Also note that if you rock the stamp back and forth, there may be stray and undesirable ink outside of the image and too much pressure will cause the ink to smear.

Second row, left to right:

Cover as much of the surface with protective tracing paper as possible to protect against stray ink spots.

When you are ready to apply the inked stamp to the surface, move in closely so that registration to the measurement marks is clearly seen. Be accurate; you have only one chance to print. Errors cannot be corrected. Apply even pressure from the top down and do not rock the stamp.

Pull the stamp straight up to remove. The ink is very wet. The drying time varies with the type of ink used (blues take longer to dry, for instance). We suggest that drying time is at least two hours.

Finished comp.

The composition for this example was provided by fourth-year student, Sylvia Miller, and re-created for this illustration by the authors.

The "dies" used for desktop stamping are usually flat rubber plates, vinyl pads, or foam that is cut and mounted onto a block of wood or foamboard. The plate surface can be carved into a complex or simple shape; the foam is cut with precision scissors and/or a craft knife. Stamps can be flat single images or designs, or they can be fitted onto a roller to allow multiple inline repetitions of the same image by rolling the inked tool over paper.

The resulting shaped rubber is then pressed into ink. The inked stamp is then pressed onto the surface of paper or other substrate. Obviously, a smooth surface will take the ink best. Textured papers may not allow for a complete, flat coverage. For the latter, a foam stamp is more flexible for forcing into the crevices of textured substrates.

Supplies for desktop stamping can be purchased through craft and art supply retailers. Do not look for "foil stamping." Rather, supplies will be found under the name "stamping." For studio simulations and comps, you can either carve the rubber plate or have a stamp made at a retailer such as Staples, Office Depot, or other office supply stores. See Figures 9-15 and 9-16 for two versions of the desktop stamping process.

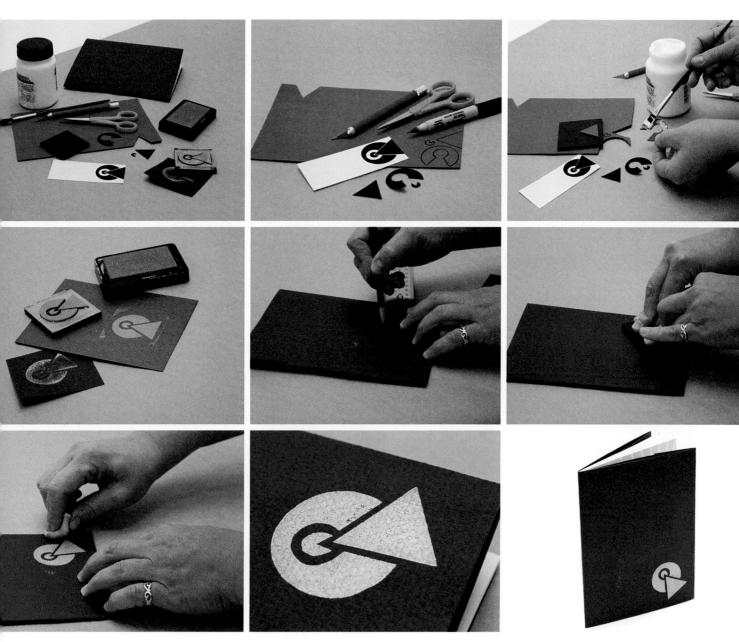

Figure 9-16

Handmade Stamp and Printing Step by Step

First row, left to right:

Design the image or shape to be used as the stamp. Print the design out in the full size, and carefully cut out the shape with a craft knife and/or scissors.

Trace the paper cutout(s) with a marker onto a piece of craft foam. Again using a knife and/or scissors, cut the shapes out of the foam.

Using a brush, spread a viscous glue such as PVA on the reverse side of the foam shapes, and carefully place those shapes on a cut piece of foamboard. Allow the glue to dry thoroughly before proceeding.

Second row, left to right:

Apply ink to the stamp and test on a scrap of the substrate or a similar one. Note coverage and compensate with more or less ink for the final.

Using a soft pencil and a ruler, measure and mark for placement on the final design piece.

With sufficient ink applied, move the stamp into place, using the pencil marks as a guide. Push the stamp down, applying even pressure. Do not rock the stamp back and forth. There may be stray and undesirable ink outside of the image. Also, too much pressure will cause the ink to smear. Pull the stamp straight up to remove.

Third row, left to right:

Use a kneaded eraser to clean up any stray ink if necessary.

Allow sufficient time for the ink to dry.

The final result.

Do *not* use premade stamps with images that are not of your own design. Strive for creative originality. Although you may hire an illustrator when you are a professional art director, at a student level, conceptualize, design, and make your own images—always be honest and authentic. When a potential employer asks if you created an illustration in a particular design within your portfolio, the answer should be "yes."

heat it up

Thermography is a relatively inexpensive specialty printing technique that employs heat to melt powder resin on the surface of a substrate. The melted resin creates a raised textured surface. Like stamping, thermography is employed for a conceptually smart, creative textural effect and in a practical way is used to print on substrates that do not take to conventional full-color printing. See Figures 9-17, 9-18, and 9-19 for thermography in action on professional work.

thermographic character

Both stamping and thermography are most commonly used for small areas of the design. Commercially printed stamping and thermography can be accomplished on intricate designs or for extensive coverage.

Figure 9-17
Invitation: Joe & Josie's 50th Anniversary
Creative Director: Rose Gonnella
Designer: Joseph Konopka
Studio: Water-born
Client: Josephine and Joseph Gonnella
Thermographic printing was used to create the faux wax seal on the envelope for this invitation. An actual wax seal would have been cost prohibitive; however, the ochre color thermography ink was an excellent substitute. The seal referenced both the official nature of the invitation and the historic event.

Figure 9-18
Book cover: Satchmo/The Wonderful World and Art of Louis Armstrong
Creative Director: Steven Brower
Designer (and author): Steven Brower
Studio: Steven Brower Design
Client: Abrams
The raised surface created by the thermography references the collage imagery created by Louis Armstrong found in the content of the book. It creates an attractive tactile surface, much like the art medium of collage.

Figure 9-19
Page spread: The Tate Residences
Creative Director: Roy Poh
Studio: Kinetic, Singapore
Client: Hong Leong Holdings Ltd.
A fine use of thermography to raise the texture of type for a soft touch (similar to the texture of a pearl). The oyster has a layer of spot varnish. Detail of the thermography is also pictured.

On the desktop, as with varnishing or stamping, we recommend that thermography printing is best used only in spots or limited discrete areas. Do not expect refined and perfectly sharp lines either. Thermography yields a pitted and uneven result. But do think of the resulting texture as a positive (not negative). Develop the design concept within the character of the technique—do not look for the medium to be something other than itself.

In the craft world, *thermography* is often used interchangeably with the term *embossing* (discussed further along in this chapter). That is unfortunately both misleading and inaccurate. Thermography specifically requires the use of heat to melt powders to create the desired effect, whereas embossing does not. However, when shopping for thermography supplies in the average art supply retailer, you're likely to find thermography supplies under the "embossing" label. Thermography powders, like stamping inks, are available in a wide array of rich colors (see Figure 9-20) including metallic, white, and clear.

Figure 9-20
Thermography powders melted on vellum.

Thermographically printed images can be produced relatively simply; the desktop process is linked to stamping. Adhesive ink must be first applied to a paper or other substrate, either from an inkpad or specialty pens/brushes. The thermographic (embossing) powder is sprinkled over the wet ink/adhesive. Excess is blown away or otherwise removed, and then heat is applied to the remaining powder. Use of a specialty heat gun is necessary because a hair-dryer won't produce enough heat. When the powder is heated to its critical temperature, it begins to coalesce into a continuous, raised surface.

comp it up: thermo!

For practice purposes, you will need to design a simple, flat shape for the adhesive ink and stamp method and a printed typeface (headline text) for the adhesive ink/pen method.

Refer back to foil stamping in regard to the procedure for creating a stamp. Once the stamp is fabricated, you can move along to the thermographic simulation process for comps. See Figures 9-21 and 9-22 for the stamp pad option and the adhesive pen option, respectively, for simulating thermography and for a visual explanation.

through the screen

Screen printing (sometimes referred to as silkscreen) is a specialty printing process by which an image is imposed onto a thin screen or fine mesh of materials such as silk, nylon, or even stainless steel. The positive (inked) image area remains uncovered while an impermeable substance masks off the nonimage areas. After the image is fixed, ink is forced through the open screen areas onto the printing surface—which can be virtually any substrate from papers to fabrics to plastics.

The screen printing method is often used to print on substrates that can't be sent through standard offset presses. Primarily, however, this printing process is valued for the ink's high opacity and utter brilliance and depth of color. Applications range from handheld invitations and printed matter contained in envelopes and folders to large posters; see Figure 9-23.

We don't have a step-by-step guide for screen printing due to its complicated procedure. Instead we suggest that you begin with the supplies themselves and accompanying instructions. There are desktop screen printing kits available that include complete instructions. Kits usually contain a frame and screen with a base, **squeegee** (the tool for pushing ink through the screen mesh), photo emulsion and acetate sheets (for masking), ink, and printed or DVD instructions. See Figure 9-24 for an example of the squeegee in action.

Figure 9-21
Thermography Step by Step
Create the stamp and application.

First row, left to right:
Measure for position and ink the stamp.

Ink the stamp and apply to the substrate (be sure to test).

Clean stray ink with a kneaded eraser.

Second row, left to right:
Sprinkle thermo powder liberally to cover the image.

The powder should adhere only to the inked area; lift the substrate and knock off the excess powder. You might want to shake it onto another sheet or right back into the jar of powder, as to minimize the waste.

Remaining powder particles can be brushed away.

Third row, left to right:
Use a craft knife to remove stubborn stray particles.

Ready to melt—aim the heat gun at the shape from about 3–4 inches from the surface. Be careful not to get too close—you will scorch the paper.

FYI: Paper combusts at 451 degrees Fahrenheit (thank you Ray Bradbury). Keep the heat going until the powder has completely melted. Turn off the heat gun.

The final result.

This hardcover book was produced through Lulu.com and then altered on the desktop. The cover paper is Gund Bronze. Stamp crafted by Christopher J. Navetta; book design by Rose Gonnella.

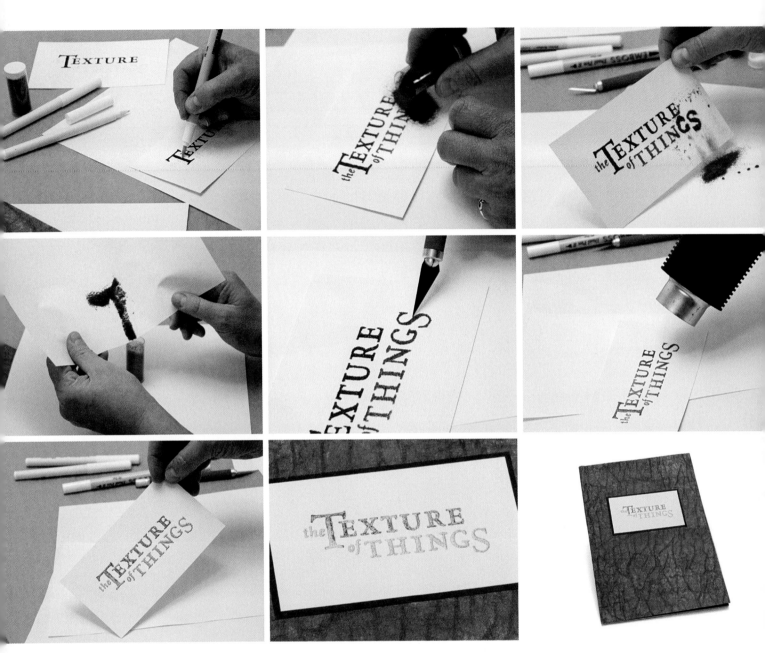

Figure 9-22

Thermography simulation using adhesive pen.

Print the image (or in this case the type) onto the substrate. The color used below the thermography powder will affect the final result. Experimentation and testing are necessary. Notice that we have a black ink and light grey ink outline.

First row, left to right:

Use the pen and ink over the shapes of the letters. If you have many words and letters, ink and print only a small group at one time.

Sprinkle thermography powder over the adhesive-covered portion of the image.

Knock off the excess. Repeat until all letters are completely inked and covered with powder.

Second row, left to right:

No waste—return excess to its container.

Brush away stray particles if necessary, and use a craft knife to remove any remaining particles.

Heat and melt powder (as noted in previous instruction).

Third row, left to right:

Final result.

Note the difference in colors due to the contrast of color in the base ink.

In application: a handmade book with a painted fabric cover and tipped-on typographic image.

The typography for this example was created by Christopher J. Navetta and applied to a book designed by Brett Magretto for the purpose of demonstration. The distressed typeface, Celestia Antiqua, was selected to work with the rough surface created by thermography.

Figure 9-23
Poster: Thinking Creatively Design Conference
Studio: The Design Studio at Kean University
Art Director and Designer: Steven Brower
Client: Kean University, Department of Design
Printing: Coe Displays
Left to right:
The poster was produced using a six-color silk screen (even though Steven specified only three colors)—two extra hits of black and two of white were generously added by the printer. The white is opaque ink, *not* a knock out. Although it is impossible to get the full sensation of the print quality in this reproduction, we vouch that the color of this poster is densely saturated and brilliant because of the specialty printing process with which it was produced.

Detail: dot (halftone) pattern used to simulate a grey shadow.

Figure 9-24
Silkscreen tools in action.
Silk screen print

© Vladimir Kinetic | Dreamstime.com

Even though the process is not simple, it can be accomplished on the desktop—albeit on a wide work table where a mess can be made without concern over staining its surface. Although we are not covering the exact steps in the process, we do offer the following tips for beginners relative to designing for screen printing:

◻ Keep the composition and the shapes bold and simple.

◻ Keep each color discrete.

◻ Do not layer colors; transparencies are possible but are an advanced level.

◻ Do not depend on exacting alignment of colors; rather let the white of the paper separate images.

◻ Test the substrate.

◻ Be prepared to practice and then attempt a final comp.

If a desktop printing seems too daunting or is not possible due to space and time limitations, there are outlets where screen printing can be purchased for relatively inexpensive rates. The cost will vary depending on the complexity of the image, the substrate, and the number of copies ordered.

venerable specialties

As listed at the start of this chapter, there are several processes that are *not* possible to simulate on the desktop or that are only possible with highly specialized presses. We are compelled to mention several of these printing processes because of their unique visual and/or textural qualities. Be aware of these specialty printing processes, and pursue further understanding (and use) when possible and appropriate in your professional career.

Several historic printing processes are still in use in the professional field. These processes include letterpress, engraving, and hand printing processes such as intaglio and woodblock.

back in time

Considered the oldest printing technique, **letterpress** is a process by which a letter (type) or an image is cut from wood or molded out of metal, then set together in rigid form, rolled over with ink, and sent through a press where the type and image are transferred (pressed) into the paper. Originally the letters or type blocks were made of wood, but as technology evolved, metal (usually lead) was the material of choice for fabricating the blocks; see Figure 9-25 for an example of wood type blocks.

Letterpress printing is a rewardingly tedious process prized for its subtle and elegant tactile qualities. Because of the high cost of printing, letterpress is primarily used for a small number of printed copies (a short run) and for applications such as stationery, business cards, invitations, posters, fine art broadsides, and limited edition art books.

You cannot fully simulate letterpress on the desktop. However, there are small desktop machines (found in craft stores) with a limited variety of typefaces to choose. Alternatively, if you have local access to fine arts studios where the art of the book is offered, there is very likely a letterpress in action. You can continue to research letterpress by visiting the sites of the book arts centers mentioned previously in Chapter 5, the College and University Letterpress Printers Association (CULPA), and commercial letterpress printers and book arts centers such as those in the following brief list:

- Aldine
- The Art Craft Company
- The Ligature
- Piccolo Press USA
- Precise Continental

Figure 9-25
Historic wooden type.
Wood Type 2
© Mark Fairey | Dreamstime.com

Figure 9-26
Professionally printed engraving sample from All State Legal, NJ.
Sample provided courtesy of All State Legal.

fine engraving

Engraving is a fine printing process. Much like letterpress, the only way to truly understand the tactile quality of engraving and get a feel for its beauty is to, well, *feel* it. Skim your fingertip across the slightly raised surface; bring the printed result close to your eyes to see the utter fineness of line quality and richness of the solid areas of color. There isn't another process quite like it; see Figure 9-26 for an example. Please realize that the full impact of engraving cannot be felt in a photograph.

Unfortunately, there is no desktop engraving process and since it would not be cost-effective to actually add an engraved image to this textbook, we urge you to seek out samples through your instructors or otherwise. The next time you attend a national American Institute of Graphic Arts (AIGA) conference, be sure to seek out samples of engraving and other specialty printing processes. Or visit the International Engraved Graphics Association (IEGA; www.iega.org) to request engraving examples from its members.

To learn more about the engraving process, as well as how and when to use it, the professionals at All State Legal and the International Engraved Graphics Association (IEGA; www.iega.org) have kindly provided us with a written guide to designing with engraving in mind; see the feature article in this chapter.

fine arts printmaking

If you are studying design in a university, college, or school that has fine arts studio programs, we strongly recommend that you peer into the book arts and printmaking studios. Likely (and luckily) you may find the presses and equipment for the studio versions of historic printing processes such as letterpress, woodcut, and *intaglio* (etching, engraving, drypoint, mezzotint), as well as screen printing.

In the printmaking studios, you can explore and learn as well as get hands-on experience with the historic printing and contemporary studio adaptations of the historic processes. Take classes for personal enrichment. Adapt what you have learned as a student designer or simply enjoy the process of creating your own engraved images and producing "hand-pulled" multiples.

back to the future

There are two twentieth-century specialty print processes worth noting for fun and flashiness. These processes include lenticular and anaglyph—both are *illusionary* three-dimensional printing. Only anaglyph printing can be simulated on the desktop.

Lenticular printing involves creating the illusion of depth or movement of images as they are viewed from different angles. At least two images are interlaced in this process. An image is sliced into strips, then interlaced with one or more other images; the strips are printed on plastic that on the reverse side has a series of long thin lens molded into it. The lens are lined up with each image interlaced so that light reflected off each strip is refracted in a slightly different direction—thus the illusion of flickering movement. See Figure 9-27 for an image of lenticular printing in use on a book cover. Developed in the 1940s, lenticular printing has recently been adapted to large scale as well and can be seen on movie posters and airport graphics—appropriately flashy.

Figure 9-27
Book cover: SVA Student Portfolio
Creative Director: Richard Wilde
Designers: Various
Studio: School of Visual Arts
Client: School of Visual Arts
Left to right:
The board cover of the book employs lenticular printing. There are approximately 120 images in total. Each unit in the grid has three images that can be seen depending on the angle of how the book is held.

the benefits of engraving

The following article on engraving was kindly provided by All State Legal and the International Engraved Graphics Association.

introduction to engraving

Engraving brings unparalleled elegance and dimension to everything it touches. Regarded as the finest way to set ink on paper, engraving lends a look of prestige to any design. Though the engraving process may add some time and cost, the results will set you apart with a classic quality and successful style that reflects the best image. Combining tactile interest with rich opaque colors, engraving has the legendary ability to reproduce fine lines and solids with stunning clarity and consistency.

how engraving works

Engraving is a form of intaglio printing. An intaglio *(in-tal'-yo)* is a design carved into the surface of hard metal. Born in the fifteenth century, this unique process entails cutting or etching fine lines onto the surface of a metal plate called a "die." Historically these lines were hand cut, causing engraving to be labor intensive and costly. Since the late 1970s, engravers have used photo-etching and other high-speed techniques that enable the process to be timely, very competitive, and affordable.

The die is then positioned on a press, coated with ink, and wiped so that only the etched areas of the plate remain filled. Exerting tremendous pressure (up to 4,000 pounds per square inch), the image is transferred from die to paper producing a finely detailed, raised image on the surface with a subtle reverse indentation on the back.

the evolution of engraving techniques

Engraving techniques appeared simultaneously in Germany and Italy around 1450, coinciding with Gutenberg's introduction of the printing press. Maso Finiguerra of Florence, and Schongauer, Graff, and Albrecht Durer of Germany were acknowledged early masters. Etching plates with acid was introduced at the beginning of the sixteenth century. Through a process called "stopping out," some areas of plates are exposed to acid longer than others, allowing the artist to obtain rich gradations and delicate atmospheric effects. Rembrandt is considered the greatest etcher of this period.

Mezzotint engraving was invented in Germany in 1642. In a mezzotint, the engraver burnishes areas of a plate or die to produce an unlimited gradation of tone. Because this captures the effects of light and shadow so well, early mezzotint engraving was often used to reproduce famous paintings, broadening their audience and appeal.

Aquatint engraving, invented by Jean Baptiste Leprince in France, combines etched lines with clearly differentiated tonal areas. The result resembles the flat tints of an ink or wash drawing. Spanish artist Francisco Goya was the acknowledged master of the aquatint technique.

benefits of engraving

Ironically, though hundreds of years old, the engraving process blends traditional craftsmanship with state-of-the-art technology for optimal quality. Today's creative community embraces engraving as one of the most creative and time-tested options for realizing their clients' identities as tangible assets.

The engraving process possesses several inherent benefits:

- **Stay true design.** Ability to reproduce fine lines and solids with stunning clarity and consistency ensures faithfulness to a designer's intentions.

- **Stay true color.** Engraving ink is designed to keep a uniform PMS color throughout any project.

- **Flexibility.** Engraving allows for the placement of light color inks over dark backgrounds creating tactile textures and images. The use of burnished metallic inks can also add dimension to any design.

- **Compatibility with desktop printers.** Engraving inks are environmentally friendly water-based compounds that do not "break down," melt, or smear when subjected to the very high temperatures in modern desktop printers.

- **Environmentally friendly.** Engraving inks are ideally suited for recycling.

- **Built-in security.** Engraving creates a superior barrier against unauthorized alterations because no scanner or color copier can duplicate the tactile features of raised ink.

These benefits are why engraving remains the universal choice for currency and negotiable instruments, as well as an excellent choice for global businesses combating counterfeit products, packaging, and marketing.

Now, get out your glasses. Technically, you can simulate an **anaglyph**—an image that has a three-dimensional illusionary effect—through Photoshop or Illustrator software. But you do need special eyeglasses to see the effect. The paper and plastic eyeglasses can be found on the web; look for "3D Glasses" or "Three D Glasses Direct."

We note the use of anaglyphs, but printing them is a novelty and can get hokey quite quickly. Yet go ahead, try creating and printing anaglyphs for zany fun; see Figure 9-28. Note that the image is a line drawing. The drawing is doubled and slightly offset in two colors: cyan and magenta. Vary the offset distance and placement (left or right) to manipulate the depth. Much experimentation is necessary. The offsetting of images creates the three-dimensional effect when viewed through the specialty glasses that have one cyan lens and one magenta lens.

Figure 9-28
Anaglyph drawing.
Illustrator: Joseph Konopka
Get out your 3D glasses to see this one. Note the line work offset.

postpress special effects

After printing has been accomplished, a number of postprinting effects can be employed to conceptually and visually enhance a design solution. The following effects are easily accomplished on the desktop and thus they are the focus of this section:

- Embossing and debossing

- Tipping on

- Die-cutting

- Laser-cutting

above or below the surface

Embossing and **debossing** are essentially the same process, the former referring to a shape that is raised above a paper's surface and the latter to a shape that's sunken below the surface.

When embossing/debossing is professionally performed, a die (metal form) must be fabricated. In this case, there are two components of the die: the female (negative) and counter die male (positive). The selected paper (or other substrate) is pressed between the two parts of the die leaving an impression on the paper.

When performed in conjunction with ink or foils (metallic, holographic, opaque colors), the process is referred to as **color register embossing.** With no inks or effects, the process is called **blind embossing.**

Within reasonable limits (and every substrate and kind of paper has its tolerances), embossing or debossing can add as much as 1/8" of depth. Deeper impressions often have to feature beveled edges as not to tear or cut the paper during the pressing process. Embossing can be accomplished in many layers as well. Deeply embossed, multiple layered surfaces are referred to as sculptural embossing or multilayered embossing.

why emboss?

The raised surface of an embossed substrate is like a magnet to the human hand. It seems that touch factor is again, a most powerful draw; see Figure 9-29 for a professional example of embossed typography.

Embossing is found in a great variety of applications including but not limited to book covers, brochure covers, invitations, stationery, and business cards. The raised or lowered surface of the substrate becomes a focal point and assists with the functional hierarchy of the composition. For technical reasons, when using a dark color,

Figure 9-29
Book: *Step Rd*
Creative Director: Scott Carslake
Designer: Scott Carslake
Copywriter: Step Rd Wines
Studio: Voice
Client: Step Rd Wines
Printer & Bindery: Finsbury Green Printing
Difficult to see in reproduction and impossible to touch—an embossed surface is raised to draw viewers in by their hands.

embossing or debossing could be used to impress an image on a surface that doesn't take well to standard lithographic printing, such as vinyl, leather, or textured paper stock .

comp it up, or down!

Simulating embossing or debossing by hand can be achieved in several ways, and with varying degrees of accuracy to the professional process. We have three desktop embossing/debossing techniques that start simple and get increasingly complicated (but not daunting):

- Cut and glue

- Paper stencil die

- Covered stencil and base

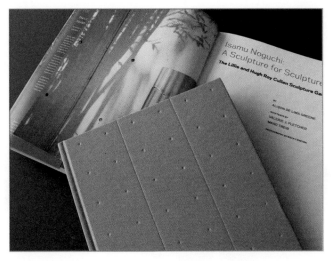

Figure 9-30
Book: *Isamu Noguchi: A Sculpture for Sculpture/The Lillie and Hugh Roy Cullen Sculpture Garden*
Creative Director: Henk van Assen
Designers: Henk van Assen, Amanda Bowers
Photographer: Rocky Kneten
Printer & Bindery: Chas P. Young
Studio: HvA
Client: Museum of Fine Arts, Houston
The embossed linen cover is a visual response to the concrete slabs used by Noguchi in the garden.

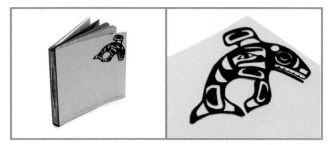

Figure 9-31
Student project: promotional brochure with embossing
Student designer: Michael Boos
(The image is based on a traditional and historic design from the Northwest Coast American Indian cultures.)
Gluing on an image raises it above the surface and simulates embossing.

Figure 9-32
Student project: menu
Student designer: Sylvia Miller
Cut out image and glue to a backing to create a simulated debossed effect.

cut out and glue method

The easiest way to simulate an embossed shape is simply to glue it onto the surface. The shape is cut from paper and adhered to the substrate, resulting in its being slightly raised from its surrounding base. This method is quick and easy, but it is the least visually appealing because it is the furthest from the actual simulation and definition of actual embossing; see Figure 9-30 for a professional example of deboss and Figures 9-31 and 9-32 for student examples of the stencil method of emboss and deboss.

paperboard die method

The **paperboard die** method is closest to simulating the industrial process. A paperboard stencil acts as a die (the tabletop is the plate). The paper is forced (rubbed) along the edges or crevices of the stencil with an embossing tool (ballpoint stylus) or a bone folder. The process "raises" the paper on the reverse side of the rubbing.

You will need cardstock or paperboard (Bristol) to make the desktop die. If the substrate paper is too thin, it will surely tear. As usual, testing is essential. Each type of paper will react differently, with some being more tolerant to this simulation process. Softer cotton papers may be easier to push into the shape, but might wrinkle more easily. Heavy or rigid wood pulp papers might not be easy to push into the shape at all and might just rip rather than conform. Testing is knowing.

Both embossing and debossing can be achieved by the paperboard stencil die method; the difference depends on which side of the paper substrate you push into the shape. See Figures 9-33 and 9-34 for a visual guide and instructions for this method (with variations).

Figure 9-33

Create and print the image to be embossed. Measure and reproduce a line art drawing of the areas to be embossed; this is the uncut stencil. Manually transfer the stencil to 140# Bristol or 120# cover weight paper (transfer can be done on a light box or cut and trace—not pictured).

First row, left to right:
Cut out the image area to be embossed.

Move to a hard, rigidly stable tabletop to implement the application. Position the stencil over the printed image to align precisely.

Carefully flip, and secure the printed design with drafting tape.

Second row, left to right:
Working on this reverse side, apply embossing tools to press and rub into the stencil. Use the larger ball of the embossing tool first and a small ball to fine-tune.

Finish completely before flipping the paper to see results.

Finished comp.

The design for this demonstration was created by Christopher J. Navetta.

Figure 9-34
Blind embossing technique.

First row, left to right:
Print the shape as an outline on index weight paper. Cut out the shape.

Measure and determine placement of the embossing.

Use drafting tape on the back of the stencil.

Second row, left to right:
Adhere the stencil to the substrate in position; all elements should be attached.

Flip the substrate to work on the reverse side; use an embossing tool to press into the edges of the stencil.

Not pictured: Once the process is complete, remove the template.

Finished result.

Third row, left to right:
After the stencil was embossed, the embossing tool was used to impress dots (to simulate salt).

Finished comp—bring mustard.

Embossed image seen in application—invitation to a book signing for *Golden Recipes from the Ballpark*.
The image for this demonstration was created by Christopher J. Navetta.

covered stencil method

A related alternative method of embossing can be achieved using cardstock or paperboard as a positive shape (stencil) that is adhered to a rigid substrate and then covered with paper.

The covering paper and its substrate base are made damp with liquid glue so that the covering paper can be pushed into and molded to the shape on the base. The result appears to be a continuous and smooth raised surface—a simulation of embossing.

Much like the previously noted stencil (die) method, start with cardstock or Bristol board. In this case, a heavyweight illustration board or other paperboard works well (for a sculptural relief). See Figure 9-35 for a visual guide and instructions.

varnish and emboss

Although we have been discussing the specialty printing methods and postpress effects individually, the processes and techniques can be combined. For instance, combine embossing or debossing with spot varnish or spot color. Thermography works well with tipped-on images—the latter discussed in the next section.

tipping-on

One of the simplest and easiest of the postpress special effects is one that you have no doubt been doing since you were very young and had access to paper and glue. Simply, a **tipped-on** element is one that is affixed on top of another (paper or a similar substrate) by means of adhesive. The image previously shown on the book cover in Figure 9-13 was printed using traditional offset lithography to keep colors true and sharp. The image subsequently was cut to size and glued (tipped-on) to the textured paper. Also noted previously, the title of the book was accomplished with opaque foil stamping.

The tipped-on element can be printed matter, a textured paper, or a small object. The element could be as basic as a photograph glued or an illustration tipped-on to a page in a book, or it can be significantly more complex depending on the item that is to be tipped-on such as a folded element, a highly textured piece of paper or other substrate, or even a booklet within a larger book.

The reasons for a tipped-on element vary. Often, the purpose is technical. For instance, the piece of printed matter will be tipped-on to a substrate that otherwise can't be printed on in a conventional way.

Or, the purpose for a tip-on may be conceptual and expressive. The tipped-on image may add a touch of textural elegance or it may be used for intrigue (to hide something below it—with only one edge glued so that the tipped-on image works like a flap). There could be any number of ideas expressed depending on the design concept.

What is important for any special effect is that its purpose should be either a technical solution to a problem or a contributing factor to the design concept, as in Figure 9-36.

Figure 9-35 (right)
This design was re-created here for demonstration purposes.

Student project: book cover.

Student designer: Michael Boos
First row, left to right:
Print image on index weight paper and cut into pieces.

Ready the substrate and the cover paper that will overlay it (work area ready for assembly).

Measure for placement.

Second row, left to right:
Using the negative stencil, trace the outline in order to place the cutout shapes on the substrate.

Apply glue to the back of the (positive) cut stencil shapes.

Using tweezers if necessary, place shapes within the outline previously drawn.

Third row, left to right:
Finished substrate ready for second-stage gluing.

Use a wide, soft bristle brush to slather the surface; work quickly so the glue does not dry.

Adhere cover paper overlay starting at one end and carefully roll it to the opposite end.

Fourth row, left to right:
Use a brayer to smooth and tighten the cover paper to the surface.

While the glue is still wet, use the embossing tool to push the cover paper into the crevices; be careful not to tear the paper by applying too much pressure. Let the tool do the job—brute strength is not necessary.

Flip over the substrate board; glue the exposed flaps of cover paper.

Fifth row, left to right:
Fold flaps over to adhere.

Final result (eventually the "embossed" board will be used as a book cover).

Close-up view of final result.

Figure 9-36
Packaging system: Fervere Handcrafted Bread
Creative Directors: Michelle Sonderegger and Ingred Sidie
Copywriter: Kerri Conan
Illustrator: Michelle Sonderegger
Printer: Hammerpress (letterpress process)
Studio: Design Ranch
Client: Handcrafted Bread
The tipped-on images enhance the handcrafted look of the packaging. Tipping-on combined with the plain kraft paper substrate also references the handcrafted character of the bakery for which the packaging serves.

comp it up: tipping-on

There are few instructions needed in describing how to simulate a commercially tipped-on image and equally few caveats. Most important, always choose an adhesive that is appropriate for the substrate. Test the glue. White glue may buckle the paper to be tipped-on if the paper is lightweight. Stick glue and double-sided tape may be preferable; both provide a very thin and usually strong layer of adhesive that will allow the attached element to lay flat—especially important if the element will only be glued along one edge as in the case of a flap.

Whatever your adhesive choice, always be as neat as possible. Smudges, fingerprints, and globs of glue peeking around the edge of a tipped-on element are not professional.

After the glue and substrates have been tested, the step-by-step procedure for a tip-on is fairly simple. Have a glue area and a clean construction area at the ready. See Figure 9-37 for a brief visual explanation for tipping-on.

N.B. To adhere a three-dimensional element (such as a button or metal clasp or hinge, for example), we suggest using hot glue. You will need a hot glue gun for this operation. We have noted the tool in Chapter 2 and its use in Chapter 3.

Figure 9-37 (right)
Erin Smith (Kean University) is the designer of this image. The book was designed and crafted by Rose Gonnella.

First row, left to right:
Print and cut out the image to be tipped-on. Measure the area to receive the tipped-on element and lightly mark the points of measurement.

Apply the liquid glue to the back of the element to be tipped-on. Make sure the glue covers the element evenly without lumps—too much will usually cause buckling. A board chip is good for this purpose.

Hold the image with a stylus so it doesn't move.

Second row, left to right:
Place the left corner of the element and align and place to the right side point. Hold the one edge and gradually place the element.

Cover with tracing paper and press with a folding tool to tighten the bond.

Voila! The final result. (For the finished book, see Figure I-4.)

cut it out

Somewhat complicated at the industrial level but relatively simple and easy on the desktop, a die cut is another postpress special effect and one that designers employ frequently when the budget allows.

The term **die cut** refers to a cut (out) made in a printed or unprinted substrate. The cutout element will either serve a conceptual/aesthetic purpose or allow for some sort of technical or mechanical function; see Figures 9-38 and 9-39 for professional examples. The possibilities for both are nearly endless and highly configurable (yes, relative to the allowable budget).

When created professionally, die cuts are made with metal knives—machine-formed into the shape of the desired cut. The metal knife shape is the "die." The size, shape, and configuration of the metal die are either standard or created by the designer.

When pushed with sufficient pressure, the metal die cleanly cuts through the paper or other substrate, and the result is a cutout shape. Slightly less pressure is sometimes used to perform a **kiss** die cut, which does not cut completely through paper or other substrate. The best example of the result of a kiss die cut is a sheet of adhesive-backed "stickers." There is enough pressure used to cut out the shape of the sticker itself but not the waxy (glue resistant) paper backing sheet.

Because of the creativity of designers, many dies have to be custom-made, significantly increasing the price. However, printers and/or postpress production companies who manufacture the die cuts often have a good deal of standard dies readily available—shapes that may suit the needs of the design solution and avoid the need for costly custom work.

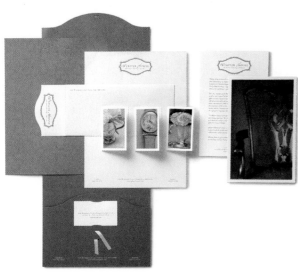

Figure 9-38
Stationery system: Webster House
Creative Directors: Michelle Sonderegger, Ingred Sidie
Designer: Rachel Karaca
Copywriter: Kerri Conan
Photographer: Gab Hopkins
Printer: M-Press
Studio: Design Ranch
Client: Webster House
Die-cutting serves both an aesthetic and functional purpose in this elegant stationery system.

Figure 9-39
Business card: EN Japanese Brasserie
Creative Director: Matteo Bologna
Designer: Andrea Brown
Printer: Diversified Graphics
Studio: Mucca Design
Paper selection: French Paper speckletone
Die-cut rounded corners are seen on this business card. Also note, as stated by the creative director, "The printing mimics a rough [hand] stamp but the debossing and heavy paper make the piece feel luxurious."

laser cutting

Beyond the metal die cuts, there is the realm of laser cutting. The process (and purpose) of cutting with a laser can yield extremely fine and intricate cutout shapes and patterns; refer back to Figure 9-1. Most specifically and for either a die cut or a laser cut, the techniques should somehow enhance the quality of shapes, images, or patterns. For example, the snowflakes that are finely laser cut in Figure 9-2 are a delightful (and thoughtful) depiction of the delicate nature of the object.

cut for a reason

A die cut or laser cut, as noted previously, should be integral to the design solution (not mindlessly decorative) or should serve a technical/functional purpose. See Figure 9-40 for an example.

Functional die cuts have a range of purposes. For example, the sides of a rectangular package might be die-cut into pointed shapes (tabs) that fit into coordinated die-cut slots on another part of the package, allowing the tab to be inserted into the slot and ultimately making the package hold its form. Die cuts are often only technical in use.

We have a recommendation relative to concept development with regard to incorporating a die cut or a laser cut.

First, ask yourself these questions:

- Can the image or shapes be an illustration or a photo instead?

- Why use a die cut or a laser cut?

We recommend that the die cut or laser cut have a specific purpose—for instance, to *surprise* the viewer. Perhaps the cutout area could be a window or "peek" hole revealing only a portion (only part of the story) of a larger image below or behind the cutout. Below the die the larger image or story is revealed; see Figure 9-41.

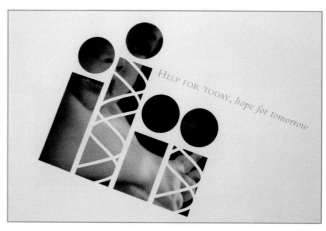

Figure 9-40
Hang tags: Forecast retail clothing
Creative Director: Jim Rivett
Art Director: Jim Rivett
Designers: Laura Treichel, Luis Avalos, and DeGaull Vang
Photographer: 44 inc.
Printer: Gift Box Corporation of America
Studio: Archetype
Client: Forecast
Die-cutting was used in these hang tags as a functional element.

Figure 9-41
Brochure cover: Huntington's Disease Society of America
Creative Director: Keith Rizzi
Designer: Keith Rizzi
Studio: Rizco Design
Client: Huntington's Disease Society of America
Laser cutting allows for delicate and fine shapes and line work. The image references a double helix DNA strand that is in direct relationship to the genetic nature of Huntington's disease (the subject matter). The cutout reveals a photograph of a baby, again making a connection to genetics and humanity.

comp it up! specialty cutting

Most clean cuts are the result of a good sharp craft knife and very steady hands. A dull blade will not cut clean and smooth and will likely tear the paper. Stay sharp! Be careful.

Work on a cutting mat, as it is soft enough to not damage the tip of your blade, but rigid enough to hold the paper flat and firmly.

Exercising patience in the hand-cutting process is a must. Patience is a virtue! Simply take your time when performing a cut. Remember the instructions discussed in Chapter 3 (and perhaps review basic techniques before proceeding). It is often necessary to cut several times slowly rather than apply too much pressure while cutting—which can make a blade wobble.

Yet, multiple passes are significantly more difficult in complex shapes, as tracing over the previous cut can be tricky. But with the alternative being a possible jagged cut or a torn paper, the multiple-pass practice is highly preferable. For slight repairs, use a very light sandpaper to smooth edges after a cut.

If the intended cutout shape is a circle or an oval, consider using a tool and template specific for the purpose (noted in Chapters 1 and 3).

A shape other than an oval or circle is fairly simple to comp. Follow the basic procedure noted in the following list:

- Ready the work area for cutting and construction.

- Test all measurements and materials involved.

The shape or patterns involved should be in the precisely desired location (there is little or no margin of error in a cut).

- Using a 5H pencil, indicate the area to be cut. The pencil line can help to score the paper—making a track in which to fit the blade. However, the track left by the pencil must be perfectly accurate and smooth; otherwise the blade will get snagged. Alternatively, make the mark for the cut without pressing with the pencil.

- Hold the substrate steady with one hand as close to the cutout shape as possible.

- Cut into the paper and slowly follow the guideline, turning the substrate and blade *together* as needed.

- The paper should cut easily and cleanly (if it does not, you may need to change the blade or the paper may be too thick).

- When complete, the cutout element should simply fall out of the substrate. If it does not, do not pull out the shape. Cut again.

- If there is a *slight* snag or a tiny tear, try using a very light sandpaper to smooth the edge. But do not rely on the sandpaper for a large nick or misplaced cut—there is nothing to do about a poorly cut shape but start over.

If attempting a complex cutout, one that simulates a laser cut, we suggest simplicity of design and a greater degree of patience. We have no other instruction than what has been stated and to make your own judgment—perhaps the laser cut is not worth the time involved. Then again, maybe it is worth all the time you have to give it; see Figure 9-42.

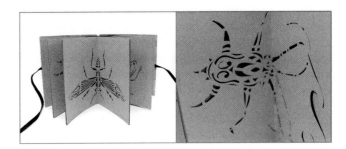

Figure 9-42

Student project: personal exploration.

Student designer: Nancy Goldberg

a decorative punch

There are also small handheld die cutting tools that will perform any one of a wide variety of cutout shapes. Available at craft and art supply stores, the handheld punches can be found in basic shapes such as circles, squares, triangles, and rectangles, as well as the more complex. There are also the sentimental and well-worn symbols such as hearts, stars, and so on. Beware of the use of these! Design with originality. Don't rely on premade shapes and cliché symbols for your design solutions *except* for the use of basic shapes (circles, squares, triangles) or if the shape is a historic classic such as a *fleur-de-lys*; see Figure 9-43 for a student example of an appropriate use of a classic, emblematic shape.

Another particular type of cutting tool is the rounded corner cutter. Exactly as its name suggests, it cuts a neat rounded corner and is available in a number of radii. A simple task like rounding the corners of a page can often prove to be somewhat difficult, especially if you're doing it in any great numbers—but this small, die-encased "clicker" (refer to Chapter 1 on tools) can make your life of comping significantly easier. And since a rounded corner softens the feel of a right angle, four rounded corners could possibly add a touch of elegance to a business card, or one rounded corner may add an asymmetrical edge—we encourage creative exploration.

Figure 9-43
Student project: business card.

Student designer: Christopher Panlillo

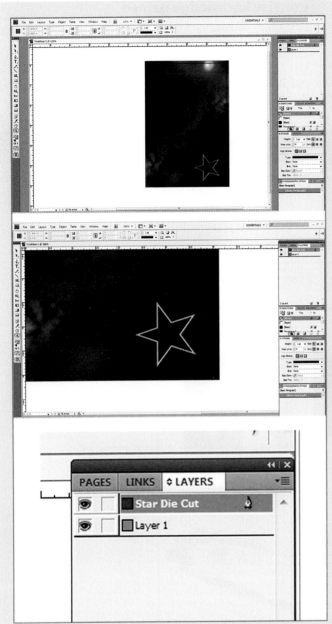

Top to bottom:

A layout for a card featuring a star-shaped cutout.

The die cut is shown in the design as a simple vector shape.

The vector shape of the star is on its own layer, named appropriately, as seen here in the layers palette.

summary:
ready, set, specialize

There is great fun in comping the specialty printing processes such as spot varnishes and colors, thermography, foil stamping, and screen printing. Die-cutting your way through paper for a visual surprise or raising the surface through manual embossing can be seductive to both the designer and audience. But once you have had your fill playing with special printing processes and postprinting special effects, do remember that in professional practice, there needs to be a balance between the creative free-for-all of design and the client's budget. Have fun. Design smart.

exercise knowledge gained

In Japanese, *kodomo no kao* refers to the look on young people's faces when they are absorbed in play.

Yes . . . it is that time once again! Collected here are several exercises and play that use the knowledge and techniques gained from this chapter and your designer's prowess to craft and produce.

1. continue to sample

Familiar now with a slew of special effects, your head should be swimming with ideas—and hopefully the inspiration to put these ideas into action!

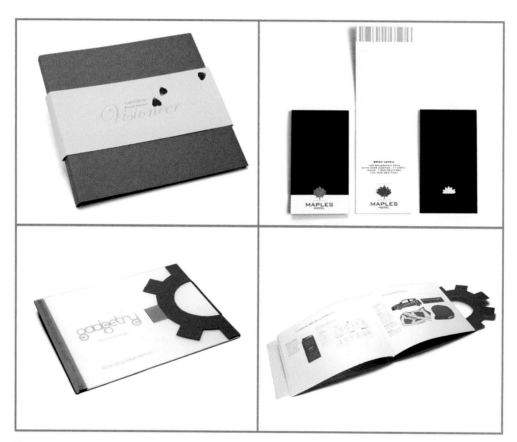

Figure 9-44
First row, left to right:
Student project: promotional brochure with "belly band" and tipped-on rose petals.

Student designer: Sylvia Miller

Student project: business card with die cut.

Student designer: Nicole Santiago

Second row, left to right:
Student project: promotional brochure with die cut (open and closed).

Student designer: Christopher Panlillo

The first thing you need to do is practice basic versions of each of the techniques. Most of the effects discussed have several variations as well as various degrees of difficulty. If you haven't done the step-by-step tests embedded in this chapter, return and complete each one on paper blanks.

Compile the blank comps and include them in your (now-bulging) binder of samples; keep the samples as a resource and for future reference.

Refer back to Chapter 1 for the sources for supplies. In addition, and specifically related to stamping, thermography, and specialty paints, we suggest the following outlets:

- Crafters Pick
- Dharma Trading Co.
- Frantic Stamper
- Ranger Ink
- River City Rubber Works
- The Ink Pad NYC

2. play and apply

You are past the basics now and have the know-how for the easy stuff. It's time to get the creative juices flowing to combine *play* with *practical application*. How can the learned specialty printing and specialty effects be applied to enhance one or more of your existing designs?

Adapt a favorite project, and explore the possibilities of enhancing it with one or more of the effects. What are the practical and aesthetic benefits? Does it simply make it look better? The effect should provide some new functionality and/or enhance the concept and composition. See Figure 9-44 for student examples.

3. be a storyteller

Begin a new project using a folded format or simple binding. Using only imagery, tell a visual story. The story can be the simplest of topics but should be conveyed in a few pages (for the sake of time and money).

In addition to the imagery, use your newfound knowledge with special printing and postpress effects to help tell that story. For instance, use spot colors or varnishes to physically illustrate the

Figure 9-45
Student project: paper company promotional brochure using die cuts and spot varnish.

Student designer and photographer: Luis Guillen

glossy nature of the story imagery. Use thermography to add tactile realism to something that feels rubbery. Emboss and deboss parts of an image to add highs and lows (and therefore depth). Die cut a shape to reveal the story below it. Design with purpose and use each effect judiciously and logically. Take your story from just the visual to the interactively tactile! See Figure 9-45 for student examples.

4. be an inventor

Learning doesn't end here. You are becoming increasingly more experienced. Now it's your turn to take matters into your own hands. Find a special effect. Using the techniques learned in this chapter, see if you can determine the best method to simulate the effect.

Lead a life of discovery. Research one avenue and you may learn something additional and unexpected along the way.

part three:
portfolio presentation

"What will differentiate individuals, corporations, educators, and countries? Generating new ideas—creative solutions to all types of problems will be the key to the future. We will need creative thinkers. We will need people whose disciplines are creatively based to inspire us all, to teach us all. We will all need to be inspired."
—*Robin Landa, educator, author, and creativity consultant*

ten
present well

chapter ten: present well

learning objectives

- Become aware of the value of a high-quality presentation.
- Acquire basic knowledge in photographing design solutions.
- Explore portfolio page compositions and book arrangement.
- Become aware of options for presentation books.

simple yet personal

Once design solutions have reached their final stage in regard to both concept and design and all the corresponding comps are perfectly constructed, you are ready to consider the presentation of your body of work.

The presentation should be of the utmost professional quality but nearly invisible—seen yes, but not "heard." After all, the presentation is meant to showcase the great work being displayed—not eclipse it. We call this type of "seen but not heard" presentation *seamless.*

We advise that the presentation be seamless, yet we are not disallowing for some personal style. Creating a presentation style could reflect your identity as a designer. Our best advice is to keep the presentation simple and well crafted and to add a touch of your personal identity. See Figures 10-1 and 10-2 for samples of student portfolios and self-promotions.

a style of thinking

You may choose to style your presentation by simply arranging each design application and solution on a single page using a screw-and-post binder. Or you may choose to display the design solutions plus your design thinking—that is, to offer insight by visualizing some aspects of your process of design. The portfolio book may even become a narrative of sorts as seen in the casebound portfolio book in Figure 10-3.

value added

The design profession is rigorously competitive at its most creative end. To reach that end, you will need every edge-up possible. Nothing trumps having a portfolio of smart design and savvy advertising concepts (a fancy self-aggrandizing presentation will not hide mistargeted or trite concepts). Yet a poor execution of comps and a shoddy or cheap presentation will not speak well of your potential in the professional arena either.

The portfolio presentation not only showcases your ideas and ability to visualize them (the design solution), it speaks of your attitude toward the profession. The excellent craftsmanship displayed in the comps and the thoughtfulness of the total presentation says the following about you to a potential employer: *I care deeply about every aspect of my work from concept through presentation.* Therefore, the employer could assume that you would bring this valuable attitude into the studio or agency.

In addition to successful and innovative design solutions, excellent craftsmanship extended beyond the comps into a final presentation adds value to your worth as a designer.

get organized

Generally speaking, the considerations for your final presentation include but are not limited to the following:

- Targeting and selecting content
- Styling and photographing three-dimensional design solutions (the comps)
- Organizing the composition of each page of the portfolio
- Organizing the order of display of the pages
- Selecting an appropriate presentation binder
- Designing an appropriate website presentation

Figure 10-2 (right bottom)
Portfolio presentation.
Student designer: Allison Grow
Pictured is a self-promotional design solution, used in a variety of applications.
First row, left to right:
Portfolio binder with hand-rendered and typeset title
(*Allison's Intergalactic Portfolio*) page.
Résumé, mini-portfolio promotional cards, business cards, self-promotional cards, sample application (*comp*), and self-promotional buttons. The résumé, business cards, and promotional cards were created on the desktop, printed on Mohawk Glacier Mist and Desert Haze text paper. Standard size envelopes were purchased. Buttons were printed and crafted through online provider Busy Beaver Button Co.
Second row, left to right:
Website home page and subpage.

Figure 10-1
Portfolio presentation.
Student designer: Michael Boos
Pictured is a self-promotional design solution, used in a variety
of applications.
First row, left to right:
Portfolio case cover with handmade spot varnish nameplate.
Résumé, mini-portfolio (cards and envelope), business card, button,
and stickers (center).
The résumé was created on the desktop, printed on Gmund duplex text.
Business cards were printed online through Overnight Prints. Standard
size envelopes were purchased in dark blue. Buttons were printed and
crafted through online provider Busy Beaver Button Co. The stickers
were printed through Zazzle.
Second row, left to right:
Website home page and subpage.

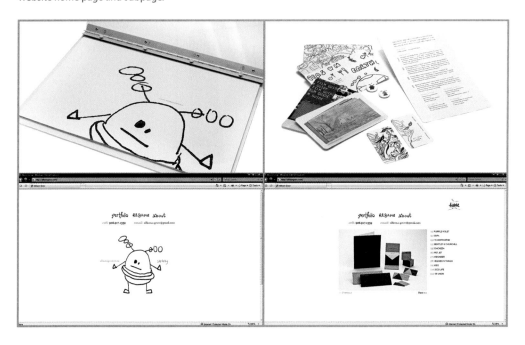

targeted content

You have spent several years developing your design thinking and visualization through an educational process that includes reading, looking, listening, and practice. Your practice design solutions are ready to present in their totality. With guidance from a mentor or through reading and understanding the requirements for entry into a particular design field such as editorial, new media, advertising, promotional, pharmaceutical, environmental, or branding, you will need to select those practice projects (or those created during an internship) to gather into the final career-launching portfolio. Two variations on content are noted in Figures 10-4 and 10-5.

We concur with the advice of the professionals in the field, national employment services, and national professional organizations such as the AIGA, the One Club, and state Art Directors Clubs in regard to the selection of work. The advice is simple: Include a limited

Figure 10-3
Student portfolio presentation
Student designer: Matthew Senna
The portfolio book is an example of a narrative style of organizing content. The pages display the designer's thought processes, influences, and general philosophy and ideas about his life as a designer as well as his work as a designer (design applications and solutions).

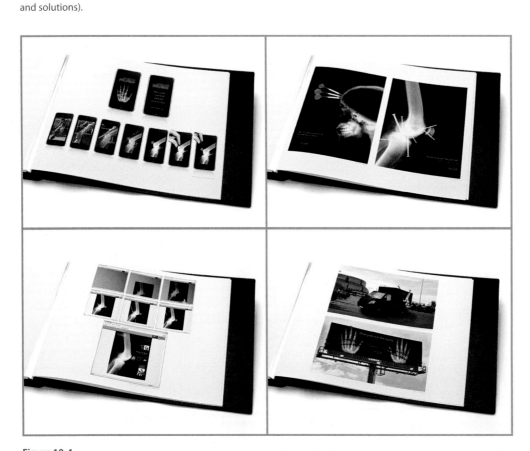

Figure 10-4
Student advertising portfolio
Student designer: Michael Fiore
An advertising portfolio typically contains five campaigns of various subject matter, exhibiting a student's knowledge of concept development across media platforms. Subject matter pictured: smart phone application; print ads, website, outdoor board, and signage for a pain reliever.

Figure 10-5
Student branding and promotional design portfolio
Student designer: Jamie Maimone
Display quality over quantity, but do include a range of subject matter, concepts, and art direction. Subject matter and application pictured: retail packaging system, promotional poster, restaurant identity (including promotional materials and menu), and real estate development stationery.

number of *only* your best design solutions. Quality, not quantity, is the paramount concern. The portfolio is all about smart ideas that display an understanding of both marketing strategy and corresponding targeted design.

The portfolio presentation should showcase a range of critical and creative thinking (smart ideas) and corresponding visualization

(art directions and design). Craftsmanship and technical skills are important in regard to presenting those ideas in the most professional manner possible.

how many?

How many design solutions should a portfolio contain? There is no magic number. And, the number is relative to the type of approach you will take in the overall presentation. However, we offer a *suggestion* of seven integrated design solutions for a graphic design portfolio and five integrated campaigns for an advertising portfolio. Cross-reference this suggestion and get more information on each area of design by consulting with employment services and professional organizations specific to the field, such as the nationally known business, the Creative Group. But do your research; not all employment agencies are reliable.

styling photographs for presentation

Your ideas and concepts are smart and on target. Your art direction and design are appropriate and engaging. Your comps are flawless (Aren't you proud of yourself?). Now how do you get the three-dimensional objects onto your portfolio or webpage? A digital rendering or layout is sufficient for logos and two-dimensional graphics such as posters, print ads, or page spreads and similar applications, but three-dimensional objects will need to be photographed. It sounds relatively simple, but popping off a digital snapshot of a design solution actually involves a complicated procedure. There are several factors that need to be taken into consideration. Some are strictly aesthetic, and others are technical. We offer general advice, direction, and guidance but not specific and detailed instruction in the technical use of the camera. Although we offer advice on lighting the objects in the photograph, lighting for photography is a complicated procedure (and one that requires some training).

N.B. If you are not equipped to photograph your own work and do not have some experience in lighting, hire a professional or a senior photography student who specializes in still life. But do read our advice because even if you decide to go with a professional, it is best to know what to consider in photographing your work.

compositional approach

The overarching goal in composing the photograph of the comp or comps of a three-dimensional design solution is to keep the arrangement as simple and clear as possible. Although portfolios could feature a combination of images including photographs of three-dimensional work and digitally generated imagery, the focus here is the arrangement of the three-dimensional comps in one composition.

For each photograph needed in a portfolio presentation, there are two different approaches: subjective and objective.

Composing the comps *subjectively* involves organizing the featured pieces in an actual environment, placing the work in a particular context. For example, a packaging application such as soda bottles could be displayed on a table with a glass (full of soda), an ice bucket, and a kitchen visible in the background. With this approach, the design application is seen in context in an appropriate setting. The result could potentially contribute to the further understanding of the concept of the design solution. The success depends on how appropriately the context is simulated. If you choose this approach, simplicity is still important. Always place the focus on the design solution and not the context itself.

Composing the comps *objectively* removes the simulated context. Only a minimal background is used—solid colored paper. The focus is placed on the design solution without offering any visual assistance for its application in context.

It is conceivable to use both approaches to the photograph's composition within the portfolio. The choice depends on the mood and message that you want to evoke or communicate. Composing subjectively brings with it many options and ultimately more to consider when setting up the objects and photographing them. Composing objectively puts the focus totally on the design solutions. With either approach, a clear arrangement and proper

Figure 10-6
Student design: Soda bottle labels
Left to right:
The bottles are pictured objectively.
The bottles are pictured subjectively.

lighting are paramount. A cluttered composition or poor lighting will surely lower the quality of the photograph and thus the whole presentation; see Figure 10-6 for examples of subjective versus objective compositions.

shooting the work

To shoot your own photographs, use the most professional or the highest quality equipment available. Even if you decide to work with a professional or senior photography student, be aware of the equipment in use.

◻ *Camera*: Your camera needs to be a quality piece of equipment. Always use the best hardware. Make sure you know how to use all the appropriate controls. Without the knowledge of how to properly operate the camera, it is likely that the photos will be of poor quality and the time wasted. And for the love of the photography gods, please use a tripod!

◻ *Lighting*: Poor lighting is the bane of an otherwise good photograph. It doesn't matter how beautiful the subject is; without proper lighting, the object is in the dark and cannot be seen well. Dark photographs are not the only problem. Poor lighting could also overpower or "blow out" an object, making the image too bright.

Although professional lighting can easily eclipse the cost of your camera, you don't need to spend a bundle to get balanced illumination. With proper placement and adjustment, almost any kind of lamp with directional capabilities will work. Pole lamps or $10 silver-cone, clip-on lamps from any hardware store make for sufficient sources of light for a desktop setup; see Figure 10-7 for an example.

Frosted plastic, even the flexible kind such as a vinyl shower curtain liner, functions relatively well as a diffuser (in front of the lamps) to help eliminate harsh shadows. Please don't place the plastic too close to light bulbs, as it will likely melt.

Bright white poster board or foamcore can be used as reflectors to bounce the light around the objects. When lighting the objects, it is most important to keep the illumination equal and balanced throughout the arrangement. There should be no dark shadows, no ultrabright areas (or "hotspots"), and no harsh and glaring reflections. A good rule of thumb is to light the arrangement of objects as they would naturally appear outside on an overcast day.

N.B. By now, you may be thinking that photographing the work is too complicated for your capabilities. Reminder: Avoid frustration, stress, and waste—hire a professional photographer who specializes in still life. Shop around; perhaps there is a generous professional willing to offer a student a discount.

◻ *Background (backdrop) material*: Keep it simple. Particularly if using an objective approach (as discussed previously), you will need a large roll of dense, opaque paper (made for photographic backdrops) that is 40–45 inches wide and several yards long. Have a few neutral colors for use relative to the content of the photograph. White, off-white, black, and grey may be necessary. The choice of background color will be determined by the amount of contrast needed or desired. See Figure 10-8 and refer back to Figure 10-1 for examples.

If you intend to digitally enhance or alter the photographs— particularly if you are intending to silhouette or isolate the objects completely—use a background color that will provide maximum contrast to more easily facilitate the Photoshop manipulation and editing efforts.

Photographic Quality

With equipment and materials in place, you need to arrange the objects in a way that will display the best qualities of each, in a way that will make the group both interact and function as a complete whole. After consultation with the pros, practice, and observation, we offer a few simple suggestions and some guidance for optimum photographs. Consider the following:

◻ Composition and arrangements

◻ Point of view

◻ Lighting

The first consideration involves selecting what part of the object will be visible. For example, in photographing a box, which side of the box will be visible to the viewer? Is the front the most important face? Yes, probably. Yet, the box can be set at a slight angle to the picture plane in order to reveal more of the design and possibly to make the box a more visually interesting shape.

Figure 10-7
Simple lighting equipment including inexpensive clip-on lamps can suffice for desktop photography, if used properly.
Cheap Lighting

© Jack Schiffer | Dreamstime.com

Figure 10-8
Student portfolio pages
Student designers: Jamie Maimone and Tricia Decker
Faculty instructing: Steven Brower
Left to right:
A white background is an excellent all-purpose backdrop to enhance a color-rich substrate. Note that a white or off-white background can also provide a neutral backdrop for work that is essentially white. The visibility and clarity of the object depend on the success of the manipulation of the lighting.
An orange-brown background complements a design solution printed on a grey substrate.
Also, refer back to Figure 10-1. The background in this image was darkened through Photoshop to provide a shade that contrasts and heightens the clarity of the design object.

When the three-dimensional object is flat or parallel to the picture plane, it is difficult to understand that it is actually a three-dimensional object. Angling a box will also assist in enhancing the three-dimensional space. One box is rather simple to photograph, but if there are multiple objects, the difficulty in arranging increases—almost exponentially. All objects should work in conjunction with each other; no single object should hide or distort any important part of another. See Figure 10-9 for a complex yet well-ordered arrangement.

Figure 10-9
Student design: Identity and packaging system for a children's clothing boutique
Student designer: Allison Grow
This complex packaging system was carefully arranged to display the essential elements of each object.

Figure 10-10
Student design: Identity and packaging system for a children's clothing boutique
Student designer: Allison Grow
Left to right:
The boxes of this student-designed identity and packaging system were photographed separately in order to display details not visible in the single group composition.

The business card needed a close view in order to realize the details. Note: The three separate photographs, one displaying the entire packaging system and the two close-ups of the details could be displayed on consecutive pages in the portfolio binder.

Figure 10-11
Student design: Packaging system for personal care products
Student designer: Michael Boos
With only one comp available but a need to display several points of view (showing the unique structure of the open and closed top), the comp of the box was photographed twice and then composited seamlessly into a single image using Photoshop.

You may find that multiple arrangements and photographs of a single design solution are necessary because all the objects cannot be clearly displayed in one composition. Or, you do not have the multiple comps of a single object that needs to be shown from various sides or in open and closed positions. The solution may be to either shoot the objects separately and composite them in Photoshop or include multiple presentation pages of the various points of view of the objects; see Figures 10-10 and 10-11 for examples.

To further assist arrangement, aids such as small cardboard boxes or wooden blocks can be used to prop up or angle an object for optimum clarity and visibility. But be aware that the propping objects also add problems of their own. Props need to be hidden from view and should not cast shadows. (This is what is meant by exponentially more difficult.) See Figure 10-12 for an example of a photo composition that required a prop to be digitally removed.

And, we offer this low-tech tip: Use the sticky power of a kneaded eraser to stop the propping box from slipping, or use it to temporarily adhere the comp to the prop. A kneaded eraser is also a handy cleanup tool in that it easily and effectively removes lint and stray particles from the background paper. But be aware that kneaded erasers can blemish or damage certain substrates. Test first to ensure that you won't ruin your comp.

Working in conjunction with the compositional arrangement of the objects, also consider the point of view. We recommend having the objects arranged slightly above eye level—set up the camera accordingly (and use a tripod for stability). See Figure 10-13 for an example of arranging the point of view.

Get as close to the picture plane as possible without distorting the perspective. Test for optimum naturalness and clarity.

Figure 10-12
Student design: Packaging system for personal care products
Student designer: Michael Boos
Some images may require additional work with Photoshop to remove the objects that are used in propping or supporting the pieces in the photographic process.
In this example, the support that held up the envelope when originally photographing the design solution can be seen in the inset. After editing in Photoshop, the supports are no longer visible in the photograph.

With objects painstakingly arranged, adjust lighting accordingly. Eliminate as many shadows as necessary and make sure all objects are as evenly lit as possible. If small parts of the designs (such as a logo) need to be clearly seen, be sure that the detail is not in shadow or bleached out by overly bright illumination; see Figure 10-14.

In addition, beware of reflections when dealing with any glossy substrates. Reflections are most difficult to counteract. Some objects (such as bottles) are inherently glossy and super-reflective. Compensate for reflection in the process of photographing the objects, as digitally fixing errors after the fact is not the best option. Do not plan to fix errors in Photoshop. Post-photography processing is time-consuming and complicated and may not lead to satisfactory results. "I'll fix it in Photoshop" is a start-up thought that can lead to more work than is necessary.

Figure 10-13
Student project: Packaging
Student designer: Michael Boos
Left to right:
With an angle too high, you're capturing too much of the top of the box, hindering the visibility of the front, which displays the logo.
The same box is shot at a more advantageous point of view. Both the object and important design elements are clearly visible.

touching up a bit

Within reason, it's safe to assume that no photo is going to be completely perfect. Fortunately, there are tools such as Photoshop to help "tweak" and edit and ultimately improve the photographs. Yet don't use Photoshop as a crutch. The software was not meant to compensate for errors and careless oversights that should have been eliminated in the setup and photo stage. Correct as many problems as possible while photographing the objects. But some

Figure 10-14
Student design: Promotional brochure
Student designer: Allison Grow
Left to right:
The photo is too dark, which obscures the design elements.

The image is too bright, which "blows out" the design elements.

Adequately balanced lighting displays the design clearly.

basic photo-editing steps are recommended at this point. Each situation carries its own variables, but as a general rule, we suggest the following considerations when editing in Photoshop:

¤　*Color:* Make sure the colors in the photo are true to the actual object. If you have a purple object, but your photograph results in a sickly blue, work with color levels and tinting to most accurately achieve the proper color.

¤　*Lighting:* Is the overall photograph too dark or too light? The lighting should have been taken into account during photography, but if necessary, tweak the appropriate levels. Lighten shadows perhaps or slightly darken bright spots.

¤　*Background:* Are there any blemishes or distracting marks in the neutral backdrop? Eliminate any stray particles with any of Photoshop's brushes or the Healing Tool or some combination therein.

After the photos are completed, print them and review quality with an objective observer such as your faculty mentor. Do not settle for a weak photographic image of your design solution. Repeat the process until the photos are of professional quality.

composing the pages

After the photographic process, there next comes the task of placement or arrangement of one photograph or several photographs on a single page (or pages). In general, the display of single or multiple photographs on an individual page should be simple, well balanced, and without clutter.

A single image of a design solution should fill the page as much as possible and be large enough to read any typographical content. The design solution could also be shown close up with the most important aspects clearly visible. Alternatively, the detail shot can be an inset of the main full-page image.

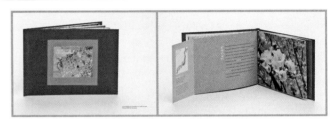

Figure 10-15
Student design: Promotional brochure biking tour company
Student designer: Megan Falb
Left to right:
Brochure cover.
Brochure page spread.

Figure 10-16
Student designers: Luis Guillen, Megan Falb
Comparison of arrangements of identity (stationery) applications
Left to right:
Arrangement of applications that have been cropped for a detailed view.
Arrangement displaying the full formats of each application.

Multiple shots of one design solution could be shown on the same page or on consecutive pages. See Figure 10-15 for an example of two consecutive portfolio pages.

In Figure 10-16, note the arrangement and placement of the photograph on the page. One student has cropped closely to show detail. In the second image, the entire objects are displayed. Either page arrangement style works well. The decision depends on how and where to place the focus and emphasis.

tech tip

Print on the highest quality, double-sided, matte paper that yields the best results with the printing hardware.

Frequently, design solutions have more than one component within the single application. For instance, an identity or a packaging system may have three to five (and beyond) individual pieces. The photographs and/or digital images displaying the components of a given application will need to be organized and composed on the printed page or webpage.

Planning the composition of the display of a multiple-part design solution on paper or a webpage depends on the number and complexity of elements in the application group. The page should include enough elements to establish and explain the design concept for the application without being redundant or cluttered. Be visually succinct, but do present all interesting aspects of the design.

displaying alternative solutions

"Nothing is more dangerous than an idea when it is the only one you have," stated the philosopher Emile Chartier. Therefore, there is often more than one design solution in consideration for an individual application. Depending on the arrangement struck with the client (or instructor), three, five, or more solutions may have been created. You may want to display the alternative solutions. Through the use and construction of a flip-out page format, a small group of alternative solutions can be displayed along with the primary (selected) design solution. See Figure 10-17 for an example.

labels

You may also choose to label each design solution (and printed page or webpage) with brief, pertinent information that will assist with a viewer's objective evaluation—a caption. If you choose to include a caption or label, keep it simple.

The caption could include the general and specific type of application, the general subject matter of the design solution, and perhaps the context and target audience (the concept should be obvious). For instance, a portfolio page/web label would read: "Identity system for an urban, boutique hotel with a young, business-oriented clientele."

Be sure to make the type grey in color as to not interfere or call too much attention to it. If the application is displayed on more than one page, the continuation could be noted on the label for that page.

page gallery

There are many ways to display a digital image, a single photograph, or multiple photographs and images on the portfolio page. It is perhaps best to see several examples to gain further understanding. In Figures 10-18 and 10-19, note in particular how the photos and images were arranged on the page. These pages also include captions.

We can never list all the options for page presentation because there are as many possibilities as there are human imaginations. Reminder: Keep the presentation simple to showcase the ideas.

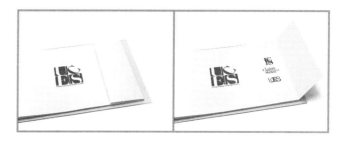

Figure 10-17
Identity: Theatre Workshop
Creative Director: Steven Brower
Student Designer: Yingyos Charyubayan
Studio: The Design Studio at Kean University
Client: Theatre Workshop, NY
Left to right:
The selected logo is displayed along with the alternative logo solutions. Displaying multiple solutions (when appropriate) to a single problem makes it known that the student can think beyond a single idea.

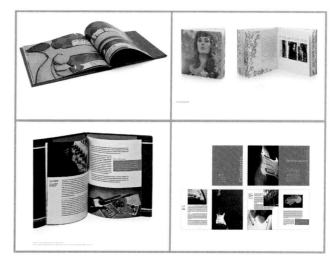

Figure 10-18
First row, left to right:
A student poster design fitting for a full-bleed spread.
Student designer: Juan Montenegro
Faculty instructing: Steven Brower
Student design: Two views of a promotional brochure composed on a single page
Student designer: Luis Guillen

Second row, left to right:
Student design: Promotional brochure
Student designer: Jamie Maimone
Photograph of the brochure (vertical and open).
InDesign page layouts printed from a PDF format.

Yet within the simplicity, there is room for some creativity—possibly employing the folds, envelopes, folders, and binding methods explored in this book. And when appropriate, design the presentation of the page to assist in highlighting a particular application or group of applications; see Figure 10-20 for examples.

Figure 10-19

First row, left to right:

Student designs: Book cover; informational brochure

Student designer: Ryan Guijo

Two views of the design solution shown separately but with a border to contain them in an orderly way.

Photograph of the brochure arranged on a single page with the corresponding InDesign page layouts.

Second row, left to right:

Student design: Concept and website design for a children's luncheonette

Student designer: Allison Grow

Website home page displayed within a browser window.

Web subpages grouped on a single page.

Third row, left to right:

Student design: Concept and website design for a cooking contest

Student designer: Jamie Maimone

Website home page displayed without browser window.

Multiple web subpages displayed to visualize the motion contained in the website. Since it is not possible to display the actual motion graphics on the printed page, several static images are necessary.

It is important to also develop the website so that any moving graphics can be seen in action. We recommend bringing a smart phone or laptop to a job interview to display any moving graphics.

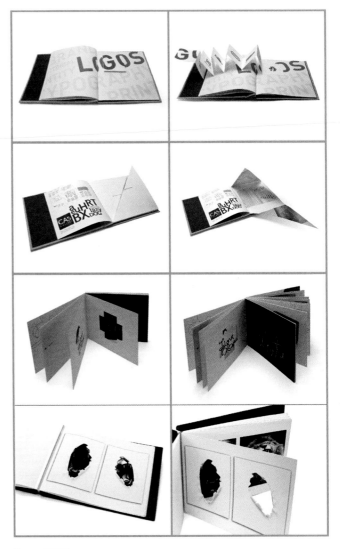

Figure 10-20

Portfolio presentation pages.

First row, left to right:

Student designer: Jason Alejandro

An accordion fold insert tipped in to a handbound book.

Second row, left to right:

Student designer: Jason Alejandro

The presentation page shown in its closed position.

The presentation page shown with page throw-outs.

Third row, left to right:

Student designer: Luis Guillen

Handmade book perfect bound; left to right pages reveal cutouts that are integral to a narrative story concerning the student designer's work philosophy.

Fourth row, left to right:

Student designer: Michael Fiore

Portfolio page showing an advertising campaign for horseradish (the product is said to have extreme bite).

The cutout page here is essential because this print ad concept would be seen in context as it is shown in the portfolio. Building the comp into the portfolio presentation is more direct than photographing the design.

order up the pages

For simple printed and bound portfolios, our suggested sequence for the order of display is as follows:

- Begin with the title page "teaser" (or web home page), name, and contact information.

- Display your best work first—the one of many great design solutions that you know is a "wow." It should be visually brilliant, innovative, successfully targeted, and well executed.

- Display the overall order of the solutions to emphasize variety rather than grouping like solutions together. In general, emphasize a range of solutions and skills.

- End with another "wow" example—your second best. Even though all are high quality, some surely have stronger impact and connection with the viewer due to the pinpoint success of the concept and art direction.

narrative content

Many student designers are opting to bind their portfolios as a casebound book—printed through one of many on-demand or one-off publishing companies such as Scribble Press Gallery Books or Lulu. This is a plausible option.

However, a casebound book also suggests that there is perhaps a story involved. The book could contain, in any order, developmental sketches for ideas, inspirational source notes, written thoughts, photographs, illustrations, and typography expressing personal ideas. Refer back to Figure 10-3 for such an example.

We cannot say with certainty if a casebound book of the content described previously will advance a young designer any further than a screw-and-post binder portfolio displaying sample design solutions only. Some creative directors (the potential employers) might find the narrative books to be engaging and compelling; the interest might lie in the unique story to be told and the practical and philosophical thinking presented.

On the other hand, an experimental presentation and content may not be seamless and may appear too self-absorbed or tedious to wade through when creative directors have so little time to look at the portfolios of aspiring designers.

Be aware that the success of the experimental, self-exploratory perfect or casebound book will depend on whether such a book is welcome. Success is also dependent on inventiveness and the *quality of ideas* presented—not the fact that the book is a story and was perfect or casebound.

We have a suggestion. If you are inclined to publish a record of your work and thinking in a book format, go ahead and do it! Your personal book could satisfy your desire for self-expression

two bright books

For every student, there is a personal style and method for ordering and displaying a body of work— the hard-earned portfolio (a.k.a. "book") of design solutions. See the accompanying figure for the title pages of two student books.

Portfolio title pages.

Top: Allison's Intergalactic Portfolio Student designer: Allison Grow
Bottom: Michael Boos

inherent in all creative people. In addition, however, also create a simple book (screw-and-post or otherwise) that showcases the best design solutions you have created.

There are no rules about how many portfolios to create. In fact, we recommend that you have several (see Figures 10-21 and 10-22), including the following:

- Screw-and-post binder

- Perfect-bound or casebound book

- Website

- Tablet computers (such as the iPad)

- A mini-book (a small size portfolio with a few examples)

- PDF samples ready for e-mail

Figure 10-21
Portfolio presentation formats.

Student designer: Luis Guillen
Left to right:
Perfect/handbound book.

Industrially bound mini-book (résumé, business cards, and handmade envelope).

Screenshot of website home page.

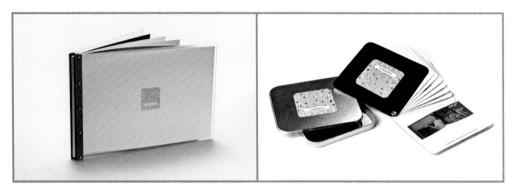

Figure 10-22
Portfolio presentation formats.

Student designer: Nicole Santiago
Left to right:
Portfolio bound using a screw-and-post book.

Handmade mini-book bound with a grommet and cased in a metal box (also shown is a magnetic business card).

portfolio presentation formats

Since we suggest that you have the five formats of portfolio presentations, we offer some further advice in their creation.

presenting on the web

An aspiring designer should have a website in order to easily display sample work to potential employers. This textbook is not meant to instruct on the technical production of a portfolio website. The concern here is in regard to the high quality of the portfolio presentation itself.

Begin by establishing a domain for your portfolio. For practical reasons, have the URL in your own name, such as www.firstname lastname.com.

The photos and digital files of the three-dimensional design solutions and the digital files of the remaining content of work can be organized in a similar way as noted for a printed book.

The site would include a limited number of *only* your best design solutions. The temptation might be to load up the site with as many images as possible (it is easy to do so), but remember that quality—not quantity—is of most concern. Show only your best, most innovative design solutions. Keep the presentation uncluttered.

Generally, follow the order of content previously presented. On the home page, clearly indicate your name and contact information. In addition, use the categories of design applications to establish the site navigation. For instance, the main navigation might include book and editorial, identity and branding, integrated advertising (perhaps with separate subject areas), environmental graphics, digital design, and mixed media.

The links to the various categories of applications can lead to a pop-up window with a simple forward/back button guiding the viewer through the work presented. (Be aware, however, that some users might block pop-up windows.) Alternatively, the links can lead to a discrete frame within the main site window also using a simple icon that allows the viewer to easily click through the sample work presented.

The site should also include your résumé and perhaps a statement of your design philosophy. This information can be included in the main navigation bar or separated relative to the emphasis desired. Refer back to Figures 10-1 and 10-2 for several webpage compositions and navigation structures.

N.B. Obviously, it is a good idea to back up all your digital files on an external hard drive and optical media such as a CD or DVD. Copy the entire original document and art files as well as all the code for the portfolio pages and the website.

binding it together

Do you have everything you need? Run through the checklist:

Ideas (check)

Comps (check)

Photos of comps (check)

Pages composed (check)

Order of pages composed (check)

Now what?

Did you forget that you need a binder, a web host, and perhaps access to on-demand publishers? Prepare well ahead of time to avoid overnight shipping charges and stress.

screw-and-post portfolio binders

Screw-and-post binders are the fastest, most economical, and potentially most environmentally friendly presentation format. The portfolio binder you purchase or construct should be—dare we say it again—*simple*. Yet it could have a touch of your identity reflected in the materials.

Screw-and-post binders are available through retail sources. Binders can be found in flat metal, perforated metal, wood, vinyl-covered board, acrylic, and canvas-covered board; several samples are shown in Figure 10-23. Also purchase or make a simple cloth case so that you can carry comps, résumés, and business cards along with the binder.

Personalize the binder covers using any of the hand-printing methods discussed in Chapter 9 or have the covers engraved or incised commercially. Or, leave the cover untouched and add a title page.

A few suggestions for binder sources include:

- Light Impressions Direct
- Lost Luggage
- Pina Zangaro
- Shrapnel Design

make it yourself: binders and books

If you are well practiced and your craftsmanship skill has developed to the level of excellence, it is possible to design and construct your own portfolio binder or book; refer back to Figure 10-21. See Figure 10-24 for an example of a handmade binder.

To accomplish the task of a handmade book, use the techniques, skills, and knowledge acquired in this book thus far; apply the learning to constructing your own portfolio binder or book. If you do not feel ready to attempt a handcrafted book, the online publishers do an excellent job for the purpose; see Figure 10-25. Do not, however, expect archival quality from the online printers and binders. Only a book made with archival ink and paper has a chance of lasting a lifetime.

We recommend that you purchase a commercially manufactured binder in addition to the handmade version—as insurance and backup. In addition, the purchased binder can be a template for the potential handcrafted one.

A handcrafted binder certainly has the potential of being unique in size and materials. But if it is not impeccably crafted . . . well, you can guess that it does you no good.

If your budget allows, there are many professional custom bookbinders that can create a personalized case. See binderies such as Brewer-Cantelmo and Cardoza-James.

caveat designer

A handcrafted portfolio book or binder can look amateurish (like a hobbyist's scrapbook). Proceed with awareness; too many different materials and fancy bindings detract from the work inside. The portfolio is all about the ideas presented and not the Japanese silk cloth used to cover the binder.

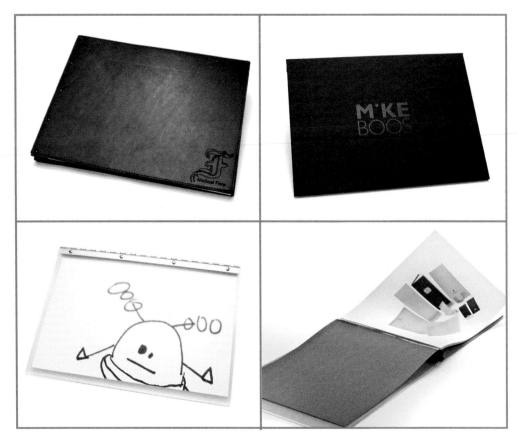

Figure 10-23

First row, left to right:
Leather cover, hinged along the left edge.

Student designer: Michael Fiore
Black canvas binder, hinged along the top (opens horizontally).

Student designer: Michael Boos

Second row, left to right:
Frosted acrylic binder with vinyl spine edge border, hinged along the top (opens horizontally).

Student designer: Allison Grow
Frosted acrylic covers tinted green with vinyl spine edge border.

Student designer: Nicole Santiago

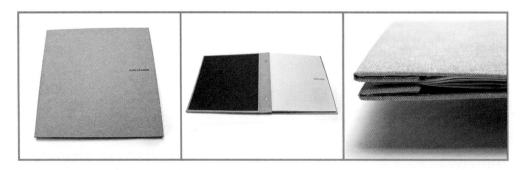

Figure 10-24
Handmade portfolio screw-and-post binder.

Student designer: Jason Alejandro
Left to right:
Canvas cover binder with screen-printed title.
Binder open to the title page.
Detail of binding.

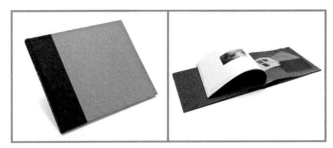

Figure 10-25
The Design Studio at Kean University portfolio (various student designers) produced by an on-demand publisher.

summary: ready, go for it!

Literally, you *made it*. With diligent study, you have applied knowledge gained and find that you are ready to present your work and launch a career. Make that presentation of the highest quality. The comps should be photographed expertly, the photographic and digital images arranged for clarity, and the portfolio book and binder selected appropriately.

Add a touch of your personal style to your presentation and show the world what you are made of!

exercise knowledge gained

Before creating a final portfolio of work, we urge you to practice the presentation techniques discussed in this chapter and reiterated in the exercises that follow. It is easy to wait until the last minute to organize a presentation of final design solutions only to find it is not at all easy to actually create one.

1. photo shoot

Do not wait until your design solutions are final. Using the guidance provided for photographing your design solutions, practice styling, lighting, and printing photos of penultimate design solutions. We suggest photographing several different types of pieces such as packaging and a multiple-piece promotional direct mail or folder. Pay close attention to the lighting and the settings on your camera. Make notes on what went well and what did not. With practice and action on your notes, the next batch of photos should improve enough to make them acceptable for final presentation purposes.

2. subjective versus objective styling

The best way to determine whether to style the design solution subjectively or objectively is to try both. Set up and photograph the design solution in both styles. Print the results. Determine whether the work is best seen subjectively or objectively.

3. mini-portfolio

Practice arranging and ordering pages by creating a "mini-portfolio." A page size that is one-quarter the size of the full-scale portfolio would be appropriate. Use all the knowledge gained in previous chapters (especially on folding and bookbinding) to create the small-scale book. Refer back to Figures 10-21 and 10-22 for examples of some mini-portfolios.

The bonus here is that the mini can also be used as self-promotion. Its small size allows you to carry the mini with you wherever you go. If you meet an art director or designer who is willing to give you an interview, you'll have samples of your work to show. Additionally, mini-portfolios are good to bring along to networking events, "jellies," and "meetups." The latter are small, local professional networking events. Research professional networking jellies and meetups online for events in your area. Be sure to get background information on any networking event to ensure its safety and credibility.

4. a presentation notebook

Did you save all your research notes, thumbnail sketches, and brainstorming notes on each of your design solutions? We hope you did because creative directors, art directors, and other potential employers often wish to see your design process.

We suggest that you bind together a book of your design thinking—the sketches, doodles, influences, personal photos, and notes that went into the design solutions in your portfolio.

Make the notebook using a simple mechanical binding or have it perfect bound on the desktop or through an online source. Tuck this presentation book into a carrying case with the main portfolio. During a job interview, if there is a question about your design process, you'll be ready with a visual (and verbal) answer.

5. narrative content

A most personal type of public portfolio is the combination of displaying your design solutions along with thumbnail sketches, notes, and other personal writing, thoughts, and images in a casebound book. If you intend to use this type of storytelling portfolio, we offer the same advice we have given throughout this chapter: Keep it simple, and keep all the images in the book pertinent. Focus the content on your creative abilities as a designer.

Finally, keep in mind this summarizing thought from Dr. Seuss: "It is fun to have fun, but you have to know how."

glossary

accordion A popular folding style with a zigzag configuration.

acrylic paint A water-soluble imaging medium that can be used in a wide range of techniques.

adhesive applicator tool A glue spreader.

adhesive ink pen A tool used to draw lines of clear ink to which the rosin or thermography powder will stick.

adhesive sheets Dry-mount adhesives.

Adobe Acrobat A software tool that "encapsulates" the components of a document, including the text, fonts, and images, making a single new document format known as a portable document format (PDF).

Adobe Dreamweaver Adobe's web development application.

Adobe Illustrator A image rendering tool that allows for the creation of sophisticated vector artwork.

Adobe InCopy A professional word processing software application built into Adobe InDesign.

Adobe InDesign A page layout/composition software tool.

Adobe Photoshop A powerful photomanipulation and editing tool for photographers, graphic designers, and web designers.

anaglyph An image that has a three-dimensional illusionary effect.

aqueous A water-based coating that is applied to a printed substrate to heighten shine, deepen color, and/or protect the surface.

awl A tool that can be used to poke tiny holes to assist in sewing or as a marking tool in measuring.

back cover The reverse of the front cover; the rear facing of a book.

base size The industry-established standard size of a sheet of paper relative to either the United States or internationally.

basic/standard A folding format style that has a single fold (horizontally or vertically) with two panels and four pages.

basis weight The ream weight of the base size.

beeswax A substance applied to thread as a coating to help it pass through a stack of paper easily and smoothly.

bevel or mat cutter A tool that will cut board at a 45-degree angle; primarily used for cutting an angled edge for the inside of a picture mat.

bindery A company that specializes in machine- and hand-binding processes.

binding The method or style used to hold a book together.

bitmap A screen-based grid.

bleed allowances The printed area beyond the dimensions of the design that are cut away in order for the image to be flush with the edge of the paper.

blind embossing Embossing performed with no ink.

book arts Art that specializes in the book and folded formats.

book block The collection and thickness of pages of a book.

bookcloth Paper-backed fabric for use specifically in bookbinding.

border area The space between a book's spine and the hinge joint.

brayer A rolling burnishing tool.

brightness The measure of paper's reflectance or luminosity.

broadside A folding option in which a sheet of paper is first folded in half before implementing a specific folding style.

burnish To rub across a surface to make it smooth.

calcium carbonate An alkaline filler that buffers the acidic nature of cellulose and makes paper relatively archival.

caliper The thickness, or bulk, of a sheet of paper.

calipers Tools that are particularly useful for measuring round and unusual-shaped objects and the thickness of paperboard.

capacity envelope or capacity folder A type of envelope or folder that has depth.

case binding A method of binding that uses a Smyth-sewn book block that is attached to board covers.

cinch stapler A heavy-duty tool that performs special tasks such as stapling through thick material.

clay An organic substance added to pulp for smoothness, to help ink adhere, and to make the paper more opaque.

CMYK The color mode that includes cyan, magenta, yellow, and black (keyline), which are the process colors of offset lithography.

color laser printer A desktop device that uses dry pigment powders (known as toner) in conjunction with a laser to adhere the colored toner to paper.

color mode A standardized method in which the software tool such as Photoshop organizes and handles the color of an image.

color register embossing Embossing that is performed in conjunction with ink or foils.

comp A shortened version of the term **comprehensive mock-up**.

comprehensive mock-up A visual, tangible simulation of the proposed outcome of a professionally printed or digitally created design solution.

content As it relates to paper, the percentage of cotton versus other fibers such as wood, hemp, bamboo, and postconsumer pulp.

converters Envelope manufacturers.

corrugation The shaping into folds or parallel and alternating ridges and grooves to increase the strength of paperboard.

craft foam Thin, compressed sponge.

craft knife A lightweight, slim-handle cutting tool.

crayons Waxy visualizing tools useful for image creation and rendering textures.

critique A written or verbal assessment of the design solution.

crossover The printing of an image or headline type across the gutter or from one page to the facing page (a spread).

cutting die A cutting tool that is fabricated and fitted in the shape of the die line; used to cut the printed substrate into the specified form.

cutting mat A smooth, movable surface used to protect the worktable.

debossing A process in which a shape is sunken below a paper's surface.

deckle The soft and uneven edge of handmade paper.

deckle-edge ripper A tool that is used to simulate the edge found on handmade paper.

decorative edger A type of specialty scissors that has blades molded into shapes to cut a decorative edge.

descreener Software that helps remove a moiré pattern during the scanning process.

die A metal form that has been fabricated into a specific image shape or typeface.

die cut A cut (out) made in a printed or unprinted substrate.

die line The flat guideline of a package, used by the designer in order to place graphics and direct construction.

digital printing A printing process using toner (dry powder ink) that goes direct to paper.

distributors Companies that buy paper from the mills and distribute to printers, designers, and other users of paper.

document A file containing image and text intended for print output.

document dimensions The height and width measurement of an image.

double-stick tape An adhesive that is useful for adhering only one edge of a paper; relatively mess-free, quick, and handy for small areas.

dpi Abbreviation for **dots per inch**; a measurement of printing resolution.

drafting table A flat, adjustable surface for sketching, drawing, and production work.

drafting tape An adhesive that temporarily secures a substrate to a surface or tests the construction before applying glue.

dyes and pigments Natural or synthetic coloring agents.

embossing A process in which a shape is raised above a paper's surface.

embossing tool A ballpoint stylus that is primarily used to push paper into a stencil to create an embossed surface.

enamels Oil-based specialty paints.

endpapers A sheet (spread) of paper on the inside facing of the front and back covers.

engraving Etching fine lines onto the surface of a metal plate, which is then positioned on a press, coated with ink, and wiped so that only the etched areas remain filled; the image is then transferred from plate to paper by pressing the paper into the etched areas.

eraser A tool used to remove graphite (pencil) from the surface of paper and other substrates.

Euro binding A type of binding that uses a cloth lining that allows the cover to lay completely flat.

felt side The "top" of the paper sheet, which comes in contact with the felt rollers during manufacture.

fiber The basic ingredient of paper.

fillers Minerals, other organic substances, and chemical agents added to pulp to improve the quality of paper.

finish The surface qualities or attributes of paper, ranging from matte to glossy, highly textured to completely smooth, and much in between.

finished size The folded state of a folded format.

finishing The final stage of the professional production of a design.

flaps Shortened panels.

flat size The unfolded state of a folded format.

flexography A printing process that involves a specially fitted web press using soft plastic plates that allow printing on unusual surfaces such as plastic film, tissue, vinyl, or paperboard.

foamboard cutter A tool used to make quick and clean-cut lines in the spongy substrate.

foil stamping A specialty postpress technique that involves impressing color film (the foil) onto the surface rather than using ink.

fold compensation A fractional measurement for shortening the dimension of the panels in order to fold them to lay flat.

folding The action of bending and creasing a piece to lay one part over another part.

folding down The process of folding from start to finish.

folding dummy A blank comp of the folded format. Also called **paper dummy** or **sequence folding dummy.**

folding format The resulting final arrangement after the printing form has been cut, bent, and folded.

folding sequence One of many variations of how a folding format can be oriented and configured.

folding tool A tool that is used to rub over the edge of a fold to make it crisp and permanent. Also known as a **bone folder.**

fore edge The outer facing of the text block; the edge opposite the spine.

French fold A single page that has been folded in half before inserting into the spine with the fold exposed along the fore edge.

French groove The hinge joint of a casebound book.

frisket Airbrush masking film.

front cover The outer facing of a book.

Galaxy Gauge A brand name for a thin plastic, highly precise measurement tool.

gate A type of fold that is characterized by its centralized symmetry. Two panels fold evenly into the center from opposite sides.

glue stick A simple, relatively mess-free, almost all-purpose adhesive.

grammage The metric equivalent of basis weight.

grade A class or level of paper quality.

gravure A printing process in which images and type are etched onto metal plates, ink is pushed into the recessed areas of the plate, the plates are fitted around cylinders, and the images are transferred to the substrate.

grind-off The process of slightly grinding down the spine width to make the spine flat and to create a pitted texture that will assist in absorbing glue.

grommets Circular metal loops that strengthen a hole cut in paper or fabric.

GSM The abbreviation for **grams per square meter**, or grammage.

gutter Within the text block, the space where two pages meet at the binding.

head/top The upper edge of a book, perpendicular to the spine.

heat gun A handheld tool that generates a low level of heat.

height The measurement of a book from the top edge to the bottom edge of the cover.

hinge joint An indented groove located parallel to the spine edge on the front and back cover of the book.

hot glue An adhesive used with a glue gun; bonds instantly and dries in seconds.

image format A specific way in which information is encoded for storage in a digital file.

image resolution Measurement of the output quality of an image.

inkjet printer The desktop device that propels liquid ink in droplets of various sizes onto paper to create images.

interpolate To generate new pixels where there are none.

jogged Vibrated to help ensure that all the sheets are perfectly aligned and ready for further processing before binding.

kirigami The Japanese art of cutting paper.

kiss cut A light cut that does not cut completely through paper or other substrate.

layflat binding A type of binding that uses a detached spine to allow books to lay flatter than perfect binding.

layout Page composition.

leaf/folio A complete page (front and back).

lenticular A type of printing that creates the illusion of depth or movement of images as they are viewed from different angles.

letter A folding format style that has two parallel folds resulting in three panels and six pages.

letterpress A historic printing technique; a process by which a letter (type) or an image is cut from wood or molded out of metal, then set together in rigid form, rolled over with ink, and sent through a press to transfer the type or image to paper.

line art Black-and-white images with no tonal variation.

linen tape An adhesive-backed strip of fabric that is useful for bookbinding.

long-handle stapler A tool that is excellent for securing a small stack of text weight papers, with the capability of reaching beyond what a standard 5-inch stapler can accomplish.

map A style of fold that is a multiple-panel accordion finished with a right-angle fold and set in a tall or narrow orientation.

markers Tools used for sketching, visualizing, and labeling.

mechanical fold A fold that is implemented as the paper passes through metal rollers that exert relative, calibrated pressure; results in an ultrasharp crease.

metal clasp An envelope seal that uses a double-prong light metal clasp for security.

milled paper Paper produced by machine.

moiré A patterned distortion.

mountain fold The peak form of a fold.

notch binding A method of binding that incorporates cutting parallel grooves into the spine perpendicular to the binding edge to allow the adhesive glue to seep into the spine and strengthen the bond. Also called **burst binding.**

off square A term describing a substrate that is not square (corners at 90 degrees).

offset lithography The printing process that involves photographically transferring an image onto a metal plate which is then inked and "offset" or transferred to a rubber blanket; that image is then transferred to paper.

opacity The amount of light that passes through a sheet of paper, determining whether the image printed on one side of the page will show through to the other side.

open-end (OE) A type of envelope that has an opening on the short dimension.

open-side (OS) A type of envelope that has an opening on the long dimension.

optical brightening agents Fillers that work by absorbing invisible ultraviolet light and converting the energy to a visible bluish white light, resulting in paper that appears brighter.

origami The Japanese art of folding paper.

output provider The person or establishment who takes the design from screen to paper or other substrates. Also referred to as **printer** or **service provider.**

page A single side of a panel.

page imposition The configuration of type and images (pages) on the printing paper.

pagination The sequence of pages.

panels The two-sided sections of the folded format.

paper mills Companies that make paper.

paperboard die An element used in simulating embossing or debossing for a comp.

parallel A folding style in which four or more panels stay parallel throughout the format.

parallel fold A fold made in the same direction (parallel) to the previous fold.

parchment paper A waxy paper that can be used as a surface on which to mix paints.

paste glue An all-purpose clear adhesive that is thick and sticky.

Peel & Seel A brand name for a type of envelope seal. A tape liner covers a resin-based adhesive; when the liner is removed and the flap is pressed down, a bond is created.

pencils Tools used for sketching and marking a line of measurement.

pens Tools used for sketching and visualizing.

perfect binding An all-purpose, fairly inexpensive adhesive binding.

perforator A small single-blade tool that cuts a perforated line.

pixels Small squares/dots of color light.

plastic comb An inexpensive binding method that uses a plastic clasp hooked onto prepunched holes and clamped.

portable document format (PDF) A file format that allows for easy document exchange from almost any application, on any computer system.

poster A folding style that is a broadside parallel or accordion configuration with a variety of sequencing possibilities.

ppi Abbreviation for **pixels per inch**; a measurement of digital image resolution.

PPI Abbreviation for **pages per inch**; determined by the thickness of pages.

precision scissors An extra-sharp cutting tool that is useful for snipping in tiny areas.

preflighting and packaging Organizing a document with all of the requirements and settings necessary for the output provider.

print run The copies printed for one job.

printing sheet The full sheet of paper on which the design solution is printed.

pulp The fiber mass before it is made into finished paper.

PUR binding A highly durable polyurethane adhesive that is flexible and will lay virtually flat.

PVA (polyvinyl acetate) A general-purpose white glue that is fast drying and creates a strong permanent bond.

razor saw A fine-toothed tool used to cut metal, wood, and plastic.

raster image An image created by the smooth gradation of color values; also known as a **tonal** or **continuous tone** image.

ream A quantity of 500 sheets of paper.

recto The front side of a leaf; in an open book, a right-hand page.

remoistenable A type of envelope seal in which the glue is activated by moistening the gummed area of the flap.

res The abbreviation for **resolution**; measured in ppi (pixels per inch).

RGB The color mode of red, green, and blue—the primary colors of light; specifically meant for on-screen applications, but not for print.

right-angle fold A fold made at a right angle to a parallel fold.

roll A folding style containing at least four panels that consecutively fold into each other.

rotary cutter A tool that is primarily used to cut fabric.

rounded-corner cutter A tool that is used to cut rounded corners.

saddle-stitch binding A method of binding that has one full single signature clamped with wire (staples) along the spine.

saddle stapler A tool that is used for stapling along a fold of several sheets of paper.

sandpaper A lightly textured surface used to grind and smooth rough edges of paper and other materials

scalable Varying size proportionately.

Schaedler Rule A brand name for a thin plastic, highly precise measurement tool.

scissors A cutting tool that is helpful for quickly cutting into large areas that do not require a precise measurement.

scoring To precisely dent, incise, or notch a line below the surface of the paper or other substrate.

scoring tool A tool that is used to incise a line that is to be folded.

screen printing A specialty printing process by which an image is imposed onto a thin screen or fine mesh of materials such as silk, nylon, or even stainless steel, after which ink is forced though the screen and onto a substrate.

serrated scissors A cutting tool that is good for thick paper.

service provider The person or establishment who takes the design from screen to paper or other substrates. Also referred to as **printer** or **output provider.**

set dividers Two-prong, sharply pointed tools that are set and locked in place at a given width; used with a ruler or straightedge to mark or check multiple units of the set measurement.

setting square The process of checking and adjusting, if necessary, all the right angles on a given substrate.

sheet fed press An offset press that prints on individual sheets of paper.

short fold The result when half of the panels of a broadside are shortened.

side-stitch binding A method of binding that uses mechanical parts (metal or otherwise) applied to the front of the book in the border area.

single fold One fold dividing the paper or substrate in half; also known as a standard or half fold.

signature One section of pages folded down (in half) into a nested group.

Singer (thread) sewn A method of binding that has a column of stitches running parallel to the spine.

Smyth (thread) sewn A method of binding that has parallel rows of stitches that cross the width of the spine.

specialty A customized fold that does not fit into one of the standard categories; also called **exotic.**

spine The edge of a book where all the pages are gathered and bound.

spine width The thickness of the spine.

spiral binding A type of binding that uses a wire or plastic spiral coil threaded through prepunched holes.

spot color An isolated application of color ink.

spot varnish An isolated application of varnishes or UV coatings.

spread Two or more pages meant to be seen or read as a whole.

spring-hinged scissors A cutting tool that is good for heavy work and thick paper.

squared A precise 90 degrees.

squeegee A tool used to push ink through a screen mesh.

stamp pad A foam base for holding the pigmented ink used for simple desktop stamping techniques.

stamping A desktop printing technique using ink and stamps made of craft foam, carveable rubber, linoleum block, and so on.

staple-free "stapler." A tool that creates a flap-joint to hold several sheets of paper together.

stock Paper of a given grade and variation.

stock image A professionally created image that can be downloaded from a provider's website, either free or for a fee.

straightedge A tool used as a cutting guide.

string and button An envelope closure that uses a string tie.

studio skills The ability to successfully choose and use the tools, materials, and techniques needed to physically create the elements of a design solution and construct a professional level, comprehensive mock-up of that solution.

substrate The material on which the design solution is created.

tail/bottom The lower edge of a book, perpendicular to the spine.

tape binding A method of binding that employs a strong (heat-activated) adhesive tape.

telescoping A condition where the inner pages of the signature are much longer than those folded on top of each other.

text Body copy, headlines/subheads, captions, and so on.

texture paint A specialty paint that is useful for painting on metal, glass, or plastic.

thermography A specialty printing technique that employs heat to melt powder rosin on the surface of a substrate.

thermography powder A rosin that melts when heat is applied over it.

thickness The measurement of paper's bulk as noted in points or mils.

thimble A tool used to protect the skin while sewing.

tipped-on A paper element that is affixed on top of another by means of adhesive.

toner The dry pigment powders used in a color laser printer.

triangle A rigid metal drafting tool that assists with measuring, drawing, and cutting angles.

T-square A steel tool that is helpful for drawing straight and 90-degree (square) lines.

utility knife A large-handle, handheld tool with a very sharp blade; recommended for cutting paper.

UV A type of nonvolatile coating that is dried or cured by ultraviolet light; applied to a printed substrate to heighten shine, deepen color, and/or protect the surface.

valley The inside of a fold.

varnish A clear oil-based coating applied to a printed substrate.

vector graphic An image that is composed of mathematically determined points, lines, or curves; also referred to as **vector art.**

Velo An inexpensive binding method that uses plastic straps clamped into prepunched holes along the border area.

verso The back side of a leaf; in an open book, a left-hand page.

wafer seal An adhesive paper circle (or other simple shape) used as a functional seal for folded paper, or used decoratively with an envelope.

web press A high-speed offset press that prints continuously using a roll of paper.

whiteness The predominant color of a sheet of white paper, either neutral white, warm white, and blue white.

width The measurement of a book from spine to fore edge.

Wire-O binding A type of binding that uses metal wire looped through prepunched holes which are then clamped to tighten into the shape of the letter O.

wire side The "bottom" of the paper sheet, which is created against the wire (screen) during manufacture.

wooden rollers A tool used for burnishing and adhering two flat substrates together. Also known as **brayers.**

index